SECURING OUR
CHILDREN'S FUTURE

Securing Our Children's Future

New Approaches to Juvenile Justice
and Youth Violence

Gary S. Katzmann

Editor

BROOKINGS INSTITUTION PRESS
Washington, D.C.

Copyright © 2002
THE BROOKINGS INSTITUTION
1775 Massachusetts Avenue, N.W., Washington, D.C. 20036
www.brookings.edu

Library of Congress Cataloging-in-Publication data

Securing our children's future : new approaches to juvenile justice and youth violence / Gary S. Katzmann, editor.
   p.   cm.
Includes bibliographical references and index.
  ISBN 0-8157-0606-5 (cloth : alk. paper)—
  ISBN 0-8157-0605-7 (pbk. : alk. paper)
  1. Juvenile delinquency—United States—Prevention. 2. Juvenile justice, Administration of—United States. 3. Juvenile delinquents—Rehabilitation—United States. 4. Problem youth—Rehabilitation—United States. I. Katzmann, Gary S.
  HV9104 .S37 2002
  364.36—dc21   2002008637

9 8 7 6 5 4 3 2 1

The paper used in this publication meets minimum requirements of the American National Standard for Information Sciences—Permanence of Paper for Printed Library Materials: ANSI Z39.48-1992.

Typeset in Adobe Garamond

Composition by Cynthia Stock
Silver Spring, Maryland

Printed by R. R. Donnelley and Sons
Harrisonburg, Virginia

THE BROOKINGS INSTITUTION

The Brookings Institution is an independent organization devoted to nonpartisan research, education, and publication in economics, government, foreign policy, and the social sciences generally. Its principal purposes are to aid in the development of sound public policies and to promote public understanding of issues of national importance. The Institution was founded on December 8, 1927, to merge the activities of the Institute for Government Research, founded in 1916, the Institute of Economics, founded in 1922, and the Robert Brookings Graduate School of Economics and Government, founded in 1924.

The Institution maintains a position of neutrality on issues of public policy to safeguard the intellectual freedom of the staff. Interpretations or conclusions in Brookings publications should be understood to be solely those of the authors.

THE GOVERNANCE INSTITUTE

The Governance Institute, a nonprofit organization incorporated in 1986, is concerned with exploring, explaining, and easing problems associated with both the separation and the division of powers in the American federal system. It is interested in how the levels and branches of government can best work with one another. It is attentive to the problems within an organization or between institutions that frustrate the functioning of government. The Governance Institute is concerned as well with those professions and mediating groups that significantly affect the delivery and quality of public services. The Institute's focus is on institutional process, a nexus linking law, institutions, and policy. The Institute believes that problem solving should integrate research and discussion. This is why the Institute endeavors to work with those decisionmakers who play a role in making changes in process and policy. The Institute currently has four program areas: problems of the judiciary; problems of the administrative state; problems in criminal justice; and challenges to the legal profession.

Foreword

JUST AS SEPTEMBER 11 no longer stands for a date on the calendar but a lasting trauma for all Americans, so the word Columbine has become a synonym for a national disgrace: students slaughtering classmates and teachers. What happened in Littleton, Colorado, on April 20, 1999, was horrible enough by itself. That similar tragedies occurred the year before in Jonesboro, Arkansas, and two years later in Santee, California, makes this particular form of violence all the more a challenge for our society, our communities, our educators, our families, and practitioners of applied social science research such as Gary Katzmann.

In the pages that follow, Gary has brought together a diverse group of practitioners and academics to examine the role of government, nonprofit, and private institutions in identifying, coordinating, and implementing strategies to combat youth violence.

This book represents an important part of the way Brookings does its work: collaboration with other nongovernmental organizations. In this case, that means with the Governance Institute, where Gary has been a fellow and director of a project, "Securing Our Children's Future: New Approaches to Juvenile Justice and Youth Violence." In this resulting volume, experts on the prosecutor's office, the defense bar, the courts, correction and probation departments, faith-based organizations, schools, the media, nonprofits, and the private sector compare experiences, insights, and strategies for a workable plan of action. The premise of this venture has been that if we are to tackle the complex problem of youth violence, the various institutions involved cannot function in isolation but must act together.

In addition to his role at the Governance Institute, Gary is a research fellow at the Program in Criminal Justice Policy and Management of Harvard University's Kennedy School of Government. A lawyer and prosecutor who has been involved in policymaking on many levels, he has written and lectured on the subject of legal and criminal process.

Gary is grateful for the support of Paul C. Light, the former director of Brookings's Governmental Studies program, and to Paul's successor, Carol Graham, under whom our program has been renamed Governance Studies—a change in terminology of which, I'm sure, Gary approves. He expresses his appreciation to Janet Walker, managing editor of the Brookings Press, who supervised the publication process; Eileen Hughes, who was a conscientious and meticulous editor; Inge Lockwood, who proofread the manuscript; Susan Fels, who prepared the index; and Elizabeth McAlpine, who provided administrative support. He also thanks Susan Woollen, Brookings art coordinator, for her expert supervision of the cover design process, and Rebecca Clark, marketing director, for her work to disseminate the findings of this project.

STROBE TALBOTT
President, Brookings Institution

Washington, D.C.
August 2002

Acknowledgments

AS IS PERHAPS APPROPRIATE for a project and book that deal with the benefits of collaboration, there are thanks to be given to various institutions and individuals.

I thankfully acknowledge the profound involvement and indispensable aid of the Charles E. Culpeper Foundation, and its president, Francis J. McNamara Jr. In providing creative support for projects to improve the administration of justice, the Culpeper Foundation occupied a unique niche. The Governance Institute—without whose support and encouragement the project on juvenile justice and youth violence on which this volume is based could not have been undertaken—was a beneficiary of the foundation's vision. I am grateful to the Governance Institute and its board of directors and officers, in particular Judge Frank M. Coffin, Judge Robert A. Katzmann, and Stephen Shannon.

The Program in Criminal Justice Policy and Management of Harvard University's Kennedy School of Government provided a wonderful environment for the project. Mark H. Moore, Guggenheim Professor of Criminal Justice Policy and Management and director of the Hauser Center for Nonprofit Organizations, offered me an appointment as a research fellow in the criminal justice program, a welcoming home from which to direct the project. I am most grateful for his continuing support and encouragement. Thanks also are owed to Susan Michaelson, Brian Welch, and Shelly Coulter for their help in project administration and to Edward Gomeau, who provided excellent assistance during the production of the manuscript.

The project and book have benefited greatly from the generous sharing of insights by numerous practitioners and academics who toil in the area of juvenile justice and youth policy. Particular mention should be made of Tom Reilly, then district attorney of Middlesex County and now Attorney General of the Commonwealth of Massachusetts; Ralph F. Boyd Jr.; Judge Gordon Martin Jr.; Judge Michael Correiro; and Shay Bilchik, who were so gracious with their thoughts and time when the project was in its formative stages. I also extend my appreciation to Justice Stephen G. Breyer, Judge Leonard B. Sand, and Judge Hugh Bownes for their interest.

Finally, I should note that I directed the project while on leave from the United States Department of Justice; the project is an independent venture. The views expressed in this volume are those of the contributing authors and should not be ascribed to the Department of Justice.

GARY S. KATZMANN
Project Director

Contents

SECURING OUR CHILDREN'S FUTURE

1

GARY S. KATZMANN

Introduction:
Issues and Institutions

NO ERA IN WORLD HISTORY has been untouched by youth violence. Tablets describing the challenges that the misbehaving young pose for society have been found that date from before 2000 B.C. Millennia later, in his annual reports to the commonwealth of Massachusetts, nineteenth-century education reformer Horace Mann pointed to the criminal behavior of young people to support his arguments for a "common school."[1] Indeed, a twenty-first-century American who traveled back two centuries would find the youth violence of the day quite familiar. The time traveler would see, for example, that in 1806 a 13-year-old girl was tried in Tennessee for the murder of her father[2] and that violent youth gangs roamed the streets of Manhattan and Philadelphia in the 1830s and after.[3] Nor would the traveler be shocked to find that before his eighteenth birthday in 1877, a gun-toting youth from a dysfunctional home—whom legend would know as "Billy the Kid"—had committed his first homicide, the beginning of a career of lethal violence.[4]

In our time, both the public and the government have felt in recent years a heightened sense of urgency and frustration about youth violence. The United States confronts the unsettling reality that the homicide rate for children under 15 far exceeds that of other industrialized countries.[5] Today, when 70.2 million Americans—more than one in four—are below age 18, the country's intense concern about youth violence has played out against a series of seemingly contradictory trends that defy easy analysis.[6] The decade beginning in 1983, which was marked by a dramatic rise in youth violence, particularly lethal violence, has been followed since 1993 by a dramatic decline. Notwithstanding an increase in the size of the juvenile population and predictions of a rise in violence, juvenile violence has fallen—although there have been suggestions of a coming upturn.[7] During this period of decline, however, a rash of shootings by young people at school—in places such as West Paducah, Kentucky; Pearl, Mississippi; Jonesboro, Arkansas; Springfield, Oregon; Littleton, Colorado; Santee, California; and Williamsport, Pennsylvania—has reverberated in the public consciousness. These tragic shootings have intensified concerns about safety—notwithstanding data showing that students are safer in school than elsewhere and that in recent years lethal crime in schools has in fact declined.

The problem of youth violence has prompted a flurry of commentary, legislative activity, scholarly studies, and government and private sector initiatives. Explanations for the fluctuations in youth violence have varied, as have proposed approaches to combating the problem. For example, in accounting for the apparent decline in youth violence, some observers have pointed to changing demographics or an improving economy, while others have pointed to successful law enforcement initiatives, such as efforts to stop the traffic in crack cocaine. The debate about how best to deal with youth violence and reduce it also has been framed in a variety of ways. Discussions sometimes have been cast in terms of law enforcement measures versus prevention programs and at other times in terms of criminal justice mechanisms versus public health or social service responses.[8] Some have focused on the etiology of violence—its "root causes"—while others have focused more on the impact of external institutions and programs. More recent discussions of policies and programs to prevent and control youth violence have increasingly focused on partnerships among the public, private, and nonprofit sectors.

All too often, discourse about "the violent crime problem" has given way to quick conclusions and subtle analysis has been supplanted by misleading categorization of the causes. The crime problem is complex and multidimensional; indeed, it is not just one problem, but many. At the end of a century that suggested some reason for optimism in addressing youth violence and at the beginning of a new century that is nevertheless fraught with uncertainty about how to proceed, the time is ripe to think about how institutions can better organize and integrate their efforts to prevent youth violence. Unless we reinforce initiatives to address the urgent problem of youth violence now, we leave yet another generation at risk.

This book focuses on the juvenile justice system and the strategic role of institutions, broadly conceived, in the identification, coordination, and implementation of anti–youth violence strategies. At a time when the direction of youth violence policy is very much the subject of debate, the Governance Institute—in cooperation with the Program in Criminal Justice Policy and Management of Harvard's Kennedy School of Government—brought together a wide range of skilled professionals and academics to participate in a project entitled Securing Our Children's Future: New Approaches to Juvenile Justice and Youth Violence. Harnessing their experience and their contributions, this volume of the same title examines, in practical terms, how institutions can be mobilized in the service of initiatives to combat youth violence. It attempts to identify promising strategies to confront the challenges of youth violence and to facilitate communication and sharing of perspectives among prosecutors, defense attorneys, the courts, correctional institutions, probation departments, faith-based groups, schools, the media, nonprofit institutions, and private entities in their efforts to develop and implement such strategies. The focus of the project and of this book is not on the root causes of violence—an important concern that has been the subject of other works—but on the conception and implementation of policy and the design of institutional processes. One purpose of this effort is to stimulate dialogue among practitioners, another is to develop a workable action plan to guide decision-making. The project considers the problems that result from viewing youth violence through different prisms; in doing so it examines strategies from the vantage of particular institutions and explores the meaning of management and leadership both within those institutions and in their relationships with others. It also examines collaborative efforts among institutions.

Before briefly describing the succeeding chapters, the remainder of this introduction relates in statistical terms the scope of youth violence and presents a snapshot of the institutional context in which the problem is addressed.

Trends in Youth Violence

Any examination of trends in youth violence must first examine the source of the statistics used; it also must clarify the definition of terms. There are two basic kinds of statistical source—official reports of law enforcement agencies and self-reports.[9] With respect to the former, a basic standard resource is the Uniform Crime Reports (UCR), an annual compilation of data on U.S. crime and arrests based on information provided to the Federal Bureau of Investigation (FBI) by local law enforcement agencies.[10] The FBI publishes its annual *Crime in the United States* report on the basis of that information.[11] We will use both of these sources for the discussion that follows. At the outset, however, it should be noted that a primary limitation on official reports arises from the fact that some criminal behavior is not reported to law enforcement agencies, and that, as a general proposition, some crimes (with the exception of murder, which is usually reported) go undetected. Moreover, UCR statistics report the number of arrests made in a particular year; they do not measure the number of crimes committed nor the number of individuals who committed crimes. A single crime committed by a youth gang may result in multiple arrests, and a single individual may be arrested repeatedly.[12] Statistics also can be misleading because of the problem of classification of offenses. While the official arrest statistics have limitations, they are the best measure of reported crime that flows into the juvenile and criminal justice systems.[13]

Because of the limitations of official reports and the fact that much criminal behavior goes undetected, policy analysts also have looked to confidential longitudinal and cross-sectional surveys that ask young people about violent acts that they may have perpetrated or been victims of over time. The recent surgeon general's *Report on Youth Violence* takes note of *Monitoring the Future*,[14] an annual cross-sectional survey of high school seniors that has been conducted since 1975.[15] Indeed, the surgeon general's report concludes that such surveys of young people establish that most crimes by young people escape the attention of the justice system.

For the purposes of preliminary analysis and statistical reference below, "youth" or "juvenile" refers to individuals who are under 18 years of age. (In fact, in 2000, the legal definition of "juvenile" in 13 states referred to persons who were younger than 17 years of age, including three states in which all 16- and 17-year-olds were defined as adults.)[16] "Violent crime" refers to the four violent crimes that make up the violent crime index of the FBI's Uniform Crime Reports—criminal homicide (murder and nonnegligent manslaughter), robbery, aggravated assault, and forcible rape.[17]

In 2000, juveniles were involved in fewer than one in six arrests for all violent crime index offenses.[18] That year, there were approximately 2.4 million juvenile arrests, of which 99,000 were for violent crime index offenses.

Of those 99,000 arrests, 1,200 were for criminal homicide, 4,500 were for forcible rape, 26,800 were for robbery, and 68,300 were for aggravated assault. For every 100,000 youths between 10 and 17 years of age, there were 309 arrests for violent crime index offenses. If each of those arrests involved a different juvenile, then about one-third of 1 percent of juveniles ages 10 through 17 years were arrested for a violent crime in 2000. Minorities were disproportionately involved in juvenile arrests. Although the racial composition of the juvenile population in 2000 was 79 percent white, 16 percent black, and 5 percent of other races (with Hispanics classified as white), 55 percent of juvenile arrests for violent crime involved white youth and 42 percent involved black youth.

The decade beginning in 1983 and ending in 1993—a period during which adult criminal violence declined[19]—saw a dramatic increase in the overall arrest rate for violent crimes committed by youths between the ages of 10 and 17.[20] The rate then fell through 2000, the most recent year for which figures are available. Between 1983 and 1993–1994, the arrest rate of youths for violent offenses increased by approximately 70 percent. During that time, both the actual number of youths who were arrested for homicide and the rate of homicide arrests nearly tripled. In the peak year of 1993, there were about 3,800 juvenile arrests for murder, but by 2000, the number fell to 1,200. The juvenile murder arrest rate dropped 74 percent from its peak in 1993 to 2000, when it reached its lowest level since the 1960s. The upsurge in juvenile lethal crimes between 1983 and 1993 was tied largely to an increase in the use of firearms by adolescents committing violent acts.[21] By 1994, 82 percent of homicides by youths were perpetrated with a firearm.[22] The dramatic drop in homicides between 1993 and 2000 coincided with a decline in firearm use.[23]

The substantial decline in juvenile arrest rates for murder should not divert attention from the reality that the statistical picture of youth violence is complex. To be sure, by 2000 the juvenile arrest rate for violent crime index offenses had fallen to its lowest level since 1985 and was 41 percent below the peak year of 1994, although marginally higher than the 1983 rate.[24] Moreover, after a 44 percent increase between 1980 and 1991, the arrest rate for forcible rape declined by 2000 to 13 percent below the 1980 rate, and the 2000 juvenile arrest rate for robbery was at its lowest level since at least 1980 and 57 percent below the peak year of 1994.[25] However, while the juvenile arrest rate for aggravated assault dropped 30 percent between 1994 and 2000, the 2000 juvenile arrest rate was 42 percent above its 1980 level.[26] Furthermore, data derived from *Monitoring the Future* show that self-reported violent behavior is at least as high today as it was in 1993.[27]

School Violence

The recent rash of highly publicized shootings in school has brought a new focus on the level of violence in U.S. schools. In fact, overall school crime has decreased since 1992.[28] In 1999, all nonfatal crimes at school against students ages 12 through 18—including theft, rape, sexual assault, robbery, aggravated assault, and simple assault—declined to 2.5 million, from 3.4 million in 1992. (In 1999, theft constituted 64 percent of all crime at school, reflecting a decline from 95 thefts per 1,000 students in 1992 to 59 per 1,000 in 1999.) In 1999, students ages 12 through 18 were the victims of 884,100 nonfatal violent crimes—that is, serious violent crimes plus simple assault—at school, reflecting a decline to 43 crimes per 1,000 students from the 1992 rate of 48 per 1,000 students. They were the victims of 1.1 million nonfatal violent crimes away from school, reflecting a decline to 39 crimes per 1,000 students from the 1992 rate of 71 per 1,000.

The rate of serious violent crime against students at school—including rape, sexual assault, robbery, and aggravated assault, but not simple assault—remained constant from 1992 to 1999. In 1999, a total of 185,600 nonfatal serious violent crimes against students were committed at school or on the way to or from school. During that year, students in urban and suburban areas were victimized by serious violent crime at school at similar rates. However, away from school, urban students were more vulnerable than suburban students to serious violent crime, and suburban students were more vulnerable to such crimes than were rural students. Nonfatal serious violent crimes against students are more likely to be committed away from school than at school. In 1999, eighteen students in 1,000 were victims of serious violent crimes while away from school; in contrast, seven in 1,000 students were victims of serious violent crime while at school or on the way to or from school. At the same time, the rate of crimes against students outside of school has declined since 1992. For example, nonfatal serious violent crimes away from school against students ages 12 through 18 declined in 1999 to eighteen students per 1,000 from thirty-two per 1,000 in 1992.

Moreover, in recent years—contrary to popular perception—weapon carrying and physical fighting by students have declined steadily. Between 1993 and 1999, there was a steady decline (from 12 to 7 percent) in the percentage of students in grades 9 through 12 who reported carrying a weapon to school on one or more days during the previous month. There also was a decline from 16 to 14 percent in the percentage of students who reported being involved in a physical fight on school property during the previous year. In 1999, about 5 percent of students aged 12 through 18 reported that they had been bullied (defined as "picked on or made to do things they did not want to do") at school during the last six months.[29] Females and males were equally likely to report that they had been bullied.

While there has been a decline since 1995 in students' fear of harm or attack at school, racial and ethnic groups differ in their perceptions of school safety. In both 1995 and 1999, larger percentages of black and Hispanic students than white students had fears of harm or attack.

Of the 2,407 murders of youth (ages 5 through 19) nationwide during the 1998–99 school year (July 1, 1998, through June 30, 1999), thirty-three were school associated—that is, committed on school property, at a school-sponsored event, or on the way to or from school or a school-sponsored event. The total number of school-associated violent deaths (including homicides, suicides, and killings of adults by law enforcement officers during the course of duty) and unintentional violent deaths declined from a high of 49 deaths during the 1995–96 school year to 47 during the 1998–99 school year. Of the forty-seven school-associated violent deaths during the 1998-99 school year, thirty-eight were homicides, six were suicides, two were caused by a law enforcement officer in the line of duty, and one was unintentional. Since the 1992–93 school year, at least one multiple-homicide event has occurred every year except for the 1993–94 school year.

Finally, it should be noted that while student behaviors such as weapon carrying and physical fighting show improvement, students have reported an increase in interruptions in class caused by student misbehavior.

Exposure to Violence and Child Abuse and Neglect

Recent estimates indicate that as many as 10 million children have witnessed or been victims of violence in their home and community. Moreover, approximately 2 million adolescents ages 12 through 17 appear to have suffered from posttraumatic stress disorder as a result of exposure to violence.[30] In 2000, public agencies received 3 million reports of alleged child maltreatment (abuse and neglect); after investigation and assessment, approximately 879,000 children were determined to be victims of child maltreatment.[31] Sixty-three percent of these child victims suffered neglect (including medical neglect); 19 percent were physically abused; 10 percent were sexually abused; and 8 percent were psychologically maltreated.[32]

The impact on children who have been exposed to violence is powerful. Whether victims or witnesses, they are at increased risk of becoming violent themselves. Such children commit nearly twice as many offenses as nonabused children, they begin committing crimes at younger ages, and they are arrested more frequently. Moreover, research has indicated that witnessing violent acts may have the same lasting emotional consequences as being directly victimized by those acts and that children who have witnessed domestic violence experience higher levels of childhood behavioral, social, and emotional problems than children who have not.[33]

Institutional and Organizational Context

Government agencies concerned with the problems of youth violence operate in the local, state, and federal spheres; within those particular spheres are a host of involved entities, ranging from law enforcement agencies to social service agencies and schools. Also involved are a variety of private and nonprofit institutions, including welfare, religious, and educational organizations.

The legal system, which is made up of the juvenile justice system, the criminal justice system, and the child protection and welfare system, is the bedrock of institutions concerned with the problems of youth violence. While the focus of this book is on conduct that falls within the ambit of the juvenile justice and criminal justice systems, a brief primer on all three components not only presents the context one needs to understand related policies and processes but also suggests the challenges of working within and among institutions to fashion viable approaches to problem solving.

Juvenile Justice System

While it is common to speak in terms of the "juvenile justice system," it should be noted at the outset that there is not one single juvenile justice "system" but rather more than fifty-one state systems, all with their own local variations. That being said, it can be further noted that juvenile justice has basically been a matter of state concern, with minimal federal judicial involvement; moreover, while there may be variations in juvenile justice systems, there are basic similarities in structure and approach that make it both appropriate and convenient to use the shorthand convention of "juvenile justice system."[34] The juvenile justice system, which deals with delinquency, status, and child neglect and abuse cases, is founded on the premise that children differ from adults and that ensuring their proper care and conduct therefore requires specialized institutions and practices. For example, the juvenile justice system assumes that children have a lesser degree of responsibility for their actions than adults, that they are in the formative stages of their development, and that rehabilitation rather than punishment should be a dominant goal in dealing with their misconduct. The jurisdiction of the juvenile justice system varies among the states. With respect to delinquency offenses—offenses that would be violations of criminal law if committed by an adult—17 years of age is the maximum age for original juvenile court jurisdiction in thirty-seven states and the District of Columbia, age 16 is the maximum in ten states, and age 15 is the maximum in three states. In most states, the juvenile court can exercise dispositional authority in delinquency matters over a youth who is adjudicated delinquent and then ages beyond the upper age of original jurisdiction, thereby permitting the court to provide services and impose sanctions for older juveniles.

In many states, there are statutory exceptions to basic age criteria. Thus some exceptions (known as statutory exclusions) related to the youth's age, alleged offense, or prior court history place the juvenile under the original jurisdiction of the criminal court. Under other exceptions related to the same factors, the youth is placed under the original jurisdiction of both the juvenile and criminal court; in such "concurrent jurisdiction" cases, the prosecutor has the authority to determine which court will handle the case. In sixteen states, statute determines the lowest age of court jurisdiction for delinquency offenses: age 6 is the minimum age in one state, with ages 7 to 10 being the minimum in fifteen states. For status offenses—behaviors such as being truant, running away, or violating curfew that are offenses by dint of the offender's juvenile status—as well as abuse and neglect matters, many states have higher upper age limits for juvenile court jurisdiction, generally through age 20.[35]

The juvenile justice system has been likened to a pipeline, with various valves at which children may be diverted from the system or continue their journey within it.[36] While, as has been noted, structures vary across the country, decisions are made at similar points. Entrance into the pipeline starts with a referral by a law enforcement official or others—such as victims, parents, social service agencies, school officials, or probation officers—or with a police arrest. Upon arrest—and after talks with both the victim and the juvenile and review of the juvenile's history—law enforcement officials usually determine whether the juvenile should proceed within the system or be diverted to a mental health and welfare agency or an alternative program. Approximately one-quarter of all arrested juveniles are handled within the police department and do not proceed further; about seven in ten are referred to juvenile court. In 1998, law enforcement officials referred 84 percent of the delinquency cases handled in juvenile court.[37]

INTAKE. On referral to juvenile court, the intake department (usually the probation department or the prosecutor's office) determines whether to dismiss the case, deal with the matter informally (including by "informal probation"), or seek formal intervention by the juvenile court. The intake department requests formal intervention either by filing a delinquency petition stating the allegation and requesting the juvenile court to hold a hearing to adjudicate the youth a delinquent—and thus a ward of the court—or by filing a petition requesting a waiver hearing in order to transfer the case to criminal court.

DETENTION. If the intake officer (generally a juvenile probation officer) determines that the matter should proceed to a hearing, the officer must determine whether the child should be sent home (with or without supervision) or held in a secure detention center or some alternative facility. If the child is detained, a court will hold a detention hearing within twenty-four to seventy-two hours. The child usually meets his or her attorney for the first time at the hearing, during which a judge determines whether the child should remain in detention.

ADJUDICATION. At the adjudicatory hearing or trial, witnesses are called and facts are presented. The juvenile is represented by counsel. Although in some states the juvenile has the right to a jury trial, in nearly all adjudicatory hearings the judge alone determines whether the juvenile was responsible for the offense. In 1998, courts with juvenile jurisdiction disposed of more than 1.7 million delinquency cases, of which more than 102,000 were violent crime index cases.[38] In the same year, juveniles were adjudicated delinquent in 63 percent of cases referred to juvenile court for delinquency, including violent crime index offenses.[39]

TRANSFER. In responding to a waiver petition filed by the prosecutor or intake officer, the juvenile court must determine whether there is probable cause to believe that the juvenile committed the alleged offense and whether the juvenile court should waive jurisdiction and transfer the case to criminal court. In making its decision, the court focuses on whether the juvenile is amenable to treatment by the juvenile justice system and considers such factors as the juvenile's history and the seriousness of the offense. In 1998, juvenile courts waived to criminal court 1.0 percent of all formally petitioned delinquency cases; 3 percent of formally petitioned violent crime index offense cases were judicially waived to criminal court.[40]

DISPOSITION. After a juvenile is judged to be delinquent, the court assesses the disposition plan developed by the probation department, which may evaluate the juvenile and available support programs. The court also may order diagnostic tests and psychological evaluation. At the disposition hearing, the court considers the recommendations of the probation officer, prosecutor, and counsel for the juvenile. The juvenile disposition may take a variety of forms. A period of probation, for example, might be fixed or indeterminate, and it might include requirements for drug counseling, a curfew, restitution to the victim or the community, or weekend confinement in a local detention center. In 1998, although formal probation was the most severe disposition ordered in 58 percent of the cases of adjudicated delinquents, juvenile courts ordered residential placement in 26 percent of cases.[41] Residential confinement may be ordered for an indeterminate or a specific term, and it may take place in a publicly or privately operated facility that may have a prison-like or an open, home-like environment. In many states, when a judge commits a juvenile to the state department of juvenile corrections, that department determines where the juvenile will be placed and when he or she will be released. In other states, the judge holds a review hearing and determines the type and length of stay.

AFTERCARE. On release from an institution, a juvenile is placed in aftercare, which is analogous to parole; during that period, the juvenile is subject to the supervision of the court or the juvenile corrections department. The juvenile must comply with the conditions of aftercare or face recommitment to a facility.

Criminal Justice System

As noted above, juveniles may enter the adult criminal justice system by means of a judicial waiver or transfer. Moreover, in more than half the states, the law requires that for certain—usually serious—offenses, juveniles must be tried as adult criminal offenders; in such instances, prosecutors are required to file the case directly in criminal court. In some states, prosecutors are given the discretion to file a case in either criminal or juvenile court. The trend toward trying juvenile offenders as adults has grown out of the perception that the juvenile justice system has not dealt successfully with serious offenders. A number of observers believe that the legal notion of parens patriae and the emphasis on rehabilitation instead of

punishment have been ineffective and that some offenders are so dangerous and some offenses so grave that the only recourse is the criminal justice
system. Proponents of trying certain juvenile offenders in criminal court
also believe that the criminal court will impose harsher, more determinate
punishment. Indeed, the language of the two systems reveals their differing
outlook—in juvenile court, the judge adjudicates the youth a delinquent
and thus a ward of the court; in criminal court, an offender is convicted
and sentenced.

Child Protective Services

Child protective services (CPS) encompass the laws and government agencies that deal with child abuse and neglect.[42] Such services are provided by
an agency authorized to act on behalf of a child when the parents are
unwilling or unable to do so. All states require these agencies to investigate
and assess reports of child abuse and neglect and to provide rehabilitative
services to families in which maltreatment has occurred or is likely to
occur. Although child protective services are concerned primarily with the
abuse and neglect of children by their parents or guardians, in many jurisdictions the CPS agency also investigates nonparental caretakers such as
teachers or day-care providers.

While state and local agencies have primary responsibility for responding to reports of child maltreatment, professionals from various organizations and disciplines are involved in the prevention and treatment of child
abuse and neglect. Apart from family members, neighbors, and friends,
other individuals who are in a position to observe children and their families—for example, school personnel, social service providers, medical professionals, daycare workers, probation officers, members of the clergy, and
mental health professionals—may report abuse. While jurisdictions vary,
the process typically has several stages. In the first stage, reporting, a mandated reporter or other person contacts the CPS agency to report suspi-
cions that a child is being abused or neglected. (Mandated reporters are
individuals such as doctors, teachers, law enforcement personnel, child-
care providers, social service providers, and clergy who often are required
by law to report evidence or allegations of abuse or neglect.) In the second
stage, screening, CPS staff determine whether the report should be investigated, "screening out" reports that fall outside the agency's mandate or
that do not provide sufficient information to locate the family. When a
report is "screened in," it is assigned to a social worker for investigation.

During investigation, the third stage, the social worker meets with the child and family and those who know them to determine whether the reports of abuse or neglect are substantiated or unsubstantiated. When the report is substantiated, the social worker opens up a case to formulate a plan for ongoing services for the child and family to prevent further maltreatment. When the child is at immediate risk of harm or cannot be protected at home, the CPS agency may file a complaint in juvenile court to remove the child from the home. Adjudicatory hearings in juvenile court address the validity of the allegations, while dispositional hearings focus on the agency's case plan (including supervision, placement, and services to be rendered). Dispositional options include providing services to the child and family through the CPS agency, granting temporary custody of the child to the state CPS agency, placing the child in foster care, terminating parental rights, giving permanent custody to the state CPS agency, and giving legal custody to a relative or other person.

In most cases that are opened for investigation, children remain in their own homes with oversight by a social worker. In those cases, the CPS agency assesses the child's situation and plans appropriate services, provides ongoing services, reviews the case periodically, and eventually closes the case.

Managing Youth Violence

The various formal legal arrangements employed in managing youth violence have a strong effect on how policies are devised and implemented. As noted, the premise of this volume (and the project from which it arises) is that we can better understand the possibilities and limits of those arrangements if we explore the perspectives of the various entities and actors involved, not simply in isolation but as parts of an interrelated system. To that end, the following chapters bring together a diverse group of practitioners and experts to examine the role of the prosecutor, the defense attorney, the courts, the corrections department, the probation department, faith-based institutions, schools, nonprofit organizations, and the media— and to explore collaborations among them.

The Prosecutor

The role of the prosecutor in addressing youth violence has evolved dramatically in recent years. In their chapter, Catherine Coles and George Kelling show how various forces, including changes in jurisdiction and legal doctrine, the rise in youth crime, and institutional capacity, have combined to establish a new prosecutorial mission in dealing with youth violence. As they note, until the 1960s, prosecutors had rather little involvement in juvenile crime, which was essentially the concern of the juvenile court and the probation officer. The advent of *Kent* v. *United States* and *In re Gault* and their progeny—which established a due process model for juveniles, changing the existing process to one of adversarial proceedings—gave the prosecutor a more central role in dealing with juvenile crime. This institutional prosecutorial presence arising from *Kent* and *Gault*—which necessarily required greater resources and an increase in staffing—was only reinforced by the rise in juvenile crime. The prosecutor, who was increasingly viewed as the community's leader in confronting adult crime, was now being called on to address youth violence. This new focus was intensifying as the community prosecution movement took root, marked by prosecutors who emphasized working at the grass-roots level with citizens, law enforcement agencies, social service agencies, and the private sector in an effort to better assess and respond to crime problems. While prosecutors were charging serious juvenile offenders in criminal courts, they also were learning that fixing broken windows, for example, and maintaining order by dealing forcefully with lower-level offenses, such as misdemeanors, could be effective in preventing the development of more serious crime. Prosecutors were becoming increasingly proactive in dealing with crime rather than simply reacting when the police brought in a case for processing, and they also were beginning to view dealing with youth violence as a matter of problem solving. The movement toward community prosecution, the initiation of partnerships with schools, and an approach to juvenile violence that called for a holistic focus on families were all part of the new, problem-solving approach.

The Defense Attorney

If the role of the prosecutor in dealing with youth violence has evolved to encompass an array of enforcement and prevention mechanisms that extend far beyond the processing of individual cases, what of the role of the defense counsel? In presenting their perspective as defense attorneys for juvenile offenders, Randy Hertz, Barbara Fedders, and Stephen Weymouth weave together several themes. First, they suggest that today's defense attorney labors in an environment in which offending youths are no longer viewed as ultimately redeemable. The harm inflicted by juveniles' use of lethal weapons, coupled with the reinforcement in popular media, such as

films, of the notion that the youths of today are inherently more dangerous than their predecessors, has shaped the public's perception of juveniles
and the day-to-day work of the juvenile defender. Second, they suggest
that while *In re Gault* was unequivocal in its declaration of the right to
counsel for juveniles, all too often those who represent juveniles have failed
to be effective. They argue for greater funding of organizations that provide
defense services to indigents, whose budgets are far outmatched by that of
the prosecutor's office; they also contend that norms of representation must
be established and enforced.

Third, they reimagine the role of the juvenile defender, calling for juvenile defense offices that "differ from adult criminal defense offices in that
they go beyond obtaining the best possible result in court" to "view the
legal representation of a child in trouble as a unique opportunity for positive intervention in the child's life." They urge that representation by juvenile defense attorneys should be as comprehensive as the best representation in adult criminal cases. They also maintain that the juvenile defense
model should observe the basic norms of the adult criminal defense model
for representation at sentencing—namely, that the client controls the decision regarding what sentence to seek and that the lawyer seeks to obtain
that sentence. The new juvenile defender paradigm goes further in that it
seeks to identify various emotional and educational needs that may have
been ignored or undetected by a child's family and school in order to create a plan for the child's welfare that relates not only to his or her court case
but also to life after court.

Hertz, Fedders, and Weymouth point to multidisciplinary programs in
which lawyers work in collaboration with other professionals such as psychologists, social workers, and community outreach workers not only to
counsel juveniles through the uncertainties of the legal process or to advocate for a particular disposition but also to help them understand their
own behavior and avoid offending conduct in the future. They argue that
such multidisciplinary programs not only can provide juveniles with
needed help and present their case in a fuller personal context before the
court, but also that they can inform the court of the "larger structural
forces" or root causes of delinquent behavior, such as poverty and child
abuse and victimization. In the authors' view, those forces make it more
appropriate for the court to treat their clients as redeemable individuals
rather than as hardened criminals who ought not be helped so much as
punished. The authors urge that "a caring defense attorney, with adequate
resources," may begin to address a child's needs: "The time in which a

child's case is pending in court can, ideally, be a window during which he or she can receive needed support and services."

The Courts

The judiciary is by nature reactive and concerned with individual cases. What of the role, then, of the courts in the management of youth violence? David Mitchell, writing from his perspective as a juvenile court judge and a judge of general jurisdiction, and his co-author Sara Kropf suggest in their chapter that the central issues for the court in the management of youth violence are those of mission and capacity. As they point out, the concerns of the judicial system have changed over the years. The adjudication of youthful offending was largely a matter for the juvenile court, which focused on delinquency, status offenses, and neglect cases. The mission of the juvenile court was basically one of rehabilitation, premised on a distinctive view of juveniles as individuals with differing capacities for decisionmaking that called for differing forms of punishment. That view was manifested in differing notions of due process, procedural protections, and sentencing sanctions. Over time, as the notions of rehabilitation and punishment began to clash and some critics lost confidence in the juvenile court's rehabilitative mission, the mission has become more complex,. The intersection of judicial precedent (emanating from *Kent*, *Gault* and their progeny) and discontent with what was perceived to be the inadequacy or ineffectiveness of what some considered a "benevolent juvenile court" has led to a dramatic shift in recent years in the way that the judicial system has dealt with juveniles. Youth crime has become a matter of concern not only for the juvenile court, but also for the adult court.

Legislation has changed the jurisdiction of the courts and with it the landscape of juvenile justice. As noted, legislation and statutory waiver (which have made particular kinds of offenses the exclusive purview of criminal courts), prosecutorial "direct file" (which has moved locus of forum discretion to the prosecutor and away from the judge), and judicial waiver (which leaves the determination of juvenile or adult adjudication with the court) have altered the role of particular courts and reflect their changed mission. In a regime that permits heavier punishments, they also have sought to recognize, in particular cases, the hybrid nature of young offenders. Blending sentencing schemes (which permits the juvenile court to impose adult correctional sanctions on adjudicated delinquents so as to extend the term of confinement beyond the upper age of juvenile jurisdiction) is an example of such efforts. Judges also have attempted, with leg-islative authorization, to focus on youth violence in other new ways, by, for example, establishing specialized courts such as weapons and drug courts and calling for post-adjudication interventions such as aggressive supervision. Mitchell and Kropf argue that judges must assert leadership—ranging from implementing management information systems to track juvenile offenders to facilitating communication among courts—if their goal is to establish an effective presence in the lives of young offenders and those at risk of offending.

Corrections

The increase in the population of violent juvenile offenders poses particular challenges for the management of juvenile correctional facilities, among them protecting staff and nonviolent youth; meeting the programming and supervision needs of juveniles; and designing programs to reintegrate the juvenile into mainstream society. As Gerald Gaes observes, management problems are magnified because a variety of facilities, public and private, are used to confine youthful offenders, including detention centers; shelters; reception/diagnostic centers; training schools, ranches, camps, and farms; and group homes and halfway houses. Further complicating matters is the increasing trend toward sentencing juvenile offenders to adult correctional facilities, which typically do not provide the special programs or individual supervision that young offenders need.

Gaes writes that improving classification and programming can improve the efficiency and impact of corrections facilities without increasing costs. He defines "classification" as the "process of estimating an individual's likelihood of continued involvement in delinquent behavior and making decisions about the most appropriate type of intervention given the identified level of risk." To improve decisionmaking, Gaes urges jurisdictions to adopt scientifically based classification tools and procedures for every stage of the juvenile and adult criminal justice process: arrest/referral, adjudication/sentencing, probation/confinement, and post-release supervision. Sound classification procedures at each stage can make the decisionmaking process more rational (by improving officials' ability to accurately predict juveniles' behavior and thus the appropriateness of decisions to detain them, place them in a residential facility, and release them); more efficient (by promoting the more efficient allocation of resources); more just (by promoting uniformity and consistency in decisionmaking); and better managed (by facilitating the collection of information to be used to project potential offender populations and to allocate resources).

Gaes contends that it is useful to think of corrections as one link in the chain of the juvenile justice process and calls for continuity not only in the collection of information at every stage in the process, but also in programming for juveniles moving from residential to postresidential supervision.

Probation

Partnerships forged through crisis characterize the reinvention of the probation officer in the management of youth violence. Ronald Corbett Jr. uses as his starting point Operation Night Light, a Boston probation-police department partnership involving intensive contact with high-risk offenders during evening hours, both at home and in the street.

Traditionally, the probation officer has had three major responsibilities: intake, screening, and assessment (which involves making recommendations to the juvenile court judge as to whether juveniles arrested for minor offenses should be subjected to the formal court process or an informal process); conducting presentencing investigations to assist the court in determining an appropriate sentence and disposition; and, most important, supervising youth placed on probation by the courts. The supervisory function, which constitutes the major component of the probation officer's work, involves enforcing court orders regarding curfews or restitution and maintaining regular contact with the offender. In addition, the officer engages in collateral work with parents, schools, agency personnel, and employers; he or she may also ask for revocation of probation and perhaps imposition of a more serious sentence when the offender fails to comply with the conditions of probation. The potential impact of probation practices becomes self-evident when one considers that nationally 60 percent of all offenders under supervision of corrections departments are on probation.

Because of the increase in the number of violent juvenile offenders and the growing danger that probation officers would be assaulted in the line of duty, officers began to engage in less direct contact with the offenders they were charged with supervising and to maintain less of a physical presence on the street. As Corbett writes, "[Operation] Night Light rested on the stunningly simple premise that 'you can't fight fires from the station house' and was designed to reverse the trend of desk-bound probation officers working primarily out of their offices with little visible presence in the community, in an anemic form of community corrections disparagingly referred to as 'fortress probation.'"

Operation Night Light, as Corbett explains, was born out of the collaboration between the gang unit of the Boston police department and members of the probation department, who seized upon the insight that "they were watching the same youthful offenders from two different points on the perimeter of the revolving door." Using information obtained from their dealings with gang members and intelligence from their contacts with the gang unit, probation officers began to ask judges to include curfews and area restrictions in the conditions of probation for high-risk offenders. The Night Light strategy was based on the notion that such offenders required a short leash and that tighter supervision would reduce the number of new arrests as compliance with curfews, area restrictions, and other probation conditions increased. Typically, a one- or two-person probation team, matched with a similar team from the gang unit, would meet at gang unit headquarters to review the ten or fifteen probationers who the probation officers thought were evading compliance or were active on the street.

The Boston probation-police department collaboration has yielded great benefits to both partners. By facilitating closer surveillance of probationers and tighter enforcement of probation conditions, the partnership enables the police to deter probationers from offending again. It affords probation officers increased safety when entering crime-ridden areas in the evening and also brings new credibility to the supervisory function and to the enforcement of curfews and area restrictions.

Finally, the boldness in thinking about mission that can flow from a successful collaboration can result in creative new partnerships. Thus, as Corbett notes, in the community-based justice program spearheaded by Tom Reilly, a former Middlesex County (Massachusetts) district attorney, probation officers, school officials, and prosecutors are now working toward redefining their relationship and tearing down the "fire wall" that has impeded collaboration and sharing of information among them.

Faith-Based Institutions

The authors in this volume suggest that the traditional roles of the institutions involved in dealing with youth violence ought to be redefined, and they stress the importance of collaboration and partnerships with other institutions in improving outcomes. Recent experience has suggested that intermediary institutions typically divorced from a law enforcement function can play an important role. Pointing to the Boston experience,

Christopher Winship and Jenny Berrien discuss the role of a faith-based group, the Ten Point Coalition, in reducing youth violence. The Ten Point Coalition, which is led by three ministers and has about forty member churches, was formed in 1992 "to mobilize the Christian community around issues affecting black and Latino youth, especially those at risk for violence, drug abuse and other destructive behavior." The key contribution of the coalition, Winship and Berrien argue, rests not in establishing outreach programs for at-risk youth but in acting as intermediary between the police and the inner-city community. Noting the tensions that had existed between the minority community and the police, Winship and Berrien contend that the Ten Point Coalition, using its unique status as a moral force in the community, has created an "umbrella of legitimacy" for law enforcement efforts. That umbrella, and the new relationship between the police and the community, rests on several implicit understandings. They include the understanding that youth violence should be treated as a criminal problem that warrants the jailing of some youths for their own good and the good of the community; that a small number of offenders generates most of the violent crime and that members of the coalition will help identify them; that the ministers will have input in the treatment of specific individuals; and that the ministers will, through the media, monitor police behavior.

Interagency Strategy and Coordination

It is one thing to address youth violence from the perspective of a particular agency; it is another to create and coordinate interaction among agencies in order to establish a common strategy. David Kennedy, the director of the Boston Gun Project, writes of the latter effort. He discusses the development of a strategy—first through Operation Scrap Iron (an effort to clamp down on gun trafficking led by the Boston police department) and then through the Boston Gun Project working group (made up of members from the police department's gang unit, the probation department, the gang-outreach streetworker program, and academic researchers)—that culminated in Operation Ceasefire (a coordinated citywide strategy involving law enforcement and criminal justice agencies). Kennedy demonstrates that the practitioners were correct in their judgment that in Boston, juvenile violence was gang violence. Gun Project research showed that 1,300 individuals, many of them older than juveniles, in sixty-one identifiable street gangs were responsible for more than 60 percent of the killings of persons age 21 and under in Boston. Discussions within the working group resulted in the hypothesis that a dynamic of violence among the "1,300 and 61" had been established and that the risk and fear of gun violence was leading to gun carrying, gun use, preemptive and retributive shootings, proviolence street norms, and a self-perpetuating dynamic of violence. A further hypothesis was that the dynamic itself should be a target for deliberate intervention—that in a sense it was a "cause" to be attacked, like family and community problems and other risk factors. If the dynamic could be interrupted, then safer streets might result. As Kennedy further details, using research data and practitioner knowledge, the Boston Gun Project diagnosis was elaborated on as follows: homicides were being committed by juveniles and youths (not simply juveniles) in chronically offending groups (not limited to those that fit the technical law enforcement definitions of "gangs") by various means (although most of the violence was gun violence and the disruption of the illegal sale and possession of firearms would be a prime focus of the strategy).

Noting that successful interventions appear to have been implemented in diverse jurisdictions and that those jurisdictions vary in their organization and the nature of their problems, Kennedy offers some basic lessons regarding the framework that should be in place.

The Neutral Convener

Approaches to problem solving vary with the size, demographics, and history of jurisdictions. Frank Hartmann discusses Safety First, a partnership of criminal justice agencies, city agencies, and community groups and residents in Lowell, Massachusetts, a mid-sized urban city with a population of approximately 100,000. Lowell has had the benefit of dynamic community-based justice efforts spearheaded by then district attorney Tom Reilly and continued by his successor, Martha Coakley. In Hartmann's view, Safety First shows how supplementary efforts using nonprofit organizations, supporting academic research, and "a powerful neutral convener" can facilitate cross-cutting dialogue in a working group. The powerful neutral convener, who chairs the working group (and who in Lowell is the publisher of the local newspaper), "is someone whose professional status and personal reputation would make it difficult for local leadership to casually ignore his or her call." Hartmann explains that the behavior of youth was a top priority in Lowell, primarily because of the negative behavior of some crime-prone youths who dominated the city's large high school. He describes how twenty youths were identified as the most serious offenders/leaders, how a task force arranged meetings with each of the youths, and how the message was sent that criminality and violence would not be tolerated. The twenty offenders also were told about the availability of supportive social services. A "second tier" of thirty-five youths also was identified, and they too were informed of the new enforcement effort and the availability of services. When an offense occurred, the task force would "manage back" from the event in order to learn why it had not been anticipated and how it might have been prevented. In Hartmann's view, Safety First presents an example of how a "system" can be institutionalized to bring together parties who should be engaged in dialogue and how that dialogue can result in an improved response to the problems of crime.

Public, Private, and Nonprofit Sector Partnerships

It is instructive to think of the role of the public, private, and nonprofit sectors in the management of youth violence as well as the role of institutions. The continuing career of Amalia Betanzos has spanned those sectors for more than thirty-five years. During that time she has held the position of president of the Wildcat Academy, an alternative high school for at-risk youth, often with violent backgrounds; she also has been a member of the New York City board of education and a member of a mayoral commission on school safety. Analyzing the success of the Wildcat Academy, she points to five basic features: small class size and staffing priorities that place a premium on responsiveness to student needs; a "conspiracy of adults" who care; a longer school day; student work opportunities; a culture of self-discipline and self-respect; and the autonomy of the school from the central bureaucracy. Betanzos observes that it is useful to think in terms of mission, organization and management, measures of success, funding, partnerships, innovation, and competition in considering the roles of the public, private, and nonprofit sectors in dealing with youth violence. Betanzos concludes that to deal with school violence, we must be prepared "to tackle the conditions of chaos that have undermined the school experience," as some schools have begun to do by establishing new links with prosecutors, probation officers, the police, and mental health professionals and by expanding their curriculum to teach conflict resolution and avoidance of gangs.

The Media

It is also useful to approach the problem of youth violence by looking at institutions that contribute to the level of violence. One case in point is the media. Ronald Slaby writes that media violence appears to serve as a contributing cause of aggression, fear, callousness, and an appetite for violence. Those effects are shaped by a variety of factors, including the particular ways in which violence is presented as well as the susceptibility of viewers such as children to its effects. As to potential solutions, Slaby proposes the following: media/business remedies that focus on media industry efforts to disseminate programming designed to prevent violence and foster positive social behavior; policy/regulatory remedies directed at regulating the content of programming; public health/education remedies that use the media to educate parents, teachers, and other caregivers about early violence prevention strategies; parent/teacher remedies that focus on developing skills in young viewers that enable them to evaluate the accuracy of what they see in the media and that help youth to appreciate nonviolent alternatives; advocacy group/community remedies that promote alliances among community leaders, health professionals, educators, parents, law enforcement officials, and representatives of the media.

Networks of Capacity

As Mark Moore observes, "networks of capacity"—which encompass public-private partnerships and partnerships of local, state, and federal agencies—cross the boundaries of existing organizations. The challenge is to "take the existing uncoordinated operations of different agencies . . . and turn them into a more or less coherent and well-understood strategy for action that can be implemented successfully."

Drawing on the notion of cross-functional teams in business management and of cross-boundary management in the public sector, Moore explores the complex issues facing partnerships and collaborations. He notes, for example, how the boundaries between levels of government, between government agencies at the same level, and between government agencies and private sector enterprises pose great challenges to the management of youth violence, particularly large public sector initiatives. Moore draws lessons from the three points of the "strategic triangle"—one point focusing on the "public value" that an enterprise is trying to produce, the second focusing on the legitimacy of and support for an enterprise, and the third focusing on the operational capacity necessary to achieve the desired results. As managers and leaders strive to launch and maintain initiatives directed against youth violence, they need to consider all three points of the triangle.

Conclusion

As the director of the Securing Our Children's Future project, I posit a new collaborative framework distilled from the lessons of experience over the past decade to guide institutions and strategies in dealing with the problems of juvenile justice and youth violence. Elements of the framework include new responsibilities for the federal government and revised roles for the police, prosecutor, defense attorney, courts, probation officer, corrections, aftercare programs, schools, profit and nonprofit organizations, and the media. A new agenda is proposed that calls for building bridges between the juvenile justice system and the child welfare and protection system; enhancing mental health outreach efforts; developing a better understanding of collaboration and partnership in developing strategies to address youth violence; strengthening the research mission and the integration of research findings into action plans; and the periodic presentation by the nation's president of a "State of the Young" address.

Notes

1. Governor's Advisory Council on Youth Violence, *Analysis and Recommendations Regarding Violence in Massachusetts Schools* (Boston, 1999), p. 8.

2. Robert H. Bremner, ed., *Children and Youth in America: A Documentary History*, vol. 1 (Harvard University Press, 1970), pp. 309–11.

3. Irving A. Spergel, *The Youth Gang Problem: A Community Approach*, vol. 1 (Oxford University Press, 1995), p. 7.

4. Much legend surrounds Billy the Kid, who was born Henry McCarty in New York City in 1859 and was also known as William Bonney. He would become "the most celebrated outlaw in the old Southwest" before he was shot to death in New Mexico in 1881 by Sheriff Pat Garrett. See "Billy the Kid," in *Encyclopedia Americana* (Danbury: Grolier, 2001), p. 749. While some have attributed twenty-one killings to Billy the Kid, others have concluded that that tally is greatly exaggerated. See Time-Life Books, *The Wild West* (New York: Warner Books, 1993), p. 150. See, generally, Joseph Geringer, "Henry McCarty: The Wild West's 'Billy the Kid'" (http://www.crimelibrary.com/americana/kid/index.htm [April 2002]).

5. Howard N. Snyder and Melissa Sickmund, *Juvenile Offenders and Victims: 1999 National Report* (U.S. Department of Justice, Office of Juvenile Justice and Delinquency Prevention, 1999), p. 25; U.S. Surgeon General, *Youth Violence: A Report of the Surgeon General* (U.S. Department of Health and Human Services, 2001), p. 27.

6. U.S. Department of Justice Office of Juvenile Justice and Delinquency Prevention (OJJDP), *Statistical Briefing Book* (http://ojjdp.ncjrs.org/ojstatbb/html/qa092.html [April 2002]). The population of those under 18 is expected to increase 8 percent between 1995

and 2015. By contrast, the population of persons age 65 and older will increase 36 percent, persons ages 25 to 64 will increase 18 percent, and persons ages 18 through 24 will increase 22 percent.

7. Jeffrey A. Butts, *Youth Crime Drop* (Washington: Urban Institute, 2000). Regarding an upturn, see, for example, Francis Latour, "Crackdown on Crime in Dorchester Set to Start," *Boston Globe,* October 30, 2001, p. B1. See also Federal Bureau of Investigation, *Crime Trends: 2001 Preliminary Figures* (Washington, 2002) (volume of violent crime generally, not broken down by age, increased 0.6 percent in 2001 from the 2000 figure; murder volume increased 26.4 percent). See also Dan Eggen, "Major Crimes in U.S. Increase," *Washington Post,* June 23, 2002, p. A1, quoting Jack Riley, director of the Rand Corporation Public Safety and Justice Program, as stating that "[w]e're probably done seeing declines in crime rates for some time to come"; professor James Alan Fox is quoted as observing that "[t]he great 1990s crime drop ended with the 1990s; the new millenium brings a different picture. This tells us we can't be complacent about crime levels. We have to reintensify our efforts."

8. See, for example, Deborah Prothrow-Stith and Michaele Weissman, *Deadly Consequences* (New York: Harper Perennial, 1993); Mark H. Moore, "Public Health and Criminal Justice Approaches to Prevention," in Michael Tonry and D. P. Farrington, eds., *Crime and Justice: A Review of Research* (University of Chicago Press, 1995); Mark H. Moore and others, "Violence and Intentional Injuries: Criminal Justice and Public Health Perspectives on an Urgent National Problem," in A. J. Reiss and J. A. Roth, eds., *Understanding and Preventing Violence,* vol. 4 (Washington: National Academy Press, 1994), pp. 167–216.

9. U.S. Surgeon General, *Youth Violence,* pp. 17–19; Alfred Blumstein and Joel Wallman, "The Recent Rise and Fall of American Youth Violence," in Alfred Blumstein and Joel Wallman, eds., *The Crime Drop in America* (Cambridge University Press, 2000), p. 3.

10. U.S. Surgeon General, *Youth Violence,* pp. 17–19; Blumstein and Wallman, "The Recent Rise and Fall of American Youth Violence," p. 3.

11. Federal Bureau of Investigation, *Crime in the United States 2000* (U.S. Department of Justice, 2001).

12. Howard Snyder, *Juvenile Arrests 2000* (Pittsburgh: National Center for Juvenile Justice, 2001), p. 2.

13. Ibid.

14. Lloyd D. Johnson, Jerold G. Bachman, and Patrick M. O'Malley, *Monitoring the Future* (Ann Arbor: Institute of Social Research, 1995).

15. U.S. Surgeon General, *Youth Violence,* pp. 17–18.

16. Snyder, *Juvenile Arrests 2000,* p. 12.

17. The four violent crime index offenses are defined as follows: *Criminal homicide/murder and nonnegligent manslaughter.* The willful (nonnegligent) killing of one human being by another. *Robbery.* The taking or attempting to take anything of value from the care, custody, or control of a person or persons by force or threat of force or violence and/or putting the victim in fear. *Aggravated assault:* An unlawful attack by one person upon another wherein the offender uses a weapon or displays it in a threatening manner or the victim suffers obvious severe or aggravated bodily injury involving apparent broken bones, loss of teeth, possible internal injury, severe laceration, or loss of consciousness. *Forcible rape:* The carnal knowledge of a female forcibly and against her will. Assaults or attempts to

commit rape by force or threat of force are also included; however, statutory rape (without force) and other sex offenses are excluded. (Federal Bureau of Investigation, *Crime in the United States 2000*.)

18. The figures in this paragraph come from Snyder, *Juvenile Arrests 2000*, pp. 3, 4, 6, and 10.

19. Blumstein and Wallman, "The Recent Rise and Fall of American Youth Violence," p. 17.

20. The following figures come from Snyder, *Juvenile Arrests 2000*, pp. 1, 4, and 6.

21. Snyder, *Juvenile Arrests 2000*, p. 8; U.S. Surgeon General, *Youth Violence*, p. 21; Philip J. Cook and John H. Laub, "The Unprecedented Epidemic in Youth Violence," in Tonry and Moore, eds., *Youth Violence,* pp. 27–64.

22. U.S. Surgeon General, *Youth Violence*, p. 20.

23. Ibid.

24. Snyder, *Juvenile Arrests 2000*, p. 4; U.S. Surgeon General, *Youth Violence*, p. 20.

25. Snyder, *Juvenile Arrests 2000*, p. 6.

26. Ibid.

27. U.S. Surgeon General, *Youth Violence*, p. 33.

28. The data that follow are taken from U.S. Department of Education, U.S. Department of Justice, *Indicators of School Crime and Safety 2001* (2001), pp. 1–30; and U.S. Department of Education, U.S. Department of Justice, *2000 Annual Report on School Safety* (2000), pp. 3–11.

29. U.S. Department of Education, U.S. Department of Justice, *Indicators of School Crime and Safety 2001*, p. 13.

30. Kristen Kracke, "Children's Exposure to Violence: The Safe Start Initiative" (U.S. Department of Justice, Office of Juvenile Justice and Delinquency Prevention, April 2001).

31. U.S. Department of Health and Human Services, "National Child Abuse and Neglect Data System (NCANDS), Summary of Key Findings from Calendar Year 2000" (http://www.calib.com/nccanch/prevmnth/scope/ncands.cfm [April 2002]); see, generally, Jane Waldfogel, *The Future of Child Protection: How to Break the Cycle of Abuse and Neglect* (Harvard University Press, 1998), pp. 6–8.

32. U.S. Department of Health and Human Services, "National Child Abuse and Neglect Data System (NCANDS), Summary of Key Findings from Calendar Year 2000."

33. Kracke, "Children's Exposure to Violence," p. 1.

34. Richard A. Mendel, *Less Hype, More Help: Reducing Juvenile Crime, What Works— And What Doesn't* (Washington: American Youth Policy Form, 2000), p. 47. With respect to the limited federal judicial involvement with juveniles, statistics reveal that during the period October 1, 1998, through September 30, 1999, there were only 459 convicted federal offenders between the ages of 16 and 18, constituting 0.8 percent of all convicted offenders, and 1.6 percent of violent offenses. U.S. Department of Justice, *Compendium of Federal Justice Statistics, 1999* (Bureau of Justice Statistics, 2001), p. 59. Federal statutes setting forth the restrictions on proceedings against juveniles are found in Title 18 of the United States Code, Sections 5031–39.

35. Snyder and Sickmund, *Juvenile Offenders and Victims*, p. 93.

36. Thomas Grisso and Robert G. Schwartz, eds., *Youth on Trial: A Developmental Perspective on Juvenile Justice* (University of Chicago, 2000), pp. 14–19. The description of

the juvenile justice and "adult" criminal system draws on Grisso and Schwartz and Snyder and Sickmund, *Juvenile Offenders and Victims,* pp. 97–100.

37. OJJDP, *Statistical Briefing Book,* (http://ojjdp.ncjrs.org/ojstatbb/html/qa181.html [May 2002]).

38. Ibid. (http://www.ojjdp.ncjrs.org/ojstatbb/html/qa179.html [May 2002]).

39. Ibid. (http://www.ojjdp.ncjrs.org/ojstatbb/asp [May 2002]).

40. Ibid.

41. Ibid. (http://ojjdp.ncjrs.org/ojstatbb/html/qa190.html [May 2002]).

42. Waldfogel, *The Future of Child Protection,* pp. 5–6. The description of child protective services draws on Waldfogel and Snyder and Sickmund, *Juvenile Offenders and Victims,* pp. 44–45.

2

CATHERINE M. COLES
GEORGE L. KELLING

New Trends in Prosecutors' Approaches to Youthful Offenders

PROLOGUE

O.K., I (KELLING, CERTAINLY NOT COLES) ADMIT IT. I am old enough to have practiced in the juvenile justice system in the pre-*Gault* days. And as long as I'm into admissions, I might as well admit that I am an unreconstructed and unrepentant pre-Gaultian: in my opinion, most of the changes in the handling of juveniles since the mid-1970s have been ill advised at best, disastrous at worst. But I will resist debating all of this here—the exaggerated preoccupation with rights, deinstitutionalization, decriminalization. The point is to share with readers not intimately familiar with practice then what it was like. It will help us understand what is happening now.

I worked in the juvenile justice system in two places: Hennepin County (Minneapolis, Minnesota) and Milwaukee County (Wisconsin) during the period 1956–63. The Milwaukee County system was administered by the juvenile court judge, the Hennepin County system by an administrator of court services under the direction of the county board. Hennepin County,

Research for this chapter was supported by grant number 95-IJ-CX-0096, awarded by the National Institute of Justice, Office of Justice Programs, U.S. Department of Justice. The views expressed are those of the authors and do not necessarily represent the official position or policies of the U.S. Department of Justice.

where I cut my teeth as a probation officer, was generally considered to have a highly professional system. Milwaukee County wasn't far behind.

Here's how it worked in Hennepin County. When a youth committed a crime—from vandalism to manslaughter—in St. Louis Park (one of two suburban areas to which I was assigned, both close to the city), the police would send a report to the intake division of juvenile court services. If the offense or circumstances were "serious" enough ("serious" being, of course, a relative concept depending on age, sex, demeanor, family availability, and so forth) police would take the youth to the detention home. An intake worker (a probation officer with a specific assignment) would meet with the youth—immediately if the youth was detained, otherwise, within a week or so. The intake worker had several options: counsel the youth and close the case; refer the youth for services and close the case; put the case on hold for three to six months, do nothing, and close the case if the youth committed no more offenses or seemed to be "adjusting"; meet the youth regularly, although informally; or schedule a hearing for the youth. The intake officer often contacted me for cases in my areas to find out whether I knew much about the youth, event, family, or impact of the offense. Sometimes, if I knew or was working with the family, the intake officer would refer the case directly to me for intake screening.

When a hearing was scheduled, I would receive the police incident form and a report from the intake worker. My job then was to prepare a history and make a recommendation to the court. Depending on the youth, the offense, and the judge, I might approach the court clerk (whom all the probation officers knew well) to reschedule the case, changing the date, the judge, or both. It was common among probation officers to share the lore about judges: "Don't let Judge X get a sex case [usually consensual sex between youth] unless the kid is really in a lot of other trouble. For sure, Judge X will hit him hard." To compile the history, I would conduct several interviews with the youth as well as school officials, parents, police, representatives of involved social agencies, and the pastor, priest, or rabbi. I would meet with other family members if necessary and often with the victim, especially when restitution seemed appropriate. Jewish Family and Children's Service often contacted me about Jewish youth after an offense occurred but before intake processed the case. They were always intimately involved in whatever planning I did and in shaping my recommendation. No other agency was as aggressive: in one case of chronic truancy, they contacted me even before the school and police reported the problem. The history that I prepared would conclude with a recommendation to the court: counsel the youth and close the case; continue to keep the youth under informal supervision for a specified number of months; place the youth on probation; commit the youth to the county home school for boys (Milwaukee had no county home school but had several private institutions that offered similar services), suspend the commitment, and put the youth on probation; commit the youth to the county home school for boys; commit the youth to the custody of the state for placement in a state institution for boys, stay the sentence, and place the youth on probation; and finally, commit the youth to the state. The judge, of course, had the option of transferring the case to adult court; however, I was never involved in such a case.

The hearing itself was informal. Although the judge wore robes, he sat at the head of two conference tables. Often the parents, the youth, a court reporter, and I were alone with the judge; frequently, clergy and social agency representatives were there as well. A couple of times a newspaper reporter was allowed in the courtroom, with the understanding that the confidentiality of the youth would be protected. A defense attorney was present in no more than three of my cases over a two-year period. Generally, I viewed the defense attorney as one more resource to use in planning for the youth, a role that the defense attorneys found appropriate. None ever objected to my recommendations. (One, in a manslaughter case, went out of his way to praise me at the end of the hearing—praise that was timely because I was in the dog house with the judge involved.) The judge would begin by asking the youth whether he had committed the crime in question. Admission was almost universal. I would not let a case reach that point if there was any question about culpability; it would have gone back to intake or even to the police. The judge would generally talk with the family—counseling, reprimanding, or exhorting, depending upon the judge—and then ask me to give a verbal report, including my recommendation. Parents and youth always knew what I was going to recommend. The judge probably agreed with my recommendation 95 percent of the time. That concluded the hearing.

I need not go on except to make a couple of important points: first, I never saw a prosecutor. Period. (Well, that's not entirely true—we did bowl against each other in the county employees' league.) Second, in stayed sentences I had the authority to immediately take, or have a youth taken, into custody if he reoffended, a power that the judge and I were very explicit about with youthful offenders: "Offend or violate probation and you spend the night in our bed." Truancy or minor offenses might not mean going to the county home school or into state custody, but they probably meant a few nights in detention. Given the close relationship that I had with the police, they didn't even bother with intake. They would contact me immediately if youths on stayed commitments offended or violated their probation—again, for minor as well as major offenses. And I had a caseload under fifty and rarely did more than two or three prehearing reports a month.

REFLECTING ON THESE REMINISCENCES in light of our current research into changes in policing and prosecution over the last decade or two, we (Kelling *and* Coles) are struck by the parallels between the goals, objectives, and tactics of juvenile probation officers of the 1960s in dealing with youthful offenders and those of many district attorneys and county prosecutors today, especially those who identify themselves with the "community prosecution" movement. Both recognize the importance of addressing misdemeanors as well as violent crime. Both work at building partnerships with representatives of other criminal justice agencies and the private sector to address crime and public safety issues. Both are concerned with the welfare of the community. Both work to prevent juvenile crime rather than simply respond to a crime after it has been committed. And both take a comprehensive, problem-solving approach to controlling youth crime, making use of a broad range of tactics including treatment, diversion, intermediate sanctions, and other alternatives to direct court involvement and incarceration.

These characteristics are not unique to developments in prosecution or juvenile justice, but they are central to new trends in criminal justice administration across the country. Spurred on by the apparent success of community-oriented policing in working with probation departments, state and federal prosecutors, local government officials, and citizens themselves to lower the crime rate, many prosecutors and other practitioners are rethinking their overall goals and mission. Some also are feeling increased pressure to move beyond previous definitions of acceptable performance. The development of community-oriented policing, the adoption of problem solving as a key tactic by police as well as other agencies,[1] the creation of community courts,[2] the decentralization of operations by some prosecutors as they move their offices into neighborhood storefronts and police stations,[3] and the consideration of restorative and community justice approaches to corrections[4] all reflect the critical self-examination taking place. Whether prosecutors themselves are merely receptive to such changes, aggressively pursuing them, or charting a middle course, chances are that they are testing some of them in the area of juvenile justice. Today, juvenile safety, crime, and violence are high priority.

But these are relatively recent developments in prosecution. Over the last thirty years, the prosecutor's role in juvenile justice has undergone a fundamental transformation, from nearly complete lack of involvement (except in cases of murder or repeated violent felonies) to unquestioned dominance. A due process model of juvenile justice—entailing greater formality, legalism, and adversarial proceedings—has come to replace the informal workings of the earlier juvenile court. Yet innovative prosecutors today are using their power and influence not only to prosecute violent and repeat youthful offenders vigorously, but to create, and channel offenders into, a network of community-based crime diversion programs. They are expanding their role to include crime prevention as well as prosecution, working with the police in problem-solving efforts to address crime and public safety issues. In many senses, they appear to have moved closer to the role of the juvenile probation officer described in the opening pages of this chapter.

In the discussion that follows we trace the growth of the considerable power and authority of today's prosecutors in addressing juvenile crime and violence and document the evolution of a new way of thinking about juvenile offenders. We focus in particular on two developments that contribute significantly to the new approach: the "broken windows" hypothesis and a newly emerging strategy, community prosecution. We briefly explore the key elements of each. Finally, we examine the policies and practices of a number of district attorneys and county prosecutors around the country, many of whom identify with the community prosecution strategy, in dealing with troubled and troublesome youth. Throughout, we discuss not only juveniles as they are defined in law (which varies from state to state), but youth more broadly, encompassing those in their early twenties as well. Where we describe particular laws, programs, or policies, we adopt the terminology they use.

The Historical Legacy in Prosecution

The involvement of state court prosecutors in, and their power over, the prosecution of juvenile crime increased dramatically during the second half of the past century. In part this was due to changes in the functioning of the juvenile courts themselves, as the informal manner in which the judge and court personnel once made decisions about how best to handle juvenile cases gave way to a due process model governed by formal legal proceedings, in which prosecutors play a dominant role. Prosecutors' increased involvement in juvenile justice is tied also to an increase in their overall power in criminal justice processes. In the area of juvenile prosecution, this increase is evident not only in the juvenile court but in the waiver process—the transfer of juveniles to adult criminal courts.

From the 1930s until the Supreme Court's decisions in *Kent* v. *United States* (1966) and *In re Gault* (1967), juvenile proceedings were conducted separately from criminal court proceedings; they were directed toward rehabilitation rather than punishment; and they used largely informal procedures.[5] The premise was that children under the age of sixteen (later eighteen) who committed crimes (except perhaps murder) should be helped by the juvenile court rather than prosecuted in criminal court.[6] The court's operations were governed by discretionary dispositions made by the juvenile court judge, with significant input from probation officials and intake workers, all of whom sought a resolution "in the best interests of the child." As Barry Feld describes it, "In their social and psychological inquiry into the whole child, the specific criminal offense a child committed was of minor significance because it indicated little about a child's 'real needs.' The misdeeds that brought a child before the court affected neither the intensity nor the duration of intervention because each child's 'real needs' differed and no limits could be defined in advance. Indeterminate, nonproportional dispositions could continue for the duration of minority."[7] Dispositions in juvenile courts provided for individualized treatment and social controls, with services provided by private and, to a lesser extent, public agencies in the community.[8]

During most of the intervening decades, juvenile court trials rarely took place. State or local prosecutors were present only infrequently in juvenile courts; they would appear, for example, when a judge requested that they present evidence in a case that was contested. Prosecutors no doubt believed they had "more important things to do in the criminal courts."[9] Until the mid-1970s, police prosecutors worked in juvenile courts in Boston and in other locations, while in California and other states, probation officers performed the role of prosecutor.[10] Intake was often in the hands of the police, probation officers, intake personnel who worked for the court or probation department, and the court clerk.[11] Judicial waiver was always an option. Judges could transfer any offenders to criminal courts, and they usually did so in highly visible or serious cases, with little or no formality.[12]

Prosecutors Enter the Juvenile Courts

A number of Supreme Court decisions in the 1960s heralded dramatic changes for both juvenile courts and prosecutors' involvement in them. These decisions grew out of concerns surrounding the lack of due process protections and the potential for arbitrary and unfair punishment of children accused of crimes or status offenses in the informal functioning of the juvenile courts. The two cases having the most extensive implications were *Kent* v. *United States* and *In re Gault*. In *Kent*, the Court held that before being waived to criminal court, a juvenile was "entitled to a hearing, including access by his counsel to the social records and probation or similar reports which presumably are considered by the court, and to a statement of the reasons for the Juvenile Court's decision."[13] One year later, in *Gault*, the Court set out a detailed list of rights that were to be accorded juveniles in court hearings: notification of charges; protections against self-incrimination; and the right to confront and cross-examine witnesses, to have a written transcript of proceedings, and to counsel.[14] In subsequent decisions the Supreme Court held that the government had to prove delinquency beyond a reasonable doubt (the prior standard accepted was a preponderance of the evidence)[15] and ruled that the double jeopardy clause prevented retrying a youth in adult criminal court after his case had been adjudicated in juvenile court, thereby recognizing both juvenile and criminal court proceedings as "essentially criminal."[16]

Characterizing the effects of these decisions, former Denver juvenile court judge Ted Rubin noted that "the defense attorneys came first, stimulated by the *Gault* decision. . . . The former model of the judge, assisted by probation officers, as representative of the state's interest in behalf of children and the community was no longer appropriate to a more legally based and adversarial court."[17] In its 1967 report, the President's Commission on Law Enforcement and Administration of Justice emphasized the need for defense counsel to be present in juvenile courts but downplayed the need for the prosecutor: "To the extent that the presence of counsel for the child . . . in contested adjudicatory proceedings . . . would result in a closer approximation of the adversary system, the presence of counsel on the other side may be necessary to achieve the virtues of that system. Using the public prosecutor may be too great a departure from the spirit of the juvenile court. But experience may show some legal representative of the public, perhaps a corporation counsel or a lawyer from the welfare department, to be desirable in many cases."[18]

Nevertheless, the adversarial processes and legal formality introduced into the juvenile court by the Court's decisions could not help but bring the prosecutor in to balance the presence of the defense counsel in the courtroom. Once prosecutors became involved in juvenile court proceedings, they grew concerned about the intake process as well, and they soon sought to influence and even control it. As Rubin noted:

> Prosecutors began to object when a judge gave them a contested case to prosecute and the petition was improperly prepared, probable cause was absent, evidence had been gathered contrary to constitutional requirements, witnesses had not been interviewed, or the case was de minimus and did not merit prosecution. The adult processing model, with its increased use of prosecutor screening of police reports and criminal charges, enhanced prosecutor interest in developing a parallel approach for juvenile justice.[19]

Rubin was writing (in 1980) of the "emerging dominance" of prosecutors in the intake process, but it was not only in intake that their power would grow. Gradually, prosecutors found that they needed to be present at every stage, from screening and pretrial hearings through post-trial functions. Several factors facilitated the growth of their involvement and power in the juvenile court. First, police and prosecutors' perspectives on crime control aligned more closely with each other than they did with the perspective of probation officers (especially, according to Rubin, when a probation officer might reject filing because of the contrition or cooperation of the juvenile, while the police and prosecutor would support filing). In addition, prosecutors used their influence to secure legislative changes that increased their role in juvenile court; juvenile court judges accepted the prosecutor's role as a "politically useful buffer between the police and the court"; and defense attorneys preferred prosecutors' predictable, legally based actions to the irregularity of earlier juvenile court proceedings.[20]

With the new due process orientation of the juvenile court firmly established, in 1977 the Law Enforcement Assistance Administration's advisory committee on standards for the administration of juvenile justice formally recommended that prosecutors be involved in juvenile court at virtually all stages of legal proceedings:

> The state should be entitled to be represented by counsel in all proceedings arising under the jurisdiction of the family court in which the state has an interest.

Counsel for the state in matters before the family court should be from the office that normally represents the state in criminal proceedings before the highest court of general jurisdictions. Offices with six or more attorneys should establish a separate family court section, including legal, professional, and clerical staff.[21]

Also in 1977, the National District Attorneys Association adopted national prosecution standards, including one governing juvenile delinquency, that asserted the need for prosecutors' involvement in all stages of court proceedings. According to these standards, the prosecutor should make the final decision regarding filing, and while the prosecutor's primary concern should be the interests and well-being of the community, he or she should remember the purpose and philosophy of the juvenile court. The prosecutor should be present at detention, waiver, adjudication, and dispositional proceedings; should play an adversarial role during adjudication; and should be able to make independent recommendations at disposition hearings.[22]

Even as the presence of prosecutors in juvenile courts grew, however, in practice the general orientation and operations of juvenile courts did not immediately change.[23] Looking at the juvenile courts of Middlesex County, Massachusetts, John Laub and Bruce MacMurray found as late as 1984 that although prosecutors' involvement had increased, the courts remained essentially "dispositional" rather than "prosecutorial." The court was still fundamentally committed to rehabilitating and providing services to delinquent children, and judges and probation officers were still the dominant actors. Prosecutors found themselves outsiders who had to learn to work within the court's unique setting and rules. It is no wonder that juvenile court prosecutions remained a low priority for many prosecutors.[24]

Power Shifts to the Prosecutor

Although not all prosecutors rapidly embraced their new position in the juvenile court, their role continued to expand. With the noticeable rise in youth violence that took place from the 1970s and particularly the 1980s on, pressure began to build on prosecutors as well as police to "do something." Prosecutors were no longer removed and distant, but along with police and other criminal justice officials, they had come to "own" the problems of youth crime and violence. Increasingly it would be the prosecutor who was called upon to represent the public interest with respect to youth violence in both the courtroom and the community.

Two factors afford prosecutors special opportunity and responsibility for influencing local policy toward youth violence in the community and the treatment of juveniles in the courts. First, the district attorney, county prosecutor, or state's attorney generally is elected and often is the most powerful elected criminal justice official at the local level. The prosecutor therefore can assume the role of leader in the community as well as in the courtroom. Second, the prosecutor has a significant degree of discretionary authority and power over the disposition of juvenile cases (after arrest) through charging decisions (determinations of whether and what charges to file against an offender), as well as in adjudicatory, detention, disposition, and probation hearings. James Shine and Dwight Price point out the importance of these factors: "[I]f prosecutors choose to fully utilize this influence, they can become the 'quarterback' within the juvenile system. They can help to promote a fair and just system, one that protects the public but is also concerned with the welfare of each juvenile."[25]

Recognizing the prosecutor's responsibility and potential influence, the National District Attorneys Association in 1989 adopted revised standards relating to juvenile delinquency that fully accepted the new due process model of the juvenile courts and sought to guide prosecutors in redefining their role within this context.[26] The standards called for involving prosecutors in all stages of proceedings, including disposition; establishing programs for serious juvenile crime; assigning experienced prosecutors to handle or supervise juvenile court cases; using victim witness advocates (nonlawyer personnel trained to work directly with victims, facilitating their participation in prosecutions but also assisting them by providing support and referrals to service providers); and actively involving prosecutors in diversion opportunities and programs.

Once prosecutors began to be seen as legitimate players in juvenile court proceedings, no doubt they sought, in organizational terms, to maximize their power, authority, and leverage vis-à-vis other criminal justice officials. Their ability to do so was enhanced by the concomitant growth in their overall power within the courts and criminal justice processes in general, especially as greater controls were placed on other agencies. For example, the Supreme Court sought to limit police use of discretion by imposing restrictions on search and seizure procedures, treatment of offenders in custody, and police use of force, while sentencing guidelines and mandatory minimum sentencing statutes reduced the power of judges. Many such attempts to reduce the discretion of other officials merely shifted power to the prosecutor, who exercised it less visibly in charging, called by some "the single most important decision made in an individual case."[27] When states around the country began, through legislation, to reduce the jurisdiction of the juvenile court, permitting and even mandating greater use of provisions for the transfer of violent juvenile offenders to criminal court, the effects again were "to expand the role of the prosecutor while constricting the role of the juvenile court judge."[28]

All states today have provisions of some sort for trying certain youth as adults in criminal court; most have a combination of different types of transfer.[29] Although there are three types of transfer—or waiver—the prosecutor retains considerable discretion in each one through the charging decision and, in effect, frequently can choose the forum in which a case will proceed.

Under *judicial waiver*—the most common way to transfer juvenile offenders to criminal court—a judge is the primary decisionmaker in determining whether juvenile court jurisdiction should be waived. Specific guidelines, most of which are set out in *Kent v. United States,* identify particular criteria to be considered, such as the age of the offender at the time of the offense, the nature of the offense, and the youth's past history of offenses, ultimately going to consideration of whether the youth poses a danger to the public and is amenable to treatment. Frequently, however, the process of judicial waiver is initiated by the prosecutor. Under *statutory waiver*, state legislation excludes from juvenile court jurisdiction certain categories of offenders depending on the offender's age, the crime committed, the offender's record, or a combination of these factors. Since 1992, there has been a notable increase in the enactment of such provisions by states. By 1998, twenty-eight states provided for statutory exclusion; in addition, fourteen provided for mandatory waiver and fourteen plus the District of Columbia for presumptive waiver, using similar criteria. Again, the charging decision is the prosecutor's. Finally, *prosecutorial waiver*, or *direct file*, expands the power of the prosecutor to the greatest degree. Here, juvenile and criminal courts in fourteen states and the District of Columbia have concurrent jurisdiction in all or in designated juvenile cases, and the prosecutor's decision to file in one court or the other is not subject to appellate review.[30] In a few states, such as Florida, legislation requires prosecutors to develop detailed guidelines and policies for filing juvenile cases in criminal court.[31]

In addition to these types of transfer, many states have "safety valve" provisions that permit judges to send a matter back to juvenile court; these provisions apply on a case-by-case basis where broad exclusion or concurrent jurisdiction provisions are in effect. Finally, several states have "once an adult, always an adult" provisions, whereby criminal court jurisdiction is mandatory in all subsequent cases involving juvenile offenders who are either waived from juvenile court or convicted in criminal court.[32]

The power of the prosecutor is considerable, then, with respect to waiver. Eric Klein concludes that "the prosecutor's decision of where to file, how to charge, or whether to move for waiver is a threshold decision that is completely within the prosecutor's discretion and is almost completely unchecked. The only system which affords a check on this decision is . . . judicial waiver, where the juvenile court judge is forced to either ratify or deny the prosecutor's decision. As an additional check on any arbitrary exercise of authority, the judge's decision is then appealable to a higher court."[33] More than a few observers, among them Charles Thomas and Shay Bilchik, have pointed out the potential danger in the manner and context in which prosecutors' discretion with respect to waiver is exercised and the absence of mechanisms for managing it or holding prosecutors accountable for its use:

> [T]here is a truly awesome difference in our legal system between the potential for abuse of judicial and of prosecutorial powers. Many if not most of the powers vested in the judiciary are exercised in open court and, at least in relative terms, those offended by the exercise of judicial discretion have access to various avenues of appeal. The same is far from true with regard to the exercise of prosecutorial powers. Those powers are exercised in contexts . . . shielded from public scrutiny. They equally often reflect the preferences of individual and sometimes inexperienced prosecutors rather than officially promulgated administrative guidelines devised by senior and experienced personnel—and this is most particularly true with regard to the nation's juvenile court prosecutors. Even when guidelines do exist, mechanisms for effectively monitoring compliance with them seldom exist. Finally, appellate attacks on prosecutorial decisions are almost doomed to fail in all but cases involving the most grievous abuses. Thus, whether for better or for worse, the fact is that the most peculiar feature of our juvenile and criminal justice process is that it involves a fairly elaborate set of checks and balances on the conduct and the decisions of all but one set of actors: prosecutors.[34]

Prosecution of youthful offenders is shared by district attorneys and county prosecutors, attorneys general working with state prosecutors, prosecutors employed directly by a few family courts, city and municipal attorneys (particularly in the area of status offenses and misdemeanors), and federal prosecutors (who handle the most serious violent crimes). Most cases, by far, are handled by district attorneys and county prosecutors.[35]

According to the 1994 National Survey of Prosecutors, 94 percent of state court prosecutors (district attorneys and county prosecutors) were responsible for handling juvenile cases. Of these, 86 percent handled delinquency cases; 84 percent handled requests to transfer juveniles to criminal courts; 70 percent handled abuse and neglect cases; 64 percent handled noncriminal misdemeanor cases, including status offenses (running away, incorrigibility, truancy, and others); and 45 percent handled dependency reviews.[36] A few states, such as Missouri, have family courts in which juvenile delinquency cases are heard, along with cases involving abuse and neglect, status offenses, and family matters, with prosecutors employed directly by the court administration. Of prosecutor's offices that handled juvenile cases, about two-thirds transferred at least one juvenile case to a criminal court in 1994. Among offices that carried out such transfers, "37% transferred at least one aggravated assault case, 35% at least one burglary case, 34% at least one robbery case, and 32% at least one murder case," and waivers based on violent offenses were more numerous than those based upon property offenses.[37] The 1996 National Survey of Prosecutors reported that three-fourths of all prosecutor's offices proceeded against juveniles in criminal court: the median number of juveniles proceeded against was ninety-three by full-time large offices; twenty-four by full-time medium-sized offices; four by full-time small offices; and three in part-time offices. One-third of offices had a specialized unit or attorneys handling criminal court prosecution of juveniles (most often large and medium offices), and 12 percent reported having written guidelines governing such proceedings.[38]

In 1938, Congress passed the first Juvenile Justice Act, under which juveniles could be prosecuted in federal courts. Until fairly recently, however, this option was not pursued. Today, juveniles may be adjudicated as adults in federal court if the offense is a violent felony or involves drug trafficking and was committed after a juvenile's fifteenth birthday but before the age of eighteen; or if the youth possessed a firearm during a violent offense and was at least thirteen at the time of the offense. In order to proceed against a juvenile in a delinquency adjudication, a U.S. attorney must certify to the court a "substantial Federal interest" in the case and at least one of the following claims: the state either does not have, or refuses to assume, jurisdiction; the state lacks adequate programs or services for juvenile offenders; the offense charged is one of those noted above.[39] During 1995, federal prosecutors filed cases against 240 persons for juvenile delinquency and adjudicated 122 of them; from October 1993 through September 1994, sixty-five additional juveniles were referred to federal prosecutors for prosecution as adults.[40]

These statistics relate, however, to only one portion of prosecutors' activities—formal prosecution and case processing. Yet prosecutors engage in a range of other activities through which they seek to reduce and prevent youth crime as well as to increase efficiency, effectiveness, and justness in case processing. The sheer number and diversity of these practices represent the development of a new prosecution strategy and a new way of thinking about how best to address youth crime and violence.

The Evolution of a New Prosecutorial Strategy for Addressing Troubled Youth

As prosecutors' ownership of the problem of youth violence grew, the pronounced surge in violent crime and in the number of youthful perpetrators and victims in the 1980s and early 1990s troubled some prosecutors as much as it did the police. With their greater power, these prosecutors sensed that they might be missing an opportunity. Although case processing and prosecution had grown more sophisticated and efficient, crime remained high, the quality of life in cities was threatened, and jails and prisons were overflowing. Citizens, especially in minority communities, were becoming increasingly insistent in their demand for a more comprehensive response to crime in their neighborhoods, one that went beyond strict law enforcement. Innovative responses by prosecutors to these challenges led to the development of a new strategy—community prosecution—which is increasingly evident, albeit still evolving, among prosecutors in mid-sized to large cities in the United States. Although community prosecution encompasses more than issues of youth crime and safety, it was motivated in large part by concern for them.[41] Furthermore, the roots of the new strategy grew in part from a set of ideas emphasizing the importance of dealing with lower-level crimes and misdemeanors that pervaded policing before spreading into prosecution and throughout criminal justice.

The "Broken Windows" Hypothesis: Enter the Prosecutors

Several reasons account for the new focus on misdemeanors and low-level offenses in criminal justice and for the fact that it has become a core component of recent changes taking place in prosecutors' offices. First, as police and prosecutors seek to build community partnerships, they learn that one of the top concerns of private citizens is the quality of life in their own neighborhoods. Citizens want something done about low-level offenses, and their priorities are being adopted by justice agencies. Second, many misdemeanors are serious, and it may be possible to prevent the escalation of violence and crime by dealing with them early on. For example, domestic violence and drunk driving, which often are treated as misdemeanors, are highly destructive offenses that can easily result in serious harm. Third, more than a few police departments are making the claim that linkages between misdemeanors and felonies are not trivial and that steps taken to address misdemeanors can have a significant impact on felony crime. Career felons also commit misdemeanors, and they can be apprehended, prosecuted, and taken off the streets on misdemeanor charges. Youthful "wannabes" may learn clear lessons from seeing police and prosecutors take misdemeanors seriously. In Boston's Dorchester community, gang members were stunned when another member who was on federal probation was sent to prison for nineteen years after being apprehended with two bullets in his pocket.

Underlying the new focus is what has come to be known as the "broken windows" hypothesis, which posits that just as ignoring a broken window will lead to more broken windows and damage, so too ignoring low-level crime and disorderly behavior will beget more crime by indicating to potential offenders and good citizens alike that no one cares. Sensing the absence of control emanating from such conditions, law-abiding citizens withdraw from public places in fear, leading to the loss of social control on streets and in parks. Conditions ripe for an influx of more violent crime and the neighborhood's spiral into urban decay become more pronounced. Sooner or later, a tipping point may be approached beyond which only a major effort can restore public safety in the area.

Looking back, the 1982 *Atlantic Monthly* article from which "broken windows" takes its name was less a discovery of an important idea than it was a rediscovery and reemphasis of an idea that had been around for a long time.[42] Public drunkenness, prostitution, panhandling, and other such problems have always been police concerns. The history of the police retreat from these problems during the middle of the last century is complicated: in large part it grew out of attempts to stem police abuse of vagrancy and loitering laws as well as the belief that scarce police resources should be concentrated on combating the most serious offenses, felonies.

Despite efforts to focus police attention on felonies, research conducted from the 1950s through the early 1970s demonstrated that only a small portion of police time was spent on "serious" crime, while a lot more was directed at managing disputes and maintaining order. [43] These latter activities are largely unofficial: they lie outside mainstream policing and management, no records are kept of them, and until very recently, they were largely denigrated in policing as "junk" work. But they are a core component of the routine activities of police.

Likewise, there is nothing new about the link between disorderly behavior and citizen fear. It has been known since the 1960s that disorderly behavior elicits higher levels of fear than index crimes.[44] While not intuitively obvious—after all, "serious" crimes like armed robbery would, superficially at least, seem more likely to generate higher levels of fear than disorderly conduct—virtually every report from surveys or focus groups since then has confirmed this finding. And people act on this fear: they restrict their activities and take protective action, they withdraw from civic life, they lose confidence in government, and many move from cities. That this finding has not been given more importance in crime control policy, at least until very recently, has had enormous consequences for urban life.

Yet attempts to incorporate in criminal justice policy the insight that disorder and fear are linked have caused considerable consternation in criminological and criminal justice circles. As noted, order maintenance was devalued work for police, unmanaged and performed grudgingly. Moreover, for a good share of mainstream criminologists, disorderly behavior was so closely associated with cultural diversity and pluralism (one person's traditions are disorderly behavior to another), homelessness, and race that actions to control disorder were often represented as de facto racism and imperialism. Also, many criminologists dismissed disorderly behavior and minor offenses as "victimless" crime that did not hurt anyone. Despite such views, by the late 1980s, local officials, especially mayors and overseers of public spaces like parks and public services such as transportation, understood that the situation was getting out of control and heard the demand for order that was rising in neighborhoods and communities across the country.

The significant implications for public policy of the "broken windows" theory went beyond recognition of the relationship between disorderly behavior and fear, however. "Broken windows" also hypothesized that disorderly behavior creates the context in which more violent crime can flourish: citizens become afraid and withdraw from urban life, social control diminishes, and an environment is created that attracts predators who can operate with impunity. This hypothesis, widely shared by citizens, was the second half of the broken windows metaphor: disorder, fear, felonies, and urban decay are sequentially linked. The implications were important. They suggested that if disorder led to fear and serious crime, restoring order in public spaces could not only reduce fear but also reduce crime. They also challenged the prevailing paradigm that dominated criminal justice and criminology into the 1990s.

In essence, the 1967 report by the President's Commission on Law Enforcement and Administration of Justice articulated this reigning paradigm. Its assumptions were drawn from those that gave rise to the War on Poverty: crime is caused by poverty, racism, and social injustice, and in order to deal with crime, society must deal with these "root causes." The criminal justice system is essentially reactive, responding after a crime is committed by processing offenders rapidly, fairly, and toughly. Police action might push crime around or displace it, but to the extent that the criminal justice system prevents crime, it does so through incarceration and primary and secondary deterrence. Except for token units in police departments that advise citizens about locks and other protective paraphernalia, crime prevention occurs outside of the criminal justice system and properly focuses on broad social change.

The broken windows hypothesis challenged this paradigm by suggesting that crime could be prevented by means more modest than broad social change, namely by restoring order in public spaces. Routine activities analysis, situational crime prevention, and crime prevention through environmental design represented other approaches to preventing crime that showed considerable promise during the 1980s. However, for our purposes, "broken windows" was significant because it raised the importance of a set of police activities that had been largely out of view, conducted unofficially, and considered police "dirty work." Many of those activities were directed at minor offenses by youth: alcohol consumption, vandalism, intimidating obstreperousness, gang-related behaviors, truancy, and other such activities.

Bringing order maintenance "out of the shadows" in policing had at least two ramifications. First, it made order maintenance official. While most police efforts to maintain or restore order were conducted as they always had been—through persuasion, education, warning, and threatening—official actions such as citation or arrest gained new importance. In the past, the police had considered most citations or arrests for disorderly behavior as ends in themselves, used when police confronted an incident about which they had to do something. Now, at least some police responses to disorderly behavior are seen as problem solving—that is, police interests extend beyond resolving an incident to maintaining order as a means of regaining control of public spaces.

Consider "squeegeeing," the unsolicited "washing" of car windows, primarily by youth.[45] Squeegeeing had been a problem in New York City for years. Most police responses to it were desultory: they ignored it, threatened offenders, occasionally conducted "sweeps" and jailed squeegeemen on some minor offense, or gave a desk appearance ticket (the equivalent of a traffic ticket that specifies a fine for a minor offense). DATs, as desk appearance tickets were known, were also called "disappearance tickets," since few troublemakers bothered to appear in court or pay their fines. They were a joke, to both police and offenders. By the early 1990s, squeegeeing came to be symbolic of all that was wrong with New York City. Police came under strong public and political pressure to do something about it. Yet it was clear that they could not manage the problem alone: the involvement of prosecutors was essential to bringing the problem under control.

In the case of squeegeeing, a relatively trivial but organizationally unorthodox effort was required of prosecutors: send the warrants that were issued when squeegeemen did not pay their fines or appear in court directly back to the police officers who had written the original DAT. Squeegeeing may not have been a jailable offense, but contempt of court was. Armed with the "or else" of the warrants, police and prosecutors together ended squeegeeing in three weeks. The demands on the prosecutor's office were not great, but prosecutors had to change their priorities to manage the problem. The "minor" offense of squeegeeing required special prosecutorial attention.

With the squeegeeing issue, public and political concern about an offense that was minor in individual cases but that became a serious problem in the aggregate filtered through police departments to prosecutors. Seattle city attorney Mark Sidran has made the same point: "Community prosecution or prosecutor problem solving is at least as likely to be driven by the police and police problem-solving initiatives as it is by anything prosecutors begin to initiate."[46] During the 1990s, however, prosecutors themselves began to demonstrate an increased willingness to initiate crime prevention activities, especially in dealing with youth.

Prosecutors soon discovered that concentrating on misdemeanors was not of value to police alone in solving problems, but benefited themselves as well. According to Sidran, who prosecutes misdemeanors in his juris-diction, "misdemeanors matter for a number of reasons . . . they are the sin-gle most neglected tool, in my view, in the criminal justice system's tool box."[47] Growing numbers of prosecutors adopted the use of misdemeanor enforcement for a broad range of purposes, including addressing troubled and troublesome youth. Seeking methods for both preventing delinquency and reining in repeat and violent juvenile offenders, prosecutors found that minor offenses provided the authority for them to intervene. For very youthful offenders, minor offenses were often a precursor to more serious offenses, and they provided prosecutors (insofar as they had the institu-tional capacity) the opportunity for early intervention, not just with the child, but with the child's family. Early interventions could range from var-ious forms of family assistance to punishment and restitution through community service. For older repeat or violent offenders, minor offenses, when taken seriously by officials, provided the means to "pull them up short" when they threatened others or began to misbehave in the commu-nity. These interventions could range from enforced curfews to reinstitu-tionalization. Moreover, if carried out properly, quick and appropriate responses to serious offenders, especially in gang-related circumstances, sent a message to "wannabes" that they lived in a world of consequences.

In many other ways, misdemeanors came to matter in the efforts of prosecutors. In particular, a focus on misdemeanors contributed to the development of, and moved to occupy a central place in, the new strategy of prosecutors—community prosecution. With its broader mission and more diverse tactics, community prosecution provides prosecutors with an arsenal of more diverse and powerful tools available to reduce youth crime and violence.

The Development of Community Prosecution

Grounded as it is in evolving prosecutorial practices, community prosecu-tion (as prosecutors themselves and many examining them refer to the new organizational form) is a movement in the process of defining itself. Nev-ertheless, it encompasses a number of identifiable elements, which, taken together, represent real and significant changes from the way that prosecu-tors previously defined and carried out their work.

—*A new mission for a new crime problem*: Community prosecutors are developing a new mission to address a newly defined crime "problem." This involves redefining their overall mission (previously to "achieve jus-tice" through efficient, effective felony case processing) to include the prevention of crime in addition to full prosecution. As part of this new vision, prosecutors are recognizing the need to view crime more broadly, not only in terms of index crime, but low-level, quality of life offenses as well, and to consider the linkages between the public's fear of crime and crime itself. The priorities of citizens themselves take on special importance—resulting in more direct accountability on the part of the prosecutor to address safety and crime problems neighborhood by neighborhood, rather than city- or countywide.

—*Problem solving and new tactics for crime prevention and reduction*: Community prosecutors are moving away from a traditional reliance on the criminal law and criminal prosecution to building a "problem-oriented prosecution" strategy into their operations. In other words, prosecutors' tactics are expanding and changing. In formal case processing, prosecutions begin to emphasize misdemeanors and quality of life offenses in addition to felonies. Moving beyond criminal prosecution to crime reduction and prevention, prosecutors are increasingly adopting and using civil remedies such as nuisance abatement, injunctions (sometimes in the form of stay-away or restraining orders), trespass statutes, and health and safety code enforcement. Problem-solving efforts tend to focus on specific neighborhoods or local areas and to encompass prevention and reduction as well as minimizing the effect of completed crimes. For example, prosecutors in many locations are helping to train landlords and property owners in how to prevent and recognize crime before it destroys their property. To accomplish these tasks, prosecutors' offices are hiring more non-lawyer specialists who bring extra-legal skills in areas such as public health, substance abuse treatment, and social services; public relations and community organizing; marketing and journalism; and crime prevention. Former Jackson County (Kansas City, Missouri) prosecutor Claire McCaskill, whose office has hired more of these specialists than most, credits them with constantly prodding prosecutors into thinking "outside the box."[48]

—*Collaborating with other agencies and the community*: Community prosecutors are collaborating more closely with other criminal justice agencies, with local government, with the private sector, and with citizens themselves. To be effective in their new role, prosecutors believe they must work with citizens and other agencies to identify priorities jointly, improve their prosecutorial skills through an increased understanding of crime problems and community contexts, and lend their expertise to collaborations engaging in problem solving to reduce and prevent crime. In many cases, prosecutors convene and lead these collaborations, but the goal is often for citizens themselves eventually to shoulder primary responsibility for many prevention efforts and much of the problem solving, with prosecutors and police as a backup. Responses to participation by prosecutors from their collaborating partners are overwhelmingly positive. In the words of one police officer, community prosecution is "what makes community policing work." Citizens feel that they have a strong ally who brings, and can leverage, additional resources and tools to make their neighborhoods safer.

These three elements are found together only in a number of larger prosecutor's offices in major urban centers, but many smaller jurisdictions have adopted them in a more limited fashion. Prosecutors in small offices and communities may already possess a knowledge of the local area and have the close ties with citizens, police, other criminal justice agencies, and local governments that urban prosecutors have to work to build. Nevertheless, today all these elements are increasingly visible in prosecutors' offices across the country.

Thinking Differently About Youth Crime and Violence

Many experienced prosecutors recall learning the ropes in a district attorney's office by starting out in a juvenile prosecution unit. Such sections, along with misdemeanor units, frequently were a dumping ground for prosecutors whose litigation skills were not good enough to move up to the felony prosecution team. No longer: the prosecution of juvenile cases now is considered a high priority. Today, prosecutors clearly are thinking differently about youth crime and violence. An understanding of the value of misdemeanor enforcement and commitment to the principles emerging in community prosecution figure prominently in the changes prosecutors are making—as they develop new office policies and guidelines for prosecution, restructure juvenile prosecution activities, build a range of skill capacities and seek different qualities in their personnel, and initiate more community outreach programs.

In prosecution offices that have created juvenile units, cases frequently are handled through vertical prosecution, particularly if they involve repeat or violent offenders, who also are targeted through priority prosecution programs. Specialized gang units (reportedly found in 30 percent of prosecutor's offices in large jurisdictions and in 5 percent in small jurisdictions) and multiagency task forces also have been formed. Most of these units focus on prosecution, although some, such as in San Diego, are moving into prevention.[49] The gang unit in the district attorney's office in Boston provides an example: gang unit attorneys share information with the Youth Violence Strike Force (the Boston police department's anti-gang unit), the U.S. attorney's office, and the Bureau of Alcohol, Tobacco, and Firearms and also with assistant district attorneys working in neighborhoods as part of the city's Safe Neighborhood Initiatives and in other sections of the office. Although the unit is heavily oriented toward investigation and prosecution, the district attorney's office is considering the potential benefits of reaching out more directly to the community, not just to obtain better cooperation from witnesses but also to prevent violence. Victim witness advocates already work with community members, and assistant district attorneys have begun speaking in local high schools with Youth Violence Strike Force officers, bringing in prison guards to tell students about what incarcerated offenders face. In Indianapolis, a deputy prosecutor from the county prosecutor's office serves as legal adviser to the Metro Gang Task Force and has been cross-designated an assistant U. S. attorney (AUSA) so that he can prosecute cases generated by the task force in both state felony courts and federal courts. The task force is part of the Regional Gang Intervention Program, a collaborative effort drawing together prosecutors, including AUSAs, police agencies, and federal agencies in central Indiana, whose mandate is to suppress, intervene in, and prevent criminal activity.

But these changes are only the tip of the iceberg. Employing a problem-solving approach within a mission that includes prevention as well as reactive case processing, prosecutors think holistically: they see youthful offenders and victims coming from the same families and groups within neighborhoods and seek to create opportunities to prevent further victimization. For example, District Attorney Ronald Earle, in Austin (Travis County), Texas, has created a family justice division in his office to handle all matters involving children and families, including civil and criminal child abuse, death reviews, civil and criminal neglect, juvenile prosecutions, and gang prosecution.[50] Growing numbers of prosecutors approach misdemeanor delinquency cases as one opportunity for early intervention, pursuing—and sometimes taking the lead in creating—diversion and intermediate sanction programs that provide for or require counseling, community service, restitution, mentoring, mediation, substance abuse treatment, and other options. Often prosecutors themselves take part in collaborative crime prevention and reduction efforts, along with police, probation officers, school officials, social service providers, and others in the local community. Even where prosecutors lack formal jurisdiction over juvenile prosecutions, they are turning aggressively to crime prevention and reduction, providing support for other criminal justice agencies and using other available tactics.

Perhaps harder to observe and measure than structural and tactical alterations is the gradual change in the culture of the prosecutor's office that appears to be occurring. In Boston, Suffolk County district attorney Ralph Martin explains how he has communicated to his assistant district attorneys that he "means it" when he says that the office will do more than simply prosecute juveniles:

> It's one thing to make people do what you want them to do. It's another thing to make them want what you want . . . . So, when I started talking . . . about the importance of identifying juvenile offenders, before they become at risk, and trying to intervene with them earlier, a lot of people said, "Oh, that's just the boss being political. He's got to get elected, so he's going to say stuff like that." Then, when I started putting some of the bright, young, talented prosecutors in the juvenile unit, to establish a priority prosecution unit, and then I started moving prosecutors to convene working groups in the schools . . . . [t]hey said, "Well, geez, maybe he means this stuff." And . . . when I started paying people a little extra to do this . . . . [a]nd when I started saying, "if you want to do well in the office, this is one of the units you've got to go through, before you get to a felony trial team, before you get to homicide," then, that really caught people's interest. And so, now people know that the juvenile unit is a serious unit. And we've done some good things in that unit.
>
> I first started talking about [child abuse being a priority] externally, because they are the most vulnerable victims that we see. And we re-victimize them . . . when we interview them three, four, five and six times. And we've got to do a better job at that. And, at first, it was, "yeah, that's the boss, you know, being political." But then . . . when I couldn't find people internally to do the job the way we needed it to be done, I started hiring people to do it. And gave them equal status as the other felony trial team leaders. Yeah, there was some grumbling, but over time, there has been more cross-pollination of ideas . . . more respect. And as they see that the child abuse unit now generates probably twelve percent of our felony trial team indictments . . . this is serious business . . . . The same thing with domestic violence. And over time . . . we have increased the recognition that these units . . . make us a better, more responsive office.[51]

While the trends in prosecution that we have described may not be typical of all or even most prosecutors' offices around the country, the change in thinking about the role of prosecutors apparent in Martin's efforts is evident in more than a few.[52] These changes can have a significant impact on youth violence and safety—and in many cases, the effects already are visible and measurable.

Prosecutors' New Approaches to Youth Violence

In the following sections we focus on three common approaches to youth violence that we have identified through observation of policies and practices of numerous prosecutors. First we describe a bifurcated approach that calls for aggressive prosecution of violent repeat offenders but emphasizes diversion and alternatives to prosecution for less-serious offenders and early intervention for at-risk youth. Second, we look at community-based justice programs in which prosecutors work directly with school officials, service providers, police and probation departments, and citizens in local communities to identify youthful offenders or those at risk of offending and devise appropriate interventions or responses on a case-by-case basis. Third, we examine holistic programs in which prosecutors attempt to address juvenile safety and violence issues as an interrelated whole, through a focus on families. Truancy projects in which parents are held accountable for their children's truant behavior and coordination (within a prosecutor's office) of prosecutions directed at child abuse offenders and child protective service components are two examples. These three approaches are not mutually exclusive; prosecutors often implement more than one and their functions frequently overlap.

Selective Prosecution and a Two-Pronged Approach

Under the bifurcated approach adopted by many prosecutors today, the tactic for violent repeat offenders is aggressive priority prosecution, often in criminal courts. For nonviolent offenders, delinquency proceedings can be pursued in juvenile court, or for first or second offenses a range of options may be offered as part of diversion (from adjudication or sentencing) or as conditions of probation. And for youth whose behavior is troubling but who are not yet court involved, the goal is early intervention to prevent criminal behavior. This comprehensive approach can be especially effective when used by prosecutors with a record for aggressively prosecuting violent offenders: they can use their bully pulpit to advocate diversion, early intervention, and crime prevention programs for nonviolent offenders without losing face or being accused of being "soft on crime." This is also the course suggested in policy set forth by the National District Attorneys Association (NDAA).

THE NDAA POLICY ON JUVENILE OFFENDERS. The approach adopted, or at least held as an ideal, by many prosecutors toward serious, violent, and habitual juvenile offenders is set out succinctly in the NDAA's Resource Manual and Policy Positions on Juvenile Crime Issues, issued in November 1996. The policy paper defines serious offenders as those caught for the first time after committing "multiple felony offenses, a major economic crime, repeated misdemeanor crimes of violence, or other offenses defined by a local jurisdiction as serious"; violent offenders as those involved in committing "a felony crime of violence"; and habitual felony offenders as those found guilty of at least two prior felonies.[53] To deal with the technical difficulty involved in prosecutions of such offenders, the NDAA calls for use of experienced, properly trained prosecutors and, where possible, vertical prosecution and fast tracking of cases. It recommends that prosecutors make all charging decisions involving juvenile offenders; on the subject of waiver, it favors unreviewable prosecutorial discretion over where to file cases involving serious, violent, and habitual offenders fourteen years of age and above. Once a juvenile proceeding is filed in adult criminal court and a finding of probable cause is made, the NDAA advocates requiring all further prosecutions of that youth to take place in adult court. Finally, the NDAA takes a hard line on detention and sentencing of violent offenders: it makes a strong case for the revision of federal "sight and sound" regulations, arguing that although young offenders should be kept separate from older offenders, state and local government guidelines should apply.[54] Both in detention and sentencing, the NDAA proposes that "juvenile codes that set the best interest of the child as the primary consideration of sentencing should be repealed . . . . The primary factors affecting a juvenile's sentence should be protection of the community from harm and accountability to the victim and the public for the juvenile's behavior."[55]

In its policy, then, the NDAA takes the traditional adversarial stance toward prosecution of violent offenders. To this it adds recommendations for close collaboration in investigations with other law enforcement officials at local, state, and federal levels; cross-designation of prosecutors with U.S. attorney offices so that cases can be filed in federal court when necessary; "priority prosecution" that includes expedited treatment of high-profile cases; obtaining community assistance; developing witness protection programs; and other tactics. But when it comes to nonviolent offenders, prosecutors are advised to consider diversion programs for "appropriate first-time or low-level" offenders (even to go as far as to establish them) and to seek avenues for input into eligibility criteria and guidelines established for any juvenile diversion programs not administered by the prosecutor's office.

STATE ATTORNEY HARRY SHORESTEIN, DUVAL COUNTY (JACKSONVILLE), FLORIDA. One of the best-known examples of a prosecutorial program combining a "get tough" policy with early intervention, prevention, and diversion components is that of State Attorney Harry Shorestein, in Jacksonville, Florida. In Shorestein's words: "I believe we need a two-pronged approach to curtailing juvenile crime. We must incarcerate repeat and violent offenders and at the same time intervene at an early age in an attempt to educate and habilitate juveniles at risk of becoming criminals." [56] Specific programs, which have been widely covered by the media and the subject of one serious evaluation, range from early intervention collaborations with schools, to first- and second-time offender programs, to the prosecution of serious habitual juvenile offenders as adults.

Believing that juvenile crime lay at the core of Duval County's escalating crime problem, Shorestein, who was first elected in July 1991, sought early in his administration to increase the capacity of his office to deal with the community's most serious problem. First, he appointed one of his most able prosecutors to serve as the director of the juvenile justice division and assigned ten experienced prosecutors to the division—effectively reversing the office's tradition of having newly hired and inexperienced prosecutors handle juveniles.

The second major thrust by Shorestein has been the establishment of extensive interagency collaborations, especially with local schools but with other existing programs and agencies as well, such as the Duval County sheriff's office, the city health department, the National Rifle Association, the city of Jacksonville's victim services division, Mothers Against Drunk Driving (MADD), private social service agencies (such as Hubbard House, a domestic violence center), the state of Florida's department of juvenile justice, Planned Parenthood, and others. In a close collaboration with schools, Shorestein assigns prosecutors to all twenty-two middle schools in the county where they meet with staff, students, teachers, and parents; provide information about their office and its programs; and participate in efforts to prevent youth from becoming offenders. Moreover, school resource officers (security personnel) have been further empowered through a civil citation program developed by Shorestein's office in which youth who commit minor offenses in school and who admit their offenses are required to perform thirty-five hours community service under the officers' supervision. These collaborations provide for regular presentations by prosecutors in schools; diversion programs that include restitution, community service, and counseling; counseling for very young offenders and their parents; home monitoring of at-risk youth; peer mediation of conflicts; gun safety programs; truancy referral programs and attendance centers; a juvenile justice awareness program (student visits to the prosecutor's office and courthouse); victim impact panels; peer impact panels (for drinking and driving); an intervention program for children in abusive families; a multi-agency assessment program (for first-time offenders, aged ten to fifteen); special programs for girls; and drug programs, including a juvenile drug court.

Chronic and violent offenders are handled as adults by an "adult juvenile" prosecutor who reports to the director of the juvenile justice division. Shorestein's philosophy is forthright: "In an ideal system I do not believe incarcerating juveniles as adults would be the proper thing to do; however, my hands have been tied by the explosion of juvenile crime. We will stop this process only when the juvenile system has shown it is equipped to handle dangerous criminals." Shorestein has put his philosophy into practice: "When I took office our city was faced with a 27 percent increase in the number of juveniles arrested from 1990 to 1991. Since I took office we have prosecuted over 1,500 juvenile cases in adult court. Since 1993 alone over 750 juveniles prosecuted by my office have been incarcerated in the Duval County Jail and another 155 juveniles have been sentenced to extended time in the Florida State Prison, including eighteen violent juveniles sentenced to life in prison and two juveniles convicted of first-degree murder sentenced to the death penalty."[57] Counseling, education, and mentoring programs are offered in the jail. After-care programs include specialized probation (with officers having reduced caseloads), employment, and social services. Substance abuse programs are planned. Collaborating agencies include the sheriff's office, Toastmasters International, Boys and Girls Club, the Urban League, Florida National Guard (as mentors), volunteers from local churches, and other social service agencies.

In an independent evaluation of the prosecutorial programs, David W. Rasmussen and Yiwen Yu of Florida State University conclude: "This report suggests this program has contributed to public safety in Duval

County. It is estimated that about 7,200 crimes have been prevented by incarcerating chronic youthful offenders and as many as 1,500 may have been avoided by the Program for At-Risk Students [visits to prosecutor and courthouse]. Combined, the gross public benefits of this reduced level of crime can be valued conservatively at about $18 million, or about $6 million per year. This amounts to $21,400 for each offender sentenced under this program."[58] Summing up his own evaluation of the impact of his two-pronged efforts, Shorestein writes: "Our arrest statistics prove that my philosophy has made a difference. After full implementation of our program, Jacksonville experienced an approximate 30 percent decrease in juvenile arrests from 1993 to 1994. During this same period, juvenile arrests went up statewide and nationwide. Most significantly, Jacksonville's decrease included an average 47 percent decrease in juvenile arrests in the six major crime categories (weapon offenses, aggravated assault, robbery, auto theft, home burglary, sex crimes)."[59] Shorestein also provides comparative arrest data for 1993 and 1997 (see table 2-1). One final statistic: the population of juveniles incarcerated as adults has decreased from a high in 1994 of 190 to seventy in 1998, despite a state law expanding the criteria qualifying juveniles for prosecution as adults and Florida's preeminence in the nation (in 1994–95) in juvenile transfers to criminal court.[60]

Community-Based Justice Programs

The number of youth-oriented community-based justice programs in which prosecutors play a significant role is growing around the country.[61] Programs range from early intervention and prevention initiatives targeting youth who are not court involved to deferred prosecution or post-

Table 2-1. *Duval County, Florida: Number of Persons under 18 Arrested*

Crime	1993	1997	Percent change
Murder	18	4	−78
Rape/sex offenses	178	84	−53
Robbery	294	201	−32
Aggravated assault	576	489	−15
Vehicle theft	782	327	−58
Weapons	251	161	−36

Source: Harry L. Shorestein, "Statement on Juvenile Justice," unpublished document, April 1998, p. 16; statistics from Jacksonville Sheriff's Office.

adjudication diversion programs for nonviolent offenders. The community focus in these initiatives emerges in two ways: first, prosecutors work in close partnership with private citizens and groups, local government, schools and other agencies, and criminal justice officials; and second, goals include not only increasing youth safety and preventing youth crime, but reducing the risk that troublesome youth can pose to the local community and maintaining the community's well-being and quality of life. The community, then, has become a full partner, or "co-participant," whose priorities are not secondary to the interests of youth and youthful offenders; it also is expected to share the responsibility, along with the prosecutor and other criminal justice representatives, for maintaining public safety.

COMMUNITY BASED JUSTICE PROGRAM, MIDDLESEX COUNTY, MASSACHUSETTS. Middlesex County's Community Based Justice (CBJ) program is the early intervention component of a multifaceted juvenile justice team put together by former district attorney (now Massachusetts attorney general) Tom Reilly in 1991. Located to the northwest of Boston, the county is the largest in the state and eighteenth-largest in the nation, with a diverse population of approximately 1.5 million people who live in eleven cities and forty-three towns in areas ranging from urban and suburban to rural. The county has a broad range of youth crime and safety problems. When a fourteen-year-old boy was murdered on his way home from school in a racially motivated incident in Lowell, Massachusetts, Reilly decided to seek some proactive means to address an alarming increase in youth crime. He convened a meeting of prosecutors, police officials, case workers, probation and corrections officers, youth service workers, local officials, and community agency representatives, and they began to share information about the small group of young people who were creating havoc in Lowell. From this single roundtable, CBJ has grown into thirty-nine active task forces that involve most school districts in the county. President Clinton recognized CBJ as a model program in the Federal Violent Crime Control and Law Enforcement Act of 1994.

When the CBJ program was first initiated, it was essentially a priority prosecution program that focused on the roughly 5 percent of youth who could be described as serious offenders, most of whom were seventeen to twenty-one years of age. The idea was that a message of "zero tolerance" with respect to violence and substance abuse in schools would reach other juveniles as well. After a year of operation, participants realized that they should continue to reach that 5 percent but that deterrence would be greater if they also targeted more directly the thirteen- to seventeen-year-old "wannabes" who try to emulate offenders.[62] The goal now is to inter-vene as early as possible in order to turn these youth away from crime and violence and to promote social responsibility and public safety in the com-munity. The program therefore combines aggressive prosecution of serious repeat offenders with diverse community-based diversion opportunities for nonviolent offenders.

Task forces—some regional, some drawn from one school district—meet regularly throughout the county to share information about high-risk youth whose behavior poses a threat to their school and community as well as to themselves. Meetings take place at local schools, police depart-ments, or other offices. An assistant district attorney generally chairs task force meetings, which bring together local school officials, prosecutors, police, probation officers, corrections officers, youth service representa-tives, social service professionals, and sometimes community leaders, although the meetings are not open to the public. Most youth come to the attention of CBJ by engaging in violent behavior, possessing weapons, dis-tributing illegal drugs, assaulting or threatening others, intimidating wit-nesses, or committing civil rights violations such as hate crimes.[63] At most meetings, lists are circulated of individual youth involved with the courts, as well as those who are not court involved but who have come to the attention of the authorities for some kind of troublesome or antisocial behavior. For example, if one youth from a family is court involved, task force members might be especially concerned about a younger sibling "on the fringes" of dangerous activity. Discussions of individuals take place in the group with input coming from all present: police recount recent crim-inal events involving community youth; school personnel present infor-mation on disturbances that have occurred in the school and might spill over into other locations; the prosecutor reports on the status of court cases involving youth identified as high risk; and probation, corrections, and youth service officers bring in additional information on specific cases. Sometimes information is sought from sources outside the group who are brought in by a group member.

Decisions taken by the group relative to specific individuals are informed by a knowledge of the context of each case, not simply a specific offense, and reflect consensus about what should be done to address each youth's behavior. There is always a preference for nonpunitive measures and for keeping a child out of custody if the school system feels that it can manage the youth's behavior: "We will try to work with the parents, bringing them outside resources. We will involve the schools in maintaining support and attention to the child and family. We'll use mediation, counseling, and other family-support services. We will devise creative terms of probation—set specific conditions that require the youngster to go to school, abide by the rules of the school, be off the streets, and stay out of certain areas by a certain time of the day or night. We monitor the child's adherence to these conditions on a weekly basis —and they tend to stick to their agreements, knowing that if they don't we have the ability to surrender them and move them through the system toward incarceration very quickly."[64]

The seemingly easy collaboration on many task forces is not achieved without thoughtful and planned effort by the district attorney's office—an effort that usually, though not always, works. The office routinely contacts all school districts to provide information about CBJ and to ask whether the district would like to have the office involved through a CBJ program or council. The school is key to CBJ: it provides the link to the community, and school principals are especially important figures since under state law they have discretion to decide whether to expel juveniles arrested for or convicted of a felony. The district attorney's office makes clear that no privileged school records are used in task forces, offering its own carefully researched legal analysis to assure schools that no violations of confidentiality or the rights of youth take place through the CBJ. The approach is intentionally flexible, geared toward adapting to those needs identified as priorities by communities themselves. In some districts a memorandum of understanding (always recommended and available, though not always used) is signed and implemented among the partners.

Maintaining a task force once it is in place involves continuous care and attention: when participating agency officials on a task force change or are replaced, a re-education process takes place, and when a new principal comes on board, the office must work again to obtain his or her trust and commitment. For all partners, the pact and trust underlying the agreement to work together are continuously renewed through the task force's operations. Attention to local priorities and desires is the rule. Some task forces decide not to prepare actual lists of youth; in others, prevention and deterrence are the core principles, so the district attorney is a "guest" and the leadership role belongs to someone else—an arrangement that the district attorney's office accepts. Where a task force succeeds, it does so in large part because "with the cooperation, confidence, respect, and trust that has grown among the many agencies involved . . . there comes a strong sense of responsibility and accountability among the agencies, toward the youth and toward each other. If one agency agrees to take responsibility for a young person, they know they had better pay attention to that agreement, because they'll be coming back to the Community Based Justice task force table week after week to monitor the case and to answer to the task force on how it's going. No one agency wants to let the others down."[65]

The district attorney's office indicates that fewer than 5 percent of the county's youth are being tracked through CBJ at any one time. For example, as of December 1997, task forces were tracking 1,905 youth: 456 had active cases pending; 799 were on probation; 254 were committed to the department of youth services; and 121 were incarcerated. Some CBJ activities have moved toward prevention and crime reduction. In the area of hate crimes, and where racial incidents have occurred, such as in Somerville, assistant district attorneys have gone into schools to talk with students and staff. In Operation Zero Tolerance, police go into the schools with dogs to search for drugs. By prior agreement, the district attorney's office leaves it to the principal and school officials to decide whether to search a locker or to have the district attorney get a warrant to search once the dogs signal that they have found drugs. In practice, such matters are usually discussed and worked out between school officials and the district attorney's office both before and after searches take place. In Somerville, Lowell, and Framingham, truancy programs also have been implemented.

In many senses, CBJ is a flagship program in the district attorney's office. It also embodies Reilly's brand of community prosecution. Reilly's expectation for his own staff was that prosecutors would operate "outside of the courthouse—as part of, rather than apart from, the communities they serve" as well as in the courtroom.[66] Reilly himself met with task forces regularly throughout his tenure as district attorney. Under his administration, all new prosecutors coming into the office were informed that involvement in CBJ was part of the job of a district court prosecutor (CBJ is primarily a district court program).[67] More than half of the office's approximately 100 prosecutors have been extensively trained and facilitate CBJ roundtables; the remaining are involved indirectly in CBJ efforts. Advancement, promotions, and salary raises are based at least in part on their performance in CBJ, and some have in fact been held back accordingly. Reilly's staff believe that the information-sharing concept of CBJ could be spread to other areas. For example, in Somerville, a domestic violence task force has begun meeting directly after the juvenile CBJ meetings, with assistant district attorneys from the office's domestic violence unit attending.[68]

CBJ is tied closely to Project Alliance and to the juvenile prosecution unit. Project Alliance, established by former Middlesex County district attorney Scott Harshbarger, is a broad-based prevention effort to work with youth, teachers and school officials, health educators, police, and prosecutors throughout the county to encourage positive behavior by youth through training and special programs.[69] Currently Project Alliance is a nonprofit organization, administered by a director who is housed in the district attorney's office. Fifty percent of funding for Project Alliance is provided by the district attorney's office; dues paid by participating school systems also support the project.

The juvenile prosecution unit was set up following passage by the state legislature in 1996 of the Juvenile Justice Reform Act, which eliminated juvenile court jurisdiction over defendants aged fourteen and older charged with murder and created a new category of "youthful offenders"—serious, violent, or repeat juvenile offenders aged fourteen and over.[70] The decision concerning whether to proceed against a juvenile meeting the legal standard of a juvenile delinquent or youthful offender lies with the district attorney. In Middlesex County, the chief of the juvenile prosecution unit makes these decisions, frequently after consulting with the district attorney or his first assistant or with CBJ staff familiar with the offender's background.[71] Juvenile unit prosecutors handle all juvenile cases and chair many CBJ task force meetings. Since there are not enough prosecutors in the unit to cover all CBJ districts in the county, some meetings are handled by regular district court prosecutors who coordinate with the juvenile unit. The juvenile prosecution unit receives information from the various CBJ task forces and disseminates it as necessary; for example, if a youthful offender moves from one jurisdiction to another, the juvenile unit will let the incoming school district know.

Attempts to measure the results of the CBJ program will necessarily have to take into account its various goals, which seek to initiate and maintain a collaborative process and to prevent as well as reduce crime. Lowell has seen a substantial reduction in violent crime among juveniles since the CBJ program has been in operation, and many of those involved believe that CBJ, along with other local initiatives such as Safety First, has played a significant role.[72] Nevertheless, the district attorney's office has never judged the program's value by statistics alone.[73] CBJ prosecutors, like police, understand that the information sharing that takes place through CBJ can actually lead to more arrests and reported incidents. Perhaps more important, CBJ task forces are well aware of who the most troubled youth in the local community are. After passage of the Juvenile Justice Reform Act, from October 1, 1996, through the end of 1997, sixty-three youthful offenders were indicted in Middlesex County. Of those, fifty-four were known to the CBJ program: twenty-five were being tracked on the priority prosecution list, and twenty-nine had been discussed by task forces. Nine were outside of CBJ jurisdiction.[74] Although some task forces have struggled to overcome mistrust and an unwillingness to share information, many agency representatives serving on task forces report favorably—even enthusiastically—about the cooperation that has evolved, and they point to positive results for youth in individual cases following task force intervention. Prosecutors describe principals who, considering expulsion of a student, frequently consult with the CBJ assistant district attorney before making a decision and defense attorneys who, though not formally involved in CBJ, approach assistant district attorneys to ask about diversion programs and opportunities for their clients. In one courtroom, a juvenile offender, spying assistant district attorney Mike Ortiz of the Lowell CBJ task force across the room, asked the sitting judge if Ortiz could be "his lawyer."[75] Ortiz, a former gang member in Brooklyn, New York, himself, sees his contacts with youth through CBJ as an opportunity to obtain services and counseling for them and their families. He has helped facilitate the creation of numerous diversion programs and youth groups in the area and works continuously on issues related to race, ethnicity, and safety in Lowell's multicultural community, most recently to push for the development of a cross-cultural council.

A FOCUS ON YOUTH THROUGH COMMUNITY PROSECUTION, SUFFOLK COUNTY (BOSTON), MASSACHUSETTS. Since taking office in 1992, district attorney Ralph C. Martin has created several community-based prosecution initiatives in which youth safety and violence are a central focus. Among them are the Community Based Juvenile Justice (CBJJ) program that functions closely with the juvenile prosecution unit, several Safe Neighborhood Initiatives, and the Franklin Hill Gang Prevention Project. Community prosecution efforts are integrated with overall district attorney's office operations and headed by the chief of district courts, who also is the director of community prosecution.

Martin knows that citizens favor aggressive prosecution of repeat and violent youthful offenders. But he also sees such prosecutions, and tough sentences, as a way to "send a message to the good kids that getting involved with guns is a very bad idea."[76] In 1995, he coauthored the Brett-Martin Gun Bill, which took effect in February 1996, imposing a mandatory six-month sentence in a secure state department of youth services facility for any juvenile convicted of carrying an illegal firearm.[77] Juvenile offenders are prosecuted through the district attorney's office juvenile unit, headed in recent years by prosecutors with extensive experience in the gang unit. The unit's five prosecutors (assisted by a victim witness advocate and an investigator) handle delinquency proceedings and prosecute "youthful offenders" under the Youthful Offender Statute. From January 1 through December 10, 1997, approximately 134 youthful offenders were indicted: 30 percent for armed robbery; 21 percent for assault; and 9 percent for firearms violations.[78] Juvenile unit prosecutors also conduct priority prosecutions of juveniles not indicted as youthful offenders but who pose a threat to the safety of their communities and schools. Because the same prosecutors handle all pending cases against a juvenile as part of priority prosecutions, they understand the offender's continuing impact on community life, and they are better equipped to proceed with whatever cases move forward, even though some may be dismissed. These prosecutors also speak with school officials and community members who have been affected by the offender's acts and communicate the information they obtain to the court. In several district courts with a high volume of juvenile complaints, a specific assistant district attorney handles serious juvenile cases not identified for priority prosecution.

Attached to the juvenile unit and closely integrated with the priority prosecution program is the state-mandated Community Based Juvenile Justice program, established in 1994 and shaped by Martin for operation in Suffolk County. The district attorney's office focused initially on establishing roundtables in those schools with the highest number of school incidents involving violent threats or acts or the possession or distribution of drugs, alcohol, or weapons. By early 1998, one-third (six) of the high schools and about half (eight) of the middle schools in Boston participated; in addition, all high schools in the northern part of Suffolk County— Chelsea, Revere, and Winthrop—had roundtables in operation. Martin's goal is to have all schools in the county eventually participate in CBJJ.

As in Middlesex County, CBJJ roundtables, which are held every two weeks, bring together representatives from a number of agencies, in this case prosecutors, area and Massachusetts Bay Transit Authority police, school officials, juvenile probation officers, attendance officers, and representatives of the department of youth services (DYS) and the department of social services (DSS), to identify juveniles who either pose a risk to the local school or residential community or who are themselves at risk. Most roundtables represent one school or a combination of a high school and middle school(s). In rare cases, several middle schools join in a single roundtable, apart from a high school. Boston itself has a large number of schools (eighteen high schools and nineteen middle schools), and unlike in Middlesex County, Boston schools (in Suffolk County) operate under an open enrollment policy: students attend schools based on choice rather than area of residence. Thus, a student may live in one part of the city and attend school in another, requiring a significant degree of coordination among agencies citywide for successful service planning. This fact creates an extra hurdle for CBJJ roundtables.

In Suffolk County, the director of the CBJJ program (until recently, an experienced sexual assault prosecutor and former psychiatric social worker), the program administrator (a nonlawyer), or both attend most roundtable meetings on behalf of the district attorney's office; juvenile unit prosecutors from the superior court or district court juvenile prosecutors chair some roundtables. Participants identify and discuss violent and chronic offenders who are court involved, as well as those who are at risk for developing delinquent behavior. Specific plans are devised for providing services or taking action on a case-by-case basis. The project administrator prepares and keeps current confidential lists of juveniles who are being monitored and records the steps that will be taken on behalf of a particular juvenile by the next meeting and which agency is responsible for follow-up planning. She also assists in locating community service providers who may be used in referrals. Names are not removed from these lists until referral for services has been made.

The range of interventions currently available in CBJJ includes indictment as a youthful offender and/or priority prosecution; recommitment to DYS (for violating conditional release terms); revocation of probation; request for the court to impose conditions before trial or at disposition; filing a child-in-need-of-services (CHINS) petition; and referral for services available through grants linked with CBJJ or from schools or community agencies. CBJJ is involved in three federally funded community programs: SafeFutures, Youth Opportunity Area, and the Truancy Initiative. SafeFutures, funded by the U.S. Department of Justice (specifically OJJDP), is a diversion project (with a day report center) for young teenage males in the Blue Hill Avenue corridor who have committed nonviolent first offenses. The Youth Opportunity Area grant, from the U.S. Department of Labor, funds three CBJJ roundtables and provides educational and employment opportunities for youth. Finally, the Truancy Initiative, for which the district attorney's office itself obtained $216,000 in grant funds from the U.S. Department of Health and Human Services (and which is administered by the Massachusetts Department of Public Safety), is a relatively new project designed to reduce truancy among middle-school students by following up immediately after a small number of unexplained absences to offer supportive services to the youth and his or her family.

Beginning with the 1996 school year through December 1997, 552 youth were discussed by CBJJ roundtables in Suffolk County. Of those, 36 percent were not court involved; CHINS petitions were filed for 11 percent; 44 percent were court involved; and 9 percent had both court and CHINS involvement. In Suffolk County, greater numbers of youth who are not court involved are tracked by roundtables than are tracked by CBJ task forces in Middlesex County. The participating agencies face routine confidentiality issues in building the trust necessary to share information—especially in their contacts with school officials, who are at times both understandably protective of students and frustrated by their inability to obtain information from probation and other agencies about offenses committed by their students. Moreover, some private citizens (often parents) in the community have questioned whether youth who are not court involved should be tracked, concerned that the youth may be harmed by the label and attention they receive rather than helped by the intervention. (In fact, at one CBJJ roundtable, agency participants were attempting to gain entrance for just such a youth to a summer arts program—a troublesome student who nevertheless had no criminal record and possessed artistic ability that many CBJJ participants thought might be stimulated to good effect. The dilemma was how to convince a new pilot arts project to accept a youth who might be a risk.) Other issues that roundtables have struggled with include the lack of alternative education placements for students who are suspended from school and for those eighteen and older with few academic credits; problems associated with students who have spent time in adult jail returning to schools; and the lack of coordination between schools and probation officers handling CHINS cases.

Even with these challenges, participating schools and agencies report significant progress and accomplishment. Responses from annual surveys of CBJJ participants conducted by the district attorney's office indicate that when CBJJ works well, school personnel feel that they are not "alone out there"; they know whom to call with concerns and are reassured that someone will respond. There is less burn-out among staff, who recognize that things are now different from the way they were a few years ago. They also point to concrete examples of problems resolved through CBJJ: for example, transit police have worked with school principals to increase safety in transit stations that handle large numbers of youth. In Dorchester High School (where the first roundtable was established) during the winter and spring of 1998, a CBJJ-coordinated response to increasing school violence produced a rapid turnaround: probation officers walked the hallways in the school to make their presence known while a day detective from local District C-3 of the police department was assigned to work around the school; the local juvenile court judge visited the school and, finding that probationers were not attending, began cracking down in the courtroom; and a local prosecutor met with school police every other week to monitor the situation. The number of violent incidents declined, and teachers found the climate less frightening and much improved. Many participants in various roundtables express a wish for even greater involvement by the district attorney's office and for moving forward to see what more can be accomplished.

In several areas, CBJJ roundtables operate alongside community-based Safe Neighborhood Initiatives (SNI). For example, since the first SNI was established by former Massachusetts attorney general Harshbarger, district attorney Martin, and Boston police department superintendent in chief William Bratton in Dorchester in 1993, Martin has started SNIs in East Boston (1994) and Chelsea (1995) and joined with the attorney general's office in working with the Grove Hall SNI in Roxbury (1995) and in Dorchester—all areas in which CBJJ roundtables function in local schools. In every SNI, youth safety, crime, and violence are high priority. And in many aspects, services provided through the CBJJ and the SNIs complement each other.

Each SNI operates as a formal partnership of prosecutors, the police, and representatives of other criminal justice agencies (probation and parole officers and municipal, transit, and housing police), the mayor's office and city agencies, and citizens within a specific neighborhood. Elected officials send representatives to meetings and are asked to assist in furthering SNI interests rather than advancing their official agendas. In three of the four SNIs, a coordinator (an experienced victim witness advocate or community organizer) hired by the district attorney or attorney general's office organizes meetings and activities, compiles data on arrests and court activity, and is constantly available to citizens. Citizens advisory councils meet monthly, bringing citizens together with prosecutors, the police, and other agency representatives to discuss safety issues and problems of crime and quality of life. Citizens typically provide information about where incidents or problems are occurring—what street, what address—and the nature of the problem, which is as likely to be illegal parking, public drinking, prostitution, or juvenile gang members making noise at night as violent crime. Prosecutors and police listen and also report back to citizens on their recent efforts on the streets or in court, giving information on particular cases. In three of the four SNIs a steering committee, comprising prosecutors, police officers, and other law enforcement agency representatives, meets separately to devise strategies for addressing the problems that citizens have identified.

Assistant district attorneys and attorneys general work with the SNIs in both the district and superior courts. All engage in priority prosecution of key cases (including misdemeanors and quality of life offenses, as well as felonies) from the area, work closely with citizens and police to develop strategies for addressing local crime and safety problems, and get to know the neighborhood well. But prosecutors also use other tactics: where prostitution troubled residents of more than one SNI, prosecutors helped develop the "Johns Project," offering clients the option of doing community service—cleaning up local streets in full view of the media—instead of going to trial. They speak at liquor control board hearings on behalf of SNI efforts to close troublesome establishments. In court, they tell judges about neighborhood conditions and present community impact statements from residents.

In East Boston, the SNI was instrumental in initiating a CBJJ roundtable in the local high school. Local police and juvenile court probation officers are active participants on the SNI steering committee and advisory council as well as the CBJJ roundtable, and the presiding judge in East Boston's district court, who has become convinced of the value of the SNI's activities, has added his own solutions to youth crime problems, such as setting conditions of probation that can be lifted if youthful offenders make the honor roll. In Dorchester, many local service providers who are the mainstay of the SNI focus their efforts on preventing crime and violence among local youth. During 1998, for example, the Bowdoin Street Health Center and the Log School Settlement House (established twenty-five years ago as an alternative middle school, now providing a range of programs to meet community needs, such as ESL, GED, preschool, and a homework center for students ages eight to fourteen) hired community outreach workers to address increasing violence among young Cape Verdean men in the area, while the Dorchester Youth Collaborative targeted at-risk Asian,

African American, Cape Verdean, and Hispanic teens in a variety of programs. The Boston police commander of district C-11 (Dorchester) attends all Dorchester high school CBJJ roundtable meetings, and a community relations officer chairs the Dorchester SNI advisory council meetings. Potential youth gang activity and recent disturbances are discussed routinely in both these groups, and information is shared about strategies for containing it. Similar activities take place in Roxbury's Grove Hall SNI.[79]

The Franklin Hill Gang Prevention Project was funded by a Bureau of Justice Assistance federal grant obtained by the district attorney's office. Under the grant Boston became a demonstration site for a comprehensive initiative that included both an organized law enforcement component to arrest established gang members responsible for drug dealing, associated criminal activity, and violence in and around the Franklin Hill housing development, and a prevention component, through which a wide range of services was established to assist residents in developing the capacity to prevent and resist crime and improve their quality of life. The district attorney's office managed the grant, playing a major role in both the collaborative prevention and law enforcement efforts that took place. Participants adopted an explicit problem-solving approach, working closely with residents in all aspects of the project. Youth violence and safety were key issues.

To identify and address criminal problems existing in Franklin Hill, the district attorney's office established a multijurisdictional task force to conduct investigations and develop a plan of action that included compiling a database on gang members and criminal offenders active in the area, implementing sweeps, and increasing police visibility. Criminal activity decreased rapidly, as did violent incidents; at the same time, peaceful social activities and use of public spaces by residents increased. Prevention efforts were carried out through the Franklin Hill Gang Prevention Coalition, organized by the district attorney's office and made up of local, city, state, and federal criminal justice agencies; health and service providers; and community groups. The coalition conducted an extensive needs assessment with residents and then helped to put in place a range of activities and services, including social, sports, and mentoring programs for youth; neighborhood beautification and landscaping projects; food banks; educational classes; drug prevention workshops; a fatherhood program for young court-involved men; job fairs; and a neighborhood justice network to train housing development building captains and set up crime-watch groups.

These community prosecution initiatives are linked to many other individual efforts in which prosecutors have been involved that target youth violence and crime. For example, prosecutors from the district attorney's office participated in Boston's Operation Ceasefire initiative, described elsewhere in this volume. Virtually all are characterized by collaboration among agencies to solve problems within a neighborhood, an attempt to work directly with citizens and accord priority to their concerns, and an approach that seeks to prevent crime as well as prosecute offenders.

NEIGHBORHOOD CONFERENCE COMMITTEES IN TRAVIS COUNTY (AUSTIN), TEXAS. In 1996, Travis County District Attorney Ronald Earle, "in an effort to return the individual citizen to her historical role as the dominant actor of criminal justice" and in cooperation with the city of Austin's health and human services department, formed the first of several Neighborhood Conference Committees (NCC). The Austin police department, the juvenile court, area school districts, and, above all, citizens also are partners in this collaboration.[80] The NCC program, which is derived from a model developed in El Paso County, Texas, in 1979, is coordinated by a representative of the city's health and human services department. Committees formed within zip code areas handle Class A and B misdemeanors not involving weapons or serious assault committed by juveniles between ten and sixteen years old who have no prior adjudicated offenses. Cases are referred to the councils (that is, deferred from adjudication) from the juvenile court or another local court, to be heard by a panel of three to five trained adult volunteers from the offender's neighborhood. Each committee has a salaried coordinator who organizes its activities. Along with personnel from criminal justice and local government agencies, the coordinator screens and trains citizen volunteers to serve on the panels. Participation in the NCC is voluntary for offenders and their families: if they choose not to participate or comply with the contract requirements, the case is returned to the district attorney's office, which files a petition in court.

The process begins with a meeting between the NCC panel and the offender and his or her parents, held at a school or other locality in the neighborhood, to discuss (separately and then together) the offense and aspects of the youth's family and school environment. This initial session can last two to three hours or more. Afterward, panel members devise a four- to six-month contract for the offender and parents to complete. Contracts include activities that address the causes of the juvenile's delinquent behavior and specify the consequences. Typically they involve restitution for the victim, restoration of the loss to the neighborhood, and other components intended to strengthen the juvenile's ties with adults in the neighborhood, such as mentoring and counseling. Compliance conditions are spelled out precisely, including classes the offender must attend and tasks that he or she must complete.

The goals of the diversion program are several: to encourage citizen involvement in administering juvenile justice and to empower citizens to take responsibility for neighborhood safety; to facilitate the resolution of the wrongful act; to hold the youth accountable for the offense; to make him or her aware of how the offense has injured and otherwise affected individuals; to impress upon the youth that the community is concerned about his or her action; to reduce demands on the regular courts; and to develop community resources for addressing juvenile delinquency. As part of this final goal, members of the NCC panel and the community work directly with the family of the offender to offer support and advice. For example, at one meeting members of the NCC told a single mother trying to cope with several teenagers, one of whom was before them as an offender, "Like you, we are parents in your neighborhood, and we understand the problems and pressures you are facing. These are things we have tried that have worked . . . ."[81] Facilitating the growth of positive relationships between the offender and other adults in the community is another NCC objective: in another case, an angry local resident whose boat had been damaged by a youthful offender became, over time, a mentor to him. The relationship began when the offender was assigned to "pay back" the victim by working at his house on Saturdays, and then developed further.

The first NCC began operating in the Bedichek middle school area, in South Austin, early in 1996. During the first year of operation (1996), 101 cases were referred to the NCC program: 65 percent of cases were handled to completion. Of the seventy-seven signed contracts with the NCC committee, contract requirements were completed in approximately three-quarters. The recidivism rate was approximately 21 percent.

Attempts to formally evaluate the Bedicheck NCC's operations and outcomes recognized the difficulty in relying solely on numerical indicators. Adults participating in the NCCs say they welcome the opportunity to take responsibility for directly addressing crime and working with juvenile offenders in their own neighborhoods and that they find the process of working with their neighbors on panels less difficult and more rewarding than they expected. One noted, "The tough, punishment-oriented people are tempered by others"; another remarked, "We try to work together and to be proactive." They are candid about the need to involve all ethnic and cultural groups within a neighborhood, "or else the NCC could end up with volunteers being white, and offenders Hispanic or African American." In fact, the program has been spreading rapidly as more and more neighborhoods ask to form their own NCCs to deal with juvenile crime and as some participants contemplate using the format and structure for addressing other crime and safety issues.

Approaching Youth Violence through an Holistic Focus on Families

Youthful offenders and victims frequently are part of the same families— often families in which children witness domestic abuse or are themselves abused. Truancy and delinquent behavior may offer the opportunity for groups such as the CBJ and CBJJ to intervene and provide services for an individual youth, but many prosecutors believe they can go a step further by better coordinating and integrating the disparate initiatives that target children and families.

ADDRESSING FAMILIES IN THE TRAVIS COUNTY (AUSTIN), TEXAS, DISTRICT ATTORNEY'S OFFICE. In Austin, Texas, NCCs are but one part of a comprehensive effort by District Attorney Earle to coordinate both his office's and the community's planning and resources for addressing juvenile crime. Within the district attorney's office, Earle has brought together the prosecution of all family-related crime in a family justice division. His rationale for doing so was that victims and offenders often were part of the same family, and the needs of entire families could be better addressed by coordinating prosecution and other functions carried out by his office. Assistant district attorneys are encouraged to gain experience at some time in their career with a rotation in the family justice division, not to learn basic trial skills in less significant cases but because Earle believes it helps them to understand the broad, interrelated problems associated with these types of offenses.

The family justice division is a special unit outside the grand jury intake and trial division; it handles all matters involving children and families, including child abuse, death, civil and criminal neglect, and juvenile prosecutions. Earle considers this division one of the most important in his office and has been directly involved in increasing its size and functions over the years. For most of the last decade, one of his most trusted and experienced senior staff has led the division. During that time, the division has expanded from a staff of two criminal, two civil, and one and one-half juvenile prosecutors to seventeen attorneys (in 1998) who handle criminal and civil child abuse and juvenile prosecution.

Two attorneys from the division are assigned to the child protection team (CPT). The chief prosecutor of CPT is housed together with the police, sheriff's deputies, state children's protective services caseworkers, and victim counselors; she assists CPS caseworkers in presenting civil petitions to remove children from abusive households and provides legal assistance to the law enforcement officers who are investigating criminal child abuse cases. She also chairs an interagency group that reviews the death of any child in the county to oversee the exchange of related information among agencies, determine the cause of death, and try to prevent other children from dying. A second CPT prosecutor from the division is housed at the Children's Advocacy Center, where he provides legal assistance in preparing and videotaping interviews with child victims, and he presents criminal child abuse cases to the grand jury. Four attorneys from the division are assigned to handle criminal child abuse cases in the felony district courts. In the civil child abuse group, three attorneys from the division represent state children's protective services after petitions are filed removing children from abusive households. These petitions may seek court-ordered services for the family or termination of parental rights.

Finally, seven assistant district attorneys in the juvenile unit prosecute juvenile offenders between the ages of ten and seventeen in the juvenile court. Cases involve all misdemeanors except Class C (the least serious, which lie within the jurisdiction of the county and city attorneys and are processed respectively by the justice of the peace or in municipal court) and all felonies—everything from shoplifting to capital murder. Attorneys also may seek to have juvenile offenders certified for trial as adults. One assistant district attorney position is funded by a state auto-theft prevention grant (60 to 70 percent of auto theft in the county is committed by juveniles). A gang activity prosecutor prosecutes juvenile gang members who have committed gang-related offenses, attempts to have juveniles certified as adults for the most serious offenses, and works closely with police and probation officers on the gang task force.[82]

Including these diverse components, whose interests may not appear to coincide, in a single division has created constructive tension among staff, such as between attorneys who prosecute juveniles and those responsible for civil actions involving abuse and neglect. For example, juveniles whose behavior is so violent that their parents refuse to take them in and who cannot be placed in foster care may be prosecuted by the juvenile unit. Frequently they are released from the detention facility because space is needed for more serious cases only to end up in the hands of CPS and attorneys in the civil unit. Earle sees this tension as healthy: the attorneys talk to each other about the problems, just as do police and prosecutors, or service providers and prosecutors, who work on interagency teams.

Creating these structures inside the district attorney's office is only half of what District Attorney Earle has attempted to do to address juvenile crime and victimization. Earle and former juvenile justice division director Rosemary Lehmberg developed Austin's Children's Advocacy Center, bringing together local police agencies, City Hospital, and the department of protective and regulatory services to address the problems of abused children being "revictimized" as cases were investigated and prosecuted and to improve the response of criminal justice agencies to child abuse. Located in a house on the east side of Austin (from which many victims come), the center provides a welcoming milieu for children and their families to go for evaluation, crisis intervention, evidence gathering, and counseling. Investigations begin here, where counselors, social workers, an assistant district attorney, police, and medical facilities are on the premises. All child victims of violent crime, sexual abuse, and neglect and their siblings up to the age of seventeen are treated, and follow-up counseling and services are available. Responsibility for financial support and operations of the center has been turned over to the community, with substantial contributions from businesses and foundations.

To involve the wider community, Earle also helped establish the Juvenile Justice Coordinating Committee (JACC, made up of elected school and criminal justice officials) and the Management Coordination Team (MCT, representing various county agencies) to address juvenile crime in a coordinated fashion. The planning undertaken by these groups has led to programs such as First Offender: when an analysis of continually escalating recidivism among juvenile offenders revealed that no significant sanctions were being imposed for the first, often the second, and even the third arrest and that offenders were not even going to court, Earle and JACC created the program under which juvenile first offenders, even petty misdemeanants, must appear before a judge. A truancy program was also set up. The emphasis in both programs is on early intervention and provision of services to prevent involvement in more serious crime.

JACKSON COUNTY (KANSAS CITY), MISSOURI, COUNTY PROSECUTOR'S OFFICE CHILD ABUSE, TRUANCY, AND CURFEW PROGRAMS. As Jackson County prosecutor, Claire McCaskill had no authority over the prosecution of juveniles: that responsibility lies with the juvenile officer of

the family court, who oversees the prosecution of abuse, neglect, and status and delinquency (criminal) offenses, under the supervision of the
administrative judge of the family court and court administrator for the
sixteenth judicial circuit.[83] Family court operations themselves include
extensive prevention and treatment services for juveniles and families. Nevertheless, during her administration McCaskill made youth safety, including preventing juveniles from trying and using drugs, one of her highest
priorities. She brought the capacity of her own office in prevention and
treatment to bear in developing new programs; used the authority of her
office to prosecute criminal abuse and neglect of children; and worked
closely with the family court director to better coordinate child abuse and
neglect actions between the prosecutor's office and the family court.[84]

During 1996, McCaskill began to pursue an agenda involving reform of
county child abuse prosecution, treatment, and services. Often the division
of family services and the family court shared a mission that included
extensive case management, counseling to preserve the family, and rehabilitation—a mission that would collide with efforts by the prosecutor's office
to prosecute a parent for criminal abuse just when the parent was deemed
"rehabilitated." McCaskill proposed identifying a prosecutor in the sex
crimes unit of the Jackson County prosecutor's office to cross-prosecute
with a family court attorney on those cases being worked on by both agencies: the family court attorney would "second chair" the criminal proceeding, while the prosecutor's office attorney would "second chair" the family
court proceeding. As a first step, the office applied for and received a federal grant to add a case manager position to support the assistant prosecutor from the sex crimes unit in such cases.

Efforts to combat sex crimes and abuse have recently been expanded
through the new Neighborhood Justice prosecution program, which places
prosecutors in different police patrol divisions around the city. A child
protection liaison attorney, whose function is to devise strategies for reducing child abuse and neglect throughout the county, is now focusing her
efforts on the east patrol division, where the highest number of hot-line
calls originate, and the truancy coordinator is working with neighborhood
justice prosecutors to set up truancy projects in schools in their divisions.
Through the Neighborhood Justice program, these specialists are beginning to collaborate: the child protection liaison attorney is developing protocols with the truancy coordinator to assess whether truancy might result
from child abuse or neglect; she also is working with DART (the drug
abatement response team) to develop a new protocol for use with children

found in methamphetamine houses, who may be subjects of neglect or sexual abuse.

A wide-ranging program that got off the ground late in 1996, the Kansas City in-school truancy project represents a collaborative effort among the Jackson County prosecutor's office, the family court and division of family services, the mayor's office of Kansas City, the Kansas City school district, the Mayor's Urban Symposium and Tournament, and the Missouri Department of Public Safety to decrease youth involvement in crime and violence by reducing truancy among middle- and high-school students. Statistics showed that the absentee rate in 1995–96 for middle-school students was running at 14.9 percent and for high-school students at 24.4 percent and that only 63 percent of students were graduating from high school. Data on jailed offenders collected for the anti-drug tax program COMBAT by administrator Jim Nunnelly also suggested seven early warning signs in the lives of offenders that could serve as points for intervention. The truancy project was developed to identify students at risk and to intervene early and effectively by providing coordinated services to the students and their families. Three pilot middle schools and three high schools are served in the initial project period: at each, parents are notified by an attendance clerk when students have unexplained absences of one to two days; when unexplained absences of two to ten days occur, parents are informed that they must either contact the parent-school liaison or the matter will be referred to the prosecutor's office for action; and when unexplained absences reach eleven or more days, prosecution of parents may commence for failure to ensure attendance of the juveniles under the state's compulsory attendance law. Prosecution is viewed as a last resort: the goal of the project is to encourage parents to take responsibility for their children. All these actions are fully supported by needs assessments, referrals for counseling and other services made available to parents and children, and a comprehensive treatment plan for each child at risk.

Conclusions

The advent of the twenty-first century continues to produce noticeable and widespread changes in prosecution generally, with prosecutors' position in juvenile justice remaining both central and powerful. Within prosecution itself, the adoption of comprehensive problem solving, attention to local communities and neighborhoods and their priorities, expanding sets of tactics (beyond case processing) to address crime and safety issues, emphasis upon misdemeanors and quality of life offenses as well as felonies, and attempts at preventing crime have all increasingly found their way into practice.[85] At the same time, debate over the implications, potential, and challenges of community prosecution at a time of shrinking resources in most offices is contributing to organizational and policy considerations.[86] Enhancing their ability to address and even prevent youth crime and violence has remained a crucial objective of prosecutors and has given rise to a range of new efforts across the country.[87] Particularly useful, though preliminary, are emerging research reports that offer evaluations of some of these initiatives and present outcomes of specific prosecutorial actions such as waiver.[88]

Many of the trends we recognized as evident during the last few years of the twentieth century show signs of continued evolution, strengthening, and expansion. Overall, the administration of juvenile justice, as well as the assumptions framing it, has been revolutionized during the past three and a half decades. Prosecutors, non-players in the pre-1970s era in juvenile justice, have largely superseded probation officers and judges as central players. Moreover, it is not just district attorneys and county prosecutors who have moved into the juvenile justice arena, but state attorneys general and U.S. attorneys as well. In fact, even district attorneys who do not have legal responsibility for juvenile justice, such as in Kansas City, have nonetheless assumed some responsibility.

Clearly, the prosecutorial approach to youth has been bifurcated. On the one hand, violent and repeat serious youthful offenders are now approached as a distinct category of offender in need of swift and certain punishment, including being handled as an adult and even given adult sentences. Prosecutors are at the nexus of this process, from charging to disposition. On the other hand, the emphasis for first and minor offenders has been on diversion, treatment, restitution, and community service. The response of prosecutors has not only been to use available resources; in virtually every site we have studied, prosecutors have worked to increase the community's capacity to respond to both the needs of children and those of the community for protection and justice. Prosecutors also have worked to enhance existing programs and to develop new capacities where program and service gaps exist.

Their focus has become even broader, however. First, they have demonstrated renewed concern for minor offenses committed by youth, both as a means of preventing crime and reining in serious offenders. Second, prosecutors have moved into the business of delinquency prevention, for example, in collaborations with schools and service agencies to identify potentially troubled or troublesome youth and ensure that they receive services. Just as they have sought to ensure that communities have adequate services for minor offenders, prosecutors also have encouraged and sponsored the development of treatment services for troubled families and children in the name of preventing future delinquency and crime.

Prosecutors might be in a relatively stronger position to advocate for programs for minor and potential offenders than were probation officers and judges. The public perception that juvenile judges and probation officers were more concerned about the welfare of an offending child than the community —in other words, "soft" on young criminals—diminished the strength of their appeals for services for youth. Prosecutors, especially "tough" prosecutors, are in a position to use their "toughness" as well as their status as elected officials to give the crime prevention message more credibility than juvenile justice officials previously could. This approach is proving successful in many jurisdictions. Massachusetts attorney general Tom Reilly comments, "The success of community-based justice in Middlesex was one of my proudest achievements in my time as district attorney. As attorney general, CBJ is an information-sharing model that can be applied on a larger stage, not only to issues of youth violence, but to education, health, and human services and a host of other areas where different government agencies share a mandate to protect and serve our children."[89]

We have provided examples of prosecutorial programs in all aspects of their work with youth—work with repeat violent offenders, with minor offenders, and with troubled and potentially troublesome youth—that we believe respect the rights of juveniles, seek to protect the community, and serve the interests of children as well. Having said this, we nonetheless still have concerns about the increasing power and domain of prosecutors. First, as has been noted, legislative restrictions on judicial discretion and legislative and judicial restrictions on police discretion—discretion in each case that has been relatively visible—have left prosecutors with greater discretion, discretion that is comparatively invisible. Second, there is nothing about the training of lawyers that prepares them for work with juveniles beyond litigation, particularly for deciding among the various diversion and service programs available. Lawyers might be a quick study; however, learning on the job has its limitations. Third, preventive efforts, for example with schools, raise issues of confidentiality and "widening the net." Traditionally, concerns for stigmatization and not intruding into family concerns have kept public agents of control at bay. While concerns about stigmatization have, perhaps, been exaggerated, the idea that state authority should be mobilized to intervene before delinquent and criminal acts occur raises issues of just how intrusive public agents should be—even as we come to understand that the family can be a source of horrible abuse as well as of love and care. As Barry Feld has noted, even for minor offenders who are diverted, "There is no practical way to assess the legal justification for intervention."[90] The point is that an uncontrolled prosecutor—whether dealing with violent youth, minor offenders, or troubled youngsters—has the potential to create considerable mayhem.

Yet, in the vast majority of states, district attorneys are elected. As such, they are not insulated from public accountability in the same bureaucratic way that probation officers have been or in the same structural way that judges have. Perhaps such accountability will militate against abuse or zealotry. Furthermore, in many of their extraprosecution efforts, prosecutors work collaboratively and depend on the trust and continued good faith of participants from other agencies who may provide a restraining influence. Nonetheless, we are left with a dilemma: we admire much that prosecutors are doing and suspect that their reputation for toughness has allowed them to publicly demand—and legitimately obtain—services for abused and troubled youth when others' requests have previously gone unheeded; yet, their power and discretion may be cause for greater debate of public policy than has yet taken place.

Notes

1. Herman Goldstein, *Problem-Oriented Policing* (McGraw-Hill, 1987); Herman Goldstein, "Improving Policing: A Problem-Oriented Approach," *Crime and Delinquency*, vol. 25 (April 1979), pp. 236–58.

2. Michele Sviridoff and others, *Dispensing Justice Locally: The Implementation and Effects of the Midtown Community Court* (Amsterdam: Harwood Academic Publishers, 2000).

3. Catherine M. Coles and George L. Kelling, with Mark H. Moore, *Prosecution in the Community: A Study of Emergent Strategies. A Cross Site Analysis*, research report, grant 95-IJ-CX-0096, U.S. Department of Justice, Office of Justice Programs, National Institute of Justice (September 1998).

4. See, for example, David R. Karp, ed., *Community Justice: An Emerging Field* (Lanham, Md.: Rowman and Littlefield Publishers, Inc., 1998); G. Bazemore and M. Schiff, "Community Justice/Restorative Justice: Prospects for a New Social Ecology for Community Corrections," *International Journal of Comparative and Applied Criminal Justice*, vol. 20, no. 1 (Fall 1996), pp. 311–35.

5. *Kent v. United States*, 383 U.S. 541 (1966); *In re Gault*, 387 U.S. 1 (1967). See

Barry C. Feld, "Violent Youth and Public Policy: A Case Study of Juvenile Justice Law Reform," *Minnesota Law Review*, vol. 79 (1995), p. 971.

6. Francis Barry McCarthy, "The Serious Offender and Juvenile Court Reform: The Case for Prosecutorial Waiver of Juvenile Court Jurisdiction," *St. Louis University Law Journal*, vol. 38 (1994), p. 645. The roots of this approach are traced in George L. Kelling, "Social Responses to Children: The Historical Legacy of the Juvenile Court," Working Paper 85-03-02 (Cambridge, Mass.: Program in Criminal Justice Policy and Management, John F. Kennedy School of Government, Harvard University, May 1985); Barry Krisberg, *The Juvenile Court: Reclaiming the Vision* (San Francisco: National Council on Crime and Delinquency, 1988).

7. Feld, "Violent Youth and Public Policy," p. 971.

8. Krisberg, *The Juvenile Court*, p. 6.

9. Ted Rubin, *Juvenile Justice Policy, Practice, and Law*, 2d ed. (Random House, 1985), p. 247.

10. Ibid., pp. 247–48.

11. H. Ted Rubin, "The Emerging Prosecutor Dominance of the Juvenile Court Intake Process," *Crime and Delinquency* (July 1980), pp. 299, 302–03.

12. McCarthy, "The Serious Offender and Juvenile Court Reform," p. 647. McCarthy recounts that the 1933 Pennsylvania Juvenile Act provided two criteria to determine when a child might be certified for prosecution: the child had to be above the age of fourteen and the offense charged had to be punishable by imprisonment in a state penitentiary.

13. *Kent* v. *United States*, 383 U.S. 541, 557 (1966).

14. *In re Gault*, 387 U.S. 1, 33–34, 36–37, 55–56 (1967).

15. *In re Winship*, 397 U.S. 358 (1970).

16. *Breed* v. *Jones*, 421 U.S. 519, 528–31 (1975); see also Eric K. Klein, "Dennis the Menace or Billy the Kid?: An Analysis of the Role of Transfer to Criminal Court in Juvenile Justice," *American Criminal Law Review*, vol. 35 (Winter 1998), pp. 371, 380.

17. Rubin, "The Emerging Prosecutor Dominance," pp. 310–11.

18. President's Commission on Law Enforcement and Administration of Justice, "The Administration of Juvenile Justice: The Juvenile Court and Related Methods of Delinquency Control," *Task Force Report: Juvenile Delinquency and Youth Crime* (Government Printing Office, 1967), p. 34.

19. Rubin, "The Emerging Prosecutor Dominance," p. 311.

20. Ibid., p. 312.

21. *Report of the Advisory Committee to the Administrator on Standards for the Administration of Juvenile Justice*, National Institute for Juvenile Justice and Delinquency Prevention, Law Enforcement Assistance Administration (Government Printing Office, 1977), Standards 3.142, 3.143, 3.147.

22. Standard 19.2, *National Prosecution Standards* (Chicago: National District Attorneys Association, 1977).

23. Rubin suggests that the growth in prosecution staffs was not uniform and was slower in rural areas. See *Juvenile Justice Policy, Practice, and Law*, p. 250.

24. John H. Laub and Bruce K. Mac Murray, "Increasing the Prosecutor's Role in Juvenile Court: Expectations and Realities," *Justice System Journal*, vol. 12, no. 2 (1987), pp. 196–209, 203–5.

25. James Shine and Dwight Price, "Prosecutors and Juvenile Justice: New Roles and

Perspectives," in Ira M. Schwartz, ed., *Juvenile Justice and Public Policy* (Lexington Books, 1992), p. 102.

26. National District Attorneys Association Prosecution Standard 19.2, Juvenile Delinquency.

27. See Frank J. Remington, "The Decision to Charge, the Decision to Convict on a Plea of Guilty, and the Impact of Sentence Structure on Prosecution Practices," in Lloyd E. Ohlin and Frank J. Remington, eds., *Discretion in Criminal Justice* (State University of New York Press, 1993), p. 86; American Bar Association, *Standards Relating to the Prosecution Function and the Defense Function* (Chicago: 1986; originally approved 1971).

28. Klein, "Dennis the Menace or Billy the Kid?" p. 394.

29. See Patricia Torbet and Linda Szymanski, "State Legislative Responses to Violent Juvenile Crime: 1996–97 Update," *Juvenile Justice Bulletin* (U.S. Department of Justice, Office of Juvenile Justice and Delinquency Prevention, Office of Justice Programs, November 1998), p. 3; Patrick Griffin, Patricia Torbet, and Linda Szymanski, *Trying Juveniles as Adults in Criminal Court: An Analysis of State Transfer Provisions*, Office of Juvenile Justice and Delinquency Prevention Report (U.S. Department of Justice, Office of Juvenile Justice and Delinquency Prevention, December 1998).

30. Griffin, Torbet and Szymanski, *Trying Juveniles as Adults in Criminal Court*, pp. 3–9.

31. Bureau of Justice Statistics, *Juveniles Prosecuted in State Criminal Courts. National Survey of Prosecutors 1994*, NCJ-164265 (U.S. Department of Justice, Office of Juvenile Justice and Delinquency Prevention, March 1997), p. 4; Donna Bishop and others, "A Study of Juvenile Transfers to Criminal Court in Florida," *OJJDP Fact Sheet* 113 (U.S. Department of Justice, Office of Juvenile Justice and Delinquency Prevention, August 1999), p.1.

32. Griffin, Torbet, and Szymanski, *Trying Juveniles as Adults in Criminal Court*, pp. 9–11; see also Howard N. Snyder, "Juvenile Arrests 1996," *Juvenile Justice Bulletin* (U.S. Department of Justice, Office of Juvenile Justice and Delinquency Prevention, November 1997), p. 3.

33. Klein, "Dennis the Menace or Billy the Kid?" p. 398.

34. Charles W. Thomas and Shay Bilchik, "Criminal Law: Prosecuting Juveniles in Criminal Courts: A Legal and Empirical Analysis," *Journal of Criminal Law and Criminology*, vol. 76 (Summer 1985), p. 478.

35. 1999 FBI Uniform Crime Report data showed that 23 percent of arrests involving youth under eighteen and under the original jurisdiction of their state juvenile justice system were handled by the law enforcement agency. Of all those arrested, 69 percent were referred to juvenile court (up from 58 percent in 1980), 6 percent were referred directly to criminal court (the highest proportion in two decades), and the remainder were referred to a welfare agency or another police agency. See Howard N. Snyder, "Juvenile Arrests 1999," *Juvenile Justice Bulletin* (U.S. Department of Justice, Office of Juvenile Justice and Delinquency Prevention, December 2000), p. 7. The report also notes that "the proportion of juvenile arrests sent to juvenile court was similar in cities (69%), suburban areas (68%), and rural counties (69%)."

36. Bureau of Justice Statistics, *Juveniles Prosecuted in State Criminal Courts*, p. 2.

37. Ibid, p. 1.

38. Carol J. DeFrances and Greg W. Steadman, *Prosecutors in State Courts, 1996*,

Bureau of Justice Statistics Bulletin (U.S. Department of Justice, Office of Justice Programs, July 1998).

39. "Juvenile Delinquents in the Federal Criminal Justice System, 1995," *BJS Bulletin*, NCJ-163066 (February 1997), pp. 1–2.

40. Ibid., pp. 1–2.

41. See, for example, Coles and Kelling, *Prosecution in the Community*, pp. 39–44.

42. James Q. Wilson and George L. Kelling, "Broken Windows: The Police and Neighborhood Safety," *Atlantic Monthly* (March 1982), pp. 29–38.

43. See, for example, James Q. Wilson, *The Varieties of Police Behavior* (Harvard University Press, 1968); Egon Bittner, *Aspects of Police Work* (Northeastern University Press, 1990); and Mary Ann Wycoff, "*The Role of Municipal Police Research as a Prelude to Changing It*" (Washington: Police Foundation, 1982).

44. A. D. Biderman and others, *Report on a Pilot Study in the District of Columbia on Victimization and Attitudes towards Law Enforcement* (U.S. Department of Justice, 1967).

45. The New York City Police Department, under Commissioner Raymond Kelly, recruited Kelling to help solve the squeegeeing problem.

46. Coles and Kelling, *Prosecution in the Community*, p. 37.

47. Ibid., p. 45.

48. Coles and Kelling, *Prosecution in the Community*, appendix D, Jackson County (Kansas City), Missouri, case study.

49. Claire Johnson, Barbara Webster, and Edward Connors, "Prosecuting Gangs: A National Assessment," *Research in Brief* (U.S. Department of Justice, National Institute of Justice, February 1995). See also "Research Note: Preliminary Results of the 1995 National Prosecutor's Survey," *Journal of Gang Research*, vol. 2, no. 4 (Summer 1995), p. 61.

50. Coles and Kelling, *Prosecution in the Community*, p. 74. See also appendix A, Austin.

51. Ibid., pp. 60–61, and appendix B, Boston.

52. See, for example, Coles and Kelling, *Prosecution in the Community* and case studies with descriptions of Austin, Texas, Boston, Massachusetts, Indianapolis, Indiana, Kansas City, Missouri, and numerous other sites.

53. National District Attorneys Association, *Resource Manual and Policy Positions on Juvenile Crime Issues* (Alexandria, Va.: November 16, 1996). The manual was devised by its Advisory Group on Serious, Violent, and Habitual Juvenile Offenders and finalized by the Juvenile Justice Advisory Committee.

54. Sight and sound regulations arose within the Juvenile Justice and Delinquency Prevention Act of 1974, 42 U.S.C. Sec. 5633, as amended by Act of December 8, 1980, P. L. 96-509, 94 Stat. 2755 (1980). The legislation prohibited states, if they wished to be eligible for federal funds, from detaining or confining juveniles charged with criminal acts "in any institution in which they have contact with adult [inmates.]"

55. NDAA, *Resource Manual*.

56. Harry L. Shorestein, "Statement on Juvenile Justice," unpublished manuscript, April 1998, p.1.

57. Ibid., p. 15.

58. David W. Rasmussen and Yiwen Yu, "An Evaluation of Juvenile Justice Innovations in Duval County, Florida," unpublished report, Florida State University, July 1996, p. 36.

59. Shorestein, "Statement on Juvenile Justice," p. 15.

60. Shorestein, "Statement on Juvenile Justice," p. 21; Bishop and others, "A Study of Juvenile Transfers," p.1.

61. Many of these programs take a restorative justice approach. See Gordon Bazemore, *Evaluating Community Youth Sanctioning Models: Neighborhood Dimensions and Beyond*, Research Forum, Crime and Place: Plenary Papers of the 1997 Conference on Criminal Justice Research and Evaluation. U.S. Department of Justice, National Institute of Justice, 1998; G. Bazemore and S. Day, "Restoring the Balance: Juvenile and Community Justice," *Juvenile Justice Journal* (December 1996), pp. 3–14.

62. David Losier, assistant director of the CBJ program, Middlesex County district attorney's office, interview with Catherine Coles, May 4, 1998.

63. Tom Reilly, "No Time to Wait, No Time to Waste" (Cambridge, Mass.: Middlesex County District Attorney's Office, n.d.), p. 9.

64. Ibid.

65. Ibid., pp. 9–10.

66. *First Annual Report* (Cambridge, Mass.: Middlesex County Juvenile Prosecution Unit, Middlesex County District Attorney's Office, February 1998), p. vii.

67. The district court is the lowest-level trial court.

68. Gerard T. Leone Jr., deputy first assistant, Middlesex County district attorney's office, interview with Catherine Coles, October 21, 1998.

69. Student mediation programs, antiviolence task forces, and violence prevention training offered in schools have been part of a coordinated plan to assist school districts in addressing teen violence, drug and alcohol abuse, diversity issues, and hate crimes and harassment. In addition to providing training, seminars, and workshops and facilitating student action projects, Project Alliance assists schools in developing specific policies and legal protocols and in coordinating services for at-risk youth. *First Annual Report*, Middlesex County Juvenile Prosecution Unit, pp. iv–v.

70. Massachusetts General Laws Chapter 119, Sections 54, 58, 74. Murder is charged by indictment and tried in the superior court; youthful offenders are charged by indictment and tried in the juvenile court, with the possibility of enhanced commitment periods.

71. By established policy, the district attorney's office initially indicates its intent to file for youthful offender status on each incoming case that meets the minimum statutory standard. The juvenile unit chief has discretion over the final decision.

72. See Frank Hartmann, "Safety First: Partnership, the Powerful Neutral Convener, and Problem Solving," chapter 9 in this volume

73. David Losier, interview with Catherine Coles, May 4, 1998.

74. *First Annual Report*, Middlesex County Juvenile Prosecution Unit, p. iii.

75. Michael Ortiz, assistant district attorney, Middlesex County, interview with Catherine Coles, May 15, 1998.

76. "Focus On Youth," Suffolk County District Attorney's Office, unpublished document, n.d. Martin offered this remark at a criminal justice committee hearing on the proposed legislation.

77. See Massachusetts General Laws chapter 119, Sections 58, 68 (1999).

78. Ralph C. Martin II, "Report to the Legislature: The Suffolk County Community Based Juvenile Justice Program," Suffolk County District Attorney's Office, 1998.

79. See Coles and Kelling, *Prosecution in the Community*, p. 75; see also appendix B, Boston.

80. Ibid., appendix A, Austin, Texas.

81. Personal observation, Catherine Coles.

82. Coles and Kelling, *Prosecution in the Community*, appendix A.

83. McCaskill was elected state auditor in November 1998 and resigned her position as Jackson County prosecutor two years before her term as county prosecutor was completed.

84. McCaskill had extensive resources available to her office through COMBAT, the Community Backed Anti-Drug Tax, a program supported by tax funds in the county. See Gregory Mills, *Community Backed Anti-Drug Tax: COMBAT in Jackson County, Missouri* (U.S. Department of Justice, National Institute of Justice); Coles and Kelling, *Prosecution in the Community*, appendix D.

85. See, for example, Carol J. DeFrances, *National Survey of Prosecutors: State Court Prosecutors in Large Districts, 2001*, BJA special report (U.S. Department of Justice, Office of Justice Programs, December 2001); Elaine Nugent and Gerard A. Rainville, "The State of Community Prosecution: Results of a National Survey," *Prosecutor* (March/April 2001); Barbara Boland, *Community Prosecution in Washington, DC: The U.S. Attorney's Fifth District Pilot Project*, research report (U.S. Department of Justice, National Institute of Justice, 2001); Catherine Coles, Brian Carney, and Bobbie Johnson, "Crime Prevention through Community Prosecution and Community Policing: Boston's Grove Hall Safe Neighborhood Initiative," in Corina Sole Brito and Eugenia E. Gratto, eds., *Problem Oriented Policing: Crime-Specific Problems Critical Issues and Making POP Work*, vol. 3 (Police Executive Research Forum, 2000); Sarah Glazer, "Community Prosecution," *CQ Researcher*, vol. 10, no. 42 (December 15, 2000).

86. For example, see Catherine M. Coles, "Community Prosecution, Problem Solving, and Public Accountability: The Evolving Strategy of the American Prosecutor," Working Paper 00-02-04 (Program in Criminal Justice Policy and Management, John F. Kennedy School of Government, Harvard University, 2000); Brian Forst, "Prosecutors Discover the Community," *Judicature*, vol. 84 (November–December 2000).

87. See, for example, Heike P. Gramckow and Elena Tompkins, "Enhancing Prosecutors' Ability to Combat and Prevent Juvenile Crime in Their Jurisdictions" and "Enabling Prosecutors to Address Drug, Gang, and Youth Violence," *JAIBG (Juvenile Accountability Incentive Block Grants) Bulletin* (U.S. Department of Justice, Office of Juvenile Justice and Delinquency Prevention, December 1999); Bob Scales and Julie Baker, "Seattle's Effective Strategy for Prosecuting Juvenile Firearm Offenders," *Juvenile Justice Bulletin* (U.S. Department of Justice, Office of Juvenile Justice and Delinquency Prevention, March 2000).

88. For example, see Anthony A. Braga and others, "Problem-Oriented Policing, Deterrence, and Youth Violence: An Evaluation of Boston's Operation Ceasefire," *Journal of Research in Crime and Delinquency*, vol. 38, no. 3 (August 2001); John S. Goldkamp, Cheryl Irons-Guynn, and Doris Weiland, *Community Prosecution Strategies: Measuring Impact*, research report, BJA grant 99-DD-BX-K008 (U.S. Department of Justice, Office of Justice Programs). On waiver, see, for example, Vincent Schiraldi and Jason Ziedenberg, "The Florida Experiment: Transferring Power from Judges to Prosecutors," *Criminal Justice*, vol. 15, no. 1 (American Bar Association, Section of Criminal Justice, Spring 2000);

Howard N. Snyder, Melissa Sickmund, and Eileen Poe-Yamagata, *Juvenile Transfers to Criminal Court in the 1990s: Lessons Learned From four Studies,* OJJDP summary (U.S. Department of Justice, Office of Justice Programs, 2000); "Juvenile Transfers to Criminal Court in Florida: The 1994 Reforms," *OJJDP Fact Sheet* (U.S. Department of Justice, Office of Justice Programs, June 2001); "Delinquency Cases Waived to Criminal Court, 1989–1998," *OJJDP Fact Sheet* (U.S. Department of Justice, Office of Justice Programs, September 2001).

89. Personal communication to Catherine Coles, March 1999.
90. Barry C. Feld, "Violent Youth and Public Policy," p. 1097.

3

BARBARA FEDDERS
RANDY HERTZ
STEPHEN WEYMOUTH

The Defense Attorney's
Perspective on Youth Violence

ON SEEING THE TITLE OF THIS CHAPTER, readers may wonder why there is any need for reflection on the "defense attorney's perspective on youth violence."[1] Given the prevailing conception of defense attorneys as the representatives of individual clients in individual cases, it may seem that they have little to offer in a broad discussion of the management of youth violence.[2] Moreover, given the defender's public image as a single-minded crusader who seeks to "get the client off" at all costs, it may seem that a defender would approach any such discussion with an instrumentalist bent, ready to advance the not-so-hidden agenda of maximizing the liberty of his or her clients.[3]

We have actually become accustomed to the absence of the defender's voice and perspective in public debates of appropriate responses to youth violence. When the media choose to focus on the subject of youth violence—usually because of a horrific crime committed by a child[4]—politicians and prosecutors weigh in with the standard litany of calls for harsher punishments for children while defenders often seem to stand mute.[5] Politicians seek to establish themselves as "tough on crime," including juvenile crime; usually missing from the debate is a voice to plead the cause of the children.[6]

As a result, certain myths have come to dominate public discourse, with no one to gainsay them. It has become commonplace for politicians, the

media, and prosecutors to claim that the original conception of the juvenile court as a mechanism for rehabilitation[7] is no longer viable because the
"wayward child" of the past has been succeeded by the "superpredator."[8]
Movies, television shows, and the media provide the subtext for those
claims by projecting images of adolescents, particularly those who are
African American or Hispanic, as violent, explosive, and remorseless.[9]

What effects have such claims and negative images had on the juvenile
justice system? While cause-and-effect relationships are difficult to trace
when dealing with cognitive phenomena,[10] consider the following para-
doxes: Although the rate of violent crime by juveniles has been falling since
the mid-1990s,[11] the rate of pretrial detention has generally remained constant (and, in some jurisdictions, has actually increased);[12] despite evidence
that community-based programs are better at combating recidivism than
incarceration and are vastly less expensive,[13] legislators and administrators
cut funding for those programs while sinking more money into construction of adult and juvenile prisons;[14] even when community-based alternatives *are* available, judges routinely incarcerate young people, even for nonviolent crimes;[15] and, although the available evidence strongly suggests that
treating juveniles like adults does not reduce recidivism and may actually
increase the likelihood of rearrest upon release,[16] the type of systemic
"reform" that seems to be most attractive to politicians is to transfer ever
more children[17] to the adult criminal justice system.[18]

This chapter draws heavily on the perspectives of the authors as juvenile
defenders and advocates. As we argue in greater detail, the actions of legislators, prosecutors, and judges reveal a view of young people (or, more precisely, the young people who appear in juvenile court in delinquency cases)
as incorrigible and usually dangerous. We take a closer look at the manifestations of that mindset and offer our theories about its sources, exploring the myths that animate—and are used to justify—the treatment
accorded alleged delinquents. We also examine the role that the juvenile
defense bar can play in combating such myths, for example, by representing their clients more effectively in individual cases and creating a sys-
temwide mindset that is more responsive to children's needs.

Deconstructing (and Debunking) Myths about Juveniles and the Juvenile Court

Myths and idealized images have always played a fundamental role in the
juvenile court. Founded at the turn of the twentieth century at a time when

the prevailing strain of social philosophy treated poverty as a manifestation of innate bad character,[19] the juvenile court rested on a view of children—even poor children—as innocent, guileless, and ultimately redeemable.[20] The founders of the juvenile court portrayed child criminals—who, at the time, were generally prosecuted in adult court and confined in penitentiaries alongside adults[21]—as victims who had to be saved from vice and degeneracy.[22]

Largely as a result of reformers' efforts, the Illinois legislature passed the Juvenile Court Act in 1899.[23] Other jurisdictions quickly followed its example. By 1917, juvenile courts were established in forty-seven states; today, juvenile courts exist in every state, the District of Columbia, and Puerto Rico.[24] Enacting legislation typically stressed that juvenile delinquency adjudications were not criminal proceedings. Rather, the juvenile court was to assist troubled children in righting their errant ways.[25] The Massachusetts statute, for example, provided for the juvenile court apparatus to function as a sort of caring family:

> [T]he care, custody, and discipline of children brought before the court shall approximate as nearly as possible that which they should receive from their parents, and . . . as far as practicable, the [children] shall be treated, not as criminals, but as children in need of aid, encouragement and guidance. Proceedings against children under such sections shall not be deemed criminal proceedings.[26]

From the beginning, however, that philosophy was more rhetoric than reality. Notwithstanding the emphasis on "saving" children, Judge Richard S. Tuthill of the Chicago juvenile court sent thirty-seven juveniles to adult court in the first year of the new juvenile court's existence.[27] The sentences imposed in juvenile court sometimes resulted in a longer period of incarceration than a child would have received if he had been prosecuted for the same offense in adult court.[28] It is noteworthy that those sentences were imposed after trials and sentencings held in the absence of counsel[29] and without the constitutional protections to which all adult criminal defendants were entitled.[30] Summing up the realities of juvenile court practice, an influential report stated in 1978: "The theory behind the juvenile court is not merely obsolete; it is a fairy tale that never came true."[31]

In its landmark decision in *In re Gault* in 1967,[32] the Supreme Court had to deal with the tensions and even contradictory impulses within the juvenile court. The case of Gerald Gault provided a stark illustration of the juvenile court's excesses and abuses. Gault, a fifteen-year-old, was adjudicated a delinquent and sentenced to six years in a state institution for making an obscene telephone call, an offense for which the adult penal code imposed a maximum sentence of a small fine or imprisonment for not more than two months. The delinquency finding was made on the basis of a probation officer's account of what the recipient of the telephone call told him, possibly supplemented by admissions extracted from the accused by the judge,[33] with no prefatory advice about the privilege against self-incrimination and with no provision of counsel.[34] Declaring that "the condition of being a boy does not justify a kangaroo court,"[35] the Supreme Court, in an opinion by Justice Abe Fortas, ruled that due process requires that juvenile court proceedings provide the accused with at least those criminal court procedures that are essential for "fundamental fairness." Among those, the Court ruled, are the rights to fair notice of the charges, confrontation and cross-examination of one's accuser, the privilege against self-incrimination, and, perhaps most important, "'the guiding hand of counsel at every step in the proceedings against him.'"[36]

Once again, however, lofty pronouncements provided less than they promised. Within four years, the Supreme Court curtailed the advancement of juvenile rights by holding in *McKeiver* v. *Pennsylvania* that whatever else "fundamental fairness" may mean, it does not confer on juveniles the adult criminal defendant's fundamental right to a jury trial.[37] The plurality opinion announcing that ruling, written by Justice Harry Blackmun, harked back to the traditional notion of the juvenile court judge as benevolent caretaker.[38] Although the plurality asserted its confidence that judges can be as fair as juries,[39] experience suggests the contrary.[40]

Even the rights that seemed most certain in the wake of *Gault* have proven to be largely illusory. Notwithstanding *Gault's* unequivocal declaration of the right to counsel, young people often go before the court unrepresented. Three years after *Gault*, a study in one jurisdiction found that attorneys were present in only 24 percent of juvenile cases.[41] Improvements have been slow. In a study funded by the U.S. Department of Justice, 34 percent of surveyed defense lawyers reported observing young people "waive" their right to counsel at the detention hearing.[42] While a waiver is supposed to be preceded by an advisory colloquy in the presence of a judge, the colloquy reportedly occurs infrequently and is a meaningless technicality when it does.[43] Even when a juvenile is represented by counsel, a host of personal and institutional pressures impede the zealous representation that an otherwise conscientious attorney would give his or her clients. Research shows that juvenile defenders "make few evidentiary objections, few motions to suppress evidence on constitutional grounds, call few witnesses, engage only in perfunctory cross-examination, and make only minimal, if any, closing arguments."[44]

In the 1980s and 1990s, the rhetoric of juvenile justice moved into a new phase of mythmaking. Until that point the rhetoric had been relatively consistent in depicting children as able to be redeemed and worthy of society's best efforts to rehabilitate them. Justice Blackmun's opinion in *McKeiver* in 1971 is typical: he spoke of the children currently appearing in juvenile court as needing the kind of "concern, . . . sympathy, and . . . paternal attention" that a "devoted, sympathetic, and conscientious" juvenile court judge is able to provide.[45] In the past two decades, however, prosecutors and politicians increasingly have drawn a generational divide between the innocent youth of some mythical yesteryear and the violent young criminals of today. For example, in 1996 the head of the agency that prosecutes juveniles in New York City declared:

> The philosophy behind the . . . juvenile justice system might have made sense in the days when juvenile offenders stole apples and picked pockets, often driven by poverty. Such acts really might have been isolated errors of youth, so the law gave these kids another chance, saving them from the lifelong stigma of their isolated mistakes and treating them not as criminals but as children in need of the paternal care of the state. But are the teen criminals in court today, almost nine out of ten of whom are violent felons, really juvenile delinquents rather than criminals?[46]

Politicians and policy advocates have similarly urged harsher treatment for today's youthful offenders, largely on the premise that they represent a more malevolent breed of offender than their predecessors.[47] Even some of the media have rushed to embrace this form of nostalgia. In an editorial entitled "No Kid Gloves for Teen Criminals," the *New York Post* stated:

> Treating young offenders differently from adults—offering them light punishment and numerous opportunities for rehabilitation— made sense in an earlier era when juvenile delinquency meant little more than stealing hubcaps or joy-riding in stolen cars.
>
> Today's juvenile delinquents aren't petty thieves or pranksters— they're hardened criminals, many if not most beyond hope of meaningful "rehabilitation."[48]

Proponents of the dichotomy theory focus on different sectors of the population of juvenile delinquents in the two eras. The population of children prosecuted for crimes, like the population of adult defendants, has always consisted of both violent offenders and those who commit minor offenses. Although proponents of the theory act as if there were only minor offenders in the supposedly innocent past, the historical evidence readily reveals that there have always been adolescents who engaged in acts of grotesque, explosive violence.[49] When one looks through the case reporters of the first half of the twentieth century, one finds numerous examples of violent crimes committed by children.[50] Interestingly, one finds in those opinions the same kinds of expressions of alarm that one hears nowadays about the degree of violence and apparent remorselessness of the children brought before the juvenile court.[51] A perusal of the popular press from roughly the same period uncovers now-familiar expressions of horror at unprecedented levels of juvenile crime and dire predictions about the future. In a 1943 article on juvenile delinquency, for example, a journalist warned that "some experts believe that if present conditions continue, the coming generation of Americans will contain more bad citizens and bad parents than any in history."[52]

Just as proponents of the dichotomy theory ignore the violent youth of yesteryear, so too they misleadingly characterize the current generation by looking solely at the most violent juvenile offenders and ignoring the vast number of children who are brought into juvenile court for minor offenses. In representing children in juvenile court, the three authors have seen many cases of children prosecuted for taking a bag of potato chips or a cupcake from another child in the school lunchroom (sometimes prosecuted as robbery in the second or third degree) or for taking part in a schoolyard fight with another child (sometimes prosecuted as assault in the third degree or attempted assault in the second degree).[53] When one looks through the case reporters of today, one finds numerous instances in which children were prosecuted for minor crimes and, indeed, quite often convicted on evidence that was so clearly inadequate that an appellate court reversed the conviction for insufficient evidence.[54]

Politicians and prosecutors who make assertions about the enhanced violent tendencies of today's youth also tend to ignore statistical data that would refute their allegations. Although the numbers of juveniles arrested for violent crimes spiked between 1988 and 1994, the total number of juvenile arrests for violent crime index offenses—murder, forcible rape, robbery, and aggravated assault—thereafter declined in what has turned out to be a steady pattern of decreases in violent crime by youth.[55] National statistics consistently indicate that only a small minority of juvenile arrests are for violent crimes[56] and that juveniles account for only a small proportion of the violent crimes committed each year.[57]

What, then, accounts for the widespread perception that today's juveniles are more violent than their counterparts of earlier years? This view may stem in part from the role that firearms play in modern crimes. With the greater availability of firearms and technological advances that make them more lethal, the rate of death and destruction that a single youth can cause has increased exponentially. In recent years, we have seen tragic evidence of that in places such as Moses Lake, Washington; Bethel, Alaska; Pearl, Mississippi; West Paducah, Kentucky; Jonesboro, Arkansas; Springfield, Oregon; and Littleton, Colorado.[58] That tells us less, however, about the comparative character of successive generations of youth than it does about the types of weapons that they wield.

We believe that the myths can be traced, at least in part, to images that the movies and television have propagated. It is hardly a coincidence that wistful evocations of the hooligans of the past typically refer to indigent young boys stealing food or picking pockets.[59] Images such as those are engraved in our consciousness as a result of movies like *Angels with Dirty Faces*, in which three young boys—all of them indigent, growing up in the slums—are shown stealing a tomato from a vendor's cart and immediately thereafter picking the pocket of a well-dressed, apparently wealthy man.[60] Scenes like that can produce in people's minds "schemas" or "stock scripts"—cognitive structures that shape their perceptions and influence their opinions and actions.[61] Through such structures, we interpret and assign meaning to our everyday experiences.

By the same token, modern cinematic depictions of delinquents also shape our assumptions about and expectations of today's youth. What are those depictions? We have the murderous, remorseless "stone-cold killers" of *Colors, Juice, Menace II Society*, and a host of similar films.[62] What distinguishes the adolescents in such films from their cinematic forebears is not merely the types of crimes they are shown committing. There is also a racial divide at work. The youngsters in *Angels with Dirty Faces, Dead End, Boys' Town*, and other movies of the 1930s and 1940s were white. Although they could be classified as members of an "outgroup"[63] because of their low socioeconomic status and immigrant origin, they were of the same race as the mainstream population. In contrast, the murderous teens of today's films are usually African American or Hispanic.[64]

The stock scripts that we inherit from popular culture have a particularly powerful effect on our expectations and perceptions when it comes to members of another race.[65] Thus, it would hardly be surprising if prosecutors and politicians are conditioned by popular culture to expect violence and remorselessness from children who, by virtue of their race and often their attire, resemble the murderous teens of the movies and television.[66] What happens is, in essence, a feedback loop of reciprocal mythmaking. As prosecutors, politicians, and the media echo what they have learned from Hollywood, proclaiming the youth who appear in juvenile court (who are disproportionately African American and Hispanic[67]) to be more dangerous than the delinquents of previous eras, Hollywood finds validation of the images it has been propagating.[68]

What, then, should one make of the claim that delinquents of the modern generation are innately "more violent" and "more dangerous" than their forebears? We believe that it is simply the latest —although probably the most pernicious—of the myths surrounding the juvenile court. But, whether or not it is a myth (and perhaps especially if it is a myth, considering the power of myth), that claim has influenced perceptions of today's juvenile offenders and, through its effect on prosecutors as well as judges, what goes on inside the juvenile court. It is against the backdrop of such myths that defense attorneys operate. They must wend their way not only among the various myths defining the juvenile court's mission and functions but also among the myths that shape how prosecutors, judges, and probation officers view their clients.

A Paradigm for Effective Advocacy

Some juvenile defenders do so little of what must be done to represent a client effectively that the client is almost no better off than the juveniles who appeared without lawyers in the pre-*Gault* era. To bring the quality of representation in such cases up to a level of at least minimal effectiveness, certain reforms are crucial. First, state and federal government funding of organizations providing indigent defense services must be increased. A Bureau of Justice Statistics report revealed that the defense bar receives less than one-third of the federal, state, and local funds expended by the prosecution.[69] Second, norms of representation need to be established and enforced.[70] There is certainly much that could—and should—be said on those topics. However, we focus on the other side of the equation: the juvenile defender offices that not only are providing high-quality representation but also are beginning to redefine the model of juvenile representation.

Since the Supreme Court handed down the *Gault* decision and mandated counsel for the accused in delinquency proceedings, juvenile defenders have essentially taken it for granted that the model of juvenile representation should follow the basic contours of the adult criminal defense model. In the immediate wake of *Gault*, there was some debate about whether juvenile defenders should feel freer than lawyers for adults to substitute their judgment regarding the basic goals of representation for that of their clients or to sacrifice viable defenses and plead their clients guilty in order to obtain services that they need.[71] Such issues, however, have long since been settled by ethical rules and well-accepted norms of practice. There is general agreement that the zealousness and comprehensiveness of the representation that defenders provide to juvenile clients must parallel that provided to their adult counterparts.[72]

In recent years, a few juvenile defense programs across the country have begun to develop and implement a new paradigm of juvenile defense services.[73] That paradigm accepts as a given that the work that a juvenile defender does in preparing for and handling the trial—pretrial investigation, discovery, motions, development of a defense theory, cross-examination of prosecution witnesses, and presentation of defense witnesses—should be every bit as wide-ranging and exacting as the best defense representation in adult criminal cases.[74] It also accepts the basic norms of the adult criminal defense model for representation at sentencing: that the client decides what sentence to seek; that the lawyer should do all that he or she can to obtain the sentence that the client wants; and that effective representation at sentencing often requires the lawyer to enlist the aid of other professionals, such as social workers or psychologists, who can assess the psychological status and needs of the client and prepare reports for the lawyer to use in advocating for a particular sentence.[75]

The way in which the new juvenile defense model differs from the adult model is that the juvenile defenders involved strive to do more than merely obtain the best result possible in court. They view the legal representation of a child in trouble as a unique opportunity for positive intervention in the child's life. A child brought before the juvenile court because of his or her delinquent acts more often than not has a variety of educational and emotional needs that have been either undetected or ignored by the child's family and school. If the child is represented by a caring defense attorney with adequate resources, the court may begin to address those needs. The time that a child's case is pending in court can, ideally, be a time that he or she receives needed support and services.

That type of intervention is best accomplished through a multidisciplinary approach.[76] In 1992, the Committee for Public Counsel Services (the agency responsible for providing legal representation to Massachusetts's indigent criminal defendants) established the Youth Advocacy Project (YAP) to assign experienced trial attorneys to defend juveniles facing adult sentences.[77] YAP has since expanded its focus to include delinquency cases and has tripled in size. Embodying the multidisciplinary approach, five full-time attorneys—in collaboration with an on-staff psychologist, social workers, and a community outreach worker—currently represent young people in delinquency and youthful offender proceedings as well as school suspension and expulsion proceedings. The social workers and community outreach workers make appropriate referrals to counseling centers, alternative schools, and after-school and job-training programs. They also provide support to the client during a judicial process that, for children and adults alike, usually is difficult, overwhelming, and confusing.

In cases in which a client appears to have a learning disability or behavioral or emotional disorder, the lawyer refers the client to a forensic psychologist who evaluates the client's psychological functioning and its relationship to the client's current legal problem. That information is crucial in preparing the case for court, particularly if the attorney questions the client's mental competence or believes that he or she may lack the mental ability to be held criminally responsible for his or her acts. Information about a client's psychological needs can help the attorney advocate for a particular legal disposition. If a child has an emotional problem or learning disorder, for example, the lawyer can devise a plan for the court that includes therapy and special education services as an alternative to pretrial detention, or, in cases in which the child was detained by the court at initial appearance, the lawyer can move to reduce the level of detention. In the event of conviction, the lawyer can present a dispositional plan of this sort as an alternative to incarceration.

With a detailed assessment of a young person's psychological and social history, an attorney can help the judge focus not only on the young person's offense but on the whole person. Moreover, in pinpointing the problems that led to the misdeed, the lawyer often can enlist the judge in the effort to save the child from a cycle of incarceration and recidivism.

The defense team's attention focuses on more than just the court case, however. While the psychologist evaluates the client, the social workers meet with the client and his or her family; examine school, counseling, and health records; and contact teachers and guidance counselors to offer ideas about appropriate educational placement and services. Together, the members of the defense team try to steer a child into programs that will continue after the child's involvement with the juvenile court has ended. Moreover, the community outreach workers and social workers keep an eye on the potentially debilitating long-term effects on the juveniles of involvement in juvenile court proceedings. For many juveniles, appearing in juvenile court as an alleged delinquent is a humiliating experience. If they feel that at least the defense attorney and other members of the defense team respect them and are willing to listen to their side of the story, some of that shame can be abated.

The existence of YAP has helped to transform the representation of young people throughout the Boston court system. The office's social workers, psychologist, and community workers make themselves available to assist court-appointed attorneys on issues that frequently accompany juvenile court involvement. Moreover, through financial support from several private sources, including the Shaw, Boston, and Public Welfare Foundations, YAP staff also regularly conduct educational sessions on legal rights and responsibilities to young people in schools, after-school centers, and detention facilities.

A program that has shown itself to be particularly adept at developing and presenting a complete picture of a client—and using that picture both in the client's court case and in furnishing the client with long-term help—is Project TeamChild, a Seattle-based collaboration of public defenders from the Washington Defender Association and civil legal services attorneys from Columbia Legal Services. Founded in 1995 through a grant from the Office of Juvenile Justice and Delinquency Prevention (OJJDP), the project's mandate is to address the underlying causes of a juvenile's criminal behavior. The civil attorneys assist juvenile clients with a range of problems, including finding a home, obtaining welfare benefits for the child and his or her family, and gaining access to mental health and other services. A specific focus of the project is to help adolescent clients return to school after they have dropped out or have been suspended or expelled because of delinquent behavior.[78]

What YAP and Project TeamChild have realized is that effective legal representation requires using a child's involvement in the juvenile justice system to address the deeper problems that brought the child into the system. In essence, these programs attempt to realize the underlying myth of the juvenile court—that delinquents are not criminals in need of punishment but children capable of growth and change.[79]

Effective representation also requires confronting the modern myth of the innate violence of today's delinquent youth.[80] In order to provide children with the help they need, defense teams must first develop a sophisticated understanding of the roots of delinquent behavior. Only by developing and conveying to the court a perspective that encompasses the larger structural forces that underlie their clients' decisions to commit delinquent acts can lawyers persuade judges (especially those who subscribe to the modern myths) to deal with delinquents as children rather than as hardened criminals—to seek to help rather than punish.

What factors lead to a child's involvement in the juvenile justice system? They vary, of course, and often have much to do with the psychological profile and specific life circumstances of the individual child.[81] However, studies have shown and we have found in our own experiences that certain general factors predominate and affect a substantial proportion of the children who come through the doors of the juvenile court.

First and foremost among them is poverty. James Gilligan, one of the leading authorities on the etiology of violence, argues that the disparity between the income and status of those at the top and those at the bottom of the social hierarchy accounts for the shame and self-doubt that characterizes America's poorest people. Gilligan describes violence as a means for poor people, including poor children, to cast off that shame and reclaim their dignity.[82] Violent behavior is a mechanism that allows them to inflict, rather than only suffer, pain and humiliation.[83]

Racial issues exacerbate the problems in a myriad of ways. Discriminatory treatment of young African American males by store owners and employees,[84] school teachers,[85] and law enforcement officials[86] often lead to feelings of hopelessness[87] that are compounded by the readily visible demographics of the population involved in the criminal and juvenile justice systems. In 1990, almost one in four African American males in their twenties were under some form of criminal justice supervision; by 1995, the figure had increased to one in three.[88] A study in Philadelphia revealed that African American defendants charged with capital murder are nearly four times more likely than other defendants to be sentenced to death, even when the circumstances of the killing are the same.[89] Similarly skewed racial patterns are evident in the juvenile justice system. In 1999, although African Americans made up only 15 percent of the population of U.S. residents below the age of 18, they accounted for 27 percent of arrests overall and 41 percent of arrests for violent crimes.[90] Youth of color are overrepresented throughout all stages of the juvenile justice process.[91]

Saddled with societal expectations that they will be delinquent and violent, youth of color have in many cases acted according to what they believe to be a predetermined script.[92] When they are violent, the violence is usually directed at other youth of color. The 1996 National Crime Victimization Survey found that African Americans were more likely than whites to be victims of violent crime and that Hispanics were twice as likely as non-Hispanics to fall victim to robbery and personal theft.[93] Violence is the leading cause of death for African American males.[94] In what amounts to a cycle of violence, the constant exposure of many young men of color to violence and death and the lesson implicit in it—that they will not survive their childhood—further feeds their rage and despair.

The easy access that young people have to firearms makes the already potent mix of poverty and racism-fed anger and despair potentially lethal.[95] Between 1984 and 1991, the rate of homicide among teenagers more than doubled, and firearms were involved in the deaths of more than 80 percent of teenage victims. In the 1980s, the homicide death rate by firearms of young people ages fifteen to nineteen increased by 61 percent, while the nonfirearms homicide rate decreased by 29 percent. From 1983 to 1995, the proportion of homicides in which a juvenile used a gun increased from 55 percent to 80 percent.[96] In 1999, 53 percent of the 1,800 juveniles murdered were killed with a firearm.[97] Moreover, firearms availability has been found to increase the risk of homicide in urban areas among all age groups and to be associated with higher suicide risk among urban fifteen- to twenty-four-year-olds.[98]

Between 1979 and 1991, almost 50,000 American children were killed by guns—more than the number of American soldiers who died in Vietnam.[99] Many urban areas have been transformed into war zones, and the combatants are children—disproportionately indigent African American children.[100] Geoffrey Canada, who works with youth in New York's poorest areas, describes the effect that gun availability has on inner-city children:

> As the number of guns available to young people has increased so have the odds that they will be shot in a confrontation. Many young people have figured out that the best way not to be shot is to shoot first . . . . [I've heard] young teenagers saying they'd "rather be judged by twelve than carried by six." The message on the street is clear: make a preemptive strike, shoot first even if you're not sure that your life is threatened at that moment. Odds are you'll live, and if you're arrested and then convicted at least you'll still be alive.[101]

Victimization of children also contributes to young people's violent acts toward others. Gilligan describes physical violence as the "ultimate means of communicating the absence of love."[102] Children who do not receive sufficient love from others cannot build the capacity for self-love that enables functional people to survive the rejection and pain that are part of life. They sink deeper into feelings of intense shame and humiliation until they experience a "death of the self." When such children commit acts of violence, their actions function to diminish the intensity of their shame and to ward off feelings of vulnerability.

By identifying and attending to the mental and emotional wounds of violent young people, programs like YAP and TeamChild attempt to obtain a favorable outcome in individual cases while simultaneously laying the psychological groundwork for children's future development. The work that one of the authors did with a fifteen-year-old girl (whom we call by the fictitious name Natalie) illustrates how lawyers can use general information of the foregoing sort to assess a child's needs, communicate with her, and determine how to represent her effectively.

Natalie first came to the attention of YAP when she was brought to court on the charge that she had violated the terms of her probation. She had allegedly missed numerous appointments with her probation officer, skipped several days of school, and disobeyed her mother at home. Such violations, which are fairly common among young people on probation, seemed straightforward. A phone call to Natalie's school counselor revealed, however, that Natalie's problems were deeply rooted in her family relationships.

Natalie was on probation for allegedly striking her mother. In the conversation with the school counselor (which took place after YAP provided her with a release of information form that Natalie had signed), the counselor reported that Natalie's mother was only intermittently interested in raising her. Allegations of abuse and neglect had emerged years ago, when the mother's substance abuse was first discovered. The Massachusetts Department of Social Services (DSS) had taken temporary custody of Natalie, and Natalie had shuttled between foster homes and her mother's home for several years.

Further investigation into Natalie's background—through agency records, school visits, and phone calls to DSS—revealed that she had been hospitalized for a suicide attempt, following which she was prescribed a variety of psychotropic medications. Unfortunately, her chaotic living situation (which included frequent changes of address) interfered with her remembering to take her medication (and sometimes also her access to the medication), and no adult was ever interested enough to ensure that she took it. As she moved on and off her medication, Natalie experienced wild swings in mood and behavior.

When Natalie was subsequently arrested with a friend who had pick-pocketed another girl, Natalie picked up additional criminal charges for assaulting the arresting officer. As Natalie herself described it, she "went off on" the detective, who was conducting a routine pat frisk. Natalie, who had been sexually abused as a young girl, could not tolerate being touched, and she had never received counseling to help her deal with the effects of the abuse.

Without knowledge of Natalie's background, her lawyer would not have fully understood why it was so difficult for Natalie to trust her. After being mistreated or misled by every adult in her life, Natalie took it for granted that her lawyer would distort information, miss appointments, and be late. Natalie responded accordingly—and preemptively—by missing appointments and providing misleading information. Only by understanding Natalie's background could the lawyer comprehend the need for patience and quiet persistence in attempting to reach her. Only by reaching Natalie could the lawyer be an effective advocate.

That information, and the connection that the lawyer was able to foster with Natalie on the basis of the information, was quite important at Natalie's probation surrender. YAP elaborated for the juvenile court judge the myriad ways in which DSS had failed Natalie: in never finding her a permanent placement, in failing to ensure that she took her medication, in never obtaining appropriate counseling for her. YAP was able to describe the salient aspects of her mother's substance abuse history. YAP was able to persuade the judge to move beyond the simple issue of "whether Natalie had violated her probation" and to think about the role that various public agencies had played in bringing Natalie to that point and what those agencies could and should do to rectify their past mistakes.

Natalie eventually was committed to the Massachusetts Department of Youth Services (DYS). Fifteen months later, she was still an active client. Many of her numerous needs were still unmet, and she was still emotionally volatile. When she was referred for placement in a secure facility, she contacted YAP for assistance. YAP was able to use the voluminous amount of information previously accumulated about Natalie to arrange for her representation by the Boston College Juvenile Rights Advocacy Project, a law school clinic that specializes in dispositional advocacy for girls committed to DYS. Together, YAP and the law school clinic are continuing to assist Natalie.[103]

Preliminary research indicates that the multidisciplinary approach that YAP and similar programs use is effective. An assessment of Project Team-Child, for example, found that young people who received its services were positively affected in a variety of ways.[104] In one evaluation sample, 81.8 percent of clients for whom information was available were not in school at the time their case was opened because they had been expelled or suspended or had dropped out. After TeamChild representation, 77.8 percent of those not in school when their case was opened had been reinstated in school; 24.2 percent were given special education evaluations; and 33.3 percent improved their attendance. The same assessment found that many other positive outcomes were obtained. For example, 45.5 percent of this group of clients entered counseling and 18.2 percent received psychological evaluations.

YAP, TeamChild, and other programs of this sort are still relatively new and there is much that they still need to learn, both about the most effective means of diagnosing and rectifying children's problems and about the best ways to sensitize judges to the deeper issues and persuade them to give children the help they need. As the programs struggle to acquire greater expertise in both dimensions, they may find it useful to examine some of the work that is being done in the area of capital sentencing. In capital sentencing, as in juvenile sentencing, the sentencing inquiry focuses on the personal characteristics and psychological profile of the convicted person in ways that are not typical in noncapital adult sentencing.[105] Capital defenders have, by necessity, developed sophisticated techniques to investigate and present to the sentencer the psychological, social, and personal problems that led their clients to commit capital crimes.[106] In cases in which the defendant stands accused of committing a capital crime while a minor, they search for factors that cause children to engage in acts of extreme criminal violence.[107] Moreover, a social science research project, the Capital Jury Project, has been amassing extensive data about the kinds of factors, arguments, and presentations that are most likely to persuade a jury to impose a sentence of life imprisonment instead of the death penalty.[108] Although that research probably is not directly relevant to sentencing by judges in delinquency cases, there may be much that the studies can teach juvenile defenders about the best ways to help a judge empathize with the accused.[109]

The juvenile defense programs may also find it useful to reach out to law school clinics, particularly those that specialize in the representation of alleged delinquents. Among the reasons that law school clinics were created in the 1960s and 1970s was to establish "laboratories" for developing a better understanding of the court system and lawyering.[110] Some juvenile justice clinics already have helped to chart important new directions in juvenile defense work. For example, the Children and Family Justice Center of Northwestern University School of Law has done pioneering work in devising effective modes of collaboration between juvenile defense lawyers and professionals in other fields.[111] The juvenile clinic of the University of the District of Columbia's David A. Clarke School of Law has explored ways for juvenile defense lawyers to better serve their clients within the educational system.[112] Innovative work of other sorts can be found at other law schools as well.[113] Indeed, the clinics may offer the best hope of developing the techniques necessary to navigate among the myths that shape the juvenile court. In recent years, clinical law teachers have begun to make use of the teachings of cognitive psychology to develop a better understanding of the ways in which juries and judges decide cases and the techniques of advocacy that are most likely to prove effective.[114] Research of this sort may shed light on the best means to deconstruct and remedy whatever negative preconceptions about juveniles a judge may bring to a delinquency case.[115]

Conclusion

It has often been said that the Supreme Court's decision in *Gault* "revolutionized" the juvenile court process.[116] We have suggested here that, at least with respect to *Gault*'s mandate of counsel, the revolution was more promise than reality. For much of the more than three decades since *Gault*, defense representation in many parts of the country has been inadequate. Moreover, even in jurisdictions in which children could count on zealous advocacy, representation has been unduly constrained by the fact that juvenile defenders have not attempted to broaden the adult court model of criminal defense.

The juvenile defense programs that have been emerging in recent years offer the hope of truly revolutionizing juvenile defense work. If they continue in the creative spirit in which they have begun, and especially if they take advantage of the innovative work that has been done in other fields, they will make great strides toward accomplishing their goal of providing clients with the best representation possible, consistent with the juvenile court's original goal of rehabilitation. However, even more will be required of the juvenile defense bar than enhancement of representation in particular cases. Defenders must confront the absence of their voices and perspectives in juvenile justice policymaking at the federal, state, and local levels of government. Truly effective defense work in the modern era may require advocacy on the institutional as well as the individual level.

Through grassroots organizing, media campaigns, and legislative lobbying, juvenile defenders can promote a new, more humane, and more "just" vision of juvenile justice. Defenders should reject the narrow role of individual advocate and attempt to stake out a more prominent and effective role in policymaking.[117] For example, defense attorneys can offer technical assistance and guidance to community-based organizations that both provide positive alternatives to young people struggling to resist delinquent activities and organize communities to challenge the drift of the juvenile justice system away from rehabilitation and toward punishment. New York City's Youth Force, Boston's Dorchester Youth Collaborative, and San Francisco's Center for Young Women's Development are just a few examples of such groups. In addition, defenders can bring an invaluable perspective forged through day-to-day courtroom experiences and encounters with young clients to national organizations that seek to advance the cause of justice for youth.

Where can defenders find the tools they need to reshape the public's and policymakers' views of juveniles? The answer may lie in the work of organizations like YAP and TeamChild, whose successes in individual cases offer data that would be highly useful in supporting a return to the rehabilitative ideal of the juvenile court. The strategies that YAP and TeamChild use to persuade individual judges that they should take a chance on an individual child may help in crafting institutional arguments for saving current and future generations of adolescent offenders. The twentieth century, which began with the founding of the juvenile court, ended with the development of a means of providing effective representation for the individual juvenile. The twenty-first century will demand that juvenile defenders couple effective representation at the individual level with meaningful advocacy at the institutional level.

Notes

1. The "defense attorney" in a juvenile delinquency case may be a staff attorney of an institutional office that represents indigent youth (for example, a public defender's office or a nonprofit children's law center); a private attorney who is court appointed and paid by the case to represent indigent clients; private counsel retained by a parent or guardian; or a representative of a law school clinical program. Because there are no comprehensive national directories that list public and private attorneys who represent juveniles, descriptive data on attorneys who represent young people are elusive. However, the information compiled by the American Bar Association (ABA) Juvenile Justice Center in preparing a report on counsel in juvenile court is revealing. By contacting each state's administrative office of the court and the 150 members of the ABA's Juvenile Justice Committee and by consulting the directories of the National Legal Aid and Defender Association (NLADA) and the Association of American Law Schools (AALS), the center identified approximately 260 public defender's offices, 162 contract attorneys, fifty-three law schools, and thirty-three children's law centers that represent young people in delinquency proceedings. American Bar Association, *A Call for Justice: An Assessment of Access to Counsel and Quality of Representation in Delinquency Proceedings* (Washington, 1995), p. 7. This information suggests that the bulk of juvenile representation is provided by public defenders and court-appointed counsel.

2. For a discussion of this conception of the defender's role and a critique of defenders' failure to stake out a broader role, see Kim Taylor-Thompson, "Individual Actor v. Institutional Player: Alternating Visions of the Public Defender," *Georgetown Law Journal*, vol. 84 (1996), p. 2419, and Kim Taylor-Thompson, "Effective Assistance: Reconceiving the Role of the Chief Public Defender," *Journal of the Institute for Study of Legal Ethics*, vol. 2 (1999), p. 199. See also Cait Clarke, "Problem-Solving Defenders in the Community: Expanding the Conceptual and Institutional Boundaries of Providing Counsel to the Poor," *Georgetown Journal of Legal Ethics*, vol. 14 (2001), p. 401.

3. For a discussion of this image and some of its cinematic and television sources, see Anthony G. Amsterdam and Randy Hertz, "An Analysis of Closing Arguments to a Jury," *New York Law School Law Review*, vol. 37 (1992), pp. 55, 107, and n. 135.

4. See, for example, William Glaberson, "Shootings in a Schoolhouse: The Justice System; Rising Tide of Anger at Teen-Aged Killers," *New York Times*, May 24, 1998, p.14 (feature on juvenile justice, published in the wake of school shootings in Springfield, Oregon, and Jonesboro, Arkansas); Julie Grace, "There Are No Children Here," *Time*, September 12, 1994, p. 44 (profile of family members and friends of Robert "Yummy" Sandifer, killed by young people thought to be gang members after allegedly killing a fourteen-year-old girl); "Death of Eric Morse in Housing Complex Triggers National Call for End to Kids Killing Kids," *USA Today*, November 7, 1994 (report on the death of five-year-old Eric Morse at the hands of ten-year-old and eleven-year-old boys, with a focus on the reactions of federal officials). As explained in note 17 below, in this chapter, the terms "child" and "juvenile" are used interchangeably.

5. See, for example, ABC World News Tonight, "American Agenda: Juvenile Justice System," February 21, 1995 (featuring interviews with prosecutor, juvenile offender, police officer, juvenile court judge, and criminal court youth part judge); Fox Butterfield, "With Juvenile Courts in Chaos, Some Propose Scrapping Them," *New York Times*, July 21, 1997,

p. A1 (feature on juvenile justice quoting judges, chief juvenile prosecutor of New York City, probation officer, representatives of organizations that study juvenile justice issues, and academics); Glaberson, "Shootings in a Schoolhouse; Rising Tide of Anger at Teen-Aged Killers" (quoting prosecutor, judge, law professor, and juvenile justice researchers); Patrick Markey, "Hynes Calls for Tougher Sentencing: Concern over Young Offenders," *Newsday*, May 31, 1997 (reporting killing of woman by fourteen-year-old and quoting district attorney and chief of Corporation Counsel's division that prosecutes juveniles in New York City's Family Court).

6. Peter Elikann, *Superpredators: The Demonization of Our Children by the Law* (Reading, Mass.: Perseus Books, 1999), pp. 41–42, 66.

7. For discussion of the origins of the juvenile court and its underlying philosophy, see notes 19–31 and accompanying text.

8. Compare, for example, "New Approach Set to Aid 'Waywards,'" *New York Times*, April 24, 1949 (quoting New York City youth board chair Nathaniel Kaplan's statements that "the problem of *our wayward youth* cannot be solved by sensationalizing their misdeeds" and that "[w]e must go behind the causes of their delinquencies and treat the maladjustments that we find to prevent them from growing worse" [emphasis added]) with Joyce Purnick, "Youth Crime: Should Laws Be Tougher?" *New York Times*, May 9, 1996, p. B1 (quoting prosecutor's references to delinquents of today as "*superpredators*" and reporting on recommendations for "getting tougher with young criminals" [emphasis added]). The term "superpredator" is thought to have originated with political scientist John J. DiIulio Jr. See John J. DiIulio Jr., "The Coming of the Super-Predators," *Weekly Standard*, Nov. 27, 1995, p. 23. DiIulio has reconsidered the "superpredator" notion and is now a vigorous proponent of prevention programs to deal with youth violence. See Lynette Clemetson, "Questions and Answers: John DiIulio," *Newsweek Web Exclusive* (www.msnbc. com/news.htm [February 5, 2001]). For examples of claims by prosecutors, politicians, and the media that the juvenile court is an outmoded institution that is incapable of dealing with the current generation of violent youth, see notes 46–48 and accompanying text.

9. For discussion of these images, see notes 62–64 and accompanying text.

10. For discussion of the ways in which public discourse and popular culture can influence people's perceptions and actions, see notes 65–68 and accompanying text.

11. Howard Snyder, "Juvenile Arrests 1999," *Juvenile Justice Bulletin* (U.S. Department of Justice, Office of Juvenile Justice and Delinquency Prevention, December 2000), p. 1; American Bar Association Steering Committee on the Unmet Legal Needs of Children, *America's Children Still at Risk* (Chicago, 2001), p. 253. See also Mark Anderson and others, "School-Associated Violent Deaths in the United States, 1994–1999," *Journal of the American Medical Association*, vol. 286 (December 5, 2001), pp. 2696, 2699 (study by Centers for Disease Control and Pollution in collaboration with the U.S. Department of Justice and the Department of Education showing that "[t]he rate of school-associated violent death events has decreased significantly since the 1992–93 school year"). The decrease in juvenile crime is part of an overall downturn in violent crime. From 1990 to 1999, the overall violent crime rate fell 28 percent. See Federal Bureau of Investigation, *Crime in the United States: 1999* (U.S. Department of Justice, 2000), p. 11. But see Fox Butterfield, "Killings Increase in Many Big Cities," *New York Times*, December 21, 2001, p. A1 (reporting recent rise in homicide rate in large cities). See also notes 55–57 and accompanying text.

12. See Charles Puzzanchera and others, *Juvenile Court Statistics 1997* (U.S. Department of Justice, Office of Juvenile Justice and Delinquency Prevention, 2000), pp. 7–8. See, for example, Richard A. Mendel, *Less Hype, More Help: Reducing Juvenile Crime, What Works—and What Doesn't* (Washington: American Policy Forum, 2000) ("daily population of youth confined in juvenile detention centers has increased sharply—from 20,000 nationwide at the height of the juvenile crime wave in 1993 to some 24,500 youth in 1997" [p. 52]); Lisa Feldman, Michael Males, and Vincent Schiraldi, "A Tale of Two Jurisdictions: Youth Crime and Detention Rates in Maryland and the District of Columbia" (www.buildingblocksforyouth.org/dcmd/dcmd.htm [October 23, 2001]) (Maryland's youth crime rate decreased by 15 percent during the 1990s but the detention rate increased by 3 percent; although the District of Columbia showed a significant decline in the detention rate as well as crime rate during same period, reduced detention was attributable to the closing of overcrowded detention facilities and the issuing of a consent decree in a lawsuit brought by the D.C. Public Defender Service); David M. Halbfinger, "City Detaining More Juveniles before Trial: Crowding Makes Barge a Jail for Young Boys," *New York Times*, July 2, 1998 (reporting that in New York City "[t]he number of youths in detention is growing even though juvenile arrests have declined sharply" and that overcrowding in juvenile detention centers has resulted in the city's use of "a prison barge designed for adult inmates" to detain "boys as young as 10"). The same disparity is evident in the adult criminal justice system. See, for example, Fox Butterfield, "Prison Population Growing Although Crime Rate Drops," *New York Times*, August 9, 1998, p. 18; Timothy Egan, "War on Crack Retreats, Still Taking Prisoners," *New York Times*, February 28, 1999, pp. 1, 22.

13. See, for example, Michael A. Jones and Barry Krisberg, *Images and Reality: Juvenile Crime, Youth Violence, and Public Policy* (National Council on Crime and Delinquency, 1994), pp. 36–40; Richard A. Mendel, *Less Cost, More Safety: Guiding Lights for Reform in Juvenile Justice* (Washington: American Policy Forum, 2001); Steven R. Donziger, ed., *The Real War on Crime: The Report of the National Criminal Justice Commission* (Harper, 1996), pp. 136, 138–141.

14. Donziger, *The Real War on Crime*, pp. 136, 138–41; Mike A. Males, *Scapegoat Generation: America's War on Adolescents* (Monroe, Maine: Common Courage Press, 1996).

15. See Amnesty International, *Betraying the Young: Human Rights Violations against Children in the U.S. Justice System* (New York: Amnesty International USA, 1998), p. 14 ("There are several types of evidence indicating that many jurisdictions across the USA commonly detain or commit children in secure facilities when alternatives may have been appropriate"); Mendel, *Less Hype, More Help*, p. 52 ("Seventy-nine percent of all youth held in detention in 1997 were not charged with violent index crimes"). Analyses of admissions to juvenile detention facilities show that the vast majority of juvenile offenders currently housed in long-term state correctional facilities were committed for nonviolent offenses. See James C. Howell and others, eds., *Serious, Violent, and Chronic Juvenile Offenders: A Sourcebook* (Thousand Oaks, Calif.: Sage, 1995), p. 15.

16. Research shows that treating juveniles like adults has no visible impact on recidivism rates, and some studies have even found that adolescents punished as adults have higher rearrest rates than adolescents punished as juveniles. Mendel, *Less Hype, More Help*, p. 41 (describing studies showing that "juvenile offenders who are transferred to criminal court recidivate more often, more quickly, and with more serious offenses than those who are retained under juvenile jurisdiction"); ABA Steering Committee on the Unmet Legal Needs

of Children, *America's Children Still at Risk*, p. 266. See Jeffrey Fagan, "The Comparative Impact of Juvenile versus Adult Court Sanctions for Adolescent Felony Offenders," *Law and Policy*, vol. 18 (1996), p. 77; Lawrence Winner and others, "The Transfer of Juveniles to Criminal Court: Re-examining Recidivism over the Long Term," *Crime and Delinquency*, vol. 43 (1997), p. 548. In addition to subjecting children to a high risk of rape and physical assault, incarceration in adult facilities may foster recidivism by placing youth in facilities that generally lack educational and job-training services and exposing them to a violent inmate culture that encourages criminal behavior. See Jeffrey Fagan and Franklin Zimring, eds., *The Changing Borders of Juvenile Justice: Transfer of Adolescents to the Criminal Court* (University of Chicago, 2000); Martin A. Forst, Jeffrey Fagan, and T. Scott Vivona, "Youth in Prisons and State Training Schools: Perceptions and Consequences of the Treatment-Custody Dichotomy for Adolescents," *Juvenile and Family Court Journal*, vol. 39 (1989), p. 1.

17. In this chapter, we use the terms "child" and "juvenile" interchangeably to refer to the population of minors subject to prosecution in the juvenile court for delinquency offenses. In the vast majority of jurisdictions, minors up to age eighteen are subject to prosecution in the juvenile court although individual alleged offenders can be waived or transferred to adult court for prosecution as adults for statutorily specified crimes. In ten states, all minors over the age of sixteen must be prosecuted in adult court; in three states, all minors over the age of fifteen must be prosecuted in adult court. See Snyder, *Juvenile Arrests 1999*, p. 1.

18. See, for example, Glaberson, "Shootings in a Schoolhouse; Rising Tide of Anger at Teen-Aged Killers" (reporting that "[s]ince 1994, 43 states have changed their laws to make it easier to prosecute juveniles as adults" and that recently "a Texas state legislator proposed amending Texas law to permit the death penalty for murderers as young as 11"); Purnick, "Youth Crime," p. B1 (reporting that "even though the headlines blare news of a persistently dropping crime rate," Governor Pataki is seeking to "transfer all 16-year-olds in detention centers run by the State Division for Youth to the regular prison system").

19. Jane Addams, founder of the Chicago settlement house, Hull House, and one of the reformers whose efforts culminated in the creation of the first juvenile court, wrote in a critique of the early religious charities that "the charitable agent really blamed the individual for his poverty," viewing "poverty as synonymous with vice and laziness and . . . the prosperous man as the righteous man." Jane Addams, *Democracy and Social Ethics* (Macmillan, 1902), pp. 14–15. For further discussion of Addams's life, her views, and her work at Hull House, see Jane Addams, *Twenty Years at Hull-House* (Macmillan, 1910).

20. See Ellen Ryerson, *The Best-Laid Plans: America's Juvenile Court Experiment* (Hill and Wang, 1978), pp. 28–31. See also Anthony Platt, *The Child Savers: The Invention of Delinquency* (University of Chicago Press, 2d ed., 1977), pp. 28–55.

21. See Sanford J. Fox, "Juvenile Justice Reform: An Historical Perspective," *Stanford Law Review*, vol. 22 (1970), pp. 1187–89 (citing a nineteenth-century report that called attention to the "corruptive results" of the practice of incarcerating children with adults). Not all children were sent to adult penitentiaries. Some states prohibited the incarceration of young people whose offenses were less serious and whose life histories seemed to make them proper subjects for rehabilitation. Instead, such young people were sent to juvenile reform schools, the first of which was established in Massachusetts in 1846. See Jerome Miller, *Last One over the Wall: The Massachusetts Experiment in Closing Reform Schools* (Ohio State University Press, 1991), p. 16.

22. Fox, "Juvenile Justice Reform," pp. 1188–92.

23. 1899 Ill. Laws 131 (Law of April 21, 1899) ("an Act to regulate the treatment and control of dependent, neglected, and delinquent children").

24. See, generally, Samuel M. Davis, *Rights of Juveniles: The Juvenile Justice System* (New York: C. Boardman, 2d ed. 1980 and supp. 2001), § 2.6, pp. 2–14, 2–15. Although the nomenclature of these courts varies somewhat from state to state, most jurisdictions designate the court the "juvenile court" or the "juvenile division" of the local court of general jurisdiction. A well-known variant is New York City's Family Court.

25. The theoretical justification for the state's role in providing "treatment" to young offenders was the *parens patriae* doctrine. Developed in the chancery courts in England, this doctrine held that the sovereign had an obligation to oversee the welfare of children who were neglected or abused by their parents. United States reformers at the turn of the century believed that the *parens patriae* doctrine should apply not only to those children abused or neglected by their parents but to all children likely to become problematic in their communities. Fox, "Juvenile Justice Reform," p. 1193.

26. *Massachussetts General Laws*, ch. 413, section 2 (1906). As one commentator of the time observed, "The problem for determination by the judge is not, has this boy or girl committed a specific wrong, but what is he, how has he become what he is, and what had best be done in his interest and in the interest of the state to save him from a downward career. It is apparent that the ordinary legal evidence in a criminal court is not the sort of evidence to be heard in such a proceeding." Julian Mack, "The Juvenile Court," *Harvard Law Review*, vol. 23 (1909), pp. 119–20.

27. Fox, "Juvenile Justice Reform," p. 1191.

28. See, for example, Chester Antieau, "Constitutional Rights in Juvenile Courts," *Cornell Law Quarterly*, vol. 46 (1961), p. 390 (reporting that in California, a child convicted of petit larceny would be committed until age twenty-one, whereas an adult convicted of the same crime would serve only six months in jail).

29. See *In re Gault*, 387 U.S. 1, 37–41 (1967) (describing the degree to which counsel was and was not provided in the years prior to the Court's decision in *Gault*). See, for example, *In re Hurst*, 110 N.Y.S.2d 270, 271 (Dom. Rel. Ct., Children's Court Div., Bronx Co. 1952) (noting that there were "[n]o attorneys in this case," in which the court finds that the child committed manslaughter and adjudicates him a delinquent).

30. For a description of the nature of juvenile court proceedings during this era, see *In re Gault*, 387 U.S. 1, 12–27 (1967). See, for example, *Gault*, at 14, 18 ("From the inception of the juvenile court system, wide differences have been tolerated—indeed insisted upon—between the procedural rights accorded to adults and those of juveniles. In practically all jurisdictions, there are rights granted to adults which are withheld from juveniles. . . . In 1937, Dean Pound wrote: 'The powers of the Star Chamber were a trifle in comparison with those of our juvenile courts'").

31. Twentieth Century Fund, *Confronting Youth Crime: Report of the Twentieth Century Fund Task Force on Sentencing Policy toward Young Offenders* (New York: Holmes and Meier 1978), p. 6. See also, for example, President's Commission on Law Enforcement and Administration of Justice, *Task Force Report: Juvenile Delinquency and Youth Crime* (Government Printing Office, 1967), p. 9 ("In theory the juvenile court was to be helpful and rehabilitative rather than punitive. In fact the distinction often disappears, not only because of the absence of facilities and personnel but also because of the limits of knowledge and

technique. In theory the court's action was to affix no stigmatizing label. In fact a delinquent is generally viewed by employers, schools, the armed services—by society generally—as a criminal. In theory the court was to treat children guilty of criminal acts in noncriminal ways. In fact it labels truants and runaways as junior criminals").

32. *In re Gault*, 387 U.S. 1 (1967).

33. Because the trial was not transcribed, it was unclear what evidence had or had not been presented. See *In re Gault* at 6–7 (at a later habeas corpus proceeding, the judge recalled that at trial and again at a subsequent hearing Gerald admitted making the alleged lewd remarks; a probation officer recalled his making such an admission at the first hearing but not at the second; Gerald's parents "recalled that Gerald said he only dialed Mrs. Cook's number and handed the telephone to his friend, Ronald").

34. *In re Gault*, at 6–9, 43–44.

35. *Gault* at 28. See also *Gault* at 27 ("It is of no constitutional consequence—and of limited practical meaning—that the institution to which he is committed is called an Industrial School. The fact of the matter is that, however euphemistic the title, a 'receiving home' or an 'industrial school' for juveniles is an institution of confinement in which the child is incarcerated for a greater or lesser time").

36. *Gault* at 36, quoting *Powell* v. *Alabama*, 287 U.S. 45, 69 (1932).

37. *McKeiver* v. *Pennsylvania*, 403 U.S. 528, 543–51 (1971).

38. See *McKeiver* v. *Pennsylvania* at 534 (describing the potential of the juvenile court to fulfill its founders' goal of providing children with a "judge who is devoted, sympathetic, and conscientious").

39. See *McKeiver* v. *Pennsylvania* at 543, 547–48, 550.

40. See Martin Guggenheim and Randy Hertz, "Reflections on Judges, Juries, and Justice: Ensuring the Fairness of Juvenile Delinquency Trials," *Wake Forest Law Review*, vol. 34 (1998), pp. 562–82.

41. Elyce Zenoff Ferster, Thomas F. Courtless, and Edith Nash Snethen, "The Juvenile Justice System: In Search of the Role of Counsel," *Fordham Law Review*, vol. 39 (1971) pp. 375, 386.

42. ABA, *A Call for Justice*, p. 7.

43. Ibid.

44. Patricia Puritz, "The Crisis in Juvenile Indigent Defense," *Indigent Defense News*, March/April 1998, p. 3. See also Patricia Puritz and Wendy Shang, "Juvenile Indigent Defense: Crisis and Solutions," *Criminal Justice*, vol. 15 (Spring 2000), p. 1; ABA Steering Committee on the Unmet Legal Needs of Children, *America's Children Still at Risk*, pp. 256–59; American Bar Association Presidential Working Group on the Unmet Legal Needs of Children and Their Families, *America's Children At Risk: A National Agenda for Legal Action* (Chicago: ABA, 1993), p. 60. The available data and our own experiences in juvenile court suggest that the reasons for this lackluster performance include the often "cozy" courthouse culture of juvenile court, the crushing caseloads that confront most juvenile defenders, the relative inexperience of those working in the juvenile courts (see ABA, *A Call for Justice*, p. 7, reporting that 55 percent of juvenile defenders practice in juvenile court less than 24 months), and the view of some lawyers that conviction is in the child's interest because it provides a vehicle for obtaining services at sentencing. One finds an equally low level of representation in the adult criminal courts. See, for example, Randy Hertz and James Liebman, *Federal Habeas Corpus Practice and Procedure*, vol. 1 (Charlottesville, Va.:

LEXIS Law Publishing, 4th ed., 2001) § 11.2c, pp. 532–49 (describing cases in which the federal courts granted a writ of habeas corpus on the ground that defense counsel was ineffective in preparing for or handling a trial, preparing for or handling a capital sentencing hearing, advising a client with regard to a guilty plea, or representing a criminal defendant on appeal or in a postconviction proceeding). See also Jane Fritsch and David Rohde, "Lawyers Often Fail New York's Poor," *New York Times*, April 8, 2001, p. A1; Jane Fritsch and David Rohde, "For Poor, Appeals Are Luck of the Draw," *New York Times*, April 10, 2001, p. A1; John Gibeaut, "Defense Warnings," *ABA Journal* (December 2001), p. 35.

45. *McKeiver v. Pennsylvania*, 403 U.S. 528, 534, 549-50 (1971). Accord ibid. at 552 (White, J., concurring) (agreeing with plurality's view that due process does not require jury trials in juvenile court because of court's unique character, including its focus on rehabilitation and its central premise that "[r]eprehensible acts by juveniles are not deemed the consequence of mature and malevolent choice but of environmental pressures (or lack of them) or of other forces beyond their control").

46. Peter Reinharz, "Why Teen Thugs Get Away with Murder," *City Journal*, Autumn 1996, p. 47. See also, for example, Butterfield, "With Juvenile Courts in Chaos," p. B6 (quoting juvenile prosecuting agency official as saying that "the Family Court is bankrupt. . . . It's time to sell everything off and start over").

47. See Elikann, *Superpredators*, pp. 41–42, 66 (suggesting that youth, who lack access to the ballot, are vulnerable to political rhetoric); Franklin C. Zimring, *American Youth Violence* (Oxford University Press, 1998), pp. 6–7.

48. "No Kid Gloves for Teen Criminals," editorial, *New York Post*, March 7, 1995, p. 22.

49. See, for example, Harold Schechter, "A Tragedy Repeated in History," *New York Times*, May 28, 1998, p. A15 (responding to claims of an increase in violent juvenile crime by demonstrating that "homicidal children have been a subject of concern for decades. An article titled 'Youthful Killers' in *Outlook and Independent* magazine in January 1929 cited the top 10 notorious young killers of the preceding five years . . . . In the December 1959 issue of the *American Journal of Psychiatry*, Dr. Loretta Bender published 'Children and Adolescents Who Have Killed,' in which she declared that, since 1935, she had personally known 33 boys and girls who had been associated with the death of another person. In the January 1962 issue of *Social Work*, Dr. Douglas Sergeant of the Detroit Child Study Clinic flatly asserted that homicide by children was not rare and noted that nine homicide cases had been referred to the Wayne County Juvenile Court in the previous year"). See also Jerome G. Miller, "Juvenile Justice: Facts v. Anger," *New York Times*, August 15, 1998, p. A13 ("According to the Justice Policy Institute, which analyzed FBI statistics, nationally there were 25 recorded homicides committed by children under the age of 13 in 1965, versus 16 in 1996").

50. For example, focusing on just a single jurisdiction, one finds that cases such as the following came before the Children's Court of New York City in the 1940s and early 1950s: *In re Hurst*, 110 N.Y.S.2d 270, 271 (N.Y.C. Dom. Rel. Ct., Children's Court Div., Bronx Co. 1952) (thirteen-year-old boy "commit[ted] a robbery, then within the next few days stab[bed] a child for no reason, and within 45 minutes use[d] a rifle (bought with the proceeds of the robbery) to kill a boy"); *In re X, Y, and Z*, 43 N.Y.S.2d 361 (Dom. Rel. Ct., Children's Court Div., N.Y. Co. 1943) (three respondents, all under the age of 16, while acting together with other members of their gang, beat and fatally stabbed a member of a

rival gang); *In re Cotton*, 30 N.Y.S.2d 421 (Dom. Rel. Ct., Children's Court Div., N.Y. Co. 1941) (fifteen-year-old, who was a fugitive from a chain gang in Georgia, where he had been serving sentence of more than ten years, was found delinquent for raping a woman at knifepoint).

51. For example, *In re Hurst*, 110 N.Y.S.2d 270, 271 (N.Y.C. Dom. Rel. Ct., Children's Court Div., Bronx Co. 1952) ("It is sometimes very difficult for me, as it must be for other judges, to regard some children under the age of 16 as children, in face of the offenses they commit . . . . [T]heir acts are as baneful on society as if they were committed by adults"). In an interesting forerunner to modern claims that violence by children is inspired by television and movies, one finds the judge in the *Hurst* case commenting: "This boy who is before me is a product of evil, evil influences to which he has been exposed. Whatever reading he did was confined practically and wholly to what some euphoniously call comics, or funnies, but which in fact are 'tragics.' Children read 'Crime,' 'Crime Does Not Pay,' 'Horrors,' etc. It is to be expected that a child who is not given counter-influences to the pernicious effects on him, in course of time will become so conditioned that anti-social acts amounting to crime no longer shock him." Ibid. at 272–73.

52. Roger Butterfield, "Our Kids Are in Trouble," *Life*, vol. 15 (December 20, 1943), p. 98.

53. Although prosecutors, judges, and court administrators often claim to find evidence of escalating violence in increases in felony filings, such caseload shifts often reflect merely a change in local prosecutorial policies about whether to overcharge a minor offense as a felony. See, for example, Liz Trotta, "Mayhem by 'Killer Kids' Still on Rise; Rehab Backers Halt Crackdown," *Washington Times*, December 2, 1996, p. A4 (quoting Jane Spinak, then attorney-in-charge of the New York City Legal Aid Society's juvenile rights division, commenting that the New York City agency that prosecutes juveniles "files everything as a felony and then turns around and says, 'Well, felony rates are way up'"). See also Karen Dillon, "Hopeless," *American Lawyer* (January/February 1995), p. 5 (reporter who observed Judge Judy Sheindlin when she was a New York City family court judge notes that few of the approximately 200 cases heard by Sheindlin in a typical week would draw media attention because they were not serious felonies).

54. A lengthy list of such cases, gathered in a survey of a single year's worth of reversals of juvenile adjudications for insufficiency of the evidence, can be found in Guggenheim and Hertz, "Reflections on Judges, Juries, and Justice," pp. 564–66, nn. 48–55, and accompanying text. These cases include, for example, an Arkansas case in which a sixteen-year-old youth was convicted of stealing $40 from his mother's purse (*P.V. v. State*, 1997 WL 346806 [Ark. App. June 18, 1997]); a Louisiana case in which a youth was convicted of intentionally damaging a wall of a store by falling face-first into the wall during the course of a struggle with the store manager, who had caught the youth shoplifting a liquor bottle (*State in the Interest of J.C.G.*, 706 So.2d 1081 [La. App. 1998]); and a Washington case in which a youth was convicted of aiding and abetting animal cruelty in the second degree for standing by, watching, and giggling while another boy threw a pigeon into a fountain (*State v. Simon*, 1997 WL 292344, at *1 [Wash. App. June 2, 1997]).

55. Snyder, "Juvenile Arrests 1999," pp.1–6, 8–11.

56. See Snyder, "Juvenile Arrests 1999," p. 3 (of an estimated 2,468,800 juvenile arrests in 1999, there were 645,400 juvenile arrests for violent crime); Howell and others, *Serious, Violent, and Chronic Juvenile Offenders: A Sourcebook*, p. 11); Howard N. Snyder

and Melissa Sickmund, *Juvenile Offenders and Victims: 1999 National Report* (U.S. Department of Justice, Office of Juvenile Justice and Delinquency Prevention, 1999), p. 120.

57. Snyder, "Juvenile Arrests 1999," pp. 1, 4 (juveniles accounted for 16 percent of all violent crime arrests in 1999; the proportion of violent crimes cleared by juvenile arrests in 1999 was 12.4 percent); Mendel, *Less Hype, More Help*, pp. 30–32, 34–35; ABA Steering Committee on the Unmet Legal Needs of Children, *America's Children Still at Risk*, p. 254 (reporting that "in 1996, fewer than one-half of 1 percent of children aged 10 to 17 were arrested for a violent crime in the United States. Only a core group of 6 to 8 percent of juvenile offenders is responsible for most serious and violent juvenile crimes"; the ABA report stated that nonetheless "[s]tudies show that the American public shares the same misperception of violent juvenile crime that is espoused by some elected officials" [p. 255]).

58. See, for example, Anderson and others, "School-Associated Violent Deaths," pp. 2699, 2701 (study showing that although "[t]he rate of school-associated violent death events has decreased significantly since the 1992–93 school year[,] . . . [t]he rate for multiple-victim student homicides has increased since the 1994–95 school years"; "[t]he proportion of all school-associated student homicides that involved multiple victims has risen from 0 % in 1992 to 42 % in 1999"); Timothy Egan, "From Adolescent Angst to Killings at School: Patterns in the Rage," *New York Times*, June 14, 1998, p. 22 (describing five high-profile cases involving young adolescent males charged for shooting and killing their schoolmates). For further discussion of the relationship between firearms and delinquency, see notes 95–101 and accompanying text.

59. See, for example, text accompanying note 46.

60. *Angels with Dirty Faces* (Warner Bros., 1938). See also, for example, *Boys Town* (MGM, 1938) (indigent boys shown engaging in fistfights, petty vandalism, and theft of food); *Dead End* (Samuel Goldwyn, 1937) (indigent boys of the slums shown engaging in fistfights, thefts, and assaults with fists and occasionally pocketknives).

61. See Jerome Bruner, *Acts of Meaning* (Harvard University Press, 1990), pp. 33–65; Susan T. Fiske and Shelley E. Taylor, *Social Cognition* (McGraw-Hill, 1991), pp. 79–96; Naomi Quinn and Dorothy Holland, eds., "Culture and Cognition," in *Cultural Models in Language and Thought* (Cambridge University Press, 1987), pp. 3, 20. For applications of these concepts to legal settings, see, for example, Anthony G. Amsterdam and Jerome Bruner, *Minding the Law* (Harvard University Press, 2000); Jerome Bruner, "A Psychologist and the Law," *New York Law School Law Review*, vol. 37 (1992), p. 173; Peggy Cooper Davis, "The Proverbial Woman," *Record of Association of the Bar of the City of New York*, vol. 48 (1993), p. 7.

62. *Colors* (Orion, 1988); *Juice* (Paramount, 1992); *Menace II Society* (New Line Cinema, 1993). See also, for example, *Boyz 'n the Hood* (Columbia, 1991); *American Me* (Universal 1992); *Above the Rim* (New Line Productions, 1994); *Fresh* (Miramax, 1994); *Jason's Lyric* (Polygram, 1994); *Sugar Hill* (Beacon, 1994); *Clockers* (Universal, 1995).

63. For discussion of the concept of "outgroup," see, for example, Gordon W. Allport, *The Nature of Prejudice* (Reading, Mass.: Addison-Wesley Publishing Company, 1979), pp. 41-43, 153–54, 363–66; Fiske and Taylor, *Social Cognition*, p. 123.

64. This is true of each of the films cited in note 62. For a general discussion of this trend in Hollywood's depiction of African Americans and how it fits into the broader history of cinematic depictions of African Americans, see Edward Guerrero, *Framing Blackness: The African American Image in Film* (Temple University Press, 1993), pp. 182–90. Interestingly,

when the moviemakers of today set out to tell a story about a nonviolent delinquent youth, they often choose to set that story in an earlier era and to make the protagonist a white teenager. See, for example, *A Bronx Tale* (Tribeca, 1993), set in the early 1960s; *Sleepers* (Warner Bros., 1996), set in the 1960s. For a rare positive depiction of low-income youths of color, see *Stand and Deliver* (Warner Bros., 1987), based on the real-life story of Jaime Escalante, a teacher who defied conventions by successfully coaching students at an inner-city high school in East Los Angeles to pass the advanced placement calculus examination.

65. See Peggy C. Davis, "Law as Microaggression," *Yale Law Journal*, vol. 98 (1989), pp. 1559, 1561–65; Fiske and Taylor, *Social Cognition*, pp. 121–24.

66. For applications of cognitive psychology principles to the analysis of racially biased decisionmaking by actors in the criminal justice process, see, for example, Ronald A. Farrell and Malcolm D. Hunter, "The Social and Cognitive Structure of Legal Decision-Making," *Sociology Quarterly*, vol. 32 (1991), pp. 529, 532, 536 ("[c]ourt actors internalize crime stereotypes as cognitive schemata that provide a shorthand for information-processing in a system characterized by time and resource constraints"; those schemata are "reaffirmed continuously through the everyday interaction of court actors as they deal with alleged offenders"); Donald C. Nugent, "Judicial Bias," *Cleveland State Law Review*, vol. 42 (1994), pp. 19–20, 48 (author, an Ohio appellate judge and former trial judge, reviews cognitive psychology findings on schemata, notes the statistical evidence of gender and racial bias in the court systems, and explores the ways in which "judges' early lives, their experiences both on and off the bench, and their professional careers" may "lead to many distorted and systematically biased decisions").

67. See Snyder and Sickmund, *Juvenile Offenders and Victims: 1999 National Report*, p. 150; see also note 90 and accompanying text.

68. A recent study prepared by the Justice Policy Institute and the Berkeley Media Studies Group for the Building Blocks Initiative (a consortium of children's advocates, researchers, law enforcement professionals, and community organizers) documents the media's patterns of "report[ing] crime, especially violent crime, out of proportion to its actual occurrence"; "unduly connect[ing] race and crime, especially violent crime"; and unduly connecting youth, especially youth of color, with violence. See Lori Dorfman and Vincent Schiraldi, "Off Balance: Youth, Race, and Crime in the News" (www.building-blocksforyouth.org/media/media.htm [April 10, 2001]), pp. 5, 9, 13–16. For additional discussion of the role of the media in shaping the public's perceptions of the criminal and juvenile justice systems, see Joel Best, *Random Violence: How We Talk About New Crimes and New Victims* (University of California Press, 1999); Richard L. Fox and Robert W. Van Sickel, *Tabloid Justice: Criminal Justice in an Age of Media Frenzy* (Boulder, Colo.: L. Rienner, 2001).

69. See U.S. Department of Justice, *Justice Expenditure and Employment 1990* (1992); Richard Klein and Robert Spangenberg, *The Indigent Defense Crisis* (Washington: ABA, 1993), p. 1. See also Jane Fritsch and David Rohde, "For the Poor, a Lawyer with 1,600 Clients," *New York Times*, April 7, 2001, p. A16. For a discussion of techniques that chief defenders can use to become more effective at obtaining adequate funding for their offices, including linking the funding level of the defender's office to that of the local district attorney's office, see Taylor-Thompson, "Effective Assistance," pp. 206–08.

70. For an example of standards of this sort, see the New York State Bar Association Committee on Juvenile Justice and Child Welfare, *Law Guardian Representation Standards*

(June 1998). See also *Indigent Defense* (publication of the National Legal Aid and Defender Association), March/April 1998, pp. 3–11 (identifying features necessary for effective representation, including ability to control caseload size; opportunity to enter case as early as possible after arrest; flexibility to represent child in matters arising out of delinquency proceeding, such as school suspension hearings; comprehensive training; and non-lawyer support and resources).

71. For an overview of this literature, see Paul Piersma and others, *Law and Tactics in Juvenile Cases*, 3d ed. (St. Louis University School of Law, 1977), pp. 46–51.

72. See Randy Hertz, Martin Guggenheim, and Anthony G. Amsterdam, *Trial Manual for Defense Attorneys in Juvenile Court*, vol. 1, § 2.03 (Philadelphia: American Law Institute–American Bar Association Committee on Continuing Professional Education, 1991), pp. 13–14 (discussing relevant ethical rules and professional standards).

73. In this chapter, we will focus on a few programs as examples of the trends we describe. There are, however, many other programs that are doing innovative work that could have been selected. In 1998, the American Bar Association cited the following organizations for their "innovative juvenile legal service delivery": Project TeamChild in Seattle; the juvenile offender team of the Legal Aid Society in New York City; the Youth Advocacy Project of the Committee for Public Counsel Services in Massachusetts; the juvenile services project of the Public Defender Service for the District of Columbia; the Detention Response Unit and Youthful Defendant Unit of the public defender's office in Baltimore, Maryland; the youth advocacy unit of the Missouri state public defender's office; First Defense Legal Aid of Chicago; Neighborhood Defender Service of Harlem; the Children and Family Justice Center of Northwestern University School of Law; the juvenile clinic of the University of the District of Columbia's David A. Clarke School of Law; the Mandel Legal Aid Clinic of the University of Chicago School of Law; the Juvenile Rights Advocacy Project of Boston College School of Law; the Youth Law Center in Washington, D.C., and San Francisco; the Juvenile Law Center in Philadelphia; the Children's Law Center in Covington, Kentucky; the Children's Advocacy Project of the ACLU in Montgomery, Alabama; and the Juvenile Justice Project of Louisiana in New Orleans. See *Indigent Defense*, March/April 1998, p. 3.

74. For a comprehensive discussion of the tasks involved in representing a defendant in a criminal case, including analyses of relevant law and descriptions of particularly useful techniques, see Anthony G. Amsterdam, *Trial Manual 5 for the Defense of Criminal Cases* (Philadelphia: American Law Institute–American Bar Association Committee on Continuing Professional Education, 1988–89).

75. See Hertz, Guggenheim, and Amsterdam, *Trial Manual*, vol. 2, § 38.02, pp. 869–70.

76. The multidisciplinary approach described in the text may be impossible in many jurisdictions, where stringent limitations on state funds for indigent services prevent court-appointed lawyers for indigent clients from hiring the professionals from other disciplines that the approach requires.

77. For an overview of YAP, see www.youthadvocacyproject.org [January 2002]. In 2001, YAP and its director, Josh Dohan, received the Clara Shortridge Foltz award from the National Legal Aid and Defender Association (NLADA).

78. With the assistance of private funding from the Open Society Institute, the foundation of financier George Soros, the TeamChild project has expanded, so that it now has five offices in Washington state. TeamChild's work recently was recognized by the Wash-

ington State Bar Association, which presented the organization with the state bar association's annual *Pro Bono* award. See Washington State Bar Association, "TeamChild Receives WSBA Pro Bono Award" (www.wsba.org/2001/09/teamchild.htm [September 13, 2001]). TeamChild's successes have led to the recreation of the program in other states. See, for example, www.kidscounsel.org/kidscounsel/about/index.7.htm [December 2001].

79. See notes 19–31 and accompanying text.

80. See notes 8–9, 46–48, and accompanying text.

81. See, for example, Marty Beyer, "Immaturity, Culpability and Competency in Juveniles: A Study of 17 Cases," *Criminal Justice*, vol. 15, no. 2 (Summer 2000), p. 24; Marty Beyer, "Recognizing the Child in the Delinquent," *Kentucky Children's Rights Journal*, vol. 7 (Summer 1999), p. 16; Thomas Grisso and Robert G. Schwartz, eds., *Youth on Trial: A Developmental Perspective on Juvenile Justice* (University of Chicago, 2000).

82. James Gilligan, *Violence: Our Deadly Epidemic and Its Causes* (G. P. Putnam's Sons, 1996), pp. 200–01.

83. See Carl Husemoller Nightingale, *On the Edge: A History of Poor Black Children and Their American Dreams* (Basic Books, 1993), p. 56 (explaining how young people use violence as a compensatory "front"). See also Daniel Goleman, "Black Scientists Study the 'Pose' of the Inner City," *New York Times*, April 21, 1992, p. C1 ("defiant swagger," "cool pose," and such postures are techniques that inner-city young black men use to "maintain a sense of integrity and suppress rage," thereby avoiding violence; yet, those very behaviors are often misread by white principals and teachers as "aggressive and intimidating"). A similar phenomenon of use of violence to preserve self-respect has been cited as one of the reasons for the consistently high homicide rates among Southern white men. See Fox Butterfield, "Why America's Murder Rate Is So High," *New York Times*, July 26, 1998, Week in Review section, p. 1. See also Fox Butterfield, *All God's Children: The Bosket Family and the American Tradition of Violence* (Knopf, 1995), p. 119.

84. See, for example, Tamra Jones, "The Shirt Off His Back; What's the Price Tag on Dignity? A Suit Explores Racism and Retailing," *Washington Post*, September 26, 1997, p. C1 (reporting incident in which store security guard accused a sixteen-year-old African American youth of shoplifting the shirt he was wearing and forced him to remove the shirt and leave it in store; when the youth later returned to store and presented proof of purchase, the shirt was returned without apology); William Raspberry, "Automatically Suspect," *Washington Post*, Nov. 9, 1994, p. A19 (African American op ed columnist comments that "[s]ome of us . . . feel accused much of the time—by clerks who follow us around the store").

85. See, for example, Ralph Ranalli, "Official: Teachers Expect Less From Blacks, Hispanics," *Boston Herald*, February 12, 1998, p. 20 (reporting testimony of Boston public schools deputy superintendent Janice E. Jackson that "during classroom visits in 1992, 1993, and 1996," she had observed "teachers failing to call on black and Hispanic students, reprimanding those students more often than white and Asian students, and praising white students more than blacks or Hispanics").

86. See, for example, Stephen Buckley, "Confronting the Poison of Racism; Maryland Students Hold Out Dim Hope of Finding a Cure," *Washington Post*, May 9, 1992, p. D1 (recounting comments by African American high school students that police officers follow them from store to store and that mall security guards come up to groups of black youths and ask them to move on, while ignoring equally large groups of white youths); Lisa Genasci, "Success Is No Shield for Racism Discrimination: No Matter What Positives They

Hold, Blacks Say They Daily Confront Adversity that Their White Counterparts Cannot Imagine," *Los Angeles Times*, June 14, 1995, p. 9 (reporting incident in which Earl Graves Jr., a young African American business executive who attended Yale College and Harvard Business School, was detained and searched by New York City police just after he got off of a commuter train because, they claimed, he matched the description of a perpetrator, even though Graves, who is 6'4", 225 pounds, and clean shaven, obviously did not match the description of a 5'10" slim black man with a mustache); Bob Herbert, "The Silent Treatment," *New York Times*, July 25, 1999, Week in Review section, p. 15 (describing police officers' baseless arrest of an African American star of a Broadway musical who "was standing in the vestibule of his apartment building in Washington Heights when the police arrived" and who "opened the door to hold it for them, thinking they were there to help someone in distress"); Bob Herbert, "What's Going On?" *New York Times*, February 14, 1999, Week in Review section, p. 13 (recounting interviews of African American and Hispanic students in an alternative high school in Brooklyn, who consistently described incidents in which the "police treat[ed] them as lesser beings, stopping them, demanding identification, and searching their clothing and their bodies at will"). Empirical data on police conduct also provide support for anecdotal accounts of unjustified stops and seizures on the basis of race. See, generally, David Cole, *No Equal Justice: Race and Class in the American Criminal Justice System* (New Press, 1999), pp. 34–38 (presenting statistics on race-based stops of motorists by Maryland state troopers on Interstate 95 and by New Jersey state police officers on the New Jersey Turnpike); Timothy Egan, "On Wealthy Island, Being Black Means Being a Police Suspect," *New York Times*, May 10, 1998, p. 12.

87. See, for example, Marcia Slacum Greene, "Presumed Dangerous: Area's Young Black Men Confront New Stereotypes Born of Drug Crisis," *Washington Post*, Oct. 17, 1991, p. A1 (recounting interviews with two dozen black teenagers who said that the "almost daily . . . slights . . . make them feel like outcasts").

88. Marc Mauer and Tracy Huling, *Young Black Americans and the Criminal Justice System: Five Years Later* (Washington: Sentencing Project, October 1995), p. 1. For additional information about overrepresentation of African Americans in the criminal justice system, see Jerome Miller, *Search and Destroy: African-American Males in the Criminal Justice System* (Cambridge University Press, 1996); Marc Mauer, *Race to Incarcerate* (New Press, 1999); Donziger, *The Real War on Crime*, pp. 99–121. A report by the Bureau of Justice Statistics, the Justice Department's statistical branch, "found that the incarceration rate for black men in 1996 was 3,096 per 100,000, eight times the rate for white men, 370 per 100,000, and more than double the rate for Hispanic men, 1,276 per 100,000 . . . . The racial disparities were particularly striking among young men, . . . with 8.3 percent of black men ages 25 to 29 in prison in 1996, compared with 2.6 percent of Hispanic men in the same age group and 0.8 percent of white men of those ages." Fox Butterfield, "Prison Population Growing Although Crime Rate Drops," *New York Times*, August 9, 1998, p. 18.

89. See David C. Baldus and others, "Racial Discrimination and the Death Penalty in the Post-Furman Era: An Empirical and Legal Overview, with Recent Findings from Philadelphia," *Cornell Law Review*, vol. 83 (1998), p. 1638.

90. See Snyder, "Juvenile Arrests 1999," p. 4; Snyder and Sickmund, *Juvenile Offenders and Victims: 1999 National Report*, p. 192.

91. See Snyder and Sickmund, *Juvenile Offenders and Victims: 1999 National Report*, p. 193; Eileen Poe-Yamagata and Michael A. Jones, "And Justice for Some" (www.build-

ingblocksforyouth.org/justiceforsome/jfs.html [April 25, 2001]). See also Jason Zieden-
berg, "Drugs and Disparity: The Racial Impact of Illinois' Practice of Transferring Young
Drug Offenders to Adult Court" (www.buildingblocksforyouth.org/illinois/illinois.htm
[April 19, 2001]); Mike Males and Dan Macallair, "The Color of Justice: An Analysis of
Adult Court Transfers in California" (www.buildingblocksforyouth.org/colorofjustice/
color.htm [February 2, 2000]). For further discussion of overrepresentation of African
Americans in the juvenile justice system, see Miller, *Search and Destroy*, pp. 69–80, and
Donziger, *The Real War on Crime*, pp. 121–28. See also ABA Presidential Working Group
on the Unmet Legal Needs of Children and Their Families, *America's Children at Risk*, pp.
60, 61–62.

92. See Marcia Slacum Greene, "Presumed Dangerous; Area's Young Black Men Confront New Stereotypes Born of Drug Crisis," *Washington Post*, October 17, 1991, p. A1
(describing the daily regimen of "fear and hostility" that young African American males
encounter and then reporting that "[p]sychologists say that although violence is inexcus-
able, there is a recognizable vicious cycle: Feeling scorned and rejected, some youths then
fulfill the worst of people's expectations" and that "a complex web of racism, poverty and
other social problems contributes to a higher than average incidence of violence among
young black males").

93. U.S. Department of Justice, *National Crime Victimization Survey* (1996), p. 5.

94. Leonard D. Eron, Jacquelyn H. Gentry, Peggy Schlegel, eds., "Introduction," in
Reason to Hope: A Psychosocial Perspective on Violence and Youth (Washington: American Psychological Association, 1994), p. 4.

95. A report issued by the Federal Bureau of Alcohol, Tobacco, and Firearms shows
that "[a]s many as one-third of the guns used in crimes by juveniles and up to half of those
used by people aged 18 to 24 were purchased within the last three years from federally
licensed dealers." Fox Butterfield, "Study Exposes Illegal Traffic in New Guns," *New York
Times*, February 21, 1999, p. 22.

96. Stuart Greenbaum, "Kids and Guns: From Playgrounds to Battlegrounds," in
Office of Juvenile Justice and Delinquency Prevention, *Juvenile Justice*, vol. 3 (1997), p. 3.
See Snyder, "Juvenile Arrests 1999," p. 3.

97. Snyder, "Juvenile Arrests 1999," pp. 1, 3 (seventeen percent of murdered juveniles
under age thirteen were killed with a firearm; 81 percent of murdered juveniles age thirteen
or older were killed with a firearm).

98. Howell and others, *Serious, Violent, and Chronic Juvenile Offenders*, pp. 5–7.

99. Children's Defense Fund, *State of America's Children Yearbook* (Washington, 1994).

100. See, for example, Peter Applebome, "For Youths, Fear of Crime is Pervasive and
Powerful," *New York Times*, January 12, 1996, p. A12.

101. Geoffrey Canada, *Fist, Stick, Knife, Gun: A Personal History of Violence in America* (Boston: Beacon Press, 1995), pp. 68–69.

102. Gilligan, *Violence*, p. 47.

103. One of the changes in the juvenile justice system in the past decade has been a significant increase in the number of prosecutions of girls for delinquency offenses. For a discussion of this phenomenon, the systemic implications, and various issues relating to the
representation and treatment of girls in the juvenile justice system, see American Bar Association and National Bar Association, *Justice by Gender: The Lack of Appropriate Prevention,
Diversion, and Treatment Alternatives for Girls in the Justice System* (Washington, 2001);

ABA Steering Committee on the Unmet Legal Needs of Children, *America's Children Still at Risk*, pp. 273–74; Marty Beyer, "Delinquent Girls: A Developmental Perspective," *Kentucky Children's Rights Journal*, vol. 9 (2001), p. 17; Barbara Fedders, "For Girls in Trouble, Arrest Is Becoming a Rite of Passage," *Sojourner: The Women's Forum*, vol. 25, no. 8 (April 2000), p. 24.

104. Mark Ezell, *TeamChild: Evaluation of the Third Year* (Seattle: TeamChild, 1998), pp. 6–9.

105. See, generally, Amsterdam, *Trial Manual 5 for the Defense of Criminal Cases*, vol. 3, pp. 304–07.

106. See, for example, Gary Goodpaster, "The Trial for Life: Effective Assistance of Counsel in Death Penalty Cases," *New York University Law Review*, vol. 58 (1983), p. 299; Craig Haney, "Violence and the Capital Jury: Mechanisms of Moral Disengagement and the Impulse to Condemn to Death," *Stanford Law Review*, vol. 49 (1997), p. 1447.

107. See, for example, Brief of the American Society for Adolescent Psychiatry and the American Orthopsychiatric Association as *Amici Curiae* in Support of Petitioners, *High* v. *Zant* and *Wilkins* v. *Missouri* (case decided *sub nom. Stanford* v. *Kentucky*, 492 U.S. 361 [1989]); Brief of the Child Welfare League of America, National Parents and Teachers Association, National Council on Crime and Delinquency, Children's Defense Fund, National Association of Social Workers, National Black Child Development Institute, National Network of Runaway and Youth Services, National Youth Advocate Program, and American Youth Work Center as *Amici Curiae* in Support of Petitioners, *High* v. *Zant* and *Wilkins* v. *Missouri* (case decided *sub nom. Stanford* v. *Kentucky*, 492 U.S. 361 [1989]). See also Dorothy Otnow Lewis, *Guilty by Reason of Insanity: A Psychiatrist Explains the Minds of Killers* (Fawcett Columbine, 1999).

108. See "Symposium: Capital Jury Project," *Indiana Law Journal*, vol. 70 (1995), p. 1033. See also Austin Sarat, "Speaking of Death: Narratives of Violence in Capital Trials," *Law and Society Review*, vol. 27 (1993), p. 19; Scott E. Sundby, "The Jury as Critic: An Empirical Look at How Capital Juries Perceive Expert and Lay Testimony," *Virginia Law Review*, vol. 83 (1997), pp. 1109.

109. A central principle of capital defense work is that "the major task of defense counsel at the penalty phase of a capital trial is to humanize the defendant: to bring home to the jury that there is a great deal more to the defendant than the crime s/he committed." Amsterdam, *Trial Manual 5 for the Defense of Criminal Cases*, vol. 3, p. 307. This requires, among other things, that defense counsel find ways to help jurors empathize with defendants of a different race and class, who come from life circumstances that are very different than those of many jurors. See James M. Doyle, "The Lawyers' Art: 'Representation' in Capital Cases," *Yale Journal of Law and Humanities*, vol. 8 (1996), pp. 417, 434–46; Haney, "Violence and the Capital Jury," pp. 1460–67. The same barriers often separate the judge from the accused in delinquency cases. As noted in notes 90–91 and the accompanying text, children of color are disproportionately involved in the juvenile justice system. Statistics show that only 4.1 percent of state trial court judges are African American. See Sherrilyn A. Ifill, "Judging the Judges: Racial Diversity, Impartiality, and Representation on State Trial Courts," *Boston College Law Review*, vol. 39 (1997), p. 95 and notes 2–3. Although there are no comparable statistics available on the class background of judges, our experience is that juvenile court judges typically come from a middle- to upper-class background.

110. See, for example, Stephen Wizner and Dennis Curtis, "Here's What We Do: Some Notes about Clinical Legal Education," *Cleveland State Law Review*, vol. 29 (1980), pp. 673, 678–79.

111. See Bernardine Dohrn, "Justice for Children: The 'Leastwise of the Land'" (www.law.nwu.edu/depts/clinic/cfjc/cfjc-info.html [February 20, 2002]).

112. See Joseph B. Tulman, "The Best Defense Is a Good Offense: Incorporating Special Education Law in Delinquency Representation in the Juvenile Law Clinic," *Washington University Journal of Urban and Contemporary Law*, vol. 42 (1992), p. 223.

113. For example, the Mandel Legal Aid Clinic of the University of Chicago School of Law has been specializing in defending children accused of homicide. The NYU Juvenile Rights Clinic is experimenting with new kinds of relationships with the local juvenile defense provider (the Juvenile Rights Division of the Legal Aid Society) to improve both the educational experience for the students and the service provided to clients.

114. See, for example, Anthony G. Amsterdam, "Telling Stories and Stories about Them," *Clinical Law Review*, vol. 1 (1994), p. 9; Amsterdam and Hertz, "An Analysis of Closing Arguments to a Jury"; Binny Miller, "Give Them Back Their Lives: Recognizing Client Narrative in Case Theory," *Michigan Law Review*, vol. 93 (1994), p. 485.

115. For a discussion of approaches of this sort that may be useful at the trial stage of a juvenile delinquency case, see Guggenheim and Hertz, "Reflections on Judges, Juries, and Justice," pp. 586–93.

116. *In re Gault*, 387 U.S. 1 (1967). See, for example, Barry C. Feld, "The Juvenile Court Meets the Principle of the Offense: Legislative Changes in Juvenile Waiver Statutes," *Journal of Criminal Law and Criminology*, vol. 78 (1987), p. 471; Norman Lefstein, Vaughan Stapleton, and Lee Teitelbaum, "In Search of Juvenile Justice: *Gault* and Its Implementation," *Law and Society Review*, vol. 3 (1969), pp. 491, 559. For discussion of *Gault*, see notes 32–36 and accompanying text.

117. See Taylor-Thompson, "Effective Assistance," pp. 12–19.

4

DAVID B. MITCHELL
SARA E. KROPF

Youth Violence: Response of the Judiciary

THE COURTS ARE THE central institution in the juvenile justice system. They can be understood as the hub of a wheel, from which schools and other public and private social agencies draw their authority to deal with the problems of dysfunctional youth and their families. In many respects, juvenile courts reflect prevailing social attitudes regarding the proper care and treatment of children. Although individual courts may differ in their configuration and level of authority, they remain constant in their role as an essential piece in a broad mosaic of social agencies that focus on the family. Unfortunately, courts too often are the last resort of juvenile justice administrators who handle youthful offenders. Judicial intervention frequently is seen as appropriate only after a child has engaged in long-term disruptive behavior, and social agencies refer matters to the courts only when a situation has advanced beyond the point that meaningful intervention is possible without coercion.

Juvenile courts deal with three general types of offenses: delinquency, status, and dependency offenses. Delinquency offenses are acts committed by a juvenile that if committed by an adult would be a violation of criminal law; they include crimes against persons and property, crimes against the public order, and drug-related crimes. Status offenses include acts that are offenses only when they are committed by a juvenile, such as running away from home, truancy, ungovernability of the juvenile, and underage liquor and tobacco law violations. Dependency offenses involve neglect or inadequate care of minors by parents or guardians; child abuse; and maintaining improper conditions in the home.[1]

In the growing public debate regarding youth violence, delinquency offenses have had perhaps the highest profile and been the subject of greatest scrutiny. Indeed, in recent years, the "adult" criminal courts have been increasingly involved in managing youth violence because of the growing trend at the state and federal level to alter the traditionally exclusive jurisdiction of the juvenile court in matters of juvenile crime.

Juvenile courts, which in some jurisdictions are known as family courts, are organized to adjudicate juveniles who meet statutorily defined age limits.[2] The origins of juvenile courts vary. Some states mandate the establishment of juvenile courts in their constitutions; however, in most states, legislatures define the duties and functions of these courts.[3] Although states set juvenile courts' jurisdiction, there are exceptions to state provisions. If the juvenile is Native American, he or she usually is adjudicated in tribal courts when the crime is relatively minor and in federal district court if the crime is sufficiently serious.[4] When the violation is of federal law, the juvenile can be tried in federal court. Finally, the juvenile can be transferred to adult criminal court within a state.

In addition, some states have explicitly extended juvenile courts' jurisdiction to areas such as "adoptions, court-ordered support, paternity actions, divorce, permanent termination of parental rights, custody over mentally ill or retarded children, family offenses, and foster care placement and review."[5] Some innovative juvenile courts also are combining various family legal issues such as divorce and child custody in one proceeding, taking a holistic approach that views those issues as a family problem.

Juvenile courts with extended jurisdiction have the authority to intervene in cases that involve abusive domestic conditions. Children who witness violence toward a family member at home often will duplicate that behavior with their own spouse or children in later years. Sadly, at least one state's juvenile incarceration statistics revealed that a majority of inmates had a history of being abused as a child.[6] Courts therefore increasingly aim to address abusive behavior in children in an effort to prevent future criminal conduct.

Putting Youth Violence into Context

A fundamental truth should be stated at the outset: very few juveniles in the United States engage in criminal behavior. They work hard, struggle against adversity, and behave in school and at home. Indeed, less than one-half of 1 percent of juveniles are arrested for violent crime each year.[7] Despite that encouraging statistic, the social and political environment in which today's juveniles live has greatly changed, and as a result, there has been an increase in state and federal "get tough" policies regarding juvenile courts' jurisdiction over and sentencing of young offenders.[8] Juvenile courts have found themselves forced to respond to both real and perceived increases in the level of crime and violence among American youth.

Any illusion that youth violence is confined to America's urban centers has been shattered in recent years, when, in several high-profile tragedies, school children have committed murder in rural and suburban areas—areas previously considered immune in the popular imagination to such violence.[9] Indeed, youth violence cannot be defined simply by geographic, racial, economic, or other conventional distinctions. Courts in all parts of the country have found themselves addressing its causes and symptoms.

The volume of cases adjudicated in juvenile courts in the United States is staggering. In 1999, juvenile courts handled 1,755,000 delinquency cases alone.[10] Between 1988 and 1997, the number of delinquency cases processed by U.S. juvenile courts increased 48 percent, while the number of delinquency cases rose 30 percent.[11] In 1997, less than 10 percent of delinquency offenses were violent crime index offenses.[12] In 1997, property offenses (such as shoplifting, burglary, or vandalism) made up 48 percent of all delinquency offenses; crimes against persons (such as robbery or assault), 22 percent; public order offenses (such as possession of a weapon or disorderly conduct), 18 percent; and drug law violations, 9 percent.[13]

Although commentators continue to describe the current rate of juvenile violent crime as an "epidemic,"[14] juvenile crime, including violent crime, has decreased in recent years. Figures recently released for the city of Baltimore, Maryland, are representative of the trend. In 1997, arrests for violent juvenile crime fell by 7 percent, due in significant part to a 52 percent reduction in the number of juveniles charged with murder. That was the first decrease in youth violent crime in Baltimore in nine years. In addition to the drop in the arrest rate for murder, arrests of juveniles for rape fell by 19 percent, the lowest level in twenty years; robbery arrests fell 7 percent; and aggravated assaults were down 3 percent. Other nonviolent crime results were equally impressive—arrests for motor vehicle theft, illegal weapon possession, and drug possession and distribution dropped 21 percent, 5 percent, and 11 percent, respectively.[15]

Despite these encouraging figures, the demographic characteristics of the juvenile offenders adjudicated for those crimes raise troubling social concerns. Although African American youth constitute only 15 percent of youth aged ten to seventeen in the United States, they account for 26 percent of all juvenile arrests, 41 percent of juvenile arrests for violent crime index offenses, 32 percent of delinquency referrals to juvenile court, 41 percent of juveniles detained in delinquency cases, 46 percent of juveniles in corrections institutions, and 52 percent of juveniles transferred to adult criminal court after judicial hearing.[16] In 1997, the long-term juvenile court custody rate for African American youth was nearly five times the rate for comparable white youth.[17] These numbers indicate disproportionate court involvement of black children. That disproportion has been shown to be aggravated as minorities penetrate further into the juvenile and adult criminal justice systems: 28.5 percent of black males will be incarcerated in either state or federal prison at some point during their lifetime. In contrast, the rate of incarceration for Hispanics is 16 percent and for Caucasians 4.4 percent.[18]

History of Juvenile Courts: Rehabilitation and Punishment

The first juvenile court was established in Chicago in 1899, embodying the concept that youthful offenders are different from adults and therefore require a different approach to discipline[19]—one that, at least in theory, seeks to rehabilitate them in their formative years instead of merely punishing them. In the U.S. criminal justice system, the legal status of juveniles traditionally has been distinct from that of adults,[20] having its theoretical roots in the English concept of *parens patriae*—leaving to the state the responsibility to act as surrogate parents for juvenile offenders whose natural parents do not provide adequate care for them.[21]

During the Industrial Revolution in nineteenth-century America, children often were forced into urban sweatshops and exploited as cheap labor. In 1828, the Society for the Prevention of Pauperism became the first institution to deal with juveniles who were in trouble with the law. Although the society attempted to separate juvenile from adult offenders, it continued to use clearly adult forms of punishment, including restraint by ball and chain or leg irons.[22] The deplorable conditions of many of those "houses of refuge" led to a second reform movement in the mid-1800s, toward "preventative agencies and reform schools."[23] Those reform schools were publicly funded, though state and municipal governments tried to garner private support as well.[24]

Just before the turn of the century, courts began to treat juveniles differently.[25] After Illinois established the first juvenile court in 1899, other states quickly followed.[26] By 1919, nearly all states had some form of juvenile court; by 1932, more than 600 independent juvenile courts existed in the United States; and by 1970, 2,662 juvenile courts existed in all fifty states.[27] The first juvenile courts did not adjudicate guilt or innocence as do courts in the post–*In re Gault* era; instead, they prescribed treatments to help troubled youth.[28] This rehabilitative goal endures, at least in theory, in modern juvenile court systems. Because the early juvenile courts focused on the welfare of the child, the juvenile court judge would consider each juvenile's situation individually to determine the proper disposition of the case.[29]

Juveniles were treated differently from adults for several reasons. First, they were viewed as being able to change their behavior with greater success than adult offenders.[30] Second, because their behavior was considered changeable, they were theoretically responsive to different forms of disposition.[31] Thus, courts could encourage rehabilitation rather than simply impose punishment. Third, juveniles were adjudicated in separate courts in order to protect them from the stigma associated with an adult criminal conviction.[32] That is one of the underlying reasons for keeping juvenile records confidential.

The debate that rages today over the role of juvenile courts has its origin in the conflict between the courts' historical rehabilitative goal and some modern reformers' desire to replace it with a punitive model that more closely replicates that of the criminal courts.[33] The debate plays out in the very real arena of juvenile courtrooms and in the disposition of juveniles who are adjudicated and sentenced there every day. Legislative bodies also struggle to determine how to hold violent children responsible for their acts.

The Modern Juvenile Court: Process and Sentencing

Some commentators argue that the original rehabilitative mission of juvenile courts still exists today, for three reasons.[34] First, juveniles depend on adults for care and supervision. Second, juveniles are still developing intellectually and emotionally. Third, juveniles are less capable than adults of comprehending the due process issues surrounding adjudication. Juvenile courts therefore attempt to recognize those differences and treat juveniles accordingly, generally adopting a rehabilitative approach, at least in sentencing.

Because of the operating assumption that there is indeed a difference between the purposes of juvenile and adult criminal courts, the courts are considered distinct. However, with the rising concern about youth violence, juvenile courts have been placed in an awkward position in which they are expected to play a "dual role."[35] They are to rehabilitate juvenile offenders and at the same time prevent them from harming society.[36] That duality has resulted in a "nationwide dilemma" as states reformulate their juvenile codes in a "piecemeal" manner in order to strike a delicate balance between the two goals.[37] Some commentators argue that the increased punitive focus of juvenile courts and sentencing policies have eroded the need for a separate juvenile court.[38]

Nevertheless, some state courts generally indicate that rehabilitation is their primary goal. Moreover, in 1971 the U.S. Supreme Court held in *McKeiver* v. *Pennsylvania*[39] that juveniles do not have a constitutional right to a jury trial because juvenile courts are rehabilitative and are considered "civil" rather than "criminal" courts.[40] One study demonstrates, however, that state legislatures are leaning more toward punishment of juveniles and less toward rehabilitation. The legislative purpose clauses of some states' juvenile court legislation indicate that the safety of the public rather than the welfare of the child is now the primary focus of their juvenile courts.[41]

In light of increasing public concern about juvenile violence in recent years, punishment has become a more popular goal. The Supreme Court decision in *In re Gault*,[42] which ushered in the era of due process rights for juveniles, indicated that the juvenile court system was at least in part a punitive system[43] capable of depriving a juvenile of liberty without according the juvenile his or her fundamental constitutional rights. In some ways, the goal of punishment has become even more dominant as juvenile offenders are waived more often into adult criminal courts.[44]

Legislative and Jurisdictional Changes

Since 1992, more than forty-one states have limited juvenile courts' jurisdiction over serious, violent, and chronic offenders. In most states, the maximum age of the juveniles allowed in juvenile court is set by statute. In approximately thirty-five states, juveniles are defined as those individuals below the age of eighteen; in ten states, the limit is sixteen; and in three states, the limit is fifteen. However, some states are beginning to respond to pressure to lower the age limit in order to try older juveniles in adult criminal court.[45]

One widespread tactic for dealing with violent youthful offenders is to transfer or waive them to adult court. In the view of one commentator, this response to youth violence provides "a safety valve that permits the expiatory sacrifice of some youths, quiets political and public clamor, and enables legislators to avoid otherwise irresistible pressures to lower the maximum age of juvenile court jurisdiction."[46] As of 1994, every state allowed for the transfer of juveniles to adult criminal court.[47] In some states, juveniles or their parents can request a transfer;[48] however, that is usually not the case. Typical methods of transfer are prosecutorial waiver, statutory waiver, and judicial waiver. States use one or all of those methods in differing combinations.[49]

Judicial waiver is the most common method of transfer. Consistent with the individualistic approach of early juvenile courts, a judge holds a hearing to determine whether the offender should be transferred into adult court,[50] considering factors such as the youth's amenability to rehabilitation and previous contacts with the juvenile court system.[51] Judicial waiver has become increasingly common; from 1988 to 1997, the number of cases judicially waved grew by 25 percent.[52] Judicial transfer hearings are factually based adversarial proceedings with counsel present that delve into the juvenile's individual situation. For that reason, many commentators favor this method over statutory and prosecutorial waiver.[53] Judicial discretion is not complete, however, because state legislatures often define by age or crime those cases that can be judicially waived to adult court.[54]

Legislative or statutory waiver allows the legislature to manipulate juvenile court jurisdiction to accommodate public values regarding the seriousness of crimes rather than the youthfulness of the offender. This type of waiver has been criticized as being "rigid and overinclusive,"[55] but it has the advantage of leaving the transfer decision to an elected legislature and creating clear rules for transfer. It therefore reduces judicial and prosecutorial discretion. In states with statutory transfer, the legislature specifies the age at which and offenses for which a juvenile will be automatically transferred to adult court.[56] For example, some states statutorily transfer juveniles who have prior felony convictions or who have committed certain serious, violent crimes.[57]

In some states, the prosecutor has complete discretion to choose the forum for the case and thus can choose adult criminal court when he or she deems it appropriate.[58] This type of transfer is often called "direct file" because rather than having the case originate in juvenile court and then move to adult court, the case begins in adult court.[59] The main critique of prosecutorial waiver is that generally there is no verifiable reason for a prosecutor's decision and it may be grounded in considerations that should have no bearing on the case, such as race or public opinion. It also may not take into account the ability of the juvenile justice system to respond effectively to the offender. Unlike with judicial discretion, no hearing is held or written justification for the decision is issued.[60] The decision also is beyond review by the appellate courts.

Juveniles are transferred to adult court in order to punish them more severely,[61] the theory being that punishment rather than rehabilitation is the correct response to chronic delinquent acts. Ironically, for some offenses, such as certain property offenses, the transferred juvenile receives a shorter sentence in adult court than he would have received in juvenile court.[62]

Not only have states legislated punitive systemic changes—recent proposals at the federal level reflect a similar approach to youthful offenders. Such proposals would transfer to the federal courts jurisdiction over a lengthy list of offenses that previously were the exclusive jurisdiction of the states;[63] decrease confidentiality of juvenile records; increase to forty-eight hours (from twenty-four hours) the amount of time a juvenile could be held in adult detention facilities until his initial court appearance; increase use of mandatory sentencing and exercise of nonreviewable prosecutorial discretion in the waiver of juveniles into adult court; and impose longer sentences for crimes committed with firearms. Some of these measures would be achieved through federal funding paid to the states for the operation of treatment programs and the development of information handling systems.

Juvenile court statutes often contain a "purposes clause"—a preamble of sorts—that describes the goals of the juvenile court system. Many states' purposes clauses describe a punitive rather than rehabilitative focus, [64] and the method of determining sentences reflects that focus. "Indeterminate" sentencing allows a juvenile court judge to choose from among a range of sentence lengths in order to provide for the possibility of rehabilitation during incarceration of a juvenile offender. However, nearly half of the states use "determinate" sentencing, which does not allow for consideration of the individual's rehabilitation.[65]

States are also reexamining the confidentiality of juvenile court records and proceedings.[66] Many states now authorize more open court proceedings and require records of juvenile offenders to be open to the public. As of 1996, forty states had enacted legislation permitting release of the names of juvenile offenders to the media and the public, particularly if the offense involved is of a violent nature.[67] The avowed justification for this change is that protecting the confidentiality of a juvenile is inconsistent with prosecuting criminal acts such as murder or rape. If records are kept confidential, the juvenile may escape more serious punishment for a later crime. As a result, confidentiality is no longer the policy in most juvenile courts.[68] Instead, many state criminal courts and the United States Sentencing Guidelines allow prior juvenile convictions to be used to increase later sentences.[69] One significant concern that arises in allowing the use of juvenile records in determining later sentences is that juveniles receive lesser procedural protections in juvenile court. Not only are juvenile records accorded less confidentiality, but juvenile court proceedings are more likely to be open to the public—nearly half of all states allow public access when the accused youth has been charged with a repeat, violent, or serious offense.[70] Because this alteration in the operation of the courts is so new, no data have yet been compiled to determine whether the underlying premise of the argument is valid—whether, in fact, the loss of confidentiality has positively affected the behavior of juvenile offenders.

Sentencing and Punishment of Young Offenders in Adult Court

Juveniles transferred to adult courts are treated the same as adult criminals; for example, juveniles are accorded the full array of due process rights, including the right to trial by jury.[71] Increasingly, however, adult courts are confronting the question of how to manage criminal cases involving juveniles, for whom, traditionally, they have not had adjudicative responsibility. There is debate among policymakers over how to incarcerate such youthful offenders alongside their adult counterparts and how to handle pretrial detention.[72] Criminal justice institutions that restricted their facilities to adults now must arrange punishment, treatment, and rehabilitative measures for a younger population. Juveniles convicted in adult courts often are incarcerated with adults, although at least one state court system, Maryland's, attempts to separate juvenile from adult offenders.[73]

In response, states have tended to depend on such innovations as boot camps or special community-based programs targeting certain violent acts. For example, a dozen years ago Florida created the Florida Environmental Institute for violent and chronic juvenile offenders.[74] This intense treatment program was available to courts as an alternative to sentencing a juvenile to prison or long-term confinement within a juvenile facility and represented the "last chance" for the offender to avoid incarceration in an adult facility. The effectiveness of the program is evident from a recidivism rate that hovers in the low 20 percent range.[75]

Many courts simply transfer juveniles to adult criminal courts and use the same method of sentencing. Judges often are given the discretion to use youthfulness as a mitigating factor in sentencing. Whether they do or not, their discretion is granted great deference on review, with appellate courts upholding life sentences for juveniles in certain situations.[76] Some courts are experimenting with determining sentences after a juvenile is transferred to adult court. For example, in Florida, one prosecutor has worked to place juveniles convicted in adult court in local prisons that offer more educational and treatment-oriented programs rather than in state penitentiaries.[77] Mirroring the Florida example, the Indiana state legislature is considering a bill that would require separation of youthful and adult offenders in prison.[78]

Another popular method of dealing with juvenile offenders in adult court is "blended sentencing," in which both juvenile and adult sentencing procedures are used. Currently, sixteen states use some form of blended sentencing. For example, in Missouri, a juvenile is tried in adult court, but the judge can impose simultaneous adult and juvenile sentences; if the juvenile successfully completes the juvenile sentence, the adult sentence is "suspended".[79] This program is similar to one instituted in Connecticut. Minnesota also uses blended sentences but gives the judge more discretion than do Missouri and Connecticut. The adult sentence is suspended while the juvenile completes the juvenile sentence, and the judge can review the juvenile's progress to determine whether the juvenile's sentence should be reduced.[80] Texas has implemented a third method of dealing with sentencing juveniles in adult court. Using determinate sentencing, judges can send juvenile offenders to a juvenile facility until they are eighteen years old and thereafter send them to adult prison, keep them in juvenile facilities until they are twenty-one, or release them.[81]

The transfer mechanism allows for the possibility that a juvenile offender will be sentenced to death. Obviously, that raises profound concerns about criminal responsibility and fairness. Nonetheless, the United States Supreme Court has upheld capital punishment for youthful offenders,[82] and 60 percent of the public also supports the death penalty for juveniles convicted of murder.[83]

It is unclear whether the trend toward transferring juveniles to adult court and the use of adult sentencing actually helps reduce the crime rate among juveniles. A study by the National Center for Initiatives and Alternatives compared the juvenile crime rates of two states, Colorado and Connecticut. Although Connecticut transferred juveniles at a higher rate than Colorado, their juvenile crime rates were the same.[84] A study of juveniles incarcerated in adult prisons in Nevada and Florida found that juveniles "committed new crimes upon release more often than similar juvenile offenders who went through juvenile programs."[85] Indeed, some studies suggest that juveniles convicted in adult courts are 30 percent more likely to commit repeat offenses than juveniles convicted in juvenile court of the same crimes.[86]

The question also remains of whether transferring juveniles to adult court actually results in tougher treatment, its ostensible goal. A preliminary report by Maryland's department of juvenile justice suggests that juveniles are treated more leniently in adult courts because they often are considered first-time offenders.[87] As defense attorneys indicate, often it is better to keep a case in the juvenile court system in order to avoid creating a permanent criminal record and to limit sentencing to the time when the juvenile reaches age twenty-one.

New Directions in Managing Youth Violence

Courts addressing the problem of youth violence face an increasing workload, not only in the sheer number of cases, but also in their complexity. The situation may initially appear intractable, but many juvenile and adult criminal courts have begun to experiment with alternative processes in order to combat their burgeoning dockets. A survey of some resulting initiatives suggests that court processes are indeed amenable to innovation. We take note of several: restorative community-based justice programs; alternative dispute resolution; unified family courts; coordinated courts; youth parts; post-adjudication supervision; specialized courts, such as weapons or drug courts; and new information-tracking systems.

Restorative Community-Based Justice

Some policymakers and commentators have recently espoused a new concept of justice to replace the traditional concept of retributive, offender-based justice: restorative, community-based justice. Restorative justice considers the needs and interests of the three groups most affected by youth violence—crime victims, youthful offenders, and the community.[88] Among the general features of restorative justice programs are the following:

—Restitution to crime victims and opportunities for youthful offenders to earn money to repay victims with the court's supervision and support.

—Community service projects that benefit areas affected most by youth violence. Projects could be chosen by victims or victims' families.

—Victim awareness programs and victim impact statements that help the offender to understand the negative impact that his or her actions have had on others, as well as their impact on the community as a whole.[89]

These examples are only a few of the changes that could be instituted in a top-down, comprehensive approach to restorative justice. As one commentator has noted, such changes cannot be effected in a piecemeal fashion; there must be an overarching change of focus and theory to back them up.[90] The new initiatives described below frequently embody such restorative justice ideals. They include not only the courts but community groups and other citizens in their quest to ameliorate the problem of youth violence. One final introductory comment on these new programs: many have not been systematically studied for effectiveness. However, at least one meta-analysis of rehabilitative programs suggests that they do have a positive effect on recidivism.[91]

Alternative Dispute Resolution

One of the most common changes that juvenile court systems have instituted is one that many civil courts encourage as well: alternative dispute resolution (ADR).[92] Court systems have begun to rely on ADR for several reasons, according to Judge Leonard P. Edwards of the superior court of Santa Clara County, California. First, states do not have enough resources to handle the large increase in juvenile cases. Second, ADR may be preferable to formal adjudication because it allows for more creative problem solving. Third, because ADR encourages juveniles and their families to develop creative solutions, the process is "empowering" and may result in juveniles being more likely to honor agreements. Finally, ADR has very practical benefits because ADR takes less time and resources to "adjudicate" a juvenile than does the formal court system.[93] It should be noted that ADR is used most commonly for juveniles who have committed minor crimes; while ADR is not designed to adjudicate serious, violent offenders, it is hoped that, in part, it will prevent minor offenders from descending into violent, serious criminality.

There are three general types of alternative dispute resolution that juvenile courts increasingly use. Some courts use mediation. In mediation, the result is nonbinding and must be acceptable to all of the involved parties.

This method is used most often in child abuse or neglect cases rather than in delinquency cases, because it often involves bringing together family members themselves to determine the cause of problems.[94] Generally, mediation proceedings are kept confidential from the court system, thereby allowing the parties to discuss their options and possible solutions freely.

A second method of alternative dispute resolution is the family group conference. In Oregon, for example, the entire family—including extended family members—meet to discuss problems and possible solutions.[95] Like mediation, the family group conference is used most often in child abuse and neglect cases rather than delinquency cases. However, there is no reason that courts could not institute conferences to delve into the reasons behind a juvenile's behavior to determine whether neglect or abuse is a contributing factor. Courts and social agencies can thereby adopt a preventive posture to deal effectively with problems before they erupt in violence.

Another method of alternative dispute resolution is the peer court. In peer courts, which have been instituted in twenty-five states,[96] youths are trained to act as juries for juveniles accused of offenses. An example is in Monongalia County, South Carolina,[97] one of three counties chosen by the South Carolina state legislature to institute an experimental peer court program. Although a judge is always present in the courtroom, trained youths take part in the entire trial, acting as prosecutors, defense attorneys, court officials, and jurors. The peer court has very limited jurisdiction; it can hear only cases involving status offenses or first- or second-offense delinquency misdemeanors. In addition, in keeping with the due process revolution in juvenile justice, offenders must choose to take part in the program. As in some other peer courts, the Monongalia County peer court jury also recommends sentences—often community service—although the jury does not actually sentence the offender. One of the forces behind the South Carolina program is a local circuit court judge, Russell Clawges Jr., who suggests that the program helps the offenders realize that they are accountable for their actions as well as increases the confidence in the legal system of the youths who take part as court officials. The use of peer courts has been recommended by the American Bar Association, and some courts have reported successful results.[98]

Unified Family Courts

Judge Edwards has suggested that the most important change in juvenile courts has not been the institution of ADR, but the creation of unified family courts.[99] These tribunals allow for a more coordinated approach to juvenile justice by eliminating some jurisdictional barriers between courts and the practice of separating cases on the basis of the offense. These courts, which approach behavior as a dynamic of the family, allow for integrated jurisdiction over all family-related issues, including divorce, child custody, child support, paternity, domestic violence, adoption, and so forth. Rather than focus on a single malefactor, they foster a comprehensive regimen. Some states, such as New Jersey and Rhode Island, and the District of Columbia already have instituted this type of court.

Although Judge Edwards clearly believes that unified family courts allow for a holistic approach to family problems that may benefit juvenile offenders, he notes that such programs face high start-up costs because they involve changing jurisdictional procedures, moving files and information among courts, general recalcitrance regarding implementation, and the reluctance of judges to assume long-term assignment to a court of limited jurisdiction.

Coordinated Courts

Because of the problems in instituting unified family courts, some jurisdictions have tried to create coordinated courts,[100] which have many of the same features as unified family courts but attempt to eliminate some of their start-up costs and attendant problems. Establishing a family division within a court of general jurisdiction represents the coordinated court approach. Coordinated courts concentrate services and resources for families in a single location and set up regular meetings between the court and social agency personnel who deal with families in other areas of the court system. By allowing for information sharing, coordinated courts can hear together various cases dealing with one family. Computerized case-management systems permit judges to follow all court proceedings that affect the family. To protect the juvenile involved, coordinated courts have a representative who acts as his or her advocate.

Youth Parts

Some court systems have responded to increased youth violence and juvenile delinquency caseloads by creating within the adult court system a subsystem of juvenile courts that handle specific types of cases. An example is New York City's "Youth Part," which has its own intake and screening process.[101] The judge considers a report that describes the juvenile's background and relations with the community as well as his or her own evaluation of the case in deciding whether the juvenile should proceed to trial in adult criminal court or be placed under the supervision of a community-based program. Michael Corriero is the presiding judge for the Youth Part; either he or his law clerks personally check on the juveniles that he has recommended for community supervision. An important feature of the program is that juveniles who successfully complete the program have their records sealed, thereby allowing them to look for employment later without the stigma of a juvenile delinquency or criminal record.

Post-Adjudication Supervision

Court systems also are making an effort to ensure that juvenile offenders do not reappear in their courtrooms by working with them after the adjudicatory process has formally ended. One such program is Project LIFE (Lasting Intense Firearms Education) in Indianapolis,[102] which is supported by the juvenile court system. The program works only with juveniles who already have been found delinquent for weapons violations and placed on probation; attendance is mandated by the court. Like some of the ADR methods discussed above, Project LIFE involves the juvenile's family. Sessions are held in which juveniles and their parents discuss the situations that led to the juvenile's involvement with and arrest for possession of a weapon.[103] Because the program begins only after adjudication is finished, the juveniles are freer to talk about their situation.

One reason for the increased focus on working with juveniles after adjudication is that many observers believe that a minority of juvenile offenders commit a majority of crimes.[104] In other words, repeat offenders are responsible for much of the juvenile crime in the nation. At least one juvenile court, in Cleveland, Ohio, has implemented a pilot program called Multi-Systemic Therapy to reach repeat offenders and to prevent first offenders from becoming repeat offenders.[105] The program involves not only the courts but other community actors as well. Approximately 100 juveniles are involved over a three- to four-month period, during which caseworkers visit the juveniles daily at school or home to ensure that they are staying out of trouble. The program seeks to identify at-risk juveniles and prevent them from becoming adult offenders through alcohol and violence counseling. One impetus for Cleveland's program is clearly financial: boot camp costs $25,000 per year per child, a state correctional institution costs $35,000, and Multi-Systemic Therapy costs approximately $5,000. Not only is the program less expensive than many alternatives, it also has been shown to be effective. A national study indicates that participating juveniles commit about half as many new crimes as juveniles participating in other programs.[106]

One critique of the court system's role in the juvenile justice system is that it acts as an independent force rather than as a member of a broad community of juvenile justice service providers. Some jurisdictions, however, are establishing programs to address that deficiency. COMPASS (Community Providers of Adolescent Services), whose purpose is to "bring together families, schools, courts, child welfare agencies, and community organizations to form lasting support services for . . . these kids,"[107] is one such program.[108] In COMPASS, "trackers" keep up with juveniles who have been adjudicated by the courts and committed to the Massachusetts department of youth services until they reach eighteen years of age. Involvement in COMPASS, which closely monitors all aspects of a youth's community activities through an intensive intervention strategy that couples aggressive frequent contact with counseling, may in some instances replace court-imposed detention. Each tracker supervises approximately seven juveniles and keeps up with each on a near-daily basis. By using the courts to locate and focus on the offenders, COMPASS involves the juvenile court system in a broader solution to youth violence.

Specialized Courts

Some post-adjudication programs, such as Project LIFE described above, focus on juvenile offenders who have been convicted of weapons violations. However, special court programs also have been developed to deal with adjudicating these offenders. One example is the New York City juvenile weapons court.

Why do courts need to focus on weapons violations by juveniles? The statistics are startling. From 1985 to 1995, the number of homicide offenders between the ages of fourteen and seventeen more than doubled, and that increase was largely due to weapon use. The victims of the crimes also were young. In 1994, for example, 57 percent of victims were under twenty-five years of age.[109] The Vera Institute states that between "1985 and 1995, the murder rate among kids ages 12 to 17 more than doubled . . . since 1988, more than 80 percent of murder victims aged 15 to 19 were killed with a firearm, and in 1994, the number reached 90 percent."[110] Those statistics point to the need for specialized courts to respond to juvenile gun violence.

An example of an adult criminal court that takes the initiative in adjudicating weapons offenses and then providing specialized treatment to young offenders is the court of Judge Willie Lipscomb in Detroit. Lipscomb developed a handgun intervention program to address the growing problem of youth violence, although participating juveniles are considered adult offenders.[111] He uses his courtroom as a forum to encourage juvenile offenders convicted as adults to avoid the dangerous pitfalls of weapons violations and to disabuse them of the idea that guns will protect them on the street. Lipscomb brings in former offenders, who talk about their violent pasts and describe deadly outcomes of encounters involving weapons, to drive the point home to recent offenders. The program is brief, only a few hours on Saturday mornings, but some preliminary research by the Urban Institute indicates that the program has had some effect on changing the juveniles' attitudes toward guns.[112]

One of the key aspects of Lipscomb's program is that he employs it not only to emphasize the danger of weapons but to connect offenders to community services that can help them later. He admits that the court system cannot keep up with every offender or serve as a resource in every case, but he hopes that by inviting various community groups to speak to current and past offenders he will introduce recent offenders to community resources.[113] That way, should offenders feel tempted to use weapons again, they may remember a community group that can help them find alternative approaches to their problems. In one commentator's words, this type of program "connect[s] kids with adults who can support them informally over time."[114]

Mirroring the recent focus on weapons violations among juveniles, at least one jurisdiction has suggested creating a system to deal with juvenile drug offenses. In Fort Worth, Texas, officials have received a state grant to institute a juvenile drug court.[115] It is to be modeled on one already in Pensacola, Florida, that has been viewed as a success. In Pensacola, the drug court refers juvenile abusers to a drug treatment program and the juveniles must also report to the court once a week. The program generally lasts one year, but if the juvenile shows improvement, supervision becomes less intense and the juvenile may be released early from the program. The drug court in Pensacola also involves the juvenile's family in the program and may order drug treatment for the family if warranted.

The abuse of licit and illicit substances has wreaked havoc in the lives of American families. Whether a member of the family abuses alcohol or narcotics, the result often is the same—the creation of a chaotic environment for children. Recognizing that, in 1988 the Baltimore City juvenile court developed a special agency within the court with a single mission: to seek a solution to the increasing problem of substance abuse in the lives of the juveniles and parents who come to court.[116]

In February 1989, the juvenile court early intervention project (JCEIP), a collaborative effort of state and city, was implemented to identify cases in which drug-abusing parents are unable to exercise responsibility for their children and to treat the whole family for substance abuse. The program operates without regard to the reason for the family's appearance in court. In the following nine years, JCEIP screened 10,300 cases and placed 8,000 individuals in treatment. A broad spectrum of legal professionals—including prosecution and defense attorneys in delinquency proceedings and social services agencies and children's attorneys in dependency matters—can refer juveniles to the program. The treatment options range from intensive outpatient counseling and short-term detoxification to referral to long-term residential facilities. Often JCEIP will use the court's on-site drug-testing facility at the initial interview to respond to participants' denials of substance abuse. If treatment is not readily accepted by the parent, the guardian, the parent's significant other, or the child, an order for treatment is issued.

Treatment as an alternative to court has resulted in remarkable success for some participants. For example, an eighteen-year-old juvenile, a chronic glue sniffer, was ordered into treatment after his fifth arrest. Six months after he completed his one-year program, he completed basic training in the U.S. Air Force and reported to court in his new uniform. Another young man of seventeen was arrested for the second time in weeks for the felony offense of narcotics distribution. After referral to JCEIP, it was determined that his family had other problems. Although the juvenile was capable of succeeding in school, he was failing because of frequent bouts of despondency brought on by his family situation, and he was becoming enmeshed in the world of narcotics and its attendant violence. His family was headed by his mother and included his twenty-five-year-old alcoholic brother. The court and JCEIP used the unique Maryland statute to order the family into treatment. The older brother, who at times abused his mother and the juvenile, was referred to the Veterans Administration for substance abuse treatment and assistance in obtaining independent housing for himself. The mother was referred to counseling to learn how to deal more effectively with the family's problems, and the juvenile defendant also was referred for counseling. In the end, the family recovered. The defendant graduated from high school and found employment; the mother learned to handle the problems that had overwhelmed her; and the alcoholic brother recovered to the extent that he was able to find a job and live independently.

Early and meaningful intervention were the keys to successfully diverting these offenders from spiraling down into further criminal behavior. Despite such successful outcomes, the cases before the court are worsening—JCEIP is now confronted with cases such as the tragedy of a seven-year-old drug addict.

Information Systems

Some court systems, such as that in Baltimore, discussed below, have responded to increases in youth violence by trying to compile as much information as possible about juvenile offenders and their behavioral patterns. An example of this type of initiative is found in Cleveland, Ohio.[117] The Cleveland juvenile court sought to centralize the management of juvenile offender files as well as develop a system to create a schedule that will "contain vital information about each child which will be posted and updated everyday."[118]

Although changing a juvenile offender filing system may seem minor, the massive increase in juvenile offenses has left many court systems overwhelmed and unable to deal effectively with the cases before them. By streamlining and updating offender information, court systems can spend their time addressing the serious problems that are before them in the courtroom rather than dealing with administrative duties.

Managing a Juvenile Court: Baltimore

One factor that undermines the juvenile court's ability to respond effectively to youthful violence is lack of resources.[119] That lack extends across the spectrum of court activities, starting with the personnel available to the court and ending with the programs the court uses to make dispositions that are in the best interests of the juvenile and the public. The system that I administered in Baltimore for more than a decade illustrates the problem and the limitations it imposes.

Baltimore is the largest urban center in Maryland; the work of its juvenile court represents nearly one-quarter of the total juvenile cases adjudicated in the state.[120] The operations of the court have remained essentially unchanged since they were modernized after World War II. A youth arrested for an offense that did not result in immediate detention was released to a parent who was advised that the state youth services agency would contact the family and juvenile in an attempt to resolve the case informally.[121] That could not occur until city police produced the paperwork related to the arrest and forwarded it to the state agency. However, as police commanders confronted staffing shortages occasioned by budgetary shortfalls, the police youth officers who were responsible for handling the information were gradually removed from that assignment and placed in more direct police work. Youth officers were considered a low priority. Gradually, the time required to transmit information from the police to the youth services agency increased from days to months and in some instances exceeded a year. When the state agency finally received a case from the police department, information regarding the address of the youthful offender often was invalid because the family had moved. Eventually, the case was referred to the court for adjudication, but the memories of victims, witnesses, and the charged juvenile had faded. The offender received the incorrect message that society cared little about his or her misdeeds. One crime led to another, and soon the juvenile reached the classification of chronic offender before the juvenile justice system responded. Essentially, the systems stopped communicating with each other as they became mired in their own issues. Youngsters who could be rehabilitated faced restrictive alternatives because of delays in addressing their problems.

The court itself faced its own evolving crisis in information handling. When there was a court event pertaining to one case, a clerk had to make an identical data entry in seven different places. The court had nine judicial officers, but in order to schedule a future court date, each judge was required to telephone one assignment clerk who was equipped with one telephone line. Each court event produced critical information that instructed social agencies on how to handle a child; yet that information did not reach the agencies for hours, even though the court and the agencies were housed in the same building.

Although the problems were recognized by many observers, there was no concerted effort to resolve them until the court collaborated with the Maryland Bar Association in 1992 to mobilize public, media, and political support to create a better court management system, even though resources were limited. The court had to be able to respond aggressively to children at the moment of need, not later. Our solution was to establish a central location for processing of all children who were taken into police custody. In that location were concentrated police and state agency personnel who could see a child and family immediately. A triage system was established to sort cases according to the needs of the child: those that required immediate court referral were handled first, and less serious cases were resolved with immediate appointments for crisis intervention. That simple solution resulted in the reduction in 1996 of the interval between a delinquent act and court intervention from nearly a year to 45 days or less when court involvement was necessary.[122]

The other major management innovation by Baltimore courts was the implementation of a new computer and information system that provided immediate access to court dockets to parties such as police and social agencies even when the court no longer was in session. Where one clerk had been required to replicate work seven or more times, the new system substituted a single computer keystroke. Thus, scheduling of cases, docket management, production of dispositional orders, and the dissemination of vital information regarding the offender became instantaneous. The information gap was closed. Also eliminated was the waste of staff time.

These measures, along with the concerted efforts of law enforcement agencies and policy changes at the executive level of government, contributed to significant reductions in violent juvenile crime. The systems innovations in the Baltimore City juvenile court took effect in 1995. By 1997, arrests of juveniles in Baltimore decreased by nearly 10 percent and juvenile arrests for violent crime decreased by 19 percent.[123]

A Call for Judicial Leadership

To a great extent, juvenile courts are the "stepchildren" in the U.S. system of justice, a training ground where new lawyers and judges are expected to hone the skills that will make them valuable in other pursuits. Perhaps the reasoning is that because only children are involved, no one can get hurt. That attitude also is evident when resources are allocated within the system of justice. Little remains after adult corrections has received its share, and juvenile courts are left with resources that are inadequate for fashioning a rehabilitation program for troubled youngsters that might ameliorate the conditions that produce them. Similarly, inadequate resources are made available to social services agencies charged with the task of protecting children from abusive parents. It should be no surprise that unprotected children become violent youthful offenders.

Countless studies have documented that prevention and education are the most reliable and effective measures for deterring juvenile violence. During my entire eleven-year service with the court I never had occasion to deal with a child who was a senior in high school. Not once in that period did I encounter a religious leader who appeared on behalf of a juvenile delinquent who knew the juvenile through the juvenile's association with a house of worship. Children must learn first in the home that they have a responsibility to themselves and to those around them and that work precedes reward. The institutions of society are then prepared to support the family's teachings, reinforcing through school, church, and other social activities the sense of moral values instilled in the children. In my experience, children who are involved in church, school, or scouting are less prone to participate in acts that came to the attention of the juvenile and criminal courts. Good families supported by strong social institutions work, period.

When there is a breakdown in instruction within the home or when social institutions fail to support the family effectively, court involvement typically follows. The juvenile court today is far too often expected to habilitate youngsters rather than rehabilitate them. Rehabilitation presupposes the presence of a set of core values and that only a course correction is required to return the offending child to a productive path in society. At this point in history, many children unfortunately acquire deficits that leave them bereft of a sense that they are a part of society. Consequently, they become self-centered and lack empathy with other individuals; they view their behavior only in terms of its impact on themselves and are unaffected by its impact on their victims. Many juvenile justice systems now believe that replacing this fundamental lack of social conscience is at the core of the emerging concept of restorative justice. As Mark Umbreit argues, "[i]n the restorative justice paradigm, the meaning of accountability shifts the focus from incurring a debt to society to that of incurring a responsibility for making amends to the victimized person."[124]

While any discussion of the needs of the juvenile court must focus on additional resources, concentrating on that issue alone misses the point. What courts need most is a vocal, informed leadership prepared to educate the public and policymakers about the demands of the court and its constituency. Judges are the natural spokespersons for any effort to help communities understand what is necessary to reduce violence among children. The courts and juvenile agencies cannot afford to simply augment their resources or respond defensively to proposals that undermine their programs. If they fail to assume the role of advocate for the juvenile justice system, they will create a void, and into that void will step others who will make decisions on the basis of the "crime of the moment" or other information that bears little resemblance to the reality of violent crime among children.

The leadership of both the criminal and juvenile judiciary is critical to forging consensus among the disparate points of view within communities. Judges naturally must adhere to the tenants of the Canons of Judicial Ethics regarding lobbying legislatures, engaging in political activities, and presenting opinions that would cause their disqualification from a case or the court. Nonetheless, there is ample space within the rigid confines of judicial ethics for a judge to engage the community in a constructive search for solutions to the ills of society. Judges simply must dispel the notion that disabling constraints exist to participating with other professionals, including political leaders, in improving the system of justice and developing meaningful alternatives to failed policies of the past. The public awaits the unique perspectives of members of the judiciary, and it is critical that all enter the fray if public confidence in the vitality of this institution is to be restored. Judges are uniquely positioned to inform policymakers of the connection that exists among children who are exposed to harmful environmental forces, dysfunctional families, violence, poor educational opportunities, and the paucity of community-level treatment alternatives. Society's problems have a way of finding their way into the nation's courts. Our silence in the face of such provocation is deafening. A judge's role is to speak.

Postscript

I chose to follow my own advice to speak on behalf of children and the courts. After eleven years of service on the Baltimore juvenile court and in the administration of the juvenile court docket, I returned to the criminal and civil courts. In 1999, I came back to judicial administration to address a criminal court system so beset with a backlog of court cases that it was, in effect, denying offenders their right to a speedy trial—a consequence of the lack of leadership of judges and the failure of community leaders to confront longstanding deficits in the justice system. Before my departure, we experienced several major reforms. Defendants in criminal cases received swift trials, and we significantly reduced trial delays. Public confidence that judges would try cases in a timely manner returned.

A short while later I accepted the position of executive director of the National Council of Juvenile and Family Court Judges, the nation's oldest and largest voluntary association of judges. The mission of the National

Council is to promote and help provide for the training of judges, resource development, and procedural reform in the country's juvenile and family courts. My decision to leave the Baltimore court was difficult, but accepting a position in an organization that speaks with a national voice for leadership and reform in the juvenile justice system presented a tremendous opportunity.

Children require the sense of stability that a good family provides to become productive in society. The National Council predicates its work on the belief that having the community gather around and lend its support to a child and family early in a crisis is one of the most effective ways of preventing an angry, disaffected young person from venting that anger through violence. Through public and private funding, the National Council leads the struggle to reform court processes in areas such as family violence and assaults on women, research in juvenile justice, improvements in permanency planning for children who are in foster care, technical assistance for courts in systems and process analysis, and judicial training. The National Council is the primary source of statistical analysis on juvenile justice for the nation, analyzing all aspects of juvenile justice to supply policymakers with the facts from national, state, and local sources that they need to make sound decisions.

In addition, it has developed "model" courts to demonstrate the benefits of adopting changes in the ways that courts traditionally fulfill their mission. Interdisciplinary teams of community professionals such as judges, child welfare officials, police, educators, religious leaders, attorneys, and child advocates come together in the model courts to improve the practices of the social welfare agencies in their community and thereby improve decisionmaking and outcomes for children and families. The exciting work of the National Council, which strives to implement model court practices in courts as diverse as those of New York City and the Zuni Pueblo Tribal Court of New Mexico, has received the endorsement of the American Bar Association and the Conference of Chief Justices of the United States.

Significant challenges remain. The system of supervision for delinquent youth who return home after incarceration in training schools is an abysmal failure. Our communities must provide a more cohesive network of resources and services. The judicial leadership has a mandate to foster innovative concepts to support a community's efforts to reintegrate youthful offenders and help them pursue a productive life as net contributors to society rather than takers. The nation's judges also must address the question of why the juvenile and child welfare system treats children of color differently from others. We must confront as well the disgrace of the disproportional treatment of children of color in other aspects of the juvenile justice system.

The responsibility of a judge is to advocate for improvements in the law as well as to adjudicate a particular case. Most of my colleagues in the juvenile and family courts of America understand that and are comfortable with that role. I am proud to represent them.

Notes

1. Charles Puzzanchera and others, *Juvenile Court Statistics 1997* (U.S. Department of Justice, Office of Juvenile Justice and Delinquency Prevention, 2000), pp. 64–67.

2. Clifford E. Simonsen, *Juvenile Justice in America* (MacMillan, 1998), p. 225.

3. Simonsen, *Juvenile Justice*, p. 225.

4. H. Ted Rubin, "The Nature of the Court Today," *Future of Children*, vol. 6, no. 3 (Winter 1996), pp. 44–45.

5. Carol S. Stevenson and others, "The Juvenile Court: Analysis and Recommendations," *Future of Children*, vol. 6, no. 3 (Winter 1996), pp. 236–37.

6. Bureau of Justice Statistics, *Privacy and Juvenile Justice Records: A Mid-Decade Status Report*, NCJ 161255 (U.S. Department of Justice, May 1997), p. 4.

7. U.S. Department of Justice, *Combating Violence and Delinquency: The National Juvenile Justice Plan: Summary* (March 1996).

8. Barry C. Feld, "Juvenile and Criminal Justice Systems' Responses to Youth Violence," in Michael Tonry and Mark H. Moore, eds., *Youth Violence* (University of Chicago Press, 1998), p. 194.

9. William Glaberson, "Shootings in a Schoolhouse: The Justice System; Rising Tide of Anger at Teen-Aged Killers," *New York Times*, May 24, 1998, p. A1.

10. Puzzanchera and others, *Juvenile Court Statistics 1997*, p. 5.

11. Howard N. Snyder, "The Juvenile Court and Delinquency Cases," *Future of Children*, vol. 6, no. 3 (Winter 1996), p. 54.

12. Puzzanchera and others, *Juvenile Court Statistics 1997*, pp. 5, 6.

13. Ibid., p. 6.

14. Mark H. Moore and Michael Tonry, "Youth Violence in America," in Tonry and Moore, eds., *Youth Violence*, p. 7.

15. Michael Dresser, "Violent Crime by Juveniles Decreases by 7%; First Drop in 9 Years," *Baltimore Sun*, September 28, 1998.

16. Howard Snyder and Melissa Sickmund, *Juvenile Offenders and Victims: 1999 National Report* (U.S. Department of Justice, Office of Juvenile Justice and Delinquency Prevention, 1999), p. 192; Howard N. Snyder, "Juvenile Arrests 1999," *Juvenile Justice Bulletin* (U.S. Department of Justice, Office of Juvenile Justice and Delinquency Prevention, December 2000), p. 4.

17. Snyder and Sickmund, *Juvenile Offenders and Victims*, p. 197.

18. Thomas P. Bonczar and Allen J. Beck, *Lifetime Likelihood of Going to State or Fed-*

eral Prison, Bureau of Justice Statistics special report NCJ-160092 (U.S. Department of Justice, March 1997), p. 1.

19. Fatima L. Hall, "Black Boys Bear the Brunt of Youth Transfers to Adult Court," *Miami Times*, August 10, 1995, p. 1A.

20. Jennifer M. O'Connor and Lucinda K. Treat, "Getting Smarter about Getting Tough: Juvenile Justice and the Possibility of Progressive Reform," *American Criminal Law Review*, vol. 33 (1996), p. 1302.

21. Stacey Sabo, "Rights of Passage: An Analysis of Waiver of Juvenile Court Jurisdiction," *Fordham Law Review*, vol. 33 (1996), p. 1302.

22. Simonsen, *Juvenile Justice*, pp. 18-19.

23. Ibid., p. 228.

24. Ibid., p. 22.

25. Ibid., p. 29.

26. Sabo, "Rights of Passage," p. 2430.

27. Simonsen, *Juvenile Justice*, pp. 30, 229.

28. Ibid., p. 228.

29. Sabo, "Rights of Passage," p. 2430.

30. Ibid., p. 2430.

31. Ibid.

32. Ibid.

33. Barry Feld, "The Transformation of the Juvenile Court," *Minnesota Law Review*, vol. 75 (1991), pp. 7122–25.

34. Stevenson and others, "The Juvenile Court: Analysis and Recommendations," pp. 5–6.

35. Simonsen, *Juvenile Justice*, p. 230; Julianne P. Sheffer, "Serious and Habitual Juvenile Offender Statutes: Reconciling Punishment and Rehabilitation within the Juvenile Justice System," *Vanderbilt Law Review*, vol. 48 (1995), pp. 481–82.

36. Simonsen, *Juvenile Justice*, pp. 230–31.

37. Linda F. Giardino, "Statutory Rhetoric: The Reality behind Juvenile Justice Policies in America," *Journal of Law and Policy*, vol. 5 (1996), p. 224.

38. Feld, "Juvenile and Criminal Justice Systems' Responses to Youth Violence," p. 244.

39. *McKeiver v. Pennsylvania*, 403 U.S. 528 (1971).

40. Sheffer, "Serious and Habitual Juvenile Offender Statutes," p. 485.

41. Giardino, "Statutory Rhetoric," p. 223.

42. 387 U.S. 1 (1967).

43. Ibid.

44. Barry Feld, "Abolish the Juvenile Court: Youthfulness, Criminal Responsibility, and Sentencing Policy," *Journal of Criminal Law and Criminology*, vol. 88 (1997), pp. 69, 73.

45. Carol J. DeFrances and Kevin J. Strom, "Juveniles Prosecuted in State Criminal Courts," *Bureau of Justice Statistics Selected Findings* (March 1997), pp. 1–2.

46. Feld, "Juvenile and Criminal Justice Systems' Responses to Youth Violence," p. 195.

47. Melissa Sickmund, "How Juveniles Get to Criminal Court," *OJJDP Update on Statistics*, no. 150309 (U.S. Department of Justice, Office of Juvenile Justice and Delinquency Prevention, October 1994).

48. Ibid., p. 2.

49. Feld, "The Transformation of the Juvenile Court," pp. 722–25.

50. Feld, "Juvenile and Criminal Justice Systems' Responses to Youth Violence," p. 196.

51. Ibid., pp. 198–99.

52. Puzzanchera and others, *Juvenile Court Statistics, 1997,* p. 13.

53. Catherine R. Guttman, "Listen to the Children: The Decision to Transfer Juveniles to Adult Court," *Harvard Civil Rights–Civil Liberties Law Review,* vol. 30 (1995), p. 522.

54. Sickmund, "How Juveniles Get to Criminal Court," pp. 1, 2, fig. 1.

55. Feld, "Juvenile and Criminal Justice Systems' Responses to Youth Violence," p. 201.

56. Guttman, "Listen to the Children", p. 521.

57. Sickmund, "How Juveniles Get to Criminal Court," p. 3.

58. Feld, "Juvenile and Criminal Justice Systems' Responses to Youth Violence," p. 197.

59. Guttman, "Listen to the Children," p. 521.

60. Sabo, "Rights of Passage," p. 2427.

61. Guttman, "Listen to the Children," p. 509.

62. Feld, "Abolish the Juvenile Court," pp. 80–81.

63. Sara Sun Beale, "Too Many and Yet Too Few: New Principles to Define the Proper Limits for Federal Criminal Jurisdiction," *Hastings Law Journal,* vol. 46 (April 1995).

64. Feld, "Juvenile and Criminal Justice Sytems' Responses to Youth Violence," p. 222.

65. Ibid., p. 224.

66. Gordon A. Martin, "Open the Doors: A Judicial Call to End Confidentiality in Delinquency Proceedings," *Criminal and Civil Confinement,* vol. 21, no. 2 (1995), p. 393.

67. Linda A. Szymanski, "Releasing Names of Juvenile Offenders to the Media/Public," *NCJJ Snapshot,* vol. 2, no. 6 (June 1997), p. 2.

68. Bureau of Justice Statistics, *Privacy and Juvenile Justice Records,* pp. 14–15.

69. Feld, "Juvenile and Criminal Justice Systems' Responses to Youth Violence," p. 214.

70. Ibid., p. 215.

71. *McKeiver* v. *Pennsylvania,* 403 U.S. 528 (1971).

72. Feld, "Juvenile and Criminal Justice Systems' Responses to Youth Violence," p. 212.

73. Philip P. Pan, "Tougher Youth Laws Examined; In MD, It's Unclear if Prison is Effective," *Washington Post,* March 29, 1998, p. B1.

74. Cindy Ruppert, "Last Chance Camp Turning Kids Away from Crime," *Tampa Tribune,* October 15, 1995, p. C3.

75. Kale M. Kritch, *Recidivism Study 1998* (Associated Marine Institutes).

76. Feld, "Juvenile and Criminal Justice Systems' Responses to Youth Violence," p. 217.

77. Ted Guest and Victoria Pope, "Crime Time Bomb," *U.S. News & World Report,* March 25, 1996, p. 32.

78. Suzanne McBride, "Bill Might Keep Juvenile Offenders out of Adult Prisons," *Indianapolis Star,* January 21, 1998, p. B6.

79. "Adult Time for Adult Crime: Blending Is a Better Way," *USA Today,* March 20, 1998, p. 14A.

80. Ibid.

81. Tracy Everbach, "More States Treating Youths Like Adults," *Dallas Morning News,* March 26, 1998, p. 24A.

82. *Stanford* v. *Kentucky,* 492 U.S. 361 (1989).

83. John Johnson Kerbs, "(Un)equal Justice: Juvenile Court Abolition and African

Americans," *Annals of the American Academy of Political and Social Science*, vol. 564 (July 1999), p. 114 (quoting a 1994 *USA Today*/CNN/Gallup poll).

84. Sally B. Donnelly, "Teen Crime: Congress Wants to Crack Down on Juvenile Offenders," *Time*, July 21, 1997, p. 26.

85. "Adult Time for Adult Crime," p. 14A.

86. Maria Puente, "The Law Getting Tougher on Children," *USA Today*, April 1, 1998, p. A3.

87. Pan, "Tougher Youth Laws Examined," p. B1.

88. Gordon Bazemore, "The Fork in the Road to Juvenile Court Reform," *Annals of the American Academy of Political and Social Science*, vol. 564 (July 1999), pp. 88–89.

89. Ibid., at p. 89.

90. Ibid., p. 90.

91. Mark W. Lipsey, "Can Intervention Rehabilitate Serious Delinquents?" *Annals of the American Academy of Political and Social Science*, vol. 564 (July 1999), p. 143.

92. Stevenson and others, "The Juvenile Court: Analysis and Recommendations," at 21–22.

93. Leonard Edwards, "The Future of the Juvenile Court: Promising New Directions," *Future of Children*, vol. 6, no. 3 (Winter 1996), p. 133.

94. Stevenson and others, "The Juvenile Court: Analysis and Recommendations," p. 2.

95. Ibid.

96. Barbara G. Johnson and Daniel Rosman, "Recent Developments in Nontraditional Alternatives in Juvenile Justice," *Loyola University of Chicago Law Journal*, vol. 28 (1997), pp. 719, 722.

97. Rusty Marks, "Court Puts Juveniles before a Jury of Peers," *Charleston Gazette*, April 24, 1998, p. B12.

98. Johnson and Rosman, "Recent Developments in Nontraditional Alternatives," p. 724.

99. Edwards, "The Future of the Juvenile Court," p. 132.

100. Ibid.

101. Jennifer Trone and Darlene Jorif, *Teaching Brain Power, Not Gun Power: Low-Intensity, Low-Cost Programs for Juvenile Weapons Offenders*, no. 1425 (New York: Vera Institute, 1998), p. 7.

102. Trone and Jorif, *Teaching Brain Power*, p. 7.

103. Ibid., p. 13.

104. Howard Snyder and others, *Juvenile Offenders and Victims: 1996 Update on Violence and Victimization* (U.S. Department of Justice, Office of Juvenile Justice and Delinquency Prevention, February 1996), p. 14.

105. Christopher Quinn, "Juvenile Court Tries New Tack to Reform Repeat Offenders," *Plain Dealer*, June 23, 1998, p. B1.

106. Quinn, "Juvenile Court Tries New Tack," p. B1.

107. Jennifer Trone, Molly Armstrong, and Mercer Sullivan, *Beyond Blame and Panic: Institutional Strategies for Preventing and Controlling Adolescent Violence* (New York: Vera Institute, 1998), p. 11.

108. Ibid.

109. Trone and Jorif, *Teaching Brain Power*, p. 4.

110. Ibid.

111. Trone, Armstrong, and Sullivan, *Beyond Blame*, p. 9.

112. Ibid.

113. Ibid.

114. Ibid.

115. Gabrielle Crist, "Tarrant Obtains Grant to Start Juvenile Drug Court," *Fort Worth Star-Telegram*, January 4, 1998, p. B1.

116. Wilson Everett, director, Juvenile Court Intervention Project of Circuit Court for Baltimore County, unpublished work, 1998 (analysis of project's results working with juvenile substance abusers).

117. Grace Waite Jones, "Juvenile Court Announces System-Wide Initiatives," *Call and Post*, March 5, 1998, p. A4.

118. Ibid., quoting court administrator.

119. The following sections are written from the point of view of chapter author David B. Mitchell.

120. Administrative Office of the Courts, *Annual Report of the Maryland Judiciary* 1996–1997, table CC-8, p. 47.

121. Bar Association of Baltimore City, *The Drug Crisis and Underfunding of the Justice System in Baltimore City* (January 1992), p. 6.

122. Section 3-810(p), Courts and Judicial Proceedings Article, Annotated Code of Maryland (replacement volume) effective October 1, 1995.

123. Uniform Crime Reporting Program, Central Records Division, Maryland State Police.

124. Mark S. Umbreit, "Holding Juvenile Offenders Accountable: A Restorative Justice Perspective," *Juvenile and Family Court Journal*, vol. 26 (Spring 1995), p. 31.

5

GERALD G. GAES

Managing the Juvenile
Offender Population
through Classification
and Programming

THE JUVENILE JUSTICE SYSTEM has been changing rapidly. In the period
1992–95, almost every state legislature enacted laws that affect juvenile
offenders—by, for example, increasing punishment for serious and violent
juvenile crimes, limiting the confidentiality of juvenile records, extending
the rights of juvenile victims, changing the nature of juvenile correctional
programs, and expanding the jurisdiction of criminal courts in cases
involving juveniles. These changes have not occurred in a vacuum. They
are a reaction to the rise in juvenile violence that occurred from the mid-
1980s to the mid-1990s, and they have affected the confinement of juveniles and the nature of correctional programs. Despite the fact that correctional confinement budgets have continued to increase, some researchers
have asserted that resources have been diverted from the juvenile to the
adult correctional system. As a result, they say, one of the primary management problems facing juvenile corrections nationwide in recent years is
the deterioration in services and conditions of confinement, which has in
turn sparked more aggressive juvenile advocacy. Other administrative and
management problems also have arisen from the increase in the population
of serious and violent juveniles (SVJs). As a working definition of serious

The views expressed in this chapter are solely the author's and are not intended to represent the policy of the Federal Bureau of Prisons or the U.S. Department of Justice.

violent juvenile offenses, this chapter adopts the categories Howard Snyder used in his analysis of delinquent cohorts in Maricopa County, Arizona.[1] Snyder defined violent offenses using the Federal Bureau of Investigation's (FBI's) violent index crimes: rape, robbery, aggravated assault, and homicide. Serious nonviolent offenses were defined as burglary, arson, drug trafficking, motor vehicle theft, larceny, and weapons charges. Other offenses such as simple assault, disorderly conduct, vandalism, and possession of a controlled substance were considered nonserious.

This chapter presents a broad overview of the impact that recent changes in the juvenile justice system have had on juvenile corrections as well as some of the problems correctional administrators face in managing the serious violent juvenile population. It then explores broad areas of research that can help in managing these offenders: classification/assessment systems and correctional programs. These areas are easy to link conceptually; however, it is also important to link them in practice. While recent evidence stresses the importance of continuity of programming from confinement to supervision, continuity in classifying and assessing juveniles from arrest (referral) until they are released from the jurisdiction of the juvenile court also is needed. The chapter concludes with a case study of a juvenile training facility.

Trends in Juvenile Crime and the Juvenile Justice System

While there may have been exaggerations of the extent to which youth violence increased from the mid-1980s to the mid-1990s, there is substantial evidence that the rate of violent crime among youth did rise. The Uniform Crime Reports (UCR) produced by the FBI are one source of data used by researchers to index the rise in juvenile violent crime, which they do by computing the ratio of arrests of juveniles (youth ages seventeen and under) relative to the number of juveniles in the population. The rates are computed per 100,000 youth. The data reported here, which were compiled by the National Center for Juvenile Justice, come from an Office of Juvenile Justice and Delinquency Prevention (OJJDP) publication.[2] In 1985, juveniles were arrested in 9.6 percent of all violent crimes; in 1994, they were arrested in 14.2 percent of all violent crimes.

The total violent crime index is composed of homicide, robbery, aggravated assault, and rape. Each of these separate crimes shows increased youth involvement, especially from mid-1980 to mid-1990. In 1975, the juvenile arrest rate for murder and nonnegligent manslaughter was less than six per 100,000 youth, and that rate was relatively constant from 1975 to 1986. From 1986 to 1991, however, the juvenile homicide arrest rate grew to almost thirteen per 100,000, more than a 100 percent increase, and it remained about the same through 1994. The juvenile arrest rate for rape rose from less than fifteen per 100,000 in 1975 to about twenty-three per 100,000 in 1991 and fell slightly to about twenty per 100,000 by 1994. Aggravated assault composes the largest share of arrests. The juvenile arrest rate for aggravated assault was about 135 per 100,000 in 1975 and remained relatively constant until about 1985. There was a relatively steady increase in the arrest rate after 1985, however, and by 1994 it had reached almost 300 per 100,000 juveniles. Robbery arrest rates for juveniles actually declined from 160 per 100,000 in 1975 to about 120 per 100,000 in 1988. However, since 1988, the rate has risen to more than 180 per 100,000 youths. A one-year update of this information indicated that violence rates for juveniles might have peaked in 1994. The 1995, 1996, and 1997 rates were lower.[3] This is confirmed by the age-specific homicide arrest rates discussed next.

The data just discussed were calculated by distinguishing youth, ages seventeen and below, from adults, ages eighteen and above. However, a more exact way of evaluating violent trends is to examine age-specific rates over time. Graphs plotting the incidence of different index crimes have different characteristic shapes.[4] The characteristic shape of the homicide age-specific curve underwent some interesting changes from 1940 through 1980 and especially in recent years. As reported by Harer, beginning in 1987 and extending through about 1994, not only did the homicide arrest rate increase for all age groups, the peak age began to shift toward the lower age categories.[5] In 1987, the peak age was twenty-three years; by the early 1990s, it was eighteen. In recent years, the peak age has begun to shift back to the higher age groups, and the overall homicide rate is beginning to decline again.

Cook and Laub completed a comprehensive analysis of violence trends among juveniles that demonstrated that the homicide rate in 1993 was almost four times the rate in 1980.[6] Although there was a slight decline in 1994 and 1995, the increase in juvenile homicides from 1983 to 1993 was unprecedented; Cook and Laub argue that such a dramatic increase cannot be explained by changes in demographic or socioeconomic factors. They label the increase an epidemic of youth violence, suggesting that the level of violence was itself a factor that had a kind of recruitment effect—violence begetting more violence. It is not surprising that there has been an institutional response to these trends. Determining whether the legislative response to this increase has been measured and proportional is beyond the scope of this chapter; nonetheless, legislative responses have changed the contours of juvenile corrections.

Butts and Harrell have described the structural and procedural changes in the traditional juvenile court system that have evolved in recent years.[7] The juvenile court system has become more formal and its procedures more similar to those of criminal courts. Juvenile court jurisdiction has been proscribed by legislation in many localities. Although a juvenile court judge can waive jurisdiction over a case, many states have adopted other transfer mechanisms. In some jurisdictions, "legislative exclusion" requires that youth be moved to criminal court on the basis of the charged offense or other criteria, such as prior record and age. In some jurisdictions, prosecutors are given the option of charging youth in either juvenile or criminal court. Butts and Harrell describe these collective movements in structure and procedure as "going in one direction—toward abolition of the juvenile court's delinquency jurisdiction and complete convergence of the juvenile and criminal justice systems."[8] In presenting options that would once again increase the flexibility of the system in handling juveniles, they describe a "blended" justice system that includes specialty courts such as drug, gun, teen, community, and felony courts. Depending on the seriousness of the charge and the offender's situation and prior record, the offender can be referred to the most appropriate court.

Trends in the Confinement of Juveniles

What effect has the increase in juvenile violent crime and the "hardening" of the juvenile justice system had on juvenile corrections? Data available in 1991 on juvenile admissions to private and public facilities indicated that in 1991, 683,636 youth were admitted to 1,076 public juvenile facilities; 139,813 youth were admitted to 2,032 private juvenile facilities; 65,263 juveniles were admitted to adult jails; and 1,287 were admitted to state and federal adult correctional facilities.[9] More admissions were for the purpose of detention (81 percent) than commitment (19 percent). Although detention centers admit the most juveniles in a year, there is a great deal of variety in the types of facilities that house juveniles, which also include shelters, reception/diagnostic centers, training schools, ranches/camps/farms, and halfway houses or group homes. Youth are held in detention facilities pending adjudication if there is reason to believe that they constitute a threat to the community, may be at risk if returned to the community, or may fail to appear at an upcoming hearing; they also are held in these facilities pending transfer to the adult system. Reception/diagnostic centers are special types of facilities used for evaluation either before or after adjudication. Training schools, which typically are secure although some housing units may be located outside the secure zone, are used to house youth who have been adjudicated for more serious offenses. Halfway houses, group homes, ranches, and camps are used to house much smaller youth populations in nonsecure facilities that are still under the supervision of public or private agents of the state.

Most detention centers are public facilities. In 1990, 82 percent of all admissions to a public facility were to public detention centers, while only 8 percent of all admissions to private facilities were to private detention centers. Admissions to privately operated facilities were primarily to shelters (52 percent) and halfway houses and group homes (27 percent). After public detention centers, the second-greatest number of admissions to a public facility occurred at training schools (9 percent), followed by reception/diagnostic centers (3 percent). The effort to collect data on admissions and releases was discontinued in 1995; since juveniles often stayed at a facility for a very short time, it was difficult to track their coming and going. In 1994, 871,700 juveniles were released from custody, most from public facilities (83 percent).

Admissions data indicate the volume of juveniles coming into the system in a year; a one-day count indicates the number of individuals confined at a given point in time. On a given reference day in 1995, 108,746 juveniles were held in public and private juvenile facilities. Of those, 69,075 (64 percent) were held in public facilities. Among juveniles held in public facilities, 96 percent were accused or adjudicated law violators, 3 percent were status offenders, and about 1 percent were nonoffenders. Among juveniles in private facilities, about 40,000 (45 percent) were accused or adjudicated, 14 percent were status offenders, and 41 percent were nonoffenders. The nonoffending group was composed of youth who were referred for abuse, neglect, emotional disturbance, or mental retardation or who were voluntarily admitted by their parents. The one-day count rose 47 percent from 1983 to 1995. The average length of stay for juveniles in public facilities was 147 days for committed youth and fifteen days for detained youth.[10] Private facilities held youth for 109 days on average.

Public facilities were clearly more likely to hold an SVJ. In 1991, among delinquents in public facilities, 31 percent were held for violent (murder, nonnegligent manslaughter, rape, robbery, aggravated assault) or other person (negligent manslaughter, assault) offenses; 24 percent were held for serious property offenses; and 10 percent were held for drug offenses. The comparable numbers for youth held in private facilities were 10 percent for violent and other person offenses, 9 percent for serious property offenses, and 5 percent for drug offenses. In 1983, 25 percent of juveniles held in public facilities were confined for violent and other person offenses and 34 percent were held for serious property offenses. Thus in recent years a higher proportion of juveniles was being held for violent offenses but a lower proportion for serious property offenses. Comparing the 1983 with the 1995 one-day counts for public facilities shows that there was a 109 percent increase in the number of juveniles held for person offenses, a 95 percent increase in juveniles held for drug offenses, and a 17 percent decline in juveniles held for property offenses.

The Office of Juvenile Justice and Delinquency Prevention (OJJDP) redesigned its method of collecting data on juveniles held in public and private facilities and now employs a new technique called the census of juveniles in residential placement (CJRP). The first CJRP, which also represents a one-day count on a specific reference day, was conducted in 1997. A recently released OJJDP fact sheet on this census indicated that there were 125,805 young people in 1,121 public and 2,310 private residential facilities.[11] Detailed information was collected on each youth under age twenty-one who was assigned a bed on the reference day, charged with or court-adjudicated for an offense, and placed in the facility because of the offense. Among the 105,790 youth meeting those criteria, 72.7 percent resided in public facilities. OJJDP collects two types of data—data on facilities and data on the youth residing in those facilities collected through the CJRP.

Smith has mapped out many of the significant trends in juvenile custody from 1975 to 1995.[12] His analysis shows that over that period

—The number of private facilities increased more than the number of public facilities, peaking in 1987 and declining slightly since then.

—The percentage of secure facilities, both public and private, has increased.

—The proportion of public facilities operating at more than their capacity increased from 20 to 39 percent, and the number of such private facilities increased from 4 to 8 percent.

—The number of juvenile females in juvenile facilities on any given day remained fairly constant, while the number of juvenile males on any given day increased by 32,642.

—The number of juvenile offenders per 100,000 juveniles increased from 241 in 1975 to 381 in 1995.

—The proportion of African American juveniles in custody increased from 28 to 40 percent.

—The proportion of juveniles held for violent offenses increased from 20 to 31 percent.

—In 1994 dollars, per capita operating costs increased until 1990, then decreased. The 1994 per capita cost was $32,400, while the 1975 per capita cost was $31, 600.

Another way of thinking about juvenile custody is to assess the extent to which the state uses this sanction. By expressing the number of first admissions (no prior commitments) of youth taken into state custody as a fraction of the juvenile population, DeComo was able to compute state custody prevalence rates by age at admission, race/ethnicity, gender, and the particular state.[13] By adding the different rates grouped by age, he computed the likelihood that a juvenile would be taken into custody by age seventeen. For example, DeComo found that on the basis of the 1995 data for the thirty-six states that reported their numbers, 1.13 percent of all juveniles (ages twelve to seventeen) could be expected to be taken into custody. The state-by-state, race, and gender breakdowns also are quite informative. For example, the data demonstrated that the likelihood for African American juveniles was 3.3 percent, while that for white juveniles was .66 percent. The data will become more informative as researchers track prevalence rates over time and, as DeComo points out, compare them with other important social indicators.

The Direction of Change in Corrections

An increasing number of SVJ offenders are held in institutions run by state juvenile correctional agencies.[14] However, there is a trend toward establishing specialized institutions for the SVJ offender. Furthermore, with the increase in the number of juveniles sentenced as adults, correctional programming for these offenders has been approached in many different ways in different states.

According to Torbet and others, state correctional responses can be grouped into five categories:[15]

—Direct adult incarceration, which is the commitment of juveniles directly to adult facilities where there is little difference in the types of programs for adults and juveniles.

—Graduated incarceration, which involves separating juveniles from adults by placing a youth in a juvenile facility or a separate juvenile facility in an adult facility until he or she reaches a certain age. Afterward, the juvenile is transferred to an adult institution.

—Segregated incarceration, which provides separate facilities for young offenders and sometimes specialized programming.

—A special category for serious and violent youth that creates a middle ground between the juvenile and the adult system. In Colorado, for example, a youth who has been convicted of certain classes of felonies involving the use of or the threat of use of a deadly weapon is placed in the youthful offender system (YOS), where the youth is sentenced in criminal court to the adult correctional system. The sentence is then suspended pending completion of the YOS program. A court hearing is required to revoke the suspended sentence. Variations of this approach have been formulated in Kentucky, New Mexico, New York, and Wisconsin.

—An enhanced juvenile justice system that gives more punishment and rehabilitation options to the juvenile court.

Torbet and others also noted that although adult institutions have little experience in developing programs tailored to juveniles in their custody, the population of such juveniles is growing.

Conditions of Confinement

There are certain minimum conditions of confinement that must be met before it is possible to suggest improvements in the system. According to Krisberg and Howell, more resources are being provided to adult prisons and jails than to youth facilities, leading to deterioration in the conditions of confinement for juveniles in both public and privately operated facilities.[16] As Smith's data showed, crowding has increased over time in both types.

Parent and others conducted a comprehensive evaluation of conditions in juvenile detention and corrections facilities, surveying all public and private juvenile facilities except halfway houses, shelters, group homes, adult facilities housing juveniles, psychiatric facilities, and drug treatment programs.[17] They estimated that those facilities held 69 percent of all confined juveniles at the time of the study. A two-day site visit also was conducted at ninety-five randomly selected facilities to assess twelve basic features: living space; health care; food, clothing, and hygiene; living accommodations; security; controlling suicidal behavior; inspections and emergency preparedness; education; recreation; treatment; access to community; and limits on staff discretion. The authors concluded that problems in juvenile facilities—including crowding, inadequate health care, failures in security, and inadequate efforts to minimize suicidal behavior—were widespread.

The American Correctional Association (ACA) has published standards of confinement for both juvenile and adult facilities that have been developed by corrections professionals and experts to ensure the safety, well-being, and security of both confined juveniles and adults. The juvenile standards were tailored to juveniles' specific needs. ACA standards cover virtually every aspect of corrections, including food preparation, health, safety, programming, grievance procedures, and discipline. The fact that a facility has received ACA accreditation does not ensure, however, that ACA procedures are being followed. Parent and others found that confinement conditions in institutions that were accredited were no better than conditions in those that were not.

An article in the *New York Times* illustrated the most egregious of those conditions. The Tallulah Correctional Center for Youth in Louisiana was a privately operated training school housing 620 youth, ages eleven to twenty.[18] The facility, which was built and managed by a private company, Trans American, opened in 1994. According to the complaints of the juvenile residents and publicly filed reports, the conditions at the facility were inhumane. There were accusations of guard brutality, insufficient clothing, meals so meager that many of the boys lost weight, uncertified teachers, no more than one hour of instruction a day, and, until about January 1998, no books. According to the article, the sordid history of the company was the result of a confluence of social and political pressures in Louisiana at that time. Dramatic increases in the juvenile offender population and state budget constraints meant that a facility had to be built quickly and operated cheaply. State monitoring revealed problems from the beginning. A large proportion of the annual payments to the company were spent on construction of the facility, leaving relatively little money to pay for the juveniles' care and training. In 1999, the state of Louisiana assumed control of the facility. On November 5, 1998, the U.S. Department of Justice filed suit against the state of Louisiana over conditions at all of the state's juvenile correctional facilities.

Two recent reports by the American Bar Association's Juvenile Justice Center support this emerging picture of unsuitable confinement conditions in some jurisdictions. An early report revealed significant deficiencies in access to and quality of legal representation throughout the juvenile justice system.[19] The absence of representation was particularly acute for juveniles who were detained and for those who had been released from a juvenile facility but were still under the jurisdiction of the juvenile court. A second report outlined several approaches that advocates can use to improve the conditions of confinement and the services youth receive during their commitment.[20]

Under the Civil Rights of Institutionalized Persons Act (CRIPA), the U.S. Department of Justice can bring actions against state and local governments to correct systemic problems in publicly operated facilities.[21] Puritz and Scali, authors of the second American Bar Association report, noted that in January 1998, there had been investigations of seventy-three juvenile correctional institutions. As a result of CRIPA actions, the civil rights division of the U.S. Department of Justice is monitoring conditions in thirty-four juvenile correctional facilities through consent decrees in Kentucky, Puerto Rico, and New Jersey. Legal remedies can also be achieved through the Individuals with Disabilities Education Act (IDEA) for institutionalized juveniles who have learning disabilities and are receiving inadequate educational training.[22] Class action suits involving IDEA claims have been brought against detention centers and training schools throughout the United States. The American Bar Association report covers other remedial avenues. Juvenile advocacy may play an important role in raising juvenile confinement standards and the amount of resources devoted to programming, especially in systems with too few dollars and lack of appropriate oversight.

Classification and Program Solutions to the Management of the SVJ Offender

Although the growth in the confined juvenile population has paled in comparison to the increase in the number of incarcerated adults, the increased SVJ population raises special management concerns. If, as some suggest, juvenile corrections budgets are being squeezed to fund adult corrections, it will have a serious impact on the management of juvenile facilities. The data indicate that most serious violent juvenile offenders are confined in public juvenile facilities, raising many management issues, including how to protect staff and other, nonviolent youth; how to meet this population's need for special programming and supervision; and how to design programs that have a reasonable chance of reintegrating such juveniles into society.

The small proportion of SVJs that end up in adult systems also create special problems for administrators of those facilities. Youth require a great deal more supervision and direct staff contact than adult correctional systems typically provide. Furthermore, administrators of adult correctional systems are usually unfamiliar with the special programming needs of juveniles. What little research there is to date on the efficacy of transferring juveniles to criminal courts suggests that juvenile jurisdiction ought to remain with the juvenile court.[23]

Many strategies can be used to meet the special needs of juvenile populations, including increasing funding and providing special training for staff; however, there are two strategies for improving the efficiency and impact of juvenile corrections that do not require increased budgets. One, juvenile assessment and classification, can improve decisionmaking at every step of the juvenile justice process; the other, juvenile programming, may limit a youth's exposure to the juvenile justice system or reduce his or her likelihood of continuing on to the adult criminal justice system. The two strategies, classification and programming, are linked so closely that a discussion of one follows directly from a discussion of the other.

There are many levels and meanings of classification. From the clinical perspective, classification means evaluating a juvenile for mental health status and needs. From the case manager's point of view, classification means assessing the youth's education and supervision requirements. From a technical standpoint, classification seeks to identify characteristics that can predict certain types of relapse and recidivism. Will the youth take drugs after completing treatment? What is the likelihood that the youth will commit more status offenses, more serious crime, more violent crime? The definition of classification adopted by Wiebush and others is a clear concise statement: classification is "the process of estimating an individual's likelihood of continued involvement in delinquent behavior and making decisions about the most appropriate type of intervention given the identified level of risk."[24]

Because it has been demonstrated that a technically sound classification system improves decisionmaking,[25] jurisdictions should adopt scientific classification tools and procedures for use at *every* stage of the juvenile justice process. While the purpose of classification changes at each stage, it is easy to demonstrate that the information required comes from the same legal and social institutions and that there is tremendous overlap in that information. This suggests that a mechanism for collecting, sharing, and managing information could increase the knowledge base and increase the efficacy of decisionmaking. LeBlanc and Wiebush and others have done a thorough job of summarizing the current state of knowledge about the classification of the SVJ offender.[26] While the principles of classification are well documented, a great deal of empirical work still needs to be done before classification procedures can be developed that can distinguish potential serious and violent juvenile offenders from juveniles who commit nonserious offenses.

The first problem is to define the population of interest. What do we mean by serious violent juvenile offender? Snyder's analysis of youth cohorts in Maricopa County, Arizona, cited at the beginning of this chapter allowed him to disaggregate delinquent offenses into chronic/nonchronic, violent/nonviolent, and serious/nonserious categories. Assuming that Maricopa County, which includes Phoenix, is a typical urban jurisdiction, a rough estimate can be made of the proportions of the delinquent population that can be categorized as chronic, violent, or serious. Totaling the proportions for offenders who were serious and violent—whether or not they were chronic—indicated that 16 percent of the sixteen delinquent cohorts might be classified as SVJ offenders. Adding serious nonchronic offenders would increase that proportion to 33.7 percent. Whether or not it is important to distinguish the violent from the serious offender depends on the specific goals of the classification/assessment. Factors that predict violent recidivism overlap with but also are somewhat different from factors that predict serious recidivism,[27] and distinguishing between them is useful in predicting behavior and determining the appropriate level of supervision. Classification procedures also are used for purposes of intervention—for example, to reveal whether a juvenile has personal deficits that may be improved if he or she participates in a suitable program. For this diagnostic purpose, it probably is not as important to distinguish violent from serious offenders. Current juvenile intervention literature does not distinguish juveniles who commit serious offenses from those who commit violent offenses. Palmer has come to the same conclusion.[28]

There are many well-documented techniques for developing a valid, reliable classification system. Entire volumes have been devoted to the topic.[29] To understand how classification can be used to manage risk and programming needs in juvenile corrections and in the juvenile justice system in general, one need only consider each stage of the juvenile and adult criminal justice process: arrest/referral, adjudication/sentencing, probation/confinement, and post-release supervision. As noted before, the purpose of classification changes at each stage of the juvenile justice process. Youth services and probation agencies do an assessment for the purpose of informing the court's detention decisions, which are based on assessment of risk. Postadjudication classification is important for designating the level of custody required and for planning the juvenile's program needs. Risk assessment also informs decisions regarding the level of supervision during probation and any additional community programming.

Although formal classification procedures are more common than they used to be, no jurisdiction seems to use these procedures at every stage of the judicial process. For example, in Massachusetts, Hogan chaired a committee to evaluate the state department of youth services.[30] Although Massachusetts, which was one of the first states to deinstitutionalize its residential delinquent population, is considered one of the more progressive states in its treatment of juveniles, among the many recommendations of the Hogan committee was one to develop a comprehensive classification system. Apparently, placement decisions in Massachusetts for all but the most serious and violent youth were made with very little information or assessment. The committee recommended that risk assessment should be the basis of all decisions regarding placement, movement, discharge, and extension of commitment. Even the classification system for the more serious youth was based on the concept of "teaming" rather than the concept of actuarial prediction in conjunction with assessment of needs. Teaming is a term of art used in corrections to denote a group decision made by staff familiar with an individual's case. I agree with the emphasis of the Hogan committee, but I also believe that much of the same information should be used in making decisions about detention, commitment, and supervision. Barton and Gorsuch found that only about half of those states that responded to their survey reported that the state juvenile correction agencies used formal classification tools.[31]

Beginning with arrest/referral, every subsequent stage in the juvenile justice process should benefit from assessment and risk classification in the previous stage. Even though the decisions to be made vary depending on the stage, the information that is required to make those decisions can be used at almost any stage in the process. Table 5-1 lists factors that are characteristically measured by risk/classification devices and the various stages at which information on those factors is used in making decisions. While there are a great many jurisdictional variations in the use of this information, table 5-1 illustrates that there is considerable overlap in the information needed at each decision point.

Table 5-1. *Juvenile Justice Process Classification Factors*

Factor or variable	Stage of process at which factor applies[a]	Type of factor
Personality measures	P	Alterable/unalterable status
Past and instant criminal behavior	D, S, P	Historical
Past and instant aggressive behavior (including use of weapon)	D, S, P	Historical
Escape or runaway history	D, S, P	Historical
Demographic characteristics (age, race, sex)	D, S, P	Unalterable status
Drug use/abuse	D, S, P, N	Dynamic
Alcohol use/abuse	D, S, P, N	Dynamic
School behavior	D, P, S	Historical
Educational level/needs	P, N	Dynamic
Family status (single parent, foster care)	D, S, P	Alterable status
Family experience (abuse, neglect, etc.)	D, S, P	Historical/alterable status
Gang membership	D, S, P	Alterable status
Positive peer relationships	D, S, P	Alterable status
Intellectual ability/special education needs	P, N	Dynamic
Mental health	P, N	Dynamic
Physical/health problems	N	Historical/dynamic
Employment/vocational skills	P, N	Dynamic
Behavior while under control of the juvenile justice system	D, S, P	Historical
Victimization	N	Historical/dynamic
Independing living skills	N	Dynamic

a. D = Detention; N = Treatment need; P = Placement; S = Supervision.

Representing classification/assessment as a systemic problem highlights another important dimension. Clearly, the system is intended to change a juvenile's behavior. Because that is viewed as a dynamic process, the youth's response to intervention at each stage and any changes over time in his or her "risk set"—factors that indicate whether the juvenile is likely to recidivate—must be documented. The factors listed in table 5-1 can be understood to have varying degrees of malleability. Many are what some researchers call dynamic risk predictors—ones that can be modified by intervention. Drug abuse, for example, can be treated. Vocational, educational, and employment skills can be acquired or increased through training. Alterable status factors, which indicate membership in a group or a group characteristic, are difficult to change but nevertheless may be changed. Examples are gang membership and family status. Unalterable status variables, such as sex or race, are important dimensions that can lower or raise the level of risk. Some variables are historical; they represent what has happened and for that reason cannot be changed. Examples are a youth's history of criminal or aggressive behavior, which is a very powerful predictor of future behavior. However, even that variable can be viewed as somewhat dynamic: the shorter the interval between a criminal or aggressive act and the time of assessment, the higher the likelihood of recidivism.

Many of these concepts are familiar to most criminal justice practitioners. Offender classification has been around since the middle 1940s,[32] and assessment and classification are routinely used in the juvenile justice and adult criminal justice systems; however, few jurisdictions systematically collect information. Still fewer have a good strategy for sharing diagnostic and predictive information, and very few, if any, have evaluated the predictive validity of all of their classification procedures. Furthermore, no classification procedures have been developed specifically for the SVJ offender.

Parent and others also assessed the extent to which juvenile facilities conformed to certain classification standards.[33] To conform, a facility had to have a written classification procedure, base the classification on at least one of four dimensions of risk (escape risk, danger to self, danger to others, or offense history), and use the classification in making housing assignments. Overall, only 62 percent of youth (about 62,000 in this study) were housed in institutions that met those criteria. The researchers could have set an even higher standard by inquiring whether the classification process had been validated. Although a procedure may have face validity, more rigorous analysis often demonstrates that classification systems must be tailored to the population in question and can be improved by an item-by-item analysis of the procedures.

Use of validated classification procedures in juvenile and adult institutions results in an instrument that is highly predictive of serious and/or violent misconduct. However, Parent and others found that conformance to classification standards was not related to rates of juvenile injuries, lending credence to the possibility that little or no validation was required and that a great deal of improvement could be made in placement decisions.

According to Le Blanc, juvenile classification has been "informal and discretionary." Screening devices have been used inconsistently by staff who may not be well trained and who have diverging views about intervention, leading to "decisions that were often erroneous, inconsistent, inequitable, and without justification."[34] Wiebush and others have described an extensive effort by the National Council on Crime and Delinquency to improve classification procedures.[35] The authors also have made a number of recommendations to improve assessment and prediction of the behavior of SVJ offenders in particular. However, any redesign of the procedures should not only distinguish SVJ from non-SVJ offenders but also distinguish violent recidivism from nonviolent recidivism. There have been recent attempts in the adult classification literature to distinguish violent from nonviolent recidivism, with some success.[36] The literature demonstrates that generic classification systems do not do a very good job of predicting violent recidivism; however, if the classification instrument includes specific information related to violent recidivism, it can be fine tuned to predict such events.

Why are classification decisions important? Classification procedures are part of the decisionmaking processes used throughout the juvenile justice system. As such, the procedures make the process more rational, more efficient, more just, and better managed.

—It has been shown that well-designed classification procedures can be used to greatly improve the predictive accuracy of assessments, making decisions to detain, to make a residential placement, or to release more rational.

—Classification procedures can be used to allocate resources efficiently. For example, a risk assessment device can be used to classify cases by the level of supervision they require. Resources then can be allocated accordingly.

—Classification can ensure uniformity and consistency in decisionmaking, enhancing the perception of an equitable and just system. As Wiebush and others have noted, classification can also increase accountability and can be used to expedite decisionmaking. Documentation of a decision and the basis for that decision are much clearer in an objective than a subjective assessment.

—Classification can be used as a management tool. The collection of common information for all cases can be used to track and project risk pools and to request and allocate resources.

Several studies have compared placement decisions made with and without classification tools. A study by Wiebush and others showed that formal risk assessment indicated that a higher proportion of youth needed close supervision than was indicated by the informal decisions made by probation officers and their supervisors.[37] On the other hand, Krisberg and others showed that when a structured risk assessment tool was used to calculate the risk level of youths in training schools in fourteen states, the assessment indicated that 33 percent of the youth did not require secure care.[38] These studies indicate not only that these tools can improve decisionmaking, but also that they can be used to manage scarce resources.

While this is good news, the bad news is that classification devices must be tailored to the specific jurisdiction in which they are used. There are enough procedural and information-gathering differences across jurisdictions to make it unwise for one jurisdiction to uniformly adopt the classification procedures of another. Yet no jurisdiction has to start from scratch. Various classification tools and training materials are available; an analyst can build on them to tailor a device for a particular jurisdiction and a particular stage in the juvenile justice process. Nonetheless, each jurisdiction must validate its own classification system. There also are model systems that try to match an offender's risks and needs with appropriate sanctions and treatments.[39]

Classification and inmate juvenile programming are closely aligned. The risk factors in table 5-1 that can be modified, the dynamic and alterable status variables, are not only predictors of risk, they are deficiencies that can be addressed through intervention. Child development and clinical psychologists refer to three classes of intervention that correspond to a particular stage of the juvenile delinquent career. Primary prevention refers to strategies used to stop a problem from occurring. Secondary prevention refers to strategies that are adopted after there are indications or markers that a problem will occur if the secondary strategies are not successful.

Tertiary prevention refers to strategies that are employed after a problem has occurred and that are intended to limit the damage or rehabilitate the individual so that the problem does not recur.

In the context of serious violent juvenile offenders, correctional interventions are primarily of the secondary and tertiary type. If status offenses such as school absenteeism are viewed as indicators of future criminal behavior, then the interventions employed are secondary interventions.

Correctional Treatments That Work

A great deal of research has been conducted on correctional interventions for juveniles in both institutional and noninstitutional settings. Mark Lipsey's reviews of the literature have made the formidable task of interpreting that research easier.[40] Lipsey and Wilson extended Lipsey's earlier work by examining only those studies that evaluated program interventions on serious juvenile offenders.[41] By using meta-analysis, a statistical method that summarizes and synthesizes data, they were able to extract key principles and themes from those studies.

Lipsey and Wilson were able to find 200 experimental or quasi-experimental studies that involved interventions among serious juvenile offenders. For noninstitutionalized youth, the major types of intervention programs were counseling, skill-oriented programs (tutoring, social skills, vocational skills, drug abstinence), and multiple services. Institutionalized juveniles received counseling, skill-oriented programs, and community residential programs. Program length ranged from one to thirty weeks and contact occurred from between half an hour and ten hours per week. Psychologists (29 percent) conducted most of these studies, although criminologists (19 percent) and sociologists (8 percent) conducted a sizable number. Most of the studies involved juveniles whose mean age was seventeen or under (71 percent).

The analysis indicated that after their release back into the community, on average, untreated juveniles recidivated 50 percent of the time and treated juveniles recidivated 44 percent of the time. Recidivism typically was defined as a police contact or arrest. Although that represents a modest average effect, some interventions resulted in large positive effects. To refine their analysis, Lipsey and Wilson adjusted the effects observed in each study for differences in the rigor of methods used in each evaluation and by coding additional information from each of the intervention studies. Their supplementary analysis indicated that for noninstitutionalized juveniles, the success of a program depended primarily on the characteristics of the youth. The type and level of treatment were less influential, and the characteristics of the treatment were least likely to affect program success. For institutionalized juveniles, general program characteristics had the highest impact (36 percent of the variation), while characteristics of the juveniles had the least impact (10 percent of the variation). Those results were the opposite of the results for noninstitutionalized juveniles. Amount of treatment and treatment type accounted for 27 and 26 percent respectively of the effectiveness of treatment. Since a treatment provider has little or no control over the characteristics of the population he or she treats, this analysis suggests that programs may be more effective for institutionalized than for noninstitutionalized SVJs.

The interventions that were most likely to benefit noninstitutionalized youth were individual counseling, interpersonal skills training, behavioral programs, and multiple services. Counseling programs involved one-on-one sessions between a citizen volunteer and a juvenile or between a graduate student in counseling and a juvenile. Interpersonal skills training taught youth to appreciate the perspective of others and to take responsibility through commitment to one or more personal or community projects. Behavioral programs included both parents and juveniles. Multiple services included combinations of programs such as counseling and vocational training, education and employment training, and combinations of therapy and vocational placement. Among institutionalized youth, interpersonal skills training, "teaching family" homes, behavioral programs, community residential programs, and multiple services all had effects. A teaching family home was a group home for six to eight delinquents who were mentored by a couple, the "teaching parents." In this program, youths returned to their homes on the weekend and were able to remain in their schools.

Lipsey and Wilson's analysis is an important synthesis of the literature on the effectiveness of juvenile programs. However, as the researchers noted, in the 200 studies they reviewed, there were many differences in the characteristics of the juveniles sampled, a wide range of programs, and many different procedures used to evaluate the programs. When one considers all of the possible combinations of those factors, it is not surprising that very few studies focused on a specific intervention with comparable juvenile samples and similar methods. As the researchers indicated, "it makes virtually all of the principal conclusions tentative."[42]

Continuity of Institutional and Community Programs

As with the procedures and information collected at every stage in the juvenile justice process, there should be continuity between residential and postresidential supervision. The "continuity-of-care" model implies that training and interventions carried out within residential placement will be followed up in the community. Altschuler, who has written extensively on aftercare programs for at-risk youth, concluded that the reduction in juvenile recidivism would be greater "if effective institutional programs were followed up with quality (non-institutional) aftercare programs."[43] He also has recommended that community staff be integrated into institutional programs for youth. Commenting on Lipsey and Wilson's research, Altschuler noted that there was considerable overlap in the kinds of programs that seemed to be effective in institutional and noninstitutional settings for SVJ offenders. Those programs were highly structured, involved well-trained staff, and addressed social skills and conduct related to the youths' critical life domains. Altschuler argued that there are several critical life domains that must be constantly monitored to minimize recidivism: family, peers, school, and community. A classification procedure that assesses deficits and needs in those domains and measures progress from the institution to the postrelease setting would be a useful tool for monitoring and interacting with the youth.

In discussing the role of intermediate sanctions on reducing SVJ recidivism, Altschuler also notes the structural impediments to coordination and collaboration among the many different entities in the juvenile justice system. These are the same as the impediments to sharing classification and assessment information and ensuring the continuity of care necessary to maximize the effectiveness of institutional and noninstitutional programs. Of course, every jurisdiction has different lines of authority and responsibility. To coordinate activities among them, Altschuler suggests creating interagency teams composed of representatives of the court, prosecutors, state youth corrections personnel, institution staff, parole authorities, county government staff, and any other public and private service providers.

A complementary strategy is to assign one case manager to a youth whose responsibility is to orchestrate all assessment, classification, and coordination issues with the teams suggested by Altschuler. Depending on the jurisdiction, that case manager could be an employee of the youth authority or the court. Team building across agencies is a difficult enterprise. Even with an agreement and a structure for interagency cooperation, there is always pressure to compete and to justify one's own approach to serving the youth and community. It is important to study jurisdictions that are currently coordinating their juvenile services and justice systems to find the best structures and incentives to promote cooperation. Such case studies could lead to a model system for juvenile justice intervention strategies.

A Case Study

In 1998, I visited a training school in a large metropolitan area in a mid-Atlantic state. I spent a day touring the facility, which handles the most serious juvenile offenders in the state who have not been transferred to the adult system, and staff members answered any questions I asked. Afterward, I interviewed youth authority staff whose role in this particular state is to manage a case as soon as it comes to the attention of the juvenile court and to follow it until juvenile court supervision terminates.

The school houses about 350 male juveniles, most of whom are confined within a fenced compound; there are honor dorms outside the fence. At intake, school staff assess the delinquent's educational achievement, along with his psychosocial adjustment. He is interviewed about his legal history, his family background, and his attitude toward life. His mental health also is assessed, and if there is any indication of problems, he is referred to a mental health professional. The assessment can take from two to three days; however, no formal classification device is used in the assessment.

The school employs an overall program model in which the delinquent is seen as progressing through four stages in which he acquires cognitive skills related to his delinquency. In the first stage, the youth is expected to understand the behaviors that led to his placement in the school; he is expected to admit past wrongdoing and acknowledge harm to any victims. In stage 2, he is expected to understand the impact of his behavior on others. In stage 3, he is taught to problem solve. He engages in role playing and is encouraged to think through prosocial solutions to problems. In the fourth stage, the delinquent is taught relapse prevention techniques. He is taught how to recover if he does commit another delinquent act and to think through the consequences of his behavior if he does not begin to change it.

While the cognitive skills model has become very popular, especially in adult corrections,[44] there has been no systematic evaluation of such programs in juvenile corrections. The cognitive skills approach could be viewed as an extension of the behavioral programming techniques that Lipsey and Wilson found effective in a juvenile setting. Although no attempt had been made to validate this particular program in this particular setting, the program gives the school an overarching theme and structure that both staff and juveniles seemed to accept. It provides a clear set of rules, clear consequences for disobeying those rules, and a theoretical rationale for the kinds of feedback staff give to youth and for rewarding or punishing behavior. Because of that, the program is fundamental to the juveniles' perception of fairness, in addition to its utility as a behavior change strategy.

During both the morning and afternoon shifts, the youth is given feedback on his progress in thinking about and interacting with others, responding to staff, and taking personal initiative in improving his interactions. The feedback is consistent with cognitive skills training goals. Youth are evaluated on seven dimensions: their ability to positively guide others; their willingness to empathize; their ability to accept responsibility for their actions; their ability to exercise self-restraint; their ability to understand how their decisions affect outcomes; their ability to control their emotions; and their ability to fairly resolve conflicts. A youth receives a score from 0 to 4 on each dimension. Zero indicates that the youth consistently fails to respond positively to staff feedback. A score of 4 indicates that the individual takes initiative. The average score on all dimensions determines the level of privileges the youth will receive. Clearly, the frequency with which this feedback is given requires a high staff-to-juvenile ratio, and, as mentioned previously, that kind of staffing typically is not available in adult institutions. The intense supervision and frequent feedback given here probably would not be possible for juveniles housed in adult settings.

Daily life at the training school is very structured. Inside the secure perimeter, a rigid schedule allows for school, special instruction, limited exercise periods, homework, and cleaning. Even weekend activities are highly structured, and the amenities are few. The rooms and general environment are clean but spartan. Youth are allowed surprisingly few possessions. All youth wear uniforms that look like gym outfits. They are not allowed to watch television for any length of time, and their choice of programs is restricted mainly to news shows. Any television privileges are highly valued. No privileges are allowed for a student receiving an average feedback score of 1, but they increase as the youth proceeds from level 2 through 4. Privileges at the intermediate levels include staying up an extra half-hour; participating in some organized activities, including sports; and listening to a Walkman radio on occasion. At level 4, the youth can live outside the fence, go home on pass, and participate in a number of activities away from the facility.

If a youth demonstrates difficulty in adjusting at the school or if he acts negatively or threatens other youth or staff, staff convene a "grand round," a meeting held to develop the best strategy to help the youth change his behavior and to reorient him toward more prosocial activities. Participants in the grand round can include his one-on-one counselor, his unit manager, his case manager, the program director, a psychiatrist, a mental health counselor, a substance abuse counselor, his teachers, his probation officer, the supervisory probation officer, and his parents—all of whom can have a crucial influence on his social attitudes. A coordinated plan is designed. The delinquent is informed of the decisions made at the grand round and told what his future responsibilities will be.

In this particular state, the youth authority has responsibility for advising the court about the youth's background, and the authority makes recommendations for placement and supervision. If a youth is placed at the training school, a youth authority probation officer visits the youth at least twice a month to monitor his progress and discuss his case with the training school staff. After completing the training school program, the youth is released to the youth authority for follow-up supervision.

A team assessment technique is used in this particular jurisdiction to make recommendations for placement. No technical classification devices seem to be used at any decisionmaking point; risk and needs are monitored more informally. When asked about continuity of care between residential and community placement, the supervisory staff at the youth authority talked about follow-up programs for drug treatment and vocational training. Staff were aware of the training school's emphasis on cognitive skills training, but that approach was not continued after the youth was released from the school.

While there is a great deal of communication in this particular state between the court and the youth authority that advises on placement and supervision decisions, there does not seem to be any structured, systematic way that classification decisions are made and recorded. There also is not a great deal of coordination between the training school program and the post-release programs or of consistency in their content. Of the staff I interviewed, both the training school and youth authority staff seemed to be very professional and interested in doing the best job they could to help the juveniles. One of the more interesting comments was made by a member of the training school staff, who said that he did not believe in classifying delinquents; he felt that it labeled a youth and limited his potential to change. I asked whether he thought that a structured classification system would improve his decisionmaking ability. He did not think that it would. That is a typical response among staff who view using a classification system as an abdication of their responsibilities; they view the process with skepticism because they do not see how a device can capture all the nuances of a particular case. In jurisdictions where staff have been taught to use classification tools in conjunction with their own professional judgment, however, staff typically see the technique as indispensable.

Summary

This chapter has taken a broad overview of the changing nature of juvenile confinement. The juvenile justice system has undergone dramatic changes nationwide, resulting in many different correctional programs, especially for the serious violent juvenile offender. A growing proportion of confined youth are adjudicated for violent offenses. In addition, as a result of transfer provisions, more and more youth are being tried in criminal court and turned over to the jurisdiction of adult correctional agencies. Although there are no reliable data on the number of juveniles who have been transferred, there is evidence that younger offenders constitute a small (about 2 percent) but growing number of new commitments to adult prisons. As Feld has argued, this influx of youth "poses a challenge to corrections officials to develop more programming and age-appropriate conditions of confinement for young or more vulnerable inmates."[45] As exemplified in the description of the mid-Atlantic training school, youth corrections is often structured to closely monitor the juvenile's behavior, remedy educational and other deficits, and protect the youngest and most vulnerable juveniles. Even though most adult correctional systems have education and other training programs, they are not as heavily staffed as modern juvenile correctional programs. The individualized attention given in the mid-Atlantic juvenile facility described would be difficult to achieve in most adult settings.

Not only are more youth being committed for violent offenses, juveniles are more likely to commit institution infractions. Just as there is a strong relationship between age and violent crime in the free community, there also is a strong relationship between age and violent misconduct in adult correctional environments. Younger inmates commit violent infractions at a much higher rate than older inmates. That will present an interesting challenge to adult correctional systems where violent misconduct is treated with loss of privileges and segregation. In adult systems, persistent violence often is countered with transfer to higher levels of custody, where ever-more violent criminals are confined. Are adult correctional administrators and staff prepared to meet the demands of a growing stream of younger, more violent youth? Are their only options to confine these youth at higher levels of custody, where they inevitably will be forced to associate with chronically violent adults? Under a system in which juveniles are legally and practically treated as adults, the correctional programming and punishment options decline precipitously.

The education and training needs of transferred youth pose a more subtle problem. In juvenile institutions, education often is the primary program, which all other institutional functions are intended to support. A
training school is indeed primarily a school. While education is supported
and strongly endorsed in an adult correctional environment, it typically is
not the central theme. There are strong prohibitions against inmate idle-
ness in adult correctional environments, but core activities are more often
work related. How will juveniles fare in such a system? Adult correctional
administrators will have to make the education of this population one of
their priorities if transferred juveniles are to achieve the educational level of
their training school contemporaries.

Even if violence among juveniles continues to subside and there is much
less need to confine them in adult institutions, the juvenile system still has
room for improvement. Systematic assessment and classification of youth
regardless of whether they are confined in a juvenile or adult facility is one
strategy that can be adopted to make the system more efficient, rational,
and equitable. Classification and assessment in most systems typically has
been done in a piecemeal and often very informal manner. Since programming also depends on adequate assessment, a systematic approach to classification also will enhance the efficiency and impact of juvenile programs.
As the case study shows, well-meaning staff work very hard to set up a system of controls, incentives, and programs to give youth a decent chance at
changing their behavior. I believe that the success of those efforts could be
magnified if classification and assessment are carried out at every stage of
the process. The court would benefit by having a better understanding of
the nature of the problems confronting the juvenile as well as by having
more precise information for making a placement decision. The correctional agencies would benefit from a more rational use of resources. Probation officers would benefit from a technically superior system of assigning risk to their caseloads. The juvenile would benefit from programming
tailored to his or her needs. Administrators would benefit from the most
efficient and rational use of limited resources. The entire system would
benefit because a more rational system is a more equitable system.

Notes

1. Howard N. Snyder, "Serious, Violent, and Chronic Juvenile Offenders: An Assessment of the Extent of the Trends in Officially Recognized Serious Criminal Behavior in a
Delinquent Population," in Rolf Loeber and David P. Farrington, eds., *Serious and Violent*

Juvenile Offenders: Risk Factors and Successful Interventions (Thousand Oaks, Calif.: Sage Publications, 1998), pp. 428–44.

2. Howard N. Snyder, Melissa Sickmund, and Eileen Poe-Yamagata, *Juvenile Offenders and Victims: 1996 Update on Violence* (U.S. Department of Justice, Office of Juvenile Justice and Delinquency Prevention, 1996).

3. Melissa Sickmund, Howard N. Snyder, and Eileen Poe-Yamagata, *Juvenile Offenders and Victims: 1997 Update on Violence* (U.S. Department of Justice, Office of Juvenile Justice and Delinquency Prevention, 1997).

4. Darell Steffensmeier and others, "Age and the Distribution of Crime," *American Journal of Sociology*, vol. 94, no. 4 (January 1989), pp. 803–31.

5. Miles D. Harer, research analyst, Federal Bureau of Prisons, personal communication, 1998.

6. Philip J. Cook and John H Laub, "The Unprecedented Epidemic in Youth Violence," in Michael Tonry and Mark H. Moore, eds., *Youth Violence* (University of Chicago Press, 1998), pp. 27–64.

7. Jeffrey A. Butts and Adele V. Harrell, *Delinquents or Criminals: Policy Options for Young Offenders* (Washington: Urban Institute, 1998).

8. Ibid., p. 8.

9. James Austin and others, *Juveniles Taken into Custody: Fiscal Year 1993* (U.S. Department of Justice, Office of Juvenile Justice and Delinquency Prevention, 1995).

10. "Average Time in Placement for Juveniles Released from Custody" (www.ojjdp. ncjrs.org/ojstatbb/html/correctionsCJRPtime.html [March 7, 2002]).

11. Catherine Gallagher, *OJJDP Fact Sheet: Juvenile Offenders in Residential Placement 1997* (U.S. Department of Justice, Office of Juvenile Justice and Delinquency Prevention, 1999).

12. Bradford Smith, "Children in Custody: 20-Year Trends in Juvenile Detention, Correctional, and Shelter Facilities," *Crime and Delinquency*, vol. 44, no. 4 (1998), pp. 526–43.

13. Robert E. DeComo, "Estimating the Prevalence of Juvenile Custody by Race and Gender," *Crime and Delinquency*, vol. 44, no. 4 (1998), pp. 489–525.

14. Barry Krisberg and James C. Howell, "The Impact of the Juvenile Justice System and Prospects for Graduated Sanctions in a Comprehensive Strategy," in Loeber and Farrington, *Serious and Violent Juvenile Offenders*, pp. 346–66.

15. Patricia Torbet and others, *State Responses to Serious and Violent Juvenile Crime: Research Report* (U.S. Department of Justice, Office of Juvenile Justice and Deliquency Prevention, National Center for Juvenile Justice, 1996).

16. Krisberg and Howell, "The Impact of the Juvenile Justice System," pp. 346–66.

17. Dale G. Parent and others, *Conditions of Confinement: Juvenile Detention and Corrections Facilities* (U.S. Department of Justice, Office of Juvenile Justice and Delinquency Prevention, 1994).

18. Fox Butterfield, "Profits at a Juvenile Prison Come with a Chilling Cost," *New York Times*, July 15, 1998, p. A1.

19. American Bar Association Juvenile Justice Center, "A Call for Justice: An Assessment of Access to Counsel and Quality of Representation in Delinquency Proceedings" (Washington: American Bar Association, 1996).

20. Patricia Puritz and Mary Ann Scali, "Beyond the Walls: Improving Conditions of Confinement for Youth in Custody," (U.S. Department of Justice, Office of Juvenile Justice and Delinquency Prevention, 1998).

21. 42 U.S.C. §§ 1997-1997j (1988).

22. 20 U.S.C. §§ 1401-1485 (1975)

23. Jeffrey Fagan, "Separating the Men from the Boys: The Comparative Advantage of Juvenile versus Criminal Court Sanctions on Recidivism among Adolescent Felony Offenders," in J. C. Howell and others, eds., *Sourcebook on Serious, Violent, and Chronic Juvenile Offenders* (Thousand Oaks, Calif.: Sage, 1995), pp. 238–60.

24. Richard G. Wiebush and others, "Risk Assessment for Serious, Chronic, and Violent Juvenile Offenders," in Howell and others, eds., *Sourcebook on Serious, Violent, and Chronic Juvenile Offenders*, pp. 171–212, quote is on pp. 172–73.

25. James Monahan, *Predicting Violent Behavior: An Assessment of Clinical Techniques* (Beverly Hills, Calif.: Sage, 1981).

26. Marc Le Blanc, "Screening of Serious and Violent Juvenile Offenders: Identification, Classification, and Prediction," in Loeber and Farrington, *Serious and Violent Juvenile Offenders*, pp. 167–193; Wiebush and others, "Risk Assessment for Serious, Chronic, and Violent Juvenile Offenders," pp. 171–212.

27. D. S. Elliot, F. W. Dunford, and D. Huizinga, "The Identification and Prediction of Career Offenders Utilizing Self-Reported and Official Data," in J. D. Burchard and S. N. Burchard, eds., *Prevention of Delinquent Behavior* (Newbury Park, Calif.: Sage, 1987), pp. 90–121.

28. Ted Palmer, *The Re-emergence of Correctional Intervention* (Newbury Park, Calif.: Sage, 1992).

29. Donald M. Gottfredson and Michael Tonry, eds., *Crime and Justice: An Annual Review*, vol. 9: *Prediction and Classification: Criminal Justice Decision Making* (University of Chicago Press, 1987); David P. Farrington and Richard Tarling, *Prediction in Criminology* (State University of New York Press, 1985).

30. William Hogan Jr., "Department of Youth Services: A Report to the Executive Office of Health and Human Services," *New England Journal of Criminal and Civil Confinement*, vol. 21, no. 2 (1995), pp. 317–38.

31. W. Barton and K. Gorsuch, "Risk Assessment and Classification in Juvenile Justice," paper presented at the annual meeting of the American Society of Criminology, Reno, Nevada, 1989.

32. Harry E. Barnes and Negley K. Teeters, *New Horizons in Criminology* (New York: Prentice-Hall, 1945).

33. Parent and others, *Conditions of Confinement*.

34. Le Blanc, "Screening of Serious and Violent Juvenile Offenders," p. 186.

35. Wiebush and others, "Risk Assessment for Serious, Chronic, and Violent Juvenile Offenders," pp. 171–212.

36. Vernon L. Quinsey and others, *Violent Offenders: Appraising and Managing Risk* (Washington: American Psychological Association, 1998).

37. R. G. Wiebush and others, *Oklahoma Office of Juvenile Justice 1992 Workload Study: Final Report* (Madison, Wisc.: National Council on Crime and Delinquency, 1993).

38. B. Krisberg and others, "Juveniles in State Custody: Prospects for Community-

Based Care of Troubled Adolescents," *Focus* (May 1993) (San Francisco: National Council on Crime and Delinquency).

39. James C. Howell and Barry Krisberg, "Introduction," *Crime and Delinquency*, vol. 44, no. 4 (1998), pp. 483–88.

40. Mark W. Lipsey, "The Efficacy of Intervention for Juvenile Delinquency: Results from 400 Studies," paper presented at the forty-first meeting of the American Society of Criminology, Reno, Nevada, 1989; Mark W. Lipsey, "Juvenile Delinquency Treatment: a Meta-Analytic Inquiry into the Variability of Effects," in T. D. Cook and others, eds., *Meta-Analysis for Explanation: A Casebook* (New York: Russell Sage Foundation, 1992), pp. 83–128; Mark W. Lipsey, "What Do We Learn from 400 Research Studies on the Effectiveness of Treatment with Juvenile Delinquents?" in J. McGuire, ed., *What Works: Reducing Reoffending* (John Wiley, 1995), pp. 63–78.

41. Mark W. Lipsey and David B. Wilson, "Effective Intervention for Serious Juvenile Offenders," in Loeber and Farrington, *Serious and Violent Juvenile Offenders*, pp. 313–45.

42. Ibid., p. 330.

43. David M. Altschuler, "Intermediate Sanctions and Community Treatment for Serious and Violent Juvenile Offenders," in Loeber and Farrington, *Serious and Violent Juvenile Offenders*, pp. 367–88.

44. Gerald G. Gaes and others, in Michael Tonry and Joan Petersilia, eds., *Crime and Justice: A Review of Research*, vol. 26: *Prisons* (University of Chicago Press, 1999), pp. 361–426.

45. Barry C. Feld, "Juvenile and Criminal Justice Systems' Responses to Youth Violence," in Tonry and Moore, eds., *Youth Violence*, p. 219.

6

RONALD P. CORBETT JR.

Reinventing Probation and Reducing Youth Violence

IN THE EARLY 1990S, two crises converged, leading to historic changes in the criminal justice system. The first was the dramatically escalating rate of youth violence, particularly homicide, in American cities. The second was the crisis of legitimacy that beset the practice of probation across the country. During the ensuing decade, remarkable progress was made on both fronts. Their stories are intertwined.

It takes a crisis to change a bureaucracy. Overwhelmed by dramatically rising rates of youth homicide in the early 1990s, Boston probation and police officials threw out existing blueprints in a desperate search for more effective strategies. A fearsome necessity became the mother of reinvention. In 1993, a wholly new approach to combating youth violence emerged: Operation Night Light, a police-probation partnership involving intensive home and street contact with high-risk offenders during evening hours. Night Light rested on the stunningly simple premise that "you can't fight fires from the station house." At the time, desk-bound probation officers worked primarily out of their offices, with little visible presence in the community, in an anemic form of corrections disparagingly referred to as "fortress probation." Operation Night Light was designed to reverse that practice.

Night Light worked, particularly because it was combined with several other imaginative policing, prosecutorial, and community outreach strategies. Youth homicides dropped steeply, and the city grew hopeful again. The partnership's success provided momentum for a thorough rethinking of probation strategies throughout Massachusetts, which led to a new model that placed increased emphasis on tighter supervision and stricter enforcement coupled with the heightened presence of probation officers in the community. Those officers subsequently felt a new confidence in their efforts and gained greater respectability in the public eye.

A similar sense of reform and renewal emerged in a number of states around the country, notably Washington, Wisconsin, Arizona, and Virginia. Probation executives from those and a few other states networked through the American Probation and Parole Association (APPA) to share information and experiences, publicize their still-nascent efforts, and enlist converts to the cause of a reinvented philosophy of probation.[1]

This chapter focuses on Boston's Operation Night Light, presenting some of the context, operations, early experiences, and eventual results of the initiative. The chapter identifies the six major lessons learned about the nature of youth violence, the strategies that seem to avail against it, and the dynamics that such partnerships unleash. It then offers some tips on replication, combining possibly helpful hints with cautionary notes. The chapter concludes with observations on school-probation partnerships, the next frontier in redefining conventional roles and relationships.

The Genesis of Operation Night Light

In the early 1990s, communities across the country were experiencing a surge in serious juvenile violence, reflected in the increasing numbers of homicides committed by teenagers.[2] Communities' sense of urgency in the face of the problem increased following predictions by James Fox of Northeastern University, among others, that demographic changes would lead to a major increase in juvenile violence by the end of the decade.[3]

In the late winter and early spring of 1988, Boston began to experience the first effects of an emerging network of violent rival gangs. Boston public school security personnel, who witnessed the development of the gangs within the schools, compiled the first list of gangs and individual gang members and the schools they attended. The list described loosely federated groups organized around specific territories; these groups started the custom of gangs naming themselves for the street or public housing development in which their members lived.

As the police department struggled for a strategy to deal with the problem, gang activity and its effects grew more serious. That summer brought horrific incidents on the street during daylight hours, with rival gang members gunning each other down in drive-by shootings. In August 1988, the city's attention was riveted to "ground zero" in the gang violence explosion, the intersection of Humboldt Avenue and Homestead Street in Roxbury, where twelve-year-old Darlene Tiffany Moore was shot in the head and killed by crossfire as she sat atop a mailbox, talking with friends. Rival gangs transformed her into a "mushroom" (gang jargon for an innocent victim), and she became a symbol of the horror.

A city that experienced seventy-five homicides and 5,920 aggravated assaults in 1987 would see ninety-five homicides and 6,291 aggravated assaults by year-end 1988. Homicides reached an all-time annual high of 152 and aggravated assaults reached the decade-high peak of 6,960 in 1990. Eighteen of the homicide victims in 1990 were age seventeen or younger.[4] Crack cocaine arrived on the scene around that time, and the developing gangs fought each other to become distributors of this highly profitable product. In addition, traffickers in semi-automatic handguns identified a potential market for their goods and began running guns to the emerging gangs.

During this period, gang behavior in the courthouses grew bolder. Court officials described regular disruptions in the courtrooms and corridors, intimidation of witnesses, and attempted intimidation of staff. One justice in the Dorchester district court made headlines with a call to bring in the National Guard to secure the courthouse. Probation officers began to identify and catalogue gang colors and individual gang members and their affiliations. Led by Paul Evans, then patrol chief and now police commissioner, the department searched for ways to stem the bloody tide of shootings and homicides. By spring 1990, the department had developed a new strategy, the anti–gang violence unit, and it was ready to take back the streets.

To understand Operation Night Light and its unique contribution to the criminal justice arsenal requires an understanding of the traditional role of the probation office and its practices. The conventional duties of probation officers include conducting background investigations on defendants who may be placed on probation; supervising probationers, usually in accordance with a classification scheme; and initiating violation hearings against noncompliant probationers. It is clear from conversations

with a range of probation executives that over the last two decades of the
twentieth century those fundamental duties were carried out primarily
from a desk in an office, a marked and much regretted departure from earlier practice.[5]

Probation is both a sentence and a status. As a sentence, it constitutes far
and away the most popular option in use: nationwide, 60 percent of all
offenders under correctional supervision are on probation,[6] and the corre-
sponding percentage in Massachusetts is 69 percent.[7] Offenders placed on
probation are on conditional liberty, free to remain in the community provided that they comply with any conditions of their probation. Common
conditions include avoiding subsequent arrest, reporting to a probation
officer, not leaving the state without permission, and, often, paying restitution and obtaining substance abuse counseling or other appropriate
treatment. Traditionally, some judges imposed curfews for younger offenders, but the practice waned during the 1980s and early 1990s because of
difficulties in enforcing compliance. Parents were not as cooperative as they
once were, and probation officers, who were weary of returning to high-
crime areas in the evening, had become comfortable with nine-to-five
schedules.

The building blocks of what would become Operation Night Light
were laid when the new gang unit was created within the Boston police
department. Probation officers Bill Stewart and Rick Skinner and gang
unit detective Bob Merner put the first block in place in a court corridor
conversation in the summer of 1990. Realizing that they were watching the
same youthful offenders from two different vantage points on the perimeter of a "revolving door," they and others from both agencies began to
brainstorm to develop new forms of collaboration. As Dorchester chief
probation officer Bernard Fitzgerald reported, "We began seeing the same
gang unit guys in the courthouse every single day for four months."[8]

Using information from their contacts with the gang unit and from
their interactions with gang members, which provided them with insight
into when and where probationers were violating the conditions of their
release, probation officers began to ask judges to include curfews and area
restrictions in the conditions of probation. Compliance with those conditions was expected to improve as the level of supervision was increased,
leading to a reduction in the number of new arrests of juveniles on probation. The deterrent effect of curfews depended on strict enforcement, and
officers realized that high-risk offenders, who would take advantage of any
laxity, required a tight rein.

On their own, Fitzgerald, Stewart, and Skinner began to move away from the existing model of probation by getting away from their desks in the courthouse. They began approaching probationers on the street, who all but rubbed their eyes in disbelief at the sight of their probation officers on their turf. In August 1991, Stewart wrote a memo to district court judge James Dolan, recounting the open drug dealing that he witnessed by one of his clients at 2:00 p.m. on a residential street in the district. Judge Dolan, an early supporter of the collaboration, became an even more determined backer of efforts to ensure that the terms of probation had teeth.

Police officers began to see probation as a powerful deterrent—and to carve out a new role in deterrence for themselves. Informal contacts continued to grow and yield results. On November 12, 1992, Stewart and Skinner got in the back seat of a police car with Merner and partner Bob Fratalia, and Operation Night Light began. Boston began to work toward a strategy of community corrections. One Boston police detective later remarked:

> Well, when I used to watch people walk out of court with probation as the end result, I said "That's b————!" But I can see now what good, supervised probation can do—it sounds corny—for the community. I've seen gangs from a particular neighborhood decimated only because of supervised curfews and area restrictions. So again, as I touched on before, I know so much more about probation as a tool.

Operations

On a typical evening with Operation Night Light, a one- or two-person probation team is matched with a similar team from the gang unit, and they meet at gang unit headquarters to prepare for the evening's work. The probation officers will have identified some ten to fifteen probationers that they want to see that evening, concentrating on those thought to be "active" on the street or those whose compliance with probation conditions has been slipping. Operating in an unmarked car and in plain clothes, the team proceeds to the first scheduled curfew check. The police team, which is responsible for safety issues, approaches the probationer's home with sensitivity to the surroundings and keeps an eye on exit areas in case the probationer should try to evade contact. Once the security issues, which are not monumental in most cases, are addressed, the probation officer approaches the door. Once the officers are inside the home, the contact proceeds as would any typical probationary home visit. Every effort is made to ensure that parents and other family members are not alarmed, and the visit is conducted in a courteous and friendly manner.

The purpose of the visit is to determine whether the probationer is at home, as required by his or her curfew; to reinforce the importance of strict observance of all probation conditions; and talk with any parents present about the behavior of the probationer, both at home and in the community. After those basic objectives are met and any issues of concern to any parties are addressed, the team thanks all present for their cooperation and goes on to the next scheduled contact.

It is not uncommon for a team to stop at a park or street corner where youth congregate to determine whether any probationers are present. Stopping by also demonstrates that the probation and police departments are working together and that both are interested in the whereabouts and activities of young people on probation. The teams learned that word spread fast that there was a new mode of operation in probation—and a new level of jeopardy for those who were inclined to ignore their probationary obligations.

The partnership between the probation and police departments has been sustained because both sides are reaping tangible and significant benefits. Probation officers, who are not armed or equipped with telecommunications capacity, can enter the most crime-ridden areas of the city into the late evening because the police provide a high degree of security for them. Also, because of the familiarity between the departments that has grown out of Night Light, they now routinely share information regarding the identity of those on probation; any knowledge that any police officer has concerning the activities of a probationer (whether the subject of Night Light or not) can be passed on to probation. While it may seem to be an obvious strategy, in most jurisdictions the two departments do not seem to exchange information routinely. That failure robs probation of access to the contacts and observations made by police, who work the community twenty-four hours a day, seven days a week, and therefore have more "eyes and ears" on the streets than even the most proactive probation department can muster. The increased flow of information regarding probationers' activities has been one of the greatest outcomes of Night Light.

In sum, from probation officers' point of view, their supervision of probationers and enforcement of curfews and area restrictions have a new credibility that did not exist when they conducted their probation activities from nine to five. Feedback from offenders, police, parents, and community members alike indicates that the kids are aware that things have changed and that they have become more cautious, if not to say more compliant, in their behavior. That is a breakthrough.

The police, for their part, now have a tool available to them that significantly increases their power. Many police officers speak of the frustration that comes with knowing that certain offenders are active in the community but being unable to control them because of the difficulties involved in detecting crime and apprehending criminals. While not all offenders being targeted by the police are on probation, both common sense and the available data suggest that probationers account for upward of 20 percent of all serious crime.[9] Any strategy that legally targets this group through closer surveillance and supervision can have a deterrent effect. Deterrence is achieved by requiring probationers to avoid certain areas and also to be in their homes at a reasonable hour each evening, not on the streets at times when gang-related violence flourishes. While most often probationers will not be detected undertaking criminal activity, their failure to abide by court orders can put them at risk of being incarcerated as certainly as being arrested for a new offense, and the point is not lost on them. Unlike nonprobationers, they can be removed from the street for a variety of noncriminal behaviors.

The police marvel at and appreciate the power of probation officers in this respect. Members of the gang unit have often commented on how the kids fear their "P.O." more than they fear a uniformed police officer. Provided that this broader power is used fairly and judiciously, it puts a formidable crime-fighting technique on the street to supplement conventional police strategies. In the words of another Boston police officer:

> We can use Night Light to target community concerns. If we have a rash of shootings, drive-bys, drug dealing, community complaints, we can call the court, be it Roxbury or Dorchester court, and make all our area checks down here. So besides the added uniform presence, drug unit, detectives, and everybody else from here, we have probation officers down there to start shaking everybody's tree too. If nothing else, it just defuses it.

Bernard L. Fitzgerald, chief probation officer, Dorchester district court, had this to say regarding the benefits of a strong probation enforcement policy:

> One of the most striking examples [of those benefits] is that of a young man who, along with his brothers, was the leader of a very

violent drug-involved gang in the Dorchester area. His mother made a plea for him in court to prevent him from being incarcerated. She said that if the court allowed him to continue on probation she would keep him at her new home in Plymouth.

The young man's terms of probation were written so that he couldn't be in Dorchester at any time other than to go to court. Within the next two days, while riding with the gang unit, the defendant's probation officer spotted the defendant in the back of a taxi. The police stopped the taxi, and when they approached it they observed the probationer trying to hide an object, which turned out to be a nine-millimeter handgun. He was arrested for violation of his probation and possession of a firearm. He was found in violation of probation and committed to prison. By virtue of this action, we were able to put a bit of a block on the activities of this gang.

Another example of the benefit of the Night Light program is evidenced by the young man who said that his probation officer saved his life. The young man came to his probation officer on a Monday morning and said that, had it not been for fear of being caught, he would have been with three friends who were arrested for a double murder. He said that he had been asked to go with his friends to a party on Friday evening. He declined the invitation, citing the fact that he had curfew and his P.O. periodically checked him at his home and if he were out he would be found in violation and sent to jail. The probationer stayed home, and his friends tried to rob two young men of their jewelry at a party and when they resisted they shot and killed them. The probationer said that he had no doubt that he would have been part of that had he not been afraid of violating his curfew.

A Balanced Approach

It was understood by all participants in this new approach that increased enforcement had to be leavened by a commitment to provide appropriate services to youth who frequently needed help and support in finding a new, prosocial direction as they abandoned gang life. The help came in three forms: job assistance, faith-based counseling, and personal advocacy.

Employment was at the top of everyone's list. Getting jobs for kids served multiple purposes. Work kept youth busy and therefore unavailable for gang activities; it provided spending money and, in other instances, basic provisions for neglected younger siblings; and it was a way to instill the habits of punctuality, following direction, and interacting appropriately with peers and the public, all sorely needed by the targeted youth.

In the early 1990s, the city of Boston greatly expanded its summer jobs program, so all youth who were interested had a good chance of finding summer employment. Key officers in the gang unit contributed their personal time and effort to the cause and, with corporate support, developed a program that came to be known as the Summer of Opportunity. The program provided youth referred by gang unit officers with a combination of work experience and life skills training; those who successfully completed the program (which an average of 90 percent were able to do) were provided part-time jobs during the school year.[10]

At-risk youth in Boston found a second stream of support coming from an entirely new direction. In May 1992, a local Baptist church had experienced the unspeakable—a gang-related stabbing and shooting occurred during a church service. In the wake of that event, inner-city clergy mobilized to address the church's role in combating youthful violence, and a group of ministers who were committed to taking their message to the streets in the hardest-hit areas formed the Ten Point Coalition.[11] The coalition's initial forays into gang territory led to the slow but steady development of relationships between kids and clergy that evolved into court advocacy as well as church-based programs such as Gangs Anonymous meetings, sponsored and attended by church leaders.

The involvement of clergy and other church folk created a special cast to the ongoing efforts. The Ten Point Coalition sponsored prayer meetings and special liturgies where blessings were bestowed on the new strategy and those active in it. To many of those involved, this new and decidedly spiritual dimension was deeply felt. It was as if the Almighty was smiling on Boston's efforts, bestowing a welcome and amazing grace on the undertaking.

These efforts were rounded out by those of a growing corps of "streetworkers," hired by the mayor, whose charge was to hit the streets and work with young people in crisis wherever and whenever they could be found. The streetworkers were hired for their skill in developing rapport with young people and mobilizing community resources. Although they were initially greeted with suspicion by the police, in time a close, mutually respectful relationship evolved that allowed the police to get their message out to gang leaders without the static that came with direct communication. The streetworkers helped head off trouble when alerted to emerging

"beefs," worked with kids whom police or probation officers might identify as being on the cusp of serious trouble, and connected youth with services that gave them healthy options to pursue.[12]

The emphasis on services, outreach, and advocacy gave needed balance
to the Boston strategy and gave moral authority to the efforts of police and
probation officers. Both clergy and streetworkers identified with the interests of community members and would not have supported a strategy that
relied on stepped-up enforcement while neglecting services and support.
This commitment to a balanced approach, which had the manifest support
and involvement of Boston's most aggressive police officers, made uncon-
ventional alliances possible. The youth saw a new seriousness about stem-
ming youth violence coupled with a genuine, consistent campaign to identify and increase the help available to them. In the service of saving Boston's
children, stereotypes and rigid role definitions broke down.

A case study of the Boston strategy put the matter this way:

> The outreach programs established by the Gang Unit had a two-fold
> effect: they benefitted kids and gave the police the credibility it
> needed to build close ties to the Ten-Point Coalition and other ser-
> vice organizations. The presence of these relationships in turn created
> a reservoir of good will that allowed the police and other law enforce-
> ment agencies to intensify their policing efforts without alienating
> large segments of the black community.
>
> If we [the Ten-Point Coalition] had not played a role in the inter-
> vention and prevention process in Boston, what you would have had
> was something akin to apartheid," says [Reverend Jeffrey] Brown.
> "You'd have had the police versus the youth. It would have been
> Dodge City."[13]

Program Impact

What difference have the more than 7,000 Operation Night Light contacts
(home visits, street contacts, and so forth) made in the last ten years? While
direct impact is notoriously difficult to prove, the lower numbers of homicide and other violent crimes in the areas involved are encouraging. There
was one juvenile homicide during 1996, one in 1997, six in 1998, two in
1999, two in 2000, and four in 2001; in comparison, there were sixteen in
1993.[14] The data presented in figures 6-1 through 6-6 document the homicides during the period in which Night Light has operated.

Figure 6-1. *Homicides, All Ages*

Number

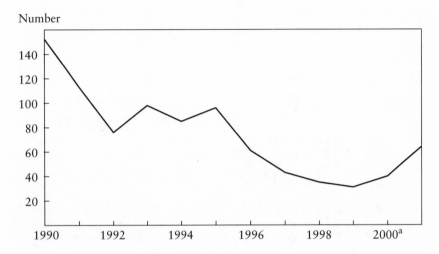

Source: Boston Police Department, Office of Police Commissioner, Office of Research and Evaluation (2002).
a. 2000 statistics include three gangland victims murdered in the 1980s whose bodies were recovered in 2000.

Figure 6-2. *Firearm Homicides, All Ages*

Number

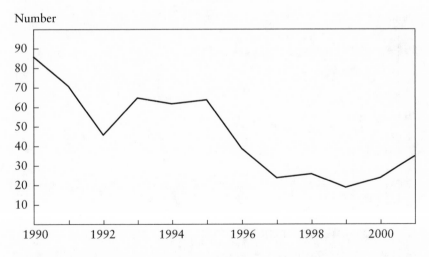

Source: Boston Police Department, Office of Police Commissioner, Office of Research and Evaluation (2002).

Figure 6-3. *Total Homicides, 16 and Under*

Number

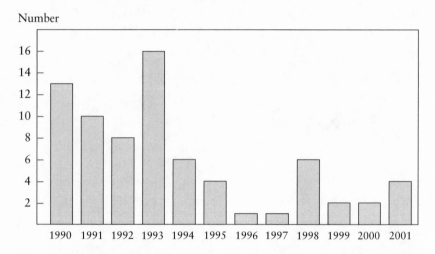

Source: Boston Police Department, Office of Police Commissioner, Office of Research and Evaluation (2002).

Figure 6-4. *Firearm Homicides, 16 and Under*

Number

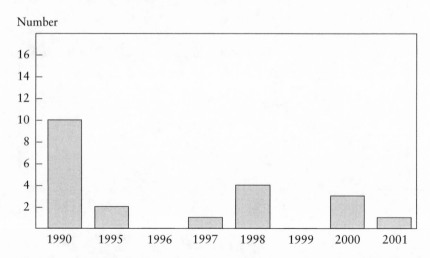

Source: Boston Police Department, Office of Police Commissioner, Office of Research and Evaluation (2002).

Figure 6-5. *All Homicides, 24 and Under*

Number

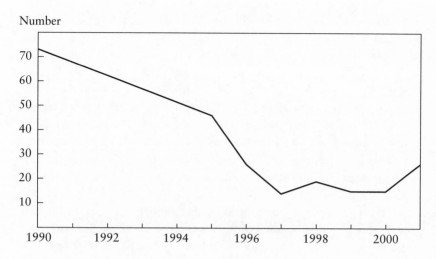

Source: Boston Police Department, Office of Police Commissioner, Office of Research and Evaluation (2002).

Figure 6-6. *Firearm Homicides, 24 and Under*

Number

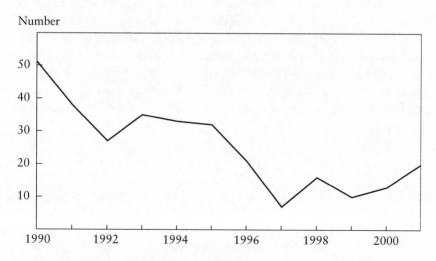

Source: Boston Police Department, Office of Police Commissioner, Office of Research and Evaluation (2002).

While no one involved in Operation Night Light claims primary credit for this positive trend, everyone believes that the partnership is at least partially responsible for the reduced levels of gang-related violence as well as increased compliance with terms of probation. Members of the network of clergy, streetworkers, community leaders, and researchers as well as criminal justice personnel that grew out of this innovation kept in regular contact with offenders in the affected neighborhoods and were unanimous in their perception that probationary sentences and those that enforce them were seen in an entirely new light. David Kennedy of Harvard University's Kennedy School of Government commented on how the gang members that he spoke to felt restrained by the curfew checks, area restrictions, and more frequent and unannounced home visits that came with the Night Light regimen.[15]

In addition, court personnel believe that probationary sentences have gained more credibility because of the stricter enforcement that Operation Night Light provides. Although it has not always been in the past, it is clear now—the word is on the street, so to speak—that those on probation must take their obligations seriously. They know now that if they do not, they will be caught and they will pay the consequences.

There is also the hard-to-measure but real reassurance felt in the neighborhoods where Night Light operates. The knowledge that probation and police officers are around to ensure that probationers are off the streets in the evening brings a measure of relief to communities hard hit by crime. It also is very clear that the parents of these young people, who often are in a losing battle to keep their sons from succumbing to the lure of the streets, genuinely appreciate the support they receive through curfew enforcement. While the program is designed primarily to prevent young offenders from committing new crimes, their parents recognize that it also serves to keep them from being victimized themselves in the mortal combat that engulfs their streets.

Promises and Perils of Partnership

As with any new public initiative, the accumulation of experiences from multiple sites and findings from sound evaluations eventually will form the basis for a reliable assessment of Operation Night Light. Though such partnerships are still in their infancy, some observations nevertheless can be offered on how they can help to address the real crisis facing contemporary probation.

First, on a practical level, the simple but consistent exchange of information between probation and police departments can serve the goals of both. If they share the surveillance task, probationers will sense the greater risk of discovery of any crime and as a result may be deterred from criminal activity. Compliance with court orders also is enhanced through police-probation department cooperation. For example, when a convicted batterer is prohibited from approaching the residence of his victim and police who patrol the area are familiar with the offender and the restriction, their chances of discovering any violation are greatly increased. The police also may be aided in investigating criminal incidents by knowing local probationers and their criminal history and by having the assistance of probation officers in identifying potential suspects. In addition, having a working relationship with the police can help probation officers apprehend absconders, who traditionally have been neglected by many probation departments due to staff shortages, insufficient staff training, or lack of appropriate equipment. Locating and arresting fugitives is second nature to law enforcement personnel, and their expertise can be shared with probation officers.

Beyond these tangible gains is the harder-to-measure but nonetheless real public relations benefit that the probation department may receive from being identified with law enforcement. The same national and local polls that reflect so poorly on probation departments give the police very high ratings.[16] There is an opportunity to ride the "coattails" of the police here, with some of the same positive sentiment that is felt for them accruing to probation officers who take on functions more akin to law enforcement and who are seen in the company of the police. To some, this may appear to be pandering, and there are attendant dangers. However, when the partnership serves legitimate correctional ends, no wise probation executive should fail to capitalize on the improved perception of probation officers that so many of the initial sites have reported.[17]

However, all the effects of partnership may not be positive. Sociologist Robert Merton was the first to introduce the concept of "unintended consequences" into policy and program analysis, and most administrators are only too familiar with its validity.[18] Initiatives undertaken with only positive intentions can perversely result in negative consequences that overshadow any gains. While it is still early in the development of these models, some potential trade-offs already have caused concern among those involved. In general, the dangers have at least the following three manifestations: mission creep, mission distortion, and organizational lag.

Mission creep. Many of these partnerships are born of or eventually connected with community policing efforts, and the demands on staff time and agency resources escalate as probation officers' role expands. Where partnerships flourish, participating probation officers engage in a variety of new collateral activities under the rubric of community building that extend well beyond the scope of normal duties. Acting as a broker for many human services, attending community functions, and responding to complaints unrelated to probation are a few common examples. For police officers who are relieved of other responsibilities or who otherwise would be conducting general patrol, that may not be burdensome. For probation officers still carrying traditional caseloads, the time conflicts are obvious, and they could easily compromise officers' effectiveness. With the right organizational and structural changes, those problems can be avoided, but often such changes are not forthcoming.

Mission distortion. Despite the best efforts of administrators who anticipate the problem and try to counteract it, there is still the real threat that partnerships with law enforcement will be perceived, particularly within probation agencies, as an abandonment of the treatment mission in favor of a nearly exclusive emphasis on enforcement. Probation has always been seen as a philosophical battleground, where the "cop" and the "social worker" types fight it out for ascendancy. A move to work with the police will almost inevitably be seen as a victory for the "cops," and that has implications for agency morale and the perceived emphasis, based on rewards, given to the different functions. In other words, the social worker types may go into a funk and wonder what's become of the agency they loved. Through Operation Night Light, the probation agency reaped a degree of positive publicity unparalleled in its 120-year history. It would be very tempting for any manager, seeing such a public relations coup, to immediately make a police partnership an overriding priority. In the meantime, attention to those functions identified with rehabilitative services could suffer, and observant staff would draw the obvious inferences.

The Greeks were right—in life, balance is everything. But in the face of rapid change, it is devilishly difficult to handle shifting priorities and new trends. It is important for administrators to remember to put only some of their eggs into each new basket and to ensure that new strategies yield to rather than obscure the agency's preexisting and, one hopes, well-thought-out mission. Furthermore, if the research in community corrections for the last fifteen years has taught us anything, it is that in the field of probation an exclusive or even primary emphasis on enforcement, surveillance, and control strategies will not succeed. Without the array of services available through the city of Boston, the business community, and the court system—including camp scholarships, summer jobs, employment training, and substance abuse treatment—the Night Light officers would have been severely hampered in their work. Whenever a high-risk probationer showed signs of wanting to get out of the "life," the supervising probation officer had referral options that enhanced the probationer's chances for success.

What was unique about Operation Night Light was not the services provided—although they were surely critical—but the fact that, for the first time in recent memory in Boston, the offenders felt that they were truly being supervised. Probation officers and the police were pooling their intelligence, and offenders knew that one or the other knew about their activities, which greatly reduced their margin for error. It is clear that because of this deterrence strategy, many more probationers than usual were amenable to "going straight."[19]

Organizational lag. Unlike the first two, the last peril is not a byproduct of police-probation partnerships but a threat to them. The correctional landscape is littered with the remains of once-promising programs that perished from lack of full institutional support. Petersilia remarks that the problem with intermediate sanctions, which she sees as having great but unfulfilled promise, is that they were never adequately supported and therefore never received a fair trial.[20] Such has been the fate of many correctional innovations.

For probation-police partnerships to take root and flourish, they cannot simply be grafted onto the existing organizational structure. Work assignment, for example, will require rethinking. Perhaps probation officers should be assigned neighborhoods instead of caseloads. Perhaps contact standards and other commonplace bureaucratic requirements should be replaced by broader, more flexible standards of practice crediting a range of actions in the community that could deter reoffending. Management information systems may need dramatic change to reward individuals who have the qualities necessary for success in this new environment.

What is more predictable is that new practices will be superimposed on existing customs, many of which have long since become obsolete. Undertaking a new approach while maintaining a traditional system of accountability will create real disincentives for interested staff, demoralize those who otherwise want the partnerships to succeed, and ultimately threaten the future of the program. To create incentives for adopting new approaches, recruitment and promotion practices must be designed so that it is clear that candidates who are committed to field-based practice are given priority. In Massachusetts, for example, the most recently negotiated union contract provides financial incentives for officers who work during nontraditional hours—evening and weekends.

As with so much else in public administration, even the best ideas cannot survive uninspired, timid management. True leadership, on the other hand, can make even flawed models work wonders.

Six Lessons Learned

Remember the importance of balance. Correctional interventions must be two-fisted. Because the problems we address never yield to one-dimensional approaches, any attempt to make real progress by using law enforcement or treatment strategies alone is doomed to failure. Nor will a one-theme approach garner critical political support. The investment in enforcement clears the path for a complementary investment in treatment. Average Americans want to see a measure of both, shifting in proportions to the realities confronted. This may be common sense, but few policymakers seem to recognize it. As Albert Camus observed, quoting the mathematician and philosopher Blaise Pascal, "'A man does not show his greatness by being at one extremity or another but rather by touching both at once.'"[21]

Publicity builds momentum and commitment. President Bill Clinton's visit to Boston in February 1997 was the culmination of an extended series of media hits for the Boston strategy. Regular coverage by both local and national media (for example, ABC Evening News, in its "Solutions" series) drew popular and, more important, internal attention to the effort. Everyone wanted to be part of the effort—there was no lack of volunteers or resources to support it.

For any new initiative to flourish, it has to create a "buzz" that draws attention and elicits support. Both an internal strategy that creates organizational incentives for involvement and an external strategy that builds political support are critical. Accordingly, new programs must attract the best and brightest employees in an agency through strong internal support and marketing by the agency's leadership. Leaders also must catch the eye of key public figures whose support is crucial to the agency. Nothing will accomplish that faster than sustained, positive media coverage.

Nurture the relationship among the partners. Partnerships of any kind are fragile affairs and sustaining them requires work. Regular communication and an honest effort to honor all partners' role and requirements are the key to longevity. In the early years of the Boston strategy, all participating agencies, including administrative and line staff, were invited to biweekly meetings. The meetings, which were well attended, served multiple functions. The frequency of the meetings allowed participants to get to know and trust each other. The opportunity to get up-to-date intelligence and to share success stories sustained interest and commitment.[22] The open forum approach, in which anyone, regardless of rank, could speak to the group, made for lively meetings where the key issues surfaced.

Use an objective outsider. Groups, particularly if they are highly charged and successful, can develop a blindness to potential mistakes and opportunities. In the flush of enthusiasm and fellow-feeling engendered by a new and exciting venture, "groupthink" can take over and reality can get lost. One antidote is to involve an outsider whose job, whether by design or happenstance, is to keep the project honest. That person stays on top of all developments, corrects flaws of logic, and points out the errors of omission and possibilities for enhancement that only a disinterested party will easily notice.

In Boston, the Boston Gun Project, led by David Kennedy and colleagues at Harvard University's Kennedy School of Government, played just such a role. Kennedy worked from a great respect for the wisdom of the participants and looked first to leverage their abilities and insights by feeding back to them in refined form the raw material of his many long and patient discussions with key players.[23]

Get good data. Although experience and familiarity with a problem may lull us into thinking that we understand its nature and dimensions, gathering hard data before undertaking a new project can still bring some surprises. At the least, it can impose needed discipline on the process. The Boston Gun Project provided an essential service by helping participants gather reliable data on the phenomenon of youth violence and on the offenders. An examination of the particulars of 155 youth homicides in Boston revealed a high correlation with gang membership and gang-related activities; it also demonstrated that both perpetrators and victims were concentrated among the relatively slim ranks of well-known chronic offenders. That information was critical to the development of the strategy.[24] In addition, tracking the results provided the documentation required by the outside world while also helping to shape and refine the emerging strategy.

Be experimental. Corrections is awash in failed strategies; the only recourse for the prudent manager is to keep trying. Moreover, trying to find entirely new ways that break from conventional approaches is especially critical. Breakthroughs in science sometimes come from exploring new avenues on the basis of nothing more than a hunch. We must be similarly foolhardy in corrections. We must adopt the long-shot, the odd-ball, the "what if" frame of mind. It is this spirit that animated the architects of the Boston strategy and accounts for much of their success. Flexibility in design and implementation is equally important. If the ideal model does not work, modify it, tweak it until it starts showing some results. Again, this is precisely how the most accomplished scientists work. They follow an iterative process, constantly testing, changing, and testing again. On the other hand, sticking with something after its shown fatal flaws is not determination but stubborn pridefulness. As Franklin D. Roosevelt remarked in an address at Oglethorpe University in May 1932, "The country needs and, unless I mistake its temper, the country demands bold, persistent experimentation. It is common sense to take a method and try it. If it fails, admit it frankly and try another. But above all, try something."

Finally, look for proof that you are attaining the desired outcome. Have a bottom line and stay with it. In Boston, the goal always was to stop the killing. The participants never looked up until the numbers began to drop dramatically. Fewer funerals was the goal, and they kept close score.

Thoughts on Replication

Principles travel, programs don't. Too often, a certain model gains popularity and becomes the darling of the correctional field. Boot camps are a good recent example; everyone has to have one. The trouble with adopting programs wholesale because they are in fashion and appear to work is that it ignores the fact that people, places, conditions, and resources vary significantly, in ways that can foster or impede success. What works for me will work for you only if you are just like me; usually, you aren't. Principles can transfer, however. Looking at the essence or core properties of a program is helpful, because they can be embodied differently depending on the key variables in the adopting jurisdiction. Custom tailor the general approach to local realities. Steal ideas, not programs.

It takes a crisis. I was part of a delegation from Boston that recently visited another state that was interested in adopting the Boston strategy. In a meeting with state officials, someone asked, "What does it take to get a program like yours started?" After a pause, I responded: "It helps if one of your churches is shot up." The tragedy at the Morning Star Baptist Church was clearly the catalyst for much of the change that began to occur in Boston. No one hopes for such an event, but the hard truth is that often it takes something of that caliber to jump-start reform efforts. Without a shared sense of urgency, the mandate for change is a weak and uncertain thing.

You cannot plan for or instigate a crisis, but you can reveal one. Sometimes, seeing that attention is drawn to otherwise little known and ominous conditions and trends can create a critical mass of concern and coverage. And having a flair for the dramatic is a well-known attribute of agents of change.

Look for natural leaders. Peter Drucker, a management guru, has observed that wherever something really great is happening, there is a monomaniac with a mission.[25] Big results require extraordinary leaders. The best ideas in corrections are never self-executing; uninspired management can undermine the best models and real leadership can breathe life into the most rudimentary ideas. New projects need champions. Agencies and jurisdictions committed to radical improvements must identify and enlist talented administrators with a passion for the enterprise and a hunger to succeed. They are few in number, but every system has them. Find one.

Start small. Don't launch the Normandy invasion if all you have to do is take a beachhead. Over-reaching squanders resources, divides attention, strains logistics, and makes retreat difficult. Learn first what it takes to succeed. Look at your most favorable circumstances and start there. To make an early victory nearly inevitable, concentrate your forces and use a small success to build momentum. By moving slowly but consistently, you can increase the scope and intensity of your impact.

Take stock of existing relationships. Citywide interventions require the support of a diverse group of public and private officials. War historians tell us that soldiers risk their lives more for their comrades than for a cause. Social action is no different. Only hard-earned mutual trust based on personal regard will get a coalition through the inevitable setbacks. The best working relationships do not come cheap. They are built around a lot of coffee cups, in the back rooms of station houses, in drafty church basements, in courthouse corridors, and at the scenes of shootings. It takes a while to learn who you can rely on, whose back you are willing to cover.

To take the lead in a new strategy, agencies must have a sufficient number of allies. If more work needs to be done on cultivating key relationships, hold off on the new initiatives and build those relationships. Your potential partners will want to know that you are a dependable, honest, and courageous team player. Show them.

School-Probation Partnerships: The Next Frontier

Traditionally, a fire wall has existed between probation and law enforcement agencies, impeding information sharing and collaboration. The experiences described earlier in this chapter reflect the progress that has been made in Boston (and, increasingly, elsewhere) in tearing down that fire wall by redefining conventional roles and relationships.

Attention should now be turned to the relationship between schools and probation agencies. Some of the same radical rethinking is needed to maximize the potential of both institutions in combating youth violence. Some reports have pointed to the need for experimentation and creativity with respect to school-based crime prevention activities.[26] Other accounts lament the fact that school officials and other adult authority figures in the community, including probation and police officers, cooperate too infrequently in supervising and supporting at-risk youth, doing a disservice to the young person, the institutions represented, and the community alike.[27]

There are some bright spots, and they offer valuable lessons.[28] Jeremy Travis, former director of the National Institute of Justice, the research arm of the U.S. Department of Justice, has reported on successful efforts to use problem-solving strategies developed first in law enforcement to address school safety issues.[29] Evaluations conducted by the Police Executive Research Forum documented strikingly positive results. For the last several years, Middlesex County in Massachusetts has experimented with creative alliances, and, in the process, recast traditional roles and ways of doing business. Three particular strategies warrant mention:

Community-based justice meetings. On the basis of a program developed originally by Tom Reilly, former district attorney and now Massachusetts attorney general, each high school in Middlesex County hosts a weekly meeting involving prosecutors, police officers, probation officers, and school officials to discuss the ongoing response to at-risk youth.[30] These meetings include the exchange of information and intelligence regarding such matters as the juveniles' school and community behavior as well as the status of any legal proceedings. In addition, participants engage in problem solving and planning to try to design a coordinated response to contain the youth while also providing needed services—a kind of carrot-and-stick approach. All participants laud the program, which already has several years of experience, and the model has been exported to all other counties in Massachusetts.

Project Firm. In Framingham, one of the largest cities in the county, the school system and the local probation office have collaborated for several years in Project Firm, a diversionary program for school offenders.[31] When students are charged with infractions of school rules that might lead to a delinquency complaint, local juvenile probation officers act as hearings officers at the schools to determine whether the infraction occurred and the nature of any appropriate sanctions and services. This process gets probation officers and school officials collaborating early on so that offending juveniles will both understand the concerns of the community and be able to access social services if indicated. The bridge established between schools and probation agencies carries over into the handling of formal delinquency complaints and has generated partnerships such as Project NIRC.

Project NIRC. Building on the success of Project Firm, school, probation, and police officials joined in a new initiative that the police dubbed NIRC (non–incident-related contact).[32] NIRC involves joint evening visits to the homes of students who are creating problems in school or in the community by three representatives, one from each partner in the initiative, to advise youth and parents of the likely consequences of further difficulty and to offer services if the family is open to them. Here again, the image portrayed to the youth and the community is that of responsible authorities working together to hold young people accountable and to offer assistance before a problem worsens.

Each of these three initiatives calls on officials to act in new and unfamiliar ways, to adopt an expanded role in which they act almost interchangeably with other officials. They eliminate the fire walls referred to earlier and replace them with bridges that facilitate communication and cooperation. Each relies on the key public institutions involved to mount a coordinated response to youthful misbehavior, leveraging and multiplying the controls and solutions that each can bring to the table in the service of community safety and individual well-being.

Albert Einstein reportedly said that insanity is doing the same old thing but expecting different results. Middlesex County is doing different things and getting different results, and its success story ranks with that of Operation Night Light in Boston.

Notes

1. Reinventing Probation Council, "Broken Windows Probation: The Next Step in Fighting Crime," Civic Report 7 (New York: Center for Civic Innovation at the Manhattan

Institute, August 1999); Reinventing Probation Council, "Transforming Probation through Leadership: The 'Broken Windows' Model" (New York: Center for Civic Innovation at the Manhattan Institute, July 2000).

2. Portions of this section are based on Ronald P. Corbett Jr., "Probation Blue: The Promise and Perils of Probation-Police Partnerships," *Correctional Management Quarterly*, vol. 2, no. 3 (1998), pp. 31–39, with permission.

3. James Alan Fox, "Trends in Juvenile Violence" (U.S. Department of Justice, March 1996), p. 4.

4. Personal communication from James Jordan, May 12, 1998.

5. Ronald P. Corbett Jr., "Juvenile Probation on the Eve of the Next Millenium," in Gary L. McDowell and Jinney S. Smith, eds., *Juvenile Delinquency in the United States and the United Kingdom* (St. Martin's Press, 1999), pp. 115–38.

6. Massachusetts Institute for a New Commonwealth, "Criminal Justice in Massachusetts: Putting Crime Control First" (October 1996), p. 21.

7. Communication with Research Department, Office of the Massachusetts Commissioner of Probation, Boston.

8. Ronald P. Corbett Jr., Bernard Fitzgerald, and James Jordan, "Operation Night Light: An Emerging Model for Police-Probation Partnership," Better Government Competition Series 6 (Boston: Pioneer Institute, 1996), p. 109.

9. Council on Crime in America, *The State of Violent Crime in America* (Washington, 1996), p. 4.

10. John A. Buntin, "A Community Response: Boston Confronts an Upsurge of Youth Violence" (Harvard University, John F. Kennedy School of Government, 1998), pp. 1–40.

11. On the Ten Point Coalition, see Christopher Winship and Jenny Berrien, chapter 7 in this volume.

12. Ibid.

13. Buntin, "A Community Response," p. 28.

14. Boston Police Department, Office of the Police Commissioner, Office of Research and Evaluation (2002).

15. See David Kennedy, chapter 8 in this volume.

16. T. J. Flanagan and D. R. Longmire, *Americans View Crime and Justice: A National Public Opinion Survey* (Thousand Oaks, Calif.: Sage Publications, 1996).

17. Meeting of National Association of Probation Executives, New York City, August 1999.

18. Robert K. Merton, *On Social Structure and Science* (University of Chicago Press, 1996), pp. 173–82.

19. Research Department, Office of the Massachussetts Commissioner of Probation, Boston (April 2000).

20. Joan Petersilia, ed., *Community Corrections: Probation, Parole, and Intermediate Sanctions* (Oxford University Press, 1998), pp. 19–27.

21. Blaise Pascal, quoted in Albert Camus, *Resistance, Rebellion, and Death* (Alfred A. Knopf, 1961), p. 1.

22. Kennedy, chapter 8.

23. Ibid.; Buntin, "A Community Response," p. 25.

24. Kennedy, chapter 8.

25. Thomas J. Peters and Robert H. Waterman Jr., *In Search of Excellence: ˹ ˻ssons from*

America's Best Run Companies (Warner Books, 1983), p. 225.

26. David C. Anderson, "Curriculum, Culture, and Community: The Challenge of School Violence," in Michael Tonry and Mark H. Moore, eds., *Youth Violence* (University of Chicago Press, 1998), pp. 317–63.

27. Stephen Marans and Mark Schaefer, "Community Policing, Schools, and Mental Health: The Challenge of Collaboration," in Delbert S. Elliott, Beatrix A. Hamburg, and Kirk R. Williams, eds., *Violence in American Schools* (Cambridge University Press, 1998), pp. 312–47.

28. Amalia V. Betanzos, chapter 10 in this volume.

29. Jeremy Travis, "Creating Safe Schools: Opening the Schoolhouse Doors to Research and Partnerships," keynote address at Conference of the Security Management Institute, New York, August 1998.

30. See Catherine Coles and George Kelling, chapter 2 in this volume.

31. Personal communication with James Poirier, July 1998.

32. Ibid.

7

JENNY BERRIEN
CHRISTOPHER WINSHIP

An Umbrella of Legitimacy: Boston's Police Department– Ten Point Coalition Collaboration

AFTER A DECADE OF sharply increased homicide rates, a host of large cities in the United States have seen a dramatic drop in the number of homicides during the 1990s.[1] For example, Boston's homicide rate dropped from 26.5 per 100,000 to 6.6 per 100,000, a decline of 75.1 percent; New York's dropped from 30.7 to 8.7, a decline of 71.7 percent; Houston's rate dropped from 34.8 to 12.0, a decline of 65.5 percent; and Los Angeles's dropped from 28.2 to 14.8, a decline of 47.5 percent. Some cities, however, saw only minimal declines. For example, Phoenix's homicide rate fell from 13.0 to 11.7, a decline of 10.0 percent; and Baltimore's fell from 41.4 to 40.3, a drop of only 2.7 percent. (See table 7-1.) In most, if not all, of those cities, the reduction has been accompanied by an even sharper decline in youth violence. Why has youth violence fallen so significantly?

The research in this chapter was supported by a grant from the Smith Richardson Foundation and the National Science Foundation. Kathy Newman provided us with extensive comments. Mary Jo Bane, Jim Quane, Gwen Dordick, John DiIulio, David Kennedy, and Ron Corbett also made many useful suggestions, as did anonymous reviewers. Participants in colloquiums at the University of Illinois-Chicago, Northwestern University, and the Center for the Study of Public Values at Harvard University as well as at the May 1998 Public-Private Ventures's Philadelphia-Boston conference provided constructive criticism. Lynne Farnum and Suzanne Washington provided valuable editorial assistance. Any errors are solely the authors' responsibility.

Table 7-1. *Homicide Rates for Major U.S. Cities, 1990 and 2000*

	1990			2000			
	Homicides	*Population*	*Homicides per 100,000*	*Homicides*	*Population*	*Homicides per 100,000*	*Percent reduction*
Boston	152	574,283	26.5	38	570,888	6.6	75.1
New York	2,245	7,322,564	30.7	673	7,746,511	8.7	71.7
Houston	568	1,630,553	34.8	230	1,920,350	12.0	65.5
Los Angeles	983	3,485,398	28.2	550	3,713,238	14.8	47.5
Washington, D.C.	472	606,900	77.8	239	572,959	41.7	46.4
Philadelphia	503	1,585,577	31.7	319	1,451,520	21.9	31.0
Phoenix	128	983,403	13.0	152	1,300,786	11.7	10.0
Baltimore	305	736,014	41.4	261	647,955	40.3	2.7

Source: U.S. Department of Justice, Federal Bureau of Investigation, *Crime in the United States 1990, 2000.*

Part of the decline in youth violence may be the result of the robust economy that the United States experienced during the 1990s, as well as the result of a drop nationwide in the number of youths aged fifteen to twenty-four, the most crime-prone age group. But those factors affect almost all cities and therefore cannot explain the discrepancy across cities. In addition, similar declines in homicide rates did not occur in the mid- and late 1980s, also a time when the U.S. economy was strong. Furthermore, the drop in the number of youths aged fifteen to twenty-four—7.7 percent from 1986 to 1996—is simply too small to account for much of the change.[2]

The story in Boston is similar to that of other cities, but it is unusual in two important respects. First, the drop in homicides has been marked by a strikingly low level of juvenile homicide victims and offenders. For the twenty-nine-month period ending in January 1998, Boston had no teenage homicide victims. There were sixteen juvenile homicides in 1993 but just one juvenile homicide during 1996, one in 1997, six in 1998, two in 1999, and two in 2000. The drop in the number of juvenile homicide offenders has also been dramatic, declining from seventeen in 1990 to zero in 1999 and one in 2000.[3]

Second, Boston is unusual in that a group of ministers, the Ten Point Coalition, is credited with playing a key role in reducing youth homicides there.[4] As far as we are aware, ministers have not been singled out as play-ing an important role in any other city where there has been a similarly sharp decline in homicides. It is noteworthy that the core of the Ten Point Coalition consists of only three ministers, Reverends Eugene Rivers, Ray-mond Hammond, and Jeffrey Brown, each of whom has had substantial additional commitments. Reverends Hammond and Brown head churches with hundreds of members, and all three ministers, who are also involved in other programs not related to youth violence, have frequent local and national speaking engagements.

This chapter addresses the question of whether the Ten Point Coalition has in fact played a significant role in reducing youth violence in Boston. On the face of it, the answer would appear to be no. Crime rates have dropped dramatically in other cities without significant involvement of the clergy. In addition, only three ministers have been centrally involved and even they have not been able to devote themselves full-time to reducing youth violence. It would seem that the churches' activities have been too limited to have played a substantial part in bringing about the observed changes. Finally, David Kennedy and Ronald Corbett have documented in this volume and elsewhere how, in a broad-based move toward community policing, new Boston police and probation department policies and prac-tices—and the new cooperative relationship between the two depart-ments—have led to more effective procedures for dealing with youth vio-lence.[5] Similar efforts have been undertaken in other cities as well. The assertion by many people that the Ten Point Coalition has been a signifi-cant facet of the effort would seem at best to be good politics and public relations.[6]

Our analysis has several goals. Most important, we want to establish that despite the above observations, the Ten Point Coalition *has* played a critical role in reducing youth violence in Boston. Second, we analyze why it has been difficult for police departments to effectively reduce violence. Certainly, racial antagonism is a problem that must be considered when assessing violence-reduction tactics in many cities. We argue more gener-ally that any police action in the inner city is inherently problematic. The decision of whether to imprison a youth who is in serious trouble is a ter-rible choice for anyone to make: either the community is left vulnerable to potentially violent acts or the community loses another child. The lack of any intermediary institution in the inner city to ensure that such decisions are made in a fair and just way is an enormous problem. As a result, it has been nearly impossible in many places to reach consensus on what constitutes legitimate and constructive police activity.

A further goal is to suggest types of policies that are likely to be effective in reducing youth violence in the inner city *over the long run*. Although many cities have successfully reduced youth violence, in some and perhaps in many cases they have done so through aggressive tactics that involve frisking and intimidating minority males on the streets. We predict that inner-city residents will find the resulting sacrifice of civil liberties simply too great to accept such tactics over the long term.

Our argument has multiple parts. Our key assertion is that a principal barrier to reducing youth violence in the inner city over the long run is the hostile and highly confrontational relationship that exists in many cities between the police (and other agents of the judicial system) and the inner-city community. That relationship has made it nearly impossible to devise legitimate and effective long-term solutions to youth violence.

The second component of our argument is that many cities (including Boston in the past) pursue an approach that is likely to succeed in the short run but not over the long term. Many inner-city residents have become so frustrated by the high levels of violence that they have had to live with that they are now willing to accept quite aggressive police tactics. Such tactics may produce immediate results, but eventually there is likely to be a community backlash, as there was in an earlier period in Boston.

A third component of our argument is that the key contribution of the Ten Point Coalition and the efforts of other church-based groups lies perhaps not so much in their work with at-risk youth as in how they have changed the ways in which the police (and other elements of the criminal justice system) and Boston's inner-city community relate to each other.[7] The coalition has done so by becoming an intermediary between the two parties. It has achieved a balance between the community's desire for safe streets and its reluctance to see its children put in jail, and in so doing it has created what we call an umbrella of legitimacy for police efforts to prevent and control crime. The coalition has served to legitimize police activities, first through a process of informal oversight and second by its willingness to go to the press when it believes that police actions have exceeded the limits of tolerance. To avoid painting an overly rosy picture, we acknowledge that the relationship in Boston between the police and the community, especially its youth, is far from completely harmonious. Much of the transformation that has taken place has involved special units of the police department that are especially sensitive to community needs and sentiments. The typical beat cop, for the most part, has not been part of this reformation. In many cases street-level patrol officers are continuing to pursue the aggressive stop-and-frisk policies of the past. Only time will tell whether their behavior will change or whether it will instead undermine the legitimacy of the partnership that has been built between the police and the Ten Point Coalition.[8]

Later in the chapter we consider how we might test our argument. Boston's earlier history serves as a control case, and the success or failure of other cities in maintaining low levels of youth violence over the long run will provide future tests. We discuss an important case that occurred in Boston, the McLaughlin murder, the details of which we were unaware of until we first presented our theory. This case reinforces our interpretation of the Boston story.

The Boston Story

Although Boston has never been considered a violence-plagued city to the extent that Los Angeles or New York has, in 1990 a record-breaking 152 homicides stunned Boston into realizing that it had a serious violence problem.[9] The roots of the problem took hold in the late 1980s, when crack cocaine was introduced in Boston's inner city, relatively late in comparison with other major U.S. cities. As the crack market developed, so did turf-based gangs. When they realized how much money they could acquire through crack sales, the gangs became increasingly protective of their turf. Gang colors and geographically based gang names, such as the "Corbett Street Posse," all showed evidence of gang identification and loyalty.

Rival gangs turned to firearms to protect and defend their turf and gang identity. One gang's show of disrespect or aggression toward another would inevitably be followed by retaliatory attacks. Gang ties and turf battles grew to such an extent that often individuals who formerly avoided gangs and the drug trade began to pursue membership for protection and camaraderie. With firearms as the primary means of aggression, the level of violence grew to a rate and severity never before seen in the Boston area.

Because Boston law enforcement agencies had little experience with turf-based violence and criminal gang activity, their initial response to the situation in the late 1980s and early 1990s was disorganized. Until 1990, police department policy directed officers and administrators to publicly deny the existence of a gang problem. Many current Boston police officers vouched for the fact that the department had no policy for dealing with the problem of violence in certain Boston neighborhoods in the late 1980s. Rather than creating a plan of attack to address the specific characteristics of gang-related violence, the police fell back on aggressive tactics. In addition, because homicide traditionally has been handled on a case-by-case basis, the police department focused primarily on making the "big hit" and arresting the "big player," rather than addressing the significance of the group-based nature of gang violence.

In 1988, the City Wide Anti-Crime Unit (CWACU), which traditionally provided intense, targeted support across district boundaries, was permanently assigned to the most violent neighborhoods in Boston's inner city. In 1989, the police department adopted a policy stating that any individual involved in a gang would be prosecuted to the full extent of the law, thereby finally acknowledging the existence of a gang problem. According to one current police captain, the CWACU was expected to "go in, kick butts, and crack heads"; the unit adopted the mentality that "they could do anything to these kids" in order to put an end to violent activity. That attitude resulted in highly aggressive and reportedly indiscriminate policing tactics.

Community Backlash

Two events in 1989, the murder of Carol Stuart and the stop-and-frisk scandal, focused community attention on the police department's initial approach to the violence crisis. Carol Stuart, a pregnant white woman, was murdered in the primarily African American neighborhood of Mission Hill. Her husband, Charles Stuart, who was with her at the time of her death, reported that a black male committed the crime. Relying on Stuart's account, the Boston police department "blanketed" the neighborhood looking for suspects. There were widespread reports of police abuse as well as coerced statements that implicated a suspect, William Bennet. Stuart himself was later alleged to be the perpetrator of the crime, but he committed suicide before an investigation could be completed. The Boston police department's unquestioning acceptance of Stuart's story about a black assailant and its subsequent mishandling of the murder investigation created extreme distrust of the department within Boston's African American community.

Community suspicion was further intensified and solidified when, in a public statement, a precinct commander labeled the then-current police approach to gang-related violence as a stop-and-frisk campaign.[10] There is some disagreement within the police department about the extent to which police policy was to indiscriminately stop and frisk all black males within high-crime areas, a practice known as "tipping kids upside down." According to several officers, they targeted individuals who either were previously spotted performing some illegal activity or were known gang members. However, officers also acknowledged that because it often was difficult to "distinguish the good guys from the bad guys," the approach was critically flawed. In addition, current members of the police force agree that there were "bad cops" who acted far too aggressively and indiscriminately. Accusations of stop-and-frisk tactics led to a court case in the fall of 1989 in which a judge threw out evidence acquired in what he considered an instance of unconstitutional search and seizure.[11]

As a result of the Stuart case and the stop-and-frisk scandal, the CWACU was disbanded in 1990. However, the department began to see significant rewards from its aggressive street practices: Boston's homicides fell from 113 in 1991 to seventy-three in 1992, and the drop reinforced belief in the efficacy of the department's heavy-handed tactics.[12] The police continued to view their actions as simple compliance with department orders. Despite that success, however, most officers acknowledged that the department's aggressive actions during that time brought community mistrust to an extreme level.

These two scandals, combined with smaller-scale, less visible incidents, eventually led the Boston press to question the police department's capacity to handle even basic policing activities effectively. In 1991, the *Boston Globe* published a harshly critical seven-part series called "Bungling the Basics," which detailed a succession of foul-ups by the department during the previous few years and reported serious failings in the department's internal affairs division.[13] Misguided investigations, problematic policing, and bad press eventually led to the appointment of the St. Clair Commission to conduct a thorough review of the Boston police department and its policies.

After all the negative publicity, the Boston police department was in desperate need of an overhaul. Steps were taken to demonstrate a real change in law enforcement policy in Boston. "Bad cops" were weeded out. The disbanded CWACU was reorganized into a new unit, the anti–gang violence unit (AGVU), which took a "softer" approach. The effective but aggressive and indiscriminate street tactics of the past were sharply curtailed. Apparently as a result, the decrease in homicides during 1991 and 1992 were followed by a sharp increase in 1993.[14]

Innovation in Police Practices

The St. Clair Commission report, released in January 1992 after a year-long investigation, cited major corruption within the department and recommended sweeping changes.[15] In 1993, Mayor Flynn resigned and Bill Bratton—who had previously been brought from New York City, where he was chief of the transit police, to be Boston's number-two cop—replaced police commissioner Mickey Roache. Bratton instilled a new philosophy and commitment to innovation to the Boston police department. Fundamental shifts occurred in overall operations. According to current police officers, the neighborhood policing tactics that formerly "just existed on paper" and had never been implemented under Roache were actively pursued under Bratton. Many officers also agreed that the new administration was simply more open-minded and willing to break away from embedded policing practices.

Street-level officers had learned from their constant exposure to the complexities of gang-related violence that innovative law enforcement strategies were needed to address the problem intelligently. The newly organized anti–gang violence unit looked for new ways to manage gang activities. First, realizing the need for community support, they were determined to follow "squeaky-clean" policing practices. Previous strategies had also failed to include collaboration with other agencies, so the AGVU began to pursue an increasingly multiagency approach to combating youth violence. In 1993, the AGVU was changed to the Youth Violence Strike Force, retaining the same key members.[16]

Other Boston law enforcement agencies were concurrently revamping their activities. Certain individuals within the probation department in particular had become quite disillusioned with the "paper-shuffling" nature of their job. Fearful of the extreme level of violence in certain Boston districts, probation officers had completely abandoned the practice of making home visits and maintaining a street presence. Consequently, there was no enforcement of probation terms such as curfew and area and activity restrictions. Without enforcement, probation became viewed as a slap on the wrist within the law enforcement community, and it was essentially ineffectual in combating youth violence.

A few probation officers began to respond to the crisis of ineffectiveness and took strong, proactive measures to readjust their approach. Informal conversations between probation officers and police officers who regularly attended hearings at Dorchester district court led to Operation Night

Light, an experimental effort in interagency collaboration that involved joint outings of probation and police officers. With police protection, probation officers were able to venture out after dark to enforce the conditions placed on probationers. Realizing that their P.O. might be out on the streets, at their house, or at their hangouts after curfew to check on them, youths began to understand that they could no longer blatantly disregard the terms of their probation. Violations would have repercussions, such as a lengthened probation sentence, stricter terms, or jail time. Operation Night Light eventually became an institutionalized practice of Boston law enforcement agencies, and it has been heavily praised by policy experts and the media across the country.[17]

Interagency collaboration to address the issue of youth violence has become standard practice in Boston. The participation of researchers (primarily David Kennedy and his associates at the John F. Kennedy School of Government) also served a vital role in bringing about a fundamental overhaul of Boston's policing strategies. The Boston Gun Project, which began in 1995, was a three-year effort to address youth violence that brought together a wide range of agencies, including the police department; the Bureau of Alcohol, Tobacco, and Firearms; the probation department; the Boston school police; the Suffolk County district attorney; and many others. The Boston Gun Project was innovative, not only because it involved collaboration but also because it used research-based information to address the problem of youth violence from a new angle. The Gun Project was able to attack the problem on the supply side by cracking down on dealers in illicit firearms and on the demand side by targeting 1,300 individuals who, although they represented less than 1 percent of their age group citywide, were identified by project research as responsible for at least 60 percent of the city's homicides.[18]

This type of interagency collaboration helped in implementing a variety of innovative strategies. In 1994, Operation Scrap Iron was initiated to target people who were illegally transporting firearms into Boston, and gun trafficking within certain areas of the city was shut down. "Area warrant sweeps," in which police would arrest all individuals with outstanding warrants within a particular housing project or neighborhood, also were used. Multiagency teams of youth workers then came in to provide follow-up services when the police presence subsided. As one police officer noted, these strategies made sure that "everyone was involved and brought something to the table. Everyone had a piece of the pie and, therefore, would get the benefits."[19] Even more impressive is that, according to the same police officer, not one civilian complaint was filed in response to the sweep tactic.

In May of 1996, this collaboration culminated in Operation Cease-Fire, which fully institutionalized interagency collaboration among Boston's crime-fighting agencies—the police and probation departments, the department of youth services, street workers, special agents from the Drug Enforcement Agency and the Bureau of Alcohol, Tobacco, and Firearms, and others already mentioned in reference to the Boston Gun Project. Key community members, primarily from faith-based organizations, also became involved in the project. These groups worked together to identify gangs responsible for violence in specific hot spots around the city. They then developed and enforced a "zero tolerance" policy toward violence within a targeted area. The contribution of the ministers' involvement in Operation Cease-Fire needs to be evaluated in future research.

Community-Based Change

Individuals within Boston's religious community were some of the most vocal and publicized critics of the police department's aggressive tactics during the late 1980s and early 1990s. Reverend Eugene Rivers, in particular, became a controversial media figure during those years because of his harsh criticism of both local law enforcement agencies and the city's black leaders. Remarkably, the same religious leaders later became active participants in law enforcement strategies such as Operation Cease-Fire. That turnaround suggests that the Boston police department has been effective in improving community relations; additionally, Boston's faith-based leaders experienced a shift in their own attitudes toward the police.

Boston's African American faith-based organizations did not begin working together as a group until 1992; until then, they had been following separate agendas, and their activities generally did not involve much street-oriented action to address youth violence within their community. Although Reverend Rivers was on the street, reaching out to gang members and other youth, his constant criticism of other clergy leaders made his effort a partnerless endeavor.

A tragic event in May 1992 finally spurred Boston's African American clergy to collaborative action.[20] Violence broke out among gang members attending the funeral at Morning Star Baptist Church of a youth murdered in a drive-by shooting, and the resulting shootout and multiple stabbing threw the congregation into chaos. The brazenness of the attack, which took place within the church sanctuary, inspired many of Boston's black clergy to take action. They realized that they could no longer hope to serve their community by remaining within the four walls of their church and ignoring the situation on the street. Instead, they needed to extend their concept of congregation to include youth and others in the surrounding troubled neighborhoods.

That incident led to the founding of the Ten Point Coalition, which represented a major step toward active collaboration within Boston's African American religious community. The coalition—which included some forty churches, with Reverends Ray Hammond, Eugene Rivers, and Jeffrey Brown as key leaders[21]—drew up and published the "Ten-Point Proposal for Citywide Mobilization to Combat the Material and Spiritual Sources of Black-on-Black Violence," a call to churches to participate in the effort to address the crisis of violence in their communities.[22] Jeffrey Brown defined the Ten Point Coalition as "an ecumenical group of Christian clergy and lay leaders working to mobilize the Christian community around issues affecting black and Latino youth—especially those at risk for violence, drug abuse, and other destructive behavior."[23]

About forty churches in the Boston area are members of the coalition, including Eugene Rivers's Azusa Christian Community, Jeffrey Brown's Union Baptist Church, and Ray Hammond's Bethel AME Church. The coalition itself employs a staff of ten. It also has a board; Ray Hammond is chairman and members of each of the aforementioned churches participate. Efforts to import the Boston Ten Point Coalition model are being pursued in several areas around the country, including Indianapolis, Philadelphia, Louisville, and Providence.

Although the formation of the Boston Ten Point Coalition represented a dramatic shift in local faith-based collaboration, relations between African American community leaders and Boston's law enforcement agencies still were strained and often antagonistic. Reverend Rivers was constantly "in the face" of Boston law enforcement officials and was viewed as a "cop basher" in police circles. He was a constant presence on the troubled streets of Dorchester and maintained contact with the same kids that the anti–gang violence unit kept an eye on. As an aggressive advocate for local youth, both in and out of the courts, Rivers had many confrontations with the AGVU and other patrol officers.

A combination of events and the strong effort made by key law enforcement officials to show that the Boston police department had changed its attitude eventually resulted in a turnaround. The antagonism subsided, replaced with effective collaboration.[24] The turnaround resulted in part from an incident in 1991 in which shots were fired into Reverend Rivers's home in Four Corners, one of the most violent areas of Dorchester, making him painfully aware of the dangers of carrying out a solitary campaign against youth violence. He acknowledged that seeing the lives of his wife and children placed in jeopardy caused a shift in his attitude, and he became more open to the possibility of allying with both other ministers and individuals in the law enforcement community.

When the Ten Point Coalition was formed in 1992, the public stature and media influence of Reverend Rivers and other key clergy members such as Ray Hammond and Jeffrey Brown increased, and they wielded their power effectively in an effort to maintain a check on police practices in Boston. In 1992, the coalition partnered with another community-based organization, the Police Practices Coalition, to establish an organized, community-based police monitoring group.

The Ten Point Coalition, especially Reverend Rivers, had habitually criticized the Boston police department. Increasingly positive interactions with individual officers, however, began to convince the group that the department could change its behavior. In 1993 the ministers acknowledged the department's progress through Youth Community Awards to publicly honor "good cops." Such positive steps eventually led to collaborative efforts like the previously mentioned Operation Cease-Fire. Cooperation among law enforcement agencies and clergy leaders, as well as various community-based groups, has continued to evolve and expand during recent years.

Current Relations

Since the mid-1990s there has been extensive interagency and community-based collaboration in Boston. A primary example is the Bloods and Crips Initiative, which was established in spring 1998 as an aggressive street-level mobilization of lay and pastoral workers to prevent youth involvement in the Bloods, the Crips, or any other gang.[25] By combining the efforts of a wide range of agency representatives, the initiative aims to approach the problem comprehensively. The Boston police and probation departments, the department of youth services, clergy members, city youth and street workers, transit authority police, the department of schools, and the school police meet weekly to share information on important developments on the street. For example, several disturbing incidents of sexual assault and harassment have occurred recently on the city's public transportation system. Transit police and city youth workers as well as clergy brought up the importance of addressing such incidents at the weekly Bloods and Crips Initiative meetings, and a task force on sexual harassment and assault was established. School presentations on the subject are planned in the future.

Another objective of the collaboration is to exhibit a strong, supportive, and unified image of authority to the targeted youth through the participation of multiple agencies and faith-based groups in all of the initiative's activities: school visits and presentations, home visits to youth suspected of gang involvement, regular street patrols, and visits to popular hang-outs during peak hours. The collaborative approach serves to notify youth of alternative options and brings them into contact with a network of resources designed to meet their specific needs.

More informal cooperation among the wide array of agencies and community groups participating in operations such as the Bloods and Crips Initiative plays an important role in achieving quick responses to tense situations and effective distribution of resources to hot spots in the city. In fall 1998, for example, a particular youth repeatedly engaged in dangerous behavior in Dorchester—holding a gun to another youth's head; firing shots in the air in the midst of young trick-or-treaters on Halloween night, shooting holes in parked cars—all within a period of a couple of weeks. Each incident had the potential to aggravate preexisting tensions among various neighborhood "crews" and to destroy any sense of community security. To avoid that risk, Reverend Rivers used his law enforcement connections to ensure the quick and effective handling of the situation.

In this case, "handling" the situation meant getting the individual off the street, for a long time.[26] At the weekly Bloods and Crips Initiative meeting, Reverend Rivers identified the youth and made law enforcement officials aware of his threat to peace in the neighborhood. Rivers and a youth worker also spoke with the youth personally to explain to him why he was being targeted. The youth was arrested and the "noise" he was causing in the community abated. Clergy leaders and law enforcement officials have thus achieved an uncommon level of collaborative action in Boston.

The Judicial System and the Inner City

Why have police departments and judicial systems been unable to deal with past or current youth violence in so many cities? Observers have pointed out that inner-city communities in America's major cities often consider themselves to be at war with the local police and local government, and they frequently compare the police to an occupying military force. The reasons for that perception are well known. While the Rodney King beating in Los Angeles is the most publicized incident of the last decade, almost every major city has its own stories of police brutality. In Boston, the most recent case occurred in January 1995. Michael Cox, a

black undercover policeman, was brutally beaten by four uniformed policemen who mistook him for a suspect. In the previous year, police mistakenly
broke into the home of Accelynne Williams, a retired black minister, during a drug bust. Williams died of a heart attack as a result of the forced
entry. We have already discussed the Stuart case and the stop-and-frisk
scandal, additional instances of allegations of racially biased and overly
aggressive policing tactics.

As disturbing as such incidents are, the response of inner-city residents
has at times been nearly as troubling. Although in most cities inner-city
residents are disproportionately the victims of crime (crimes often committed by their fellow residents), they have become increasingly unwilling
to cooperate with police or support police activities. In *Race, Crime, and the
Law*, Randall Kennedy describes the growing alienation of black inner-city
residents from the criminal justice system. Kennedy points to the lynchings
of blacks in the South as a source of the problem, quoting from Gunnar
Myrdal's 1944 book, *An American Dilemma*:

> The Negroes are hurt in their trust that the law is impartial, that the
> court and the police are their protection, and indeed, that they
> belong to an orderly society which has set up this machinery for com-
> mon security and welfare. They will not feel confidence in, and loy-
> alty toward a legal order which is entirely out of their control and
> which they see to be inequitable and merely part of the system of
> caste oppression. Solidarity then develops easily in the Negro group,
> a solidarity against the law and the police. The arrested Negro often
> acquires the prestige of a victim, a martyr, or a hero, even when he is
> simply a criminal.

Kennedy then goes on to show the same dynamic at work today:

> It largely explains why many blacks rallied around the gang of boys
> who raped a white jogger in New York's Central Park, around Mar-
> ion Barry, the mayor of Washington, D.C., who was caught red-
> handed smoking cocaine, around Alcee Hastings, the federal district
> court judge who, based on allegations of corruption, was ousted from
> office by the U.S. Senate (only to be subsequently elected to the
> House of Representatives), around Damian Williams and the other
> hooligans who gained notoriety when they were filmed beating a
> hapless white truck driver (Reginald Denny) in the early hours of the
> Los Angeles riot of 1992, and around Mike Tyson, the boxing cham-
> pion, when he was imprisoned for rape.

And the examples go on. Kennedy describes how the black criminal has been glorified in the movies and through gangster rap and records such as "Cop Killer." His point is that excesses of the criminal justice system, both past and present, have led inner-city minorities to see the system as totally lacking legitimacy and, at the extreme, to treat criminals as political dissidents and martyrs.[27]

In recent years the alienation of the inner-city community has led to a phenomenon known as jury nullification—decisions by minority juries to acquit defendants who are clearly guilty. The Marion Barry and Damian Williams cases noted above are examples. Kennedy discusses and critiques the arguments for jury nullification by Paul Butler, professor of law at George Washington University and a former federal prosecutor. Butler argues that jury nullification is justified for three reasons: there are cases when the acquittal of a guilty defendant is laudable; America has so grossly failed to keep its promises to blacks that there is no reason that blacks are obliged to uphold the law; white racism is the cause of most black criminality. Butler further argues that "the decision as to what kind of conduct by African-Americans ought to be punished is better made by African-Americans themselves based on the costs and benefits to their community than by the traditional criminal justice process."[28]

If Randall Kennedy's portrayal of minority attitudes toward police and the judicial system is even moderately accurate, as we believe it is, it should not be surprising that police have found it difficult to deal with youth violence in our inner cities. When police expect no cooperation from residents, they tend to choose aggressive broad-based tactics that only further alienate community residents. Moreover, the negative publicity they receive undermines their political support. By alienating inner-city residents, the police also lose their best potential source of community surveillance.

Randall Kennedy contends that although considerable improvements are needed in our justice system, much progress has been made. Certainly, the tense and often dangerous conditions that the police have to work in make it difficult for them to handle potentially explosive situations in a sensitive manner. We would like to suggest an additional reason. Inner-city residents have conflicting goals. On the one hand, they, like all Americans, want safe neighborhoods. On the other hand, they do not like seeing young men from their communities put in jail. As Glenn Loury has noted, "the young black men wreaking havoc in the ghetto are still 'our youngsters' in the eyes of many of the decent poor and working-class black people who are often their victims."[29] Given those conflicting desires, making decisions about whether a particular youth should be arrested or jailed is difficult. Allow him to remain in the community and perhaps endanger other neighborhood residents? Or send him to jail, depriving him of his freedom and removing yet another young man from the community? Neither option is appealing. Parents, neighbors, and other residents are likely to disagree sharply, and a decisionmaking process that would be widely perceived as fair may be unattainable.

Most inner cities simply do not have institutions that are capable of dealing with these questions in a way that would be perceived as just by both residents and society at large. The police, in addition to their history of racism, are biased in favor of safe streets by any means necessary. Social workers, street workers, and community organizers typically are sympathetic to the kids. Residents themselves are likely to differ depending on who is in trouble and their relationship to them.

We argue that in Boston, the ministers of the Ten Point Coalition have become an intermediary institution through which decisions can be made that are perceived as fair. Through their involvement with at-risk youth, the ministers have gained the legitimacy needed to convince residents that they will demand justice. They will publicly attack indiscriminate or abusive police tactics; however, they will shelter the police from broad public criticism while the police are engaged in activities that the ministers deem to be in the interest of the community and its youth, giving the police what we call an umbrella of legitimacy to work under.

An Umbrella of Legitimacy

The relationship between the Boston police and the Ten Point Coalition has progressed from hostility to stable cooperation. (Berrien provides a detailed exposition.)[30] The thesis of this chapter is that the cooperative relationship established between the Boston police and the coalition has been instrumental in reducing the level of youth violence, in two significant ways. First and more important, Ten Point has given increased legitimacy to appropriate police activities within the inner city. Second, the coalition's community surveillance may have increased police effectiveness.

If one were looking for legitimacy through a relationship, there could perhaps be no better way than through a partnership with a group of ministers. Throughout society ministers have unique moral standing. They are expected to be fair and to protect the interests of the less fortunate; because of that, they often are asked to be problem solvers and to adjudicate between conflicting parties. In the inner city, the churches are among the last formal institutions committed to the welfare of their neighborhoods, and within the black community, ministers often have been looked to for leadership. In the case of the Ten Point Coalition, two of the three core ministers live in Boston's inner city and all three are well known for their extensive work with inner-city youth, factors that give the coalition considerable credibility in speaking for Boston's inner-city community. That is not to say that Ten Point is universally seen as the legitimate representative of the black community in Boston. There have been many conflicts between Ten Point, particularly Reverend Rivers, and other representatives of the black community. Nevertheless, the *Boston Globe* has printed numerous stories praising the coalition, which also has received considerable symbolic and financial support from Cardinal Law, head of the archdiocese of Boston, and the Jewish Community Relations Council, the agency principally concerned with social justice issues within Boston's Jewish Federation. All of this has contributed significantly to Ten Point's perceived legitimacy within Greater Boston.

The new relationship between the police and Ten Point is built on a number of assumptions, each of which can support legitimate police activity. We discuss six: youth violence needs to be dealt with as a criminal problem; some kids need to be jailed for both their own good and the good of the community; a small number of youth constitute most of the problem; the ministers will work with the police in identifying problem youth; the ministers will participate in the decisions about what happens to specific individuals; and if the police use indiscriminate and abusive methods in dealing with youths, the ministers will take the story to the media.

The first assumption is that although poverty, single-parent households, poor schools, and other conditions may be factors in youth violence, any effort to reduce violence in the short run must treat it as a criminal problem. In the presentations that ministers routinely give in schools, they make it clear to the kids that they have two choices. If they go straight, the ministers will help them succeed in school, find jobs, and deal with those kids who are trying to pressure them to stay with the gang. However, if they decide to participate in gang activities, the ministers will do their utmost to see them put in jail. The ministers emphasize that the last thing they want to do is to preside over a kid's funeral—that if a kid is going to be involved in a gang, it is safer for him to be in jail than on the street.

Implicit in the "choice" that the ministers offer is a second assumption—that some kids are so out of control that they should be put in jail.

It is not apparent that the ministers held that belief initially, and the police doubted the ministers' willingness to support the incarceration of some individuals. Interview after interview with both police and ministers indicates that cooperation became possible only after the ministers publicly acknowledged (Reverend Rivers most vocally) that some kids needed to be put in jail. There was no explicit agreement about what constituted a sufficiently "out of control" kid. Cooperation between law enforcement officers and the ministers emerged through negotiations over the particular circumstances under which certain kids should be committed. With improved communication and the acknowledgment of a common objective, both parties began working with the same definition of the problem. The primary issue that remained was agreeing on what should be done in particular circumstances.

A third assumption is that only a small number of youths are responsible for most of the violence. As noted above, David Kennedy places the estimate at 1 percent of their age group—1,300 youths.[31] That is why standard stop-and-frisk procedures can be so oppressive: for every hundred kids stopped, only one is truly part of the problem. It takes only a few kids shooting off guns to terrorize a whole neighborhood. A part of the agreement is that the ministers work with the police to identify those kids who truly are problems, thereby informally providing remote surveillance for the police.[32] The information they provide makes police efforts more effective; targeting also increases police legitimacy by ensuring that the police focus on the right youth, employing appropriate measures.

The fourth assumption is that the ministers will work with the police in identifying problem youth. This is not a matter of ascertaining who are the most dangerous individuals. These are generally known to the police, ministers, and the community at large. Rather, it is a process of ongoing assessment as to which youths have the potential to get into serious trouble in the future. This work is done in both formal meetings and informal conversations, as each party attempts to understand and evaluate the youth they are working with. Through these conversations the police and ministers come to a shared understanding of the youth that then forms a basis for deciding on when and for whom interventions will occur.

A fifth assumption is that the ministers will participate in determining how particular individuals are treated by the legal system. In some circumstances that means that the ministers contact the police and ask to have certain kids arrested; the ministers may also help the police locate them. An example was related above in which Reverend Rivers contributed to the arrest of the young man responsible for repeated incidents of violence during Halloween 1998. In some cases, the ministers encourage judges to sentence troubled youths to alternative programs or regular "check-ins" at their churches, rather than time in jail; in others, the ministers appear in court to argue for a stiff sentence.

These understandings between police and the ministers are what has created what we term an umbrella of legitimacy for police activity. However, it is an umbrella that provides coverage only under specific conditions: when police focus on truly problematic youth; when they deal with these youth in what is perceived as a fair and just way; and when that is done in cooperation with the community through the ministers.

Activities that fall outside these boundaries will be publicly criticized in the media, which is the sixth assumption. The ministers' past criticism of the police in the *Globe* is well remembered. Furthermore, Reverend Rivers, the most outspoken of the ministers, is known for his willingness to criticize anyone, whether it is the police, the Urban League, or Harvard's Department of Afro-American Studies. The ministers are able to provide informal oversight of police actions in part because they are ministers, in part because they are community members and leaders, and in part because they exhibited a willingness in the past to be highly critical of the police.

How are we to understand the Ten Point Coalition's role within the inner city? In the discussion above, Myrdal and Butler argued that blacks need to have more control over the judicial process. The Ten Point Coalition has gone some if not all the way toward accomplishing that goal. Operating on the basis of these six assumptions, the coalition has created an umbrella of legitimacy for appropriate police activity. Activities carried out and decisions made under this umbrella are broadly seen by the community as being fair and just; those falling outside are brought to the attention of the media. Some youth have been sent to prison; others have been given second chances; and the vast majority are no longer being harassed on the street, or at least not as much as in the past. Because of the Ten Point Coalition's involvement, the differential treatment of individual youth is more likely to be seen by the community as legitimate. Hard decisions are being made, but they are being made in a manner that is typically viewed as fair and just.[33]

Testing the Argument

We have claimed that the Ten Point Coalition played a critical role in reducing youth violence by helping to change the relationship between the police and community from one of hostility to cooperation and thereby allowing the police to operate more effectively and with perceived legitimacy. How can our argument be tested?

Three observations are useful. First, the earlier history of Boston serves as a control case for the Ten Point story. The police, reacting to the influx of crack cocaine and guns, pursued a broad, aggressive stop-and-frisk policy that initially was successful. However, a community backlash occurred, and the police had to pull back substantially from those tactics. Without community support, they were not sustainable over the long run. Second, our theory makes important predictions about what will happen in other cities where police are pursuing heavy-handed policies to reduce youth violence. We have argued that this approach will work in the long run only if there is continued community support. We suspect that in many cities, as in Boston during the early 1990s, support will be short-lived. Most communities are unlikely to tolerate over the long term a police presence in their neighborhood that resembles an occupying military force.[34] Third, we found a practical test of our argument in a particular homicide case in Boston that illustrates how the relationship between police and the Ten Point Coalition allowed a potentially explosive situation to be handled without incident.

In May 1998, at a two-day meeting in Philadelphia to explore whether the lessons learned in Boston would be useful in Philadelphia, we made our first public presentation of our analysis of the Ten Point story. At the end of our presentation, Paul Joyce, one of the key police officers in Boston's Youth Violence Strike Force, spoke up. He said that he fully agreed with our analysis and wanted to tell us about a particular murder case that supported it.

On September 25, 1995, a white assistant attorney general, Paul McLaughlin, was shot and killed on his way home from work. The murder occurred at the commuter rail station in West Roxbury, a predominantly Irish middle-class neighborhood. McLaughlin was a well-respected prosecutor, dedicated to fighting crime, who had recently headed a task force on gang activities. The murder appeared to be a "hit" in retaliation for his gang work. His assailant was described as a "black male, about 14 or 15 years old, 5 foot 7, wearing a hooded sweat shirt and baggy jeans."[35]

Because the description could easily apply to many young black males, there was immediate concern. Reportedly, the police released the description "under intense pressure from the news media," but many feared that the public posting of such a vague description would only reinforce racial and "generational stereotypes" rather than aid the police investigation.[36]

Young black men feared being mistaken for the assailant due to their skin color, youth, and manner of dress.

Many also feared that the authority of Boston law enforcement officials could be severely damaged if the case was not handled firmly and effectively. The suspicion that McLaughlin was targeted because he prosecuted gang members left others in related professions feeling vulnerable. Calvin Wier, a criminal lawyer who lives on Dudley Street, said that he had held his head high as he walked past gang members in his neighborhood, assuming that his job sheltered him from attack. "I thought if I get killed in Roxbury, it'll be by accident. Now here's the possibility of a kid targeting someone because of his position."[37]

Due to the sensitive circumstances of the crime, Boston's African American leaders felt that they had to take immediate action. The day after it occurred, the executive committee of the Ten Point Coalition publicly condemned the murder of the assistant attorney general at a press conference, expressing concern for the McLaughlin family and strongly emphasizing the need to bring the city together to avoid the threat of polarization: "We ask the city as a whole to step back and not allow their conscious or unconscious fears to drive what happens," Reverend Hammond said. "This is a time for the city of Boston to come together and to make it clear that we will not be held hostage by either perpetrators of violence or by those who would exploit the fear of violence to promote more racial division."[38] Reverend Eugene Rivers considered the press conference critical to preventing what he termed an "open season on black youth," which he believes did occur after the Carol Stuart murder.[39] Ten Point Coalition ministers also forcefully advocated an aggressive, but fair, investigation of the murder: "Thus we wholeheartedly support all legal efforts to apprehend the perpetrators of this brutal crime."[40]

The strong stance immediately taken by leaders in the African American religious community accomplished several objectives. First, it emphasized that even a community with historically antagonistic feelings toward law enforcement officials would not tolerate retaliatory attacks against them and made it clear that the history of police abuse of African Americans in no way justified such a murder. The clergy sent the message to Boston's African American community as well as the primarily white law enforcement community that African American youth could not interpret the murder as some kind of justifiable defense of their neighborhood. At the same time, by pledging their support for a fair police effort, the clergy publicly clarified that police aggression or harassment was neither necessary or acceptable. The press conference thereby removed cause or justification for aggression on both sides.

Another major accomplishment of the immediate response from the Ten Point Coalition was to prevent damage by the media. Many newspaper articles compared the McLaughlin murder with the Stuart case, and the media were poised to report another botched investigation. However, according to one police officer who witnessed both investigations first hand, media influence was much less in the McLaughlin case. The ministers' press conference made it possible for the gang unit to investigate the murder without their actions "being misconstrued as being other than what they were; we were not followed by TV cameras, as in the Charles Stuart murder."[41] By taking a stand supporting police action, the black clergy made the media less prone to exaggerate or aggravate the tense situation.

The ministers' stance also demonstrated that a group that had been highly critical of the Boston police department in the past now believed that the department had made significant improvements. According to one police source, by the time of the McLaughlin murder, the "clergy viewed them [the police] as a much different police force" and were confident that the department would carry out a "professional investigation.[42] The clergy were adamant that the press conference was not just a political maneuver designed to avoid racial conflict or keep inner-city neighborhoods safe from the threat of police aggression. They felt that there had been a fundamental change in police practices that enabled them to "back the case," according to law enforcement officials and ministers involved.

The investigative approach taken by Boston's law enforcement officials during this tense period was markedly different from their approach to the Stuart murder. Both clergy and police were very sensitive to the racial implications of the case. Police commissioner Paul F. Evans immediately made a statement to address community fears about a repeat of the chaos that surrounded the Stuart investigation: "I'm concerned about the potential for this limited description [of the assailant] to become divisive. We're not going to let that happen. This will be a professional investigation."[43] The commissioner spoke on a radio program with a largely black audience soon after the murder to emphasize the limited value of the vague description of the assailant and to say that an effective investigation depended on cooperation between the police and the community. The commissioner also joined the ministers at the Ten Point Coalition's press conference in an additional illustration of police cooperation with, rather than antagonism toward, the African American community.[44]

Those actions might have been interpreted as a political move to avoid public anger and disorder if street-level police officers had not demonstrated equally sensitive investigative tactics. Ten Point ministers serve as community advocates, often accompanying youthful offenders to court appearances, so the ministers' statement that "they have heard of no 'indiscriminate conduct' by police accosting black youths" during the McLaughlin investigation carried a lot of weight. The way that both the police and community leaders handled the McLaughlin case illustrates the dramatic shift that had occurred in the relationship between the two groups since the late 1980s and early 1990s. In May 1998, a special grand jury indicted Jeffrey "Black" Bly for the murder of Paul R. McLaughlin. Bly was a notorious "gang banger" whom McLaughlin had tried three times, and sources who know Bly claim that he was convinced that McLaughlin was on a "vendetta against him."[45] Bly made repeated attempts to intimidate the attorney at the courthouse, and his conviction that McLaughlin was after him most likely served as his rationale for executing the prosecutor. In 1999, Jeffrey Bly was convicted by a jury for the murder of Paul McLaughlin.[46]

Conclusion

In this chapter we have argued that over the long run it is difficult if not impossible for police activity in the inner city to be successful unless it is viewed as legitimate and supported by local residents. Our argument goes further. Vigorous law enforcement initiatives and preventive tactics all have important roles in preventing and reducing youth violence.[47] We have argued also that police work dealing with youth violence is inherently problematic. Communities want safe streets, but they also want their kids to stay out of jail. Difficult choices need to be made that are likely to be seen as unjust by some residents. In this environment, it is difficult to establish legitimacy for police actions, no matter what those actions are.

We claim that in Boston the Ten Point Coalition has evolved into an institution that has at least partially ameliorated this dilemma. By supporting police activity that it believes to be beneficial to the community and criticizing activities that are not, it has created what we have called an umbrella of legitimacy for the police to work under. That in turn has allowed the police to effectively deal with youth violence by pursuing a strategy that targets the truly dangerous youth. We contend that this situation, which is far different from that in most major cities, has contributed significantly to the spectacular drop in homicide rates observed in Boston.

If our analysis is correct, it suggests that police need to create a strong community of partners who engage in a cooperative effort to deal with youth violence; there also must be a delineation of what constitutes legitimate police behavior. Police strategies can acquire true legitimacy within the inner city only if the community partner supports police tactics when they are appropriate as well as publicly criticizes activities that are not. In this role, churches and ministers are ideal partners.

The goal of our research was to establish the plausibility of the claim that the Ten Point Coalition had made a critical contribution to the dramatic reduction in homicides exhibited in Boston during the 1990s. We have argued that the coalition's primary contribution to Boston's success most likely has not been due to its street ministry, that is, its attempt to turn kids around through one-on-one counseling, but to its role in both controlling and legitimizing police activity.

While we believe that our research has established the plausibility of the Ten Point Coalition's importance, interesting questions remain. More research is needed to uncover what facets of the ministers' work have been most important. Furthermore, we do not know exactly how the three core ministers have come to obtain the power and standing they enjoy in the Boston community. If their charisma has been the critical factor, it may be difficult to replicate the Ten Point program in other cities. More generally, there is the question of why homicide rates and rate declines have varied among cities. Until we have a good understanding of what initiatives and factors have been important overall in reducing homicide rates in Boston and elsewhere, it will be impossible to determine precisely the full extent of the coalition's contribution in Boston.

As the Ten Point Coalition reaches its first decade, it does so against the backdrop of a rise in the number of homicides and juvenile homicides in Boston in 2001—to sixty-four and four, respectively—although the numbers are still below the 1992 levels.[48] The coalition remains a vigorous presence in Boston. As Reverend Ray Hammond and Reverend Wesley Roberts have observed, "in the past year alone member churches and staff of the Boston Ten Point Coalition have made more than 200 visits to the homes of high-risk youths, made presentations to more than 3,000 young people in the Boston public schools . . . worked with more than 500 high-risk youths in Department of Youth Services facilities, walked the streets (especially after several homicides), participated in crisis response teams at the funerals of several victims, and begun the mentoring and reintegration of some 20 recently released ex-offenders."[49] On behalf of a maturing coalition looking to the future, Reverend Rivers has warned of the need for a retooled grassroots effort with greater police involvement.[50] The coalition has also cautioned that the present decade poses different challenges from those of the 1990s and that there will be a need for new initiatives that target an older, ex-offender population as well as continuing interventions for high-risk youths.

The possibility that Boston has found an effective strategy for reducing youth violence without severely and broadly compromising the civil liberties of its inner-city residents is exciting. But only the future can tell whether our interpretation of the Boston story is correct. Proof or disproof of our assertions will emerge as Boston's partnership-based strategy is put to the test across the nation and produces or fails to produce substantial long-term reductions in youth homicide rates.[51]

Notes

1. Philip J. Cook and John H. Laub, "The Unprecedented Epidemic in Youth Violence," in Michael Tonry and Mark H. Moore, eds., *Youth Violence* (University of Chicago Press, 1998), pp. 27–64.

2. Many cities where there have been declines have implemented community policing programs, which typically try to be proactive rather than reactive in dealing with crime. Future research is needed to determine how important the programs might be in explaining differences across cities in the drop in homicide rates. See Alfred Blumstein and Joel Wallman, eds., *The Crime Drop in America* (Cambridge University Press, 2000).

3. See Ronald P. Corbett Jr., chapter 6 in this volume.

4. Charles Radin, "Reaching Up Against Crime: Partnerships, Awareness, Behind Boston's Success," *Boston Globe*, February 19, 1997, p. A1.

5. David Kennedy, chapter 8, and Corbett, chapter 6, in this volume. See also David Kennedy, "Pulling Levers: Chronic Offenders, High-Crime Settings, and a Theory of Prevention," *Valparaiso University Law Review*, vol. 31, no. 2 (Spring 1997), p. 449; David Kennedy, Anne M. Piehl, and Anthony A. Braga, "Kids, Guns, and Public Policy," *Law and Contemporary Problems*, vol. 59, no. 1 (Winter 1996), p. 147; and David Kennedy, "The (Un)known Universe: Mapping Gangs and Gang Violence in Boston," working paper (Cambridge, Mass.: Program in Criminal Justice Policy and Management, John F. Kennedy School of Government, Harvard University, 1996).

6. The most significant publicity that the Ten Point Coalition has received was in *Newsweek*. In the June 1998 issue the coalition's work is the feature story and Reverend Eugene Rivers's picture is on the front cover. The Coalition also has been the focus of a PBS documentary and articles in *Time* (July 21, 1997), *Sojourners Magazine*, *Impact Magazine*, the *Weekly Standard*, and several national newspapers such as the *Atlanta Journal-Constitution*, the *New York Times*, and, frequently, the *Boston Globe*.

7. Other Boston ministers, such as Reverends Bruce Wall and Michael Haynes, fellow members of the Boston Ten Point Coalition, also have engaged in intensive street ministry during the past decade. However, as we discuss later, Reverends Rivers, Hammond,

and Brown have been the key actors in establishing a partnership with the police and publicly establishing the legitimacy of their activities. As in other cities, there are many other groups in Boston involved in working with at-risk youth. Prominent examples are the Dorchester Youth Collaborative and the Boston Violence Prevention Program. Although these programs have almost certainly contributed to the dramatic reductions in crime we have seen in Boston, we believe that their direct impact on the overall homicide rate through one-on-one counseling of street youth, like that of the three Ten Point ministers, has been modest.

8. Interview with public defender.

9. The information in this section is primarily derived from interviews conducted by the authors during the fall of 1997 with members of the Boston police department, Boston probation department, employees of the city's street worker program, and David Kennedy. The Federal Bureau of Investigation's *Uniform Crime Reports* state that 143 homicides were committed in Boston in 1990; however, current Boston police statistics and current police officers report 152 homicides for that record-breaking year.

10. Interview with public defender.

11. "Events Leading to St. Clair Report," *Boston Globe*, January 15, 1992, p. 23.

12. Federal Bureau of Investigation, *Uniform Crime Reports*, 1991–1992.

13. "Events Leading to St. Clair Report," p. 23.

14. The question of timing and causality here is complex. The most aggressive period of stop-and-frisk tactics ended in 1990, yet the homicide rate continued to fall in 1991 and 1992. If one believes that the causal connection is contemporaneous, then this is evidence of lack of a causal effect. However, if the causal effect of police enforcement is lagged, then this is evidence for a causal effect.

15. James D. St. Clair, *Report of the Boston Police Department Review Committee* (Boston: January 14, 1992).

16. David Kennedy, conversation, October 1997.

17. A more extensive discussion of Operation Night Light is provided by Corbett in chapter 6 of this volume.

18. Kennedy, "Pulling Levers," p. 449.

19. Jenny Berrien, "The Boston Miracle: The Emergence of New Institutional Structures in the Absence of Rational Planning," senior thesis, Department of Sociology, Harvard University, March 20, 1998.

20. Robert A. Jordan and *Globe* staff, "Clergy's Anger Can Bring Hope," *Boston Globe*, May 16, 1992, p. 13.

21. These pastors serve different types of congregations and have very personal styles. Reverend Rivers is the pastor of the Azusa Christian Community, which has a congregation of around forty members who live mostly within the Four Corners neighborhood of Dorchester. He is sometimes accused of running a store-front church because of the surprisingly small congregation. Rivers also tends to be the most politically outspoken and controversial of the three ministers. Reverend Hammond oversees the Bethel AME church in Dorchester, a much more populous church that attracts people from a variety of neighborhoods. Hammond is described as less controversial than Rivers but equally strong in his convictions and drive for social change. Jeffrey Brown is the pastor at the Union Baptist Church in Cambridge. Brown's congregation has several hundred congregants, but like Rivers, he remains very active in street-based outreach.

22. Jordan, "Clergy's Anger Can Bring Hope," p. 13. The Ten-Point Plan to Mobilize the Churches states: "1) To establish 4–5 church cluster-collaborations which sponsor "Adopt-a-Gang" programs to organize and evangelize youth in gangs. Inner-city churches would serve as drop-in centers providing sanctuary for troubled youth. 2) To commission missionaries to serve as advocates and ombudsmen for black and Latino juveniles in the courts. Such missionaries would work closely with probation officers, law enforcement officials, and youth street workers to assist at-risk youth and their families. They would also convene summit meetings between school superintendents, principals of public middle and high schools, and black and Latino pastors to develop partnerships that will focus on the youth most at-risk. We propose to do pastoral work with the most violent and troubled young people and their families. In our judgement this is a rational alternative to ill-conceived proposals to substitute incarceration for education. 3) To commission youth evangelists to do street-level one-on-one evangelism with youth involved in drug trafficking. These evangelists would also work to prepare these youth for participation in the economic life of the nation. Such work might include preparation for college, the development of legal revenue-generating enterprises, and acquisition of trade skills and union membership. 4) To establish accountable, community-based economic development projects that go beyond "market and state" visions of revenue generation. Such economic development initiatives will include community land trusts, micro-enterprise projects, worker cooperatives, and democratically run community development corporations. 5) To establish links between suburban and down-town churches and front-line ministries to provide spiritual, human resource, and material support. 6) To initiate and support neighborhood crime-watch programs within local church neighborhoods. If, for example, 200 churches covered the four corners surrounding their sites, 800 blocks would be safer. 7) To establish working relationships between local churches and community-based health centers to provide pastoral counseling for families during times of crisis. We also propose the initiation of drug abuse prevention programs and abstinence-oriented educational programs focusing on the prevention of AIDS and sexually transmitted diseases. 8) To convene a working summit meeting for Christian black and Latino men and women in order to discuss the development of Christian brotherhoods and sisterhoods that would provide rational alternatives to violent gang life. Such groups would also be charged with fostering responsibility to family and protecting houses of worship. 9) To establish rape crisis drop-in centers and services for battered women in churches. Counseling programs must be established for abusive men, particularly teenagers and young adults. 10) To develop an aggressive black and Latino curriculum, with an additional focus on the struggles of women and poor people. Such a curriculum could be taught in churches as a means of helping our youth understand that God of history has been and remains active in the lives of all people."

23. Prepared statement of Reverend Jeffrey L. Brown, "Bringing Worlds Together," serial no. J-105-6, before the Senate Committee on the Judiciary, *Examining Efforts by Private Individuals, Community Organizations, and Religious Groups to Prevent Juvenile Crime*, 105th Cong., 1st sess., March 19, 1997.

24. Berrien, "The Boston Miracle."

25. The narrative information for this section is primarily derived from observation of weekly Bloods and Crips Initiative meetings that take place at the Ella J. Baker House (which also houses the Azusa Christian Community). A wide range of clergy and agency

partners attend these weekly meetings, including key members of the Boston police department (homicide, school police, Youth Violence Strike Force), Boston probation department (juvenile and adult probation), department of youth services, neighborhood health centers, the street worker program, and representatives from various churches in the Ten Point Coalition. The purpose of the meetings is to share information and encourage a collaborative approach to preventing and controlling gang violence in the city.

26. Information concerning this Halloween incident is based on a conversation that took place during the Bloods and Crips Initiative Wednesday meeting in November of 1998.

27. Randall Kennedy, *Race, Crime, and the Law* (Pantheon, 1997), pp. 24–25.

28. Paul Butler, "Racially Based Jury Nullification: Black Power in the Criminal Justice System," *Yale Law Journal*, vol. 105 (1995), pp. 724–25, n. 236, as cited in Kennedy, *Race, Crime, and the Law.*

29. Kennedy, *Race, Crime, and the Law*, p. 19.

30. Berrien, "The Boston Miracle."

31. David Kennedy, conversation, October 1997.

32. Some have been concerned that the ministers' role in identifying troublesome youth may allot them too much power, which is a legitimate fear. However, the Ten Point Coalition's own standing in Boston is quite fragile; it has its enemies and vocal critics. As a result, it would be difficult for the ministers to abuse their power without consequences. Moreover, the remote surveillance function, while important in terms of utilizing the coalition's presence in the community and providing a channel of communication to law enforcement, is also limited. The coalition does not have prior review power over the routine arrest and enforcement activities of the Boston Police Department.

33. An important piece of research that has not been carried out is to interview a broad section of community residents to see whether the activities and decisions that are made collaboratively by the police and the coalition are seen as just and fair. At this point, our claim is based only on the fact that there has not been any public outcry over these activities in the *Boston Globe* or the *Boston Herald* or in the local African American newspaper, the *Bay State Banner.*

34. For a discussion of recent community-police conflicts over heavy-handed policing and racism in New York City, see Andrea McArdle and Tanya Eren, *Zero Tolerance: Quality of Life and the New Police Brutality in New York City* (New York University Press, 2001).

35. Richard Chacon, "Profile of Gunman Fits Many, Youths Say," *Boston Globe,* September 27, 1995, p. 33.

36. Ibid.

37. Geeta Anand, "Stunned Community Copes with Outraged Fears," *Boston Globe*, September 27, 1995, p. 29.

38. Ibid.

39. Ibid.

40. Ten Point Coalition, "Black Leaders Speak Out on Slaying," *Boston Herald*, September 30, 1995, p. 12.

41. This information is from an interview by the author with a Boston police officer who was on the force during the Carol Stuart and the McLaughlin murder investigations.

42. Ibid.

43. Chacon, "Profiling of Gunman Fits Many, Youths Say."

44. Geeta Anand and Michael Grunwald, "Authorities Are Praised; Some Blacks Wary," *Boston Globe*, September 30, 1995, p. 80.

45. Sean Flynn, "Public Enemy," *Boston Magazine*, May 1998.

46. Ric Kahn, "Cocksure Bly Crossed the Line," *Boston Globe*, May 30, 1995, p. B5.

47. Jenny Berrien and Christopher Winship, "Lessons Learned from Boston's Police-Community Collaboration," *Federal Probation*, vol. 63, no. 2 (1999), pp. 25–32.

48. Boston Police Department Statistics. See Corbett, chapter 6 in this volume.

49. Ray Hammond and Wesley Roberts, "Renewing Efforts Against Violence," *Boston Globe*, February 19, 2002, p. A11. Reverend Roberts is president of the Black Ministerial Alliance.

50. Douglas Belkin, "Rivers Seeks New Vigor for Coalition," *Boston Globe*, January 11, 2002, p. B2.

51. See Berrien and Winship, "Lessons Learned."

8

DAVID M. KENNEDY

A Tale of One City: Reflections on the Boston Gun Project

LET US BEGIN WITH TWO IMAGES. In the first, the time is late 1994, the setting the Boston police department's special operations headquarters, a smallish and distinctly unprepossessing building on Warren Street in the city's embattled Roxbury neighborhood. As seems ever the case with anything involving law enforcement, there is never enough parking; marked and unmarked units pack the apron in front and spill over onto adjacent streets. To enter you walk up to the second floor, on poured concrete steps with a landing mid-flight, through a heavy glass door secured with a numeric keypad and then past a duty officer behind more glass on the right. Continue through a second door and you pass a battered conference room on the left, used for roll call, lunch, meetings, and, occasionally, holding arrestees. Continue further, past a copy machine stuck out in the hall, and turn left into a bullpen stuffed with desks with a pair of small offices broken out of the rear, or turn right, to another small office, also stuffed with desks. The building houses a multitude of units—motorcycle officers, arson and explosives experts, and toxics specialists come and go—but these particular spaces belong to the Youth Violence Strike Force: a gang unit, by any other name. (I once sat in the third office, which is detective space, with a trio of YVSF detectives while shots were being fired pretty close by; this was common enough to be unremarkable, and nobody got up and did anything. That, however, did seem remarkable, so we remarked on it for a bit.) Now go back to the front steps. That was where, late in 1994, a number of violent young men from Wendover Street in Dorchester—another embattled Boston neighborhood, if not quite as embattled as Roxbury—gave up their guns to detectives from the YVSF. There is a complicated story about why the young men gave up their guns. But there is also a simple story, which is that the detectives told them to and they did.

For the second image, we go forward to the fall of 1996, inside to the conference room. The room is packed to overflowing. There are two groups of people. The first, mostly seated around the conference table, mostly a bit older, mostly white, is the law enforcement group. There are about a dozen of them. They are used to being together; they have been meeting regularly in this room for almost two years. With them, making today a little special, is the U.S. attorney for the district of Massachusetts, who has not been in this room before. (Usually I chair the group at the table; today I lean against a wall behind it.) The other group, mostly seated around the periphery of the room, is mostly younger and much less white. They are streetworkers, gang outreach specialists employed by the city of Boston. There are about two dozen of them. The atmosphere in the room is civil but charged. The men and women at the table have, over the last months, orchestrated elaborate law enforcement operations against several of the city's most violent street gangs. The young men hit by those operations are young men that the streetworkers are devoted to helping, and many of the streetworkers know many of them—some now headed for federal prison—personally. Beyond that, many of the basic premises that the two groups work from are different. Both are in their own way dedicated to protecting young people and the community, but after that there is a good deal of divergence. The law enforcement group asked for this meeting, but the streetworkers are doing most of the talking. They are raising explosive matters: racism, economic opportunity and oppression, the values and motives and conduct of law enforcement officers and others in positions of authority in the city, the character of various people in the room. But part way through, one of the older streetworkers passes on a message that the street gang he works with in Mattapan—another often-troubled Boston neighborhood—asked him to convey to the men and women at the table. "Leave us alone," the streetworker repeats. "We're not doing anything." The room collapses in rueful laughter, because despite their differences both groups share the profound, weary wish for such gangs to simply stop doing violence and having violence done to them—

and also amazement that such a message could have been framed and con-
veyed and heard and welcomed. There is a complicated story about why
the young men in Mattapan were not doing anything, or at least not anything violent. But there is also a simple story, which is that the men and
women at the table told them not to and they stopped.

These images were holographic moments in the struggle to prevent
youth violence in Boston and in the genesis and playing out of Operation
Ceasefire, the youth violence prevention program that emerged from the
Boston Gun Project. The first moment was not part of the Gun Project but
of something called Operation Scrap Iron, a program that the Youth Violence Strike Force and others developed to quell violence by the Wendover
Street crew. Operation Scrap Iron preceded the Gun Project and was a central inspiration of Operation Ceasefire. The second moment came about
six months into Ceasefire and signaled that the intervention's primary aspi-
ration—to tell violent youth in Boston to stop being violent and to be
heeded—was being realized. Both are, I think, remarkable. There have
been numerous—there have been innumerable—proposals to prevent
youth violence. None of them, before Boston, contemplated simply telling
hard-core offenders to knock it off. That is what, at root, happened in
Operation Scrap Iron, and that is what, at root, happened in Ceasefire.
What follows is a meditation on that fact, on how it came to be a fact, and
on what that fact and that process might mean for preventing youth violence and, more generally, the larger enterprises of controlling crime and
promoting public safety.

It is a participant's meditation. I directed the Boston Gun Project and
chaired its core practitioner working group. Anthony Braga, Anne Piehl,
and I, who are colleagues at the Kennedy School of Government, framed
the project's activities; convened and chaired the working group; conducted research; designed and implemented the Ceasefire intervention
with the assistance of the working group and participating agencies; and
evaluated the project. That cycle was recently completed.[1] It has been an
unusual endeavor for academics, with our roles being considerably more
participatory, more fluid and open-ended, and more operations-oriented
than is the norm.[2] There are clear drawbacks here when it comes to learning lessons from and passing judgment on the enterprise. We—perhaps
particularly I—are not disinterested observers. We have striven for honesty;
whether we succeeded is for others to judge. At the same time, there are
clear advantages. We have been uniquely situated to observe and reflect on
not only the project, but also the way it has been viewed and interpreted,

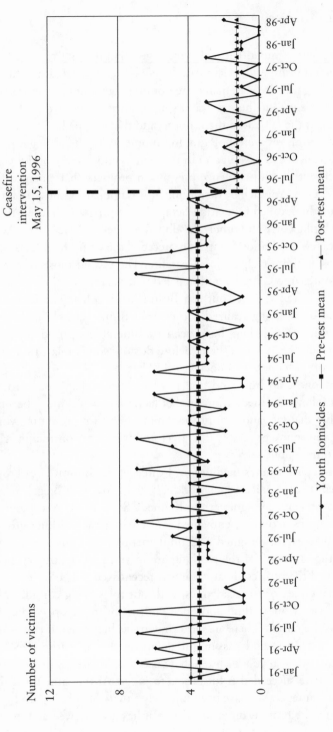

Figure 8-1. *Monthly Counts of Youth Homicides in Boston*

how it has been adopted and adapted by other jurisdictions,[3] and how its lessons and implications fit into the larger discussion of youth violence and its prevention. Herewith, some thoughts.

Preventing Violence: "Just don't do it."

The story of the Boston Gun Project and its core intervention, Operation Ceasefire, is in many ways an intricate one.[4] At the same time, there is a spine to the story, to the intervention, and to the intervention's impact on the streets that is formidably simple. The simple version goes like this: a small group of people, mostly from the law enforcement community, got together and told those most likely to both perpetrate and suffer violence to knock it off, and they did.

The impact of that simple strategy was profound. The Ceasefire working group—then consisting of Boston police officers; state and federal prosecutors; agents from the Bureau of Alcohol, Tobacco, and Firearms; probation and parole and youth corrections officers; and city of Boston gang outreach workers—first met with youth "gangs" (just what that means we will return to) and told them to stop the violence in May 1996. Over the summer and fall of 1996, youth homicide victimization (defined as those age twenty-four and under) in the city fell by about 60 percent, adult homicide victimization (defined as those age twenty-five and over) fell by about 50 percent, and youth gun assaults fell by about one-third. In November 1996, for the first time since before the epidemic years of the late 1980s and early 1990s, not a single person age twenty-four or under was killed in the city. Overall, Boston's homicide rate fell by roughly half.[5] Strict statistical analysis suggests that those reductions were real, rather than accidents of existing trends in Boston or the nation, being both larger and dramatically more abrupt than those that other American cities were experiencing during the same period.[6] One of the defining characteristics of Boston's decline in serious violence is just how sharp the reduction was: most of the decline in youth violence occurred between June and September of 1996, followed by a new, lower rate from the fall onward (see figure 8-1).

The strategy also seems to have legs. Despite an explosion of accounts and analyses suggesting that Boston was somehow unique and that various aspects of its uniqueness were essential to its ability to so dramatically control violence (those arguments we will also return to), it appears that a number of other cities implementing Boston-style strategies have managed to make their own core offenders heed the "stop it" message. In Minneapolis, after a Ceasefire-style strategy was implemented during the first week in June 1997, summer homicide victimization fell from a ten-year high of forty-two in 1996 to eight.[7] In Indianapolis, after a Ceasefire-style homicide intervention seemed to "catch" around the end of March 1999, homicide victimization fell nearly one-third for the rest of the year.[8] High Point, North Carolina, a city of about 70,000 that began experiencing big-city street violence in the mid-1990s, instituted a Ceasefire-style intervention in the last months of 1998; homicides dropped from around fifteen a year to five in 1999, with drug- and gang-related incidents being virtually eliminated.[9] None of these cities has the portfolio of historical investments and assets that some have deemed essential to Boston's success, nor did any of them frame their operations as exact duplicates of Ceasefire. Nonetheless—while observing the appropriate cautions against drawing premature conclusions—one can say that they seem to have produced promising results.

If that is true, then they have done so with remarkable speed, facility, and economy. All showed results within a year or so. All operated without doing the heavy lifting—changing neighborhoods; reforming offenders; making more, and more serious, criminal cases—usually regarded as essential to crime control. All operated without much in the way of new investments in money, personnel, and—most important, to my mind—the actual exercise of state authority; that is, they worked with the resources at hand and without draconian criminal justice measures. And all, it appears, have won not only the approval but the active support of their respective and varied communities.

All these cities did this primarily by framing new relationships with offenders: by reaching out to them directly, telling them what was expected of them, offering them help if they wanted help, and promising and delivering sanctions if sanctions were necessary. If it is true that Boston and the other cities have had an impact on serious violence, then they have done so, essentially, because they told offenders to behave and the offenders actually did so. It may even be that the offenders are *relieved* to behave.

How can it be that the most serious crimes, and the most serious criminals, are open to profound influence through what is, at bottom, talk? How is it that what appears to be our most intractable public safety problem, homicide and serious violence, can be addressed quickly, cheaply, with existing resources, without profound social change, and without much actual exercise of authority? And how is it, for that matter, that a project focusing on juvenile gun violence can end up yielding insights and operations aimed at preventing violence without regard to age or means?

The Background

The answer begins with the national epidemic of juvenile violence. This was the problem the Boston Gun Project was designed to address, by, it was hoped, coming up with an approach that would work in one city and be generalizable, in some fashion, to others.[10] The core elements of the epidemic are well known. Most of the epidemic involved handgun violence, which increased 418 percent between 1984 and 1994, mostly in poor urban communities that also suffered from a long list of other problems.[11] The juvenile violence epidemic was clearly coincident with and almost certainly caused—at least in the early stages—by the crack cocaine epidemic.[12] It hit most sharply among minority males. Homicide victimization rates for nonminority juveniles, both male and female, remained virtually unchanged.[13] The epidemic was a double crisis: not only because of the sheer numbers involved, but because the victims were children, primarily disadvantaged children from disadvantaged communities. Within those communities, not only victims but also families, friends, and community institutions like schools suffered grievously; outside them, many observers felt a special horror at what they were seeing and at the historical and continuing abuses and neglect that seemed to be fueling it.

One immediate result was an explosion of prescriptions. The juvenile violence epidemic was a public-policy Rorschach test. All of the issues apparently involved or argued to be involved in the problem or in responses to it—kids, race, firearms, poor communities, families, drugs, schools, welfare, urban policy, popular culture, helping those at risk, punishing offenders, and all the rest of a long list of candidates—aroused strong feelings in many quarters. Observers moved more or less directly from recognizing the problem—kids are killing one another—to prescribing the favored remedy of their particular ideological or professional camp. Depending on where one stood going into the debate, kids clearly needed more discipline (or more help), guns needed tighter regulation (or looser), poor neighborhoods needed more assistance (or less welfare), juvenile offenders needed to be treated more like adults (or more like kids), the drug war needed to be fought more mercilessly (or abandoned). Certain verities were established: juveniles' access to guns had increased; the schools were dangerous; the violence was widespread, random, and unpredictable; the drug epidemic and the violence epidemic were closely linked, if not one and the same thing. Passions ran high. Congress drastically upped the ante on drug violations, especially those involving crack;[14] states, alerted to a supposed wave of youthful "superpredators," retooled their juvenile justice systems;[15] public health practitioners and schools launched a wave of dispute resolution and peer mediation programs in an effort to teach kids how to deal with conflict.[16]

That, it seems to me, was essentially as it should have been. The juvenile violence epidemic was a crisis of a very high order. Nobody really understood it; nobody knew what would work. In such situations it is appropriate to act before all the evidence is in and to generate more evidence by trying various approaches and observing the results.[17] It is appropriate to apply a wide portfolio of approaches, even (or perhaps, in such situations, especially) approaches predicated on differing, even incompatible, theories. And, in the absence of well-grounded evidence and understanding, it is appropriate to fall back on strong ideas and norms—violence is learned, punishment deters—in an attempt to fill that portfolio. At the time, all the steps taken and the reasons for taking them were at least plausible.

Not all of them, in hindsight, still appear to be. A special place on that roster should be reserved for the superpredator hypothesis, which was baseless, essentially circular—violence is increasing, therefore kids' character must be worsening, therefore worsening character explains the violence— and, unfortunately, very popular indeed. Careful research by Philip Cook and John Laub has demonstrated just how baseless the idea was, in part by showing that young nonwhite males who began the epidemic years with notably low levels of violence underwent sudden and dramatic shifts to unprecedentedly high levels.[18] That is not the pattern one would expect to see in kids whose character is fundamentally rotten. "It is almost," writes Cook, "as if these rather normal cohorts were suddenly drafted into a war."[19] But the power of the superpredator idea and image—"radically impulsive, brutally remorseless youngsters"[20]—helped drive a wave of state and federal steps to stiffen procedural and sentencing regimes aimed at the supposed new breed of savages.

Some of the verities now seem less certain. There was, and is, no evidence that access to guns increased. If we now know anything about guns, it is that they are so loosely governed that if kids had wanted them before 1985 they could have gotten them; almost certainly, at least in the early years of the epidemic, most of the change was in kids' *demand* for guns—

suddenly they wanted them, and they got them.[21] The schools, far from being battlegrounds, were where kids felt safest (there was, as far as I can find, not a single urban school shooting spree, even during the worst years of the epidemic).[22] And, as I will argue below, evidence is accumulating that the violence was not about drugs—at least not for long—and that it was far from random.

Most fundamentally mistaken, I would argue, was the very framework of the discussion. *The "juvenile violence" problem was not, in fact, just about juveniles; it was but one aspect of a dramatic increase in violence among fifteen- to twenty-four-year-olds in certain hard-hit urban areas.* That is evident in the numbers, which show that violence among *nonjuvenile* minority males spiked sharply at the same time and in much the same way as it did among juveniles. Homicide commission and victimization among black males ages eighteen to twenty-four roughly doubled between the mid-1980s and early 1990s.[23] That might seem less significant than the larger percent increases among juveniles, but because the juvenile increase began from a very low starting point and the increase among eighteen- to twenty-four-year-olds from a much higher one, the older age group ends up generating considerably higher numbers. At the epidemic's peak, black juveniles were committing homicide at a rate of 120 per 100,000 juveniles and suffering homicide at a rate of about 70 per 100,000 juveniles. Their older peers, however, were committing homicide at a rate of 280 per 100,000 and suffering homicide at a rate of about 190 per 100,000.[24] The other key dimensions—the concentration of the violence in troubled urban neighborhoods, the prevalence of guns, and all the rest—were precisely the same. This core reality is also evident on the street, where juveniles and older offenders run in the same groups, manifest the same behavior, commit the same crimes, and kill and are killed alongside one another. The point is not to elevate or diminish the significance of the epidemic among one age group relative to the other. The point is that it was—and is, since it continues, albeit at levels somewhat reduced from the early-1990s peak—the *same* epidemic. We did not *have* a juvenile violence epidemic, if what we mean by that is something limited to juveniles. "Juvenile" is a meaningful legal category; it was not a meaningful distinction on the street, where juveniles, young adults, and often older males were caught up together in the same often-lethal dynamic. I think it follows that it does not make sense to craft policies and interventions that address juvenile violence as a thing in itself and not to attend to the larger context, which often involves those much older.

None of that would matter, or at least it would matter less, if the various ideas circulating at the time were producing strong, effective juvenile violence interventions. We do not have to start out in the right place in order to end up in a good place. Superpredators or not, it might have been that stricter sanctions prevented violence. Whatever was behind the violence epidemic, it might have been that attention to the crack trade prevented violence. Even if young and older individuals mixed on the street, it might have been that violence prevention programs in schools prevented juvenile violence. Even if access to guns had not increased, it might have been that gun buy-backs helped. None of that, unfortunately, appears to have been true. The available evidence suggests that stricter sentencing, increased waivers of juveniles to adult courts, and similar steps have been ineffective.[25] The logic of pursuing violence prevention by attacking drug trafficking typically foundered on the crack market's iron resistance to enforcement pressure.[26] The record of public health–style interventions is poor, at least so far, as is that of gun buy-backs.[27] This is not to say that those and other steps did no good. It is to say that if what was wanted was a *sufficient response* to the crisis—a step, or steps, that would greatly reduce the violence, reasonably quickly—then what that response should be was not apparent.

This is not very surprising. The record of *all* deliberate attempts to greatly reduce serious public safety problems is generally poor, perhaps particularly so where violence is concerned.[28] The juvenile homicide epidemic was a particularly grievous such problem. And lest there be any mistake about it, let me say that my own thinking on the subject was blessed by no special insight. I was as surprised as anybody by what emerged in Boston. When the Boston Gun Project began, it focused on a problem defined as juvenile gun violence, with the conviction that such violence was, if not random, widespread and diffuse and becoming more so. It ended focused on the problem of violence among both juveniles and those often considerably older, with the conviction that such violence was remarkably concentrated, contained, and patterned. It was the men and women at Warren Street who led us there.

The Boston Diagnosis

The Boston Gun Project, which Anne M. Piehl, Anthony A. Braga, and I designed and which was supported by a grant from the National Institute of Justice, was framed as an exercise in problem-oriented policing. Its central idea, as with other problem-oriented exercises, was to analyze and understand the problem in a way that would suggest some form of powerful, fast-acting intervention. Its core working group, composed of the Kennedy School of Government team and representatives from a wide variety of agencies, started meeting regularly in January 1995. Certain members—from the Boston police department's gang unit, the probation department, and the city of Boston's gang outreach streetworker program—had been very close to the street for a very long time. Many had been working on juvenile violence since Boston's streets exploded in 1989. And from the very first meetings, they—Paul Joyce, Bobby Fratalia, Bobby Merner, Fred Wagget, and Tito Whittington from the police department; Billy Stewart and Richard Skinner from probation; and Tracy Litthcut and James McGillivray from the streetworkers—insisted that juvenile violence in Boston was gang violence. They said that shooters were chronic offenders and gang involved; that victims also tended to be; that both victims and offenders tended to have long arrest records and probation histories; that gang-on-gang "beefs" drove the violence. They were right. Gun Project research showed that some 1,300 individuals in some sixty-one identifiable street gangs were responsible for better than 60 percent of the killings.[29] They typically had robust criminal records, and many of them were beyond juvenile age. Virtually all the gangs were involved in drug dealing, but very little of the violence was about the drug business.[30] The working group's discussions led to the idea that a freestanding, self-sustaining dynamic had established itself among the gangs: the risk and fear of violence was leading to gun acquisition, gun carrying, gun use, preemptive and retributive shootings, pro-violence street norms, and the like, all of which led to more risk and more fear, thus perpetuating the dynamic.[31]

Could that dynamic itself be a target for deliberate intervention? Was it a "cause" that could be addressed, along with crack, family and community problems, youth culture, and the rest of the more usual targets? If the dynamic could be interrupted, if a "firebreak" could somehow be cut across it, might it not be hoped that a new, safer reality could be established?

This was the Boston Gun Project diagnosis: that homicide was being driven by juveniles and youth, in chronic offending groups, in a particular dynamic—and that that dynamic needed to be addressed. It expanded the scope of the problem from "juvenile gun violence" to "'street' violence of a certain kind, regardless of age, regardless of means." Most of the violence was gun violence, of course, and illegally obtained and carried firearms continued to be viewed as a particularly important factor in creating and sustaining the dynamic, and the project's attention to illegal firearm supplies continued.

It was a fresh diagnosis. At the same time, it was utterly familiar to working group members, who, after all, had led the research team to it. The Kennedy School team's formal research refined and specified what our practitioner members already knew, but it did not change their observations in any fundamental way. The diagnosis also turns out to be essentially true in many other cities. Similar examinations in Minneapolis; High Point, North Carolina; Stockton, California; Indianapolis; and Baltimore reveal the same basic picture: a relatively small population of chronically offending, group-involved individuals is disproportionately responsible for serious violence.[32] Furthermore, since Boston I have had the opportunity to ask officers from scores of police departments a basic question about the violence they experience. Is street violence in your jurisdiction, the question goes, caused primarily by largely known chronic offenders, formed into groups of some kind or another, who hurt primarily one another? The answer is invariably affirmative; those close to the street know this to be true. Moreover, this is basic criminology. Marvin Wolfgang's pioneering 1958 analysis of 588 homicide cases in Philadelphia revealed that homicide usually occurs between nonstrangers and that a relatively high proportion of victims and offenders had a prior criminal record (about two-thirds of offenders and one-half of victims).[33] Later research by Wolfgang suggested that most crime is committed by a relatively small number of serial offenders.[34] Finally, a number of studies have found that many juveniles and youths commit crimes in groups.[35]

It's worth wondering for a moment, then, why this well-known secret took so long to surface. Remember that juvenile violence was, and often still is, described as random, unpredictable, patternless. Remember that gun violence in general is often described as the result of otherwise ordinary people having access to firearms. Neither, I think, is on balance true. What kept, and often still keeps, us from seeing through to the structure in which so much violence occurs?

One aspect, I think, is the basic intellectual, moral, and legal preconceptions that we typically bring to serious violence. Homicide involves "murderers" and "victims," and the ways we think about the two are very different. Murderers are the worst of people, predatory, guilty; victims are good people, preyed upon, blameless. We do not think of the loser of a prize fight, for example, as a "victim"; such fights are consensual and regu-

lated, and both participants are prepared. The prize fight has a winner and
a loser, not a perpetrator and a victim. The same moral framework is built
into law and into legal proceedings. Homicide is virtually never justifiable;
homicide therefore involves, almost by definition, perpetrators and victims, and all that those terms imply. It rarely matters in law and rarely
enters into the public discussion of homicide that the victims might have
been dangerous people themselves. Those close to victims rarely tell
reporters that the deceased was, at least sometimes, frightening and violent;
reporters rarely argue the point by, for instance, including victims' criminal histories in their stories. That is doubly true when the young are
involved. We generally feel quite strongly that if a juvenile has gotten to the
point that he kills someone or acts in a way that somehow contributes to
his own death, he has been failed in deeply important ways by his family,
his community, or society at large.

That is all, I think, as it should be. Nobody should be shot down in the
street, juveniles least of all. That a given victim was highly criminal and violent does not change that fact. Perhaps *something* should have been done,
by the proper authorities and under color of law, but murder is never
acceptable. The murder of a criminal does not somehow matter less; such
victims are still victims. But the heavily freighted language we use to talk
about these matters and the formal legal proceedings in which they are
addressed serve to cloud the fact that perpetrators and victims often have
much in common and that often their histories intertwine in ways that are
complicated and morally ambiguous. It is a commonplace among those in
law enforcement that today's perpetrator often is tomorrow's victim, and
that knowledge remains, essentially, an open secret.

The "group of chronic offenders" question is equally murky. Here, there
are at least three domains: the civic, the law enforcement, and the scholarly.
In all of them, "groups of chronic offenders" means, first and foremost,
"gangs," and gangs are a complicated and contentious issue. At the civic
level, the gang question resonates highly with mayors and other elected
officials and with the poor and minority communities that gangs usually
inhabit and affect. Nobody wants gangs; gangs raise unpleasant issues
about the safety of streets, the quality of civic life, the current and future
prospects of young people, the effectiveness of the police and other aspects
of the criminal justice community, and a host of usually veiled concerns
about race, minority culture, minority families, and other such hugely sensitive matters. For minority communities themselves, conversations about
gangs often are taken as a sign of, or prelude to, a blanket condemnation

of their youth, the unleashing of the police, and highly localized lapses of memory about constitutional niceties. Mayors and minority residents alike will therefore often do almost anything to avoid acknowledging a gang problem. Their job often is made easier by the fact that when most people think of gangs, they think of Los Angeles– and Chicago-style gangs—large, structured, disciplined, with delineated turf and designated leaders—and most cities do not in fact have such gangs. However, most gangs do not resemble such gangs.

A number of things happen in police departments when the issue of gangs arises. One is that the police too often view "gang" as meaning L.A. and Chicago; when they look around their own cities, they see nothing like the Bloods, Crips, or Latin Kings. Since many of them have no appropriate placeholders for other sorts of criminal groups—nothing, for all practical purposes, between solo offenders and "gangs" on the one hand and "gangs" and the Mafia on the other—the discussion stops there. The officers in such departments know perfectly well, of course, that there are various kinds of offender groups doing various sorts of things in their jurisdictions, but that knowledge typically is not translated into any kind of meaningful institutional recognition and thus fails to generate policy or action.

Another is that in departments that do recognize gangs, formal standards of various kinds force analysis and action into odd shapes. The Los Angeles police department, for example, has no trouble recognizing gangs and considers a "gang-related" crime to be any offense in which a gang member is involved. That leads to misleading results, such as characterizing gang-related an otherwise unexceptional robbery-homicide that involves a gang member. Other police departments bend in the other direction, considering "gang-related" only those incidents directly connected to gang business or ordered by gang "leadership." That leads to other sorts of misleading results, such as classifying as not gang-related homicides in long-running gang-on-gang beefs originally sparked by, say, a spontaneous "respect" clash. Still other issues are raised by formal standards for defining "membership" in gangs, such as rules that specify that three of ten criteria must be met before an individual may be considered gang-involved.[36] Many offenders in many kinds of groups do not fit neatly into such categories; at the same time, the rate of gathering, analyzing, classifying, and periodically reviewing such information is so slow that results are often badly mismatched to the much more fluid street scene.

Scholarly attention to issues relating to "groups of chronic offenders" has focused mainly on issues relating to gangs. The resulting literature is extremely rich, but the trajectory that the scholarship usually has followed—define gang, then examine issues related to those groups that fit the definition—has left a sizable gap where groups not meeting the definition are concerned. Many cities suffering from the crack epidemic, for example, found themselves with small, fluid, local groups engaged in street drug sales. Such groups fall short of many scholarly definitions of "gangs," but they became central to urban crime problems. Much gang research, furthermore, is based on surveys of and other information gathered from police departments; if the department in question does not consider the groups of chronic offenders it deals with to be gangs, then the resulting scholarship will not either. The FBI's *Supplementary Homicide Reports* (SHR), for example, allows analysis of selected circumstances relating to all homicides reported by police departments.[37] The only "group" designation allowed by SHR criteria is "gang-related." Thus, if the reporting department does not consider a small drug crew, for example, a gang, or— as is often the case—homicide investigators do not know at the time of filing that there was gang involvement, the SHR will note no group connection. The results can be quite misleading. In a comparison of SHR data on youth homicides submitted by the Boston police department and Boston Gun Project youth homicide data, more than 70 percent of the cases classified as "unknown" in the SHR data were in fact well understood by our practitioner partners. It was estimated on the basis of Boston Gun Project research that between 55 and 67 percent of the "unknown" youth homicide incidents in the SHR data were in fact gang-related.[38]

One result of such treatments of gang issues is that in many jurisdictions, much crime is committed by groups of chronic offenders and driven by dynamics among those groups without that signal fact being recognized by anyone except line law enforcement personnel—who are then left without any easy way to talk about the phenomenon, much less address it. The groups of chronic offenders addressed by Operation Ceasefire were called "gangs" by local law enforcement personnel, a usage that was picked up during the Boston Gun Project. They were, nonetheless, not at all Los Angeles– or Chicago-style gangs: they were typically small; had no formal leadership; lacked much in the way of hierarchy or structure; had "members" who sold drugs but usually without being part of a well-organized trafficking enterprise; committed episodic acts of violence without being commanded to do so; and otherwise fell short of many conceptions of "gang." They were, basically, small neighborhood groups, and Ceasefire was designed to address that fact. It is still routine, in conversations with personnel in other jurisdictions, to hear comments such as "We don't have gangs, we just have little local crews," or "We couldn't meet with gangs, our gangs don't have any leadership."

It might be best—I think it probably would be best—to sidestep the "gang" question altogether. Gangs, their nature, and their behavior will remain central questions for communities, police, and scholars. At the same time, however, where violence prevention and public safety are concerned, the gang question is simply not the central one. Much more important is, *Is what we're dealing with in large measure groups of chronic offenders and the dynamics between and within such groups?* Here, both historically and recently, the answer is overwhelmingly positive.[39]

Then, of course, there is the question of what to do about it.

Tell Them to Stop

The answer—one answer, at any rate—turns out to be profoundly simple: tell them to stop. That was the second great lesson from Warren Street.

During the Boston Gun Project, the practitioners in the working group and our own researchers were quite convincing on the "groups of chronic offenders" issue. That was rough news. In one stroke, juvenile violence turned out not to be a distinct problem but a particular aspect of a much larger group violence phenomenon. And the group violence phenomenon was, to use technical language, really, really, *really* bad. Those involved were, for the most part, serious offenders; they had had lots of apparently unproductive contact with criminal justice agencies; they faced extraordinary risks on the streets and thus had a powerful motivation to obtain, carry, and use weapons; they had real economic interests to protect; they were not the sort of people to be readily reformed by social workers and the like; and they were part of a powerfully oppositional culture. The groups involved were generating perhaps half the homicides in the city.[40] That was the problem the Gun Project was now responsible for addressing. My own reaction was not far removed from terror.[41]

Salvation lay with the Youth Violence Strike Force and Operation Scrap Iron, which had been aimed at an outbreak of violence on and around Wendover Street. Masterminded by the extraordinary detective sergeant

Paul Joyce, who then commanded the strike force, Scrap Iron had engaged in a marvelous kind of law-enforcement judo with the group-of-chronic-offenders problem.[42] The crew operating off Wendover Street, armed by a member who was running guns up from Mississippi, was the most violent group in the city during much of 1994. The genius of Scrap Iron was to turn the crew's chronic offending against it and into a tool for violence prevention. The approach was simple but profound. The YVSF and its partners, which included probation officers, corrections officers from the department of youth services, and others, systematically enforced the law against members of the Wendover Street crew. There was, by virtue of the crew's manifold misbehavior, a lot of law to enforce: members were selling drugs, selling guns, carrying weapons, walking around with outstanding warrants for their arrest, violating their terms of probation and DYS commitments, committing various kinds of misdemeanor offenses, driving unregistered cars, and so forth. From this raw material, Joyce and his partners fashioned an elaborate crackdown. In parallel, the streetworkers, probation officers, and even strike force officers did whatever they could to broker social services and other forms of assistance for those who would accept it. At the same time, the YVSF told the crew, face to face and repeatedly, that the extraordinary enforcement effort—not all legal attention, but the intense crackdown—would stop if the violence stopped. The crew capitulated and even, in the end, surrendered many of its firearms to the strike force.[43] I have never heard of such a thing occurring anywhere else.

As the Kennedy School team and the rest of the working group came to understand the Wendover Street operation, Operation Scrap Iron's potential as a "use reduction" strategy became more and more tantalizing. Nearly all the essential elements of what became Ceasefire were there: the singular focus on violence; the framing of the intervention at the group level; the direct communication; the use of multiple enforcement "levers" (thus the eventual casting of Ceasefire-like operations as "pulling levers" interventions); the simultaneous marshalling of services and other kinds of "helping" interventions. Once the logic of Operation Scrap Iron was clear, it was not such a great intellectual leap—even if a mind-bendingly demanding and uncertain enforcement task—to deciding to tell *all* of Boston's groups of chronic offenders to stop. To the inexpressible astonishment of everybody involved —logic or no logic, Ceasefire was a huge leap of faith— they pretty much did.

Why should such a tactic work? We are not really sure: the *fact* of impact now seems pretty clear, in Boston and perhaps elsewhere, but the how and why are a bit less obvious.[44] Nevertheless, it seems reasonable to speculate that Ceasefire-like interventions might play out in several interesting ways.

One way would be to confirm the "firebreak hypothesis": that in given jurisdictions groups of chronic offenders are locked into a self-perpetuating dynamic; that the dynamic can be interrupted; and that a new, less violent, street dynamic can then emerge. That seems almost too simple to be credited, and too good to be true. And yet—if offenders carry and use guns because they regularly fear being shot, and if deliberate intervention produces a situation in which offenders do *not* regularly fear being shot, might the whole situation not resolve itself into something calmer? It can be a feature of such "tipping" dynamics that very small changes in context or inputs can result in large changes in outcomes.[45] Take, for example, a group of 100 people, on a city street, with graduated tendencies for breaking windows: the first will break a window if somebody else does; the second if two other people do; and so on. In the first run of this model, no outsider breaks a window, so nothing happens: the group, and the street, stays quiet. In the second run, an outsider *does* break a window, and so does the next person, and then the next, and so on through the group: a riot. For the third run, we change the model slightly, by setting the propensity of the first person to *two* broken windows rather than one. Now an outsider breaks a window, and nothing happens.[46] Very similar basic situations; small but crucial differences in key variables; radically different outcomes.

Can the production of serious violence be regarded in any way as similar? I think it can. Group-on-group "beefs" in Boston were highly conducive to violence. If Ceasefire effectively prevented, for a number of those beefs, *the next act* in what would be a continuing cycle of violence, it could thereby interrupt the cycle and even help the beef itself fade away. Violence among chronic offenders and groups of chronic offenders often is driven by "respect" issues. Let us imagine, in another example, that in each of ten groups there is one member with a propensity to act disrespectfully; one member who feels compelled to use violence in response to disrespect; group norms requiring all group members to back any group member; and sufficient social mixing to allow plentiful contact between members. Let the wheels turn long enough and these ten groups alone can generate ninety violent beefs, with enough people involved to keep them running for a long time.

Now change a few small things. Let's say that only two groups have a member given to disrespect or allowed by other group members to show disrespect: now, we have only eighteen beefs. Let's say disrespect no longer requires a violent response: now we have no beefs—or at least no violent beefs. Let's say disrespect still counts, but the price of violence has risen to the point that group norms have changed; group members are no longer invariably willing to accept an individual member's dispute as a group dispute. Two things could happen, separately or together. First, lacking that formerly certain solidarity, members might be less willing both to give and to take offense, and beefs would decline. Second, beefs could continue to arise, but they would remain between *individuals* rather than *groups*. They would thus be contained: those involved could resolve them, including through violence, but there would be far fewer people involved and correspondingly less violence.

Ceasefire-like interventions may well produce an effect like that. They are designed to prevent violent acts, which often produce further violence. They are intended to raise the costs to the group of violent acts committed by individual members, quite possibly leading to the exercise of group control of more violent members. (It is interesting to speculate about whether this might lead to increased influence within the group of, say, the most reasonable members, the most profit-seeking members, or those members with the most to lose in their next contact with law enforcement.) They are intended to create a new norm—or allow the reemergence of an old one— that opposes violence and to provide group members, through the official threat of punishment, a way to justify nonviolence to their peers. The Ceasefire working group thought of this as the provision of an "honorable exit"—giving members a reason to eschew violence that would pass muster within their groups. They are intended to change the rules of the street for everybody at the same time. If you tell one group in fifty that it can no longer use violence to protect its drug interests, it instantly becomes bait for the other forty-nine; tell all fifty, and, none losing anything relative to the others, all just may accept the new status quo.

At the core of all such speculation is the notion that there is a *dynamic*— some kind of self-reinforcing positive-feedback *process*—driving violence, and that that dynamic can be, somehow, addressed more or less directly. That is something of a new thought in the realm of criminal justice. Root causes and other more traditional prevention theories are comfortable with the idea that certain processes lead to crime problems: That idea, in fact, almost defines those frameworks. Historical oppression leads to poor schools and poor job markets, which generates crime; domestic abuse exposes children to violence, which leads to further violence a generation later. These frameworks present a variety of points at which the cycle may be interrupted. Racism can be eliminated or reduced; job markets enhanced; domestic violence prevented or responded to today in a way that reduces generational transfer; violence, as a learned behavior, can be countered by other measures, such as in-school prevention programs. Those approaches have the appeal of being potentially very powerful and generally relying on *facilitative*—service, teaching—rather than *authority-based*—arrest, prison—interventions.[47] They have the disadvantage of typically requiring action on a very broad front—all those who are racist, all children exposed to violence—and having effects that are at best realized rather slowly.

The police and other criminal justice officials typically have not thought in such process-based terms. The job of law enforcement, at root, has been to set things right at a given moment: to patrol in a way that prevents crime, to investigate and prosecute in a way that removes offenders from the community, to impose sanctions in a way that deters potential offenders. The underlying presumption is that if such actions are abandoned, then control is lost too, in what is essentially an endless and basically static tug-of-war with offenders and potential offenders.[48] Criminal justice agencies tend not to think or operate along lines that allow them to say "here is what we will do *today* in order to create a lasting and self-sustaining improvement in this situation *tomorrow*." The obvious exceptions to this, such as the idea of rehabilitating offenders in correctional settings, have fallen into pretty severe disrepute in criminal justice circles. In practice, that means that both inside and outside criminal justice circles not much in the way of lasting improvements are expected from criminal justice interventions; conversely, it means that both inside and outside criminal justice circles the idea of *prevention* has come to mean, almost by definition, "not criminal justice."[49]

Ceasefire and Ceasefire-like interventions are not easily located along the root causes/criminal justice spectrum. Ceasefire was designed to prevent crime and violence, but to do so primarily through the exercise of authority. It was designed to have lasting impact, but without addressing the usual menu of root causes: racism, economic inequality, community conditions, or the functioning of core community institutions. It was designed to change norms and otherwise affect behavior, but without using instruments like either violence prevention programs or sustained high levels of law enforcement and negative sanctions. It was designed to facilitate fundamental improvements in the community, but through the unusual process of reducing violence and fear first and directly, so that community institutions like schools and community improvement efforts like economic development programs could function better. It was designed to do all this, as discussed, by changing the street dynamic that was believed to be driving much of Boston's violent crime—and to do so quickly and with minimal actual enforcement. Again, while what actually happened remains somewhat mysterious, it is possible that the intervention really did change that dynamic.

Is this outcome one to which criminal justice can aspire? Are there other dynamics that might be more or less substantially altered through the strategic exercise of authority? I think it is, and I think there are. We take for granted, for instance, that a certain number of young people will become socialized in such a way that they engage in criminal behavior, particularly in high-crime communities. Need we? In Winston-Salem, North Carolina, a pulling-levers intervention explicitly aims to intervene in that process. To the basic no-violence message directed at the usual groups, the intervention adds the order not to involve juveniles in crime, for example as couriers and lookouts in drug activity. Groups that involve juveniles are informed that they will be first on the list to receive special attention. Will it work? It might, to some extent at any rate. The result could be a reduction both in outright juvenile offending and victimization and in the "graduation" of youths to adult criminality as young people are exposed to fewer opportunities for offending, are drawn into fewer networks of older offenders, and as the appeal of legitimate options becomes relatively stronger and remains so for longer periods of time.[50]

Drug epidemics may be another natural target for such interventions. The crack epidemic, for example, was (and in many places still is) characterized on the supply side by high-profile street markets and on the demand side by high-rate users. The markets proved highly resistant to ordinary enforcement efforts and the users highly resistant to ordinary prevention efforts. It is reasonable to think that these were linked phenomena: the persistence of markets facilitated use, while the persistence of use strengthened markets. In the event, despite massive efforts to intercept drugs, arrest and incarcerate dealers and users, and prevent and treat drug use, the epidemic largely ran its own decade-and-longer course. We might have done and in many places still could do much better. On the supply side, we could, perhaps, eliminate street markets through the simple process of communicating, seriatim, to particular markets that they are going to come under overwhelming enforcement attention. Markets that fail to comply would be made into examples for subsequent markets. The compliance of markets that do concede to law enforcement demands might be fairly easily maintained: while a market of a few blocks with a hundred drug dealers is an enforcement nightmare, the first drug dealer to venture forth in the same few blocks after they have been purged of open dealing will stand out sharply and can be dealt with swiftly. On the demand side, we might use meaningful probation and parole supervision to control many addicts' drug use. The lion's share of both heroin and cocaine is consumed by a relatively small number of high-rate users, who frequently are on probation and parole; frequent drug testing combined with a workable schedule of swift, certain, and appropriately severe sanctions (backed up as much as possible by treatment options) might go a long way toward helping them manage their drug use.[51] The weaker the markets, the harder it is for drug users, especially new users and those on the fringes of using, to use drugs; the fewer the users, the weaker the markets. Even if such steps were successful, would they "solve the drug problem?" They would not—some dealing, some use, and the problems associated with both would remain. However, we need not stand helplessly by while this or the next drug wildfire burns out of control, all but immune to our standard enforcement and prevention techniques.

These examples may or may not work in practice. The larger point, I think, remains. Crime, offending, fear—the whole panoply of public safety concerns—often can be viewed as the outcome of different sorts of *dynamic processes*. Those processes may be amenable to strategic interventions in which relatively small alterations in the dynamic result in relatively large changes in outcomes. One approach to effecting those alterations may, in particular circumstances, be pulling-levers style interventions. But regardless of the mode of intervention, those in criminal justice and others who are concerned with the problems of crime, safety, and conditions in troubled communities should look for those dynamics and for ways to alter their course.

Learning from Boston

Much ink has been spilled over the "Boston Miracle," and many conclusions of the *post hoc, ergo propter hoc* variety have been drawn. Replicating Boston's success, we are told, requires years of prior investment in public health interventions,[52] the involvement of activist black clergy,[53] particular forms of police/probation partnerships,[54] and on and on into the finest details of Boston's particular history. There is, I think, little to be gained from that. Operation Ceasefire was constructed, quite deliberately and because there was literally no other choice, largely from the assets and capacities available in Boston at the time and equally deliberately tailored to the city's specific violence problem. There is no reason to think that everything that came before Ceasefire contributed to violence prevention in the city;[55] that the mix of capacities incorporated into Ceasefire was either ideal or essential; or that a different city or jurisdiction with a meaningfully different violence (or other) problem should look to deploy the same assets in the same ways. It is worth noting that none of the jurisdictions that have since applied Ceasefire-like interventions, with often quite promising results, have had a history of *any* of the elements some have deemed essential to Boston's success: activist clergy, police/probation partnerships, broad public health violence-prevention initiatives, or any of the rest.

Rather, an argument can be made that basic components of Boston's "architecture" should be in place. They might include the following:

A locus of responsibility. If I could banish one term from the crime-policy lexicon, it would be the inherently fraudulent "the criminal justice system." There is in fact no such thing, as anybody who spends any time at all with criminal justice agencies cannot fail to notice. Agencies work largely independently, often at cross-purposes, often without even the most basic kind of coordination, and often in an atmosphere of bitter dislike and distrust. Too often, the same is true of different elements within agencies. This is not to say that something like a system cannot be created; it can, but doing so is a major undertaking. That is the role played in Boston by the Boston Gun Project working group. Despite all the innovative and dedicated work taking place in Boston around youth violence, before the working group and Ceasefire, there was no locus of responsibility for the youth violence problem and no overall strategy for taking action. I am repeatedly asked to offer detailed insights into overcoming the presumed difficulty of "getting people to the table," but in fact I have none. My own experience and observations suggest that usually it is not hard to get people to the table: it is simply that nobody has seriously tried to do so before. It is also probably not very important who does the convening; we now have academics,[56] state and federal prosecutors,[57] and public health practitioners[58] playing that role. Exactly who they are is, I expect, probably a good deal less important than how they go about their business, meaning respectfully, with an eye to the strengths and interests of members and a commitment to drawing out of the process a new and powerful operational approach.

Attention to understanding the problem in a practically useful way, and in particular drawing on *practitioner knowledge* to do this. The whole of the problem-oriented approach that undergirds the Boston Gun Project and similar strategic crime-prevention exercises is that careful examination may reveal a way in which powerful interventions can be made. Much of what was true about youth violence in Boston was well known from existing studies concerning the national epidemic: it was concentrated in poor minority neighborhoods, it was concentrated amongst minority males, it was firearms violence, it was connected in some way to drug trafficking, and more. It was not until a new description was added, *complementary*, not *contradictory*, to all these—a small number of chronic offenders in street crews hurting one another—that the potential for a new kind of intervention began to show itself. This assessment rested on guidance from high-quality front-line practitioners—they helped the research team to understand what questions to ask—and on the systematic gathering of qualitative information from practitioners, for example to identify gangs, their sizes, their turf, and their antagonisms and alliances.[59]

Once one knows what questions to ask, the process sometimes can proceed extremely quickly and efficiently. In designing a homicide intervention in Minneapolis, the basic diagnosis was clear after a one-day, closed-door meeting with police and probation officers, prosecutors, ATF agents, state investigators, and similar law enforcement representatives. The key questions were as follows:

—Are you dealing with groups of chronic offenders?

—Do you know what these groups are and a good deal about their members and activities?

—When a homicide occurs, do you generally know in fairly short order what happened and what group or groups were involved?

—If you could design and implement a "pulling levers" strategy, would the groups as you know them respond?

The answer to each question was yes; subsequent work, based on both more detailed debriefings of practitioners and on formal quantitative data, provided a more detailed description of the problem and helped the group design and implement an actual intervention.[60] Groups working in the U.S. Justice Department's Strategic Approaches to Community Safety Initiative (SACSI) process have worked in similar ways with practitioners to address a variety of problems.[61]

The skills and the will to see the process through. The Boston Gun Project; similar enterprises, like the SACSI projects; and Ceasefire-type interventions are not particularly expensive, and it has been demonstrated that they can take place without new laws, new sanctions, and the like (which is not to say that additional resources and laws might not enhance particular interventions). What they *are* is virtually indescribably demanding of time, commitment, management, and administration—commodities not notably in oversupply in criminal justice agencies. Agency commitment must be solicited and obtained; agency representatives identified and assigned; and the working group (or similar body or bodies) convened and managed. Both existing and new information must be obtained and analyzed; problem assessments and intervention possibilities articulated and weighed; chosen interventions fully specified; operational agency commitments obtained; field operations designed and implemented; and midcourse corrections recognized and incorporated. All that must take place in an environment that inevitably will involve difficulties rooted in individual and agency conflicts and concerns about the repercussions of success as well as failure. The problem-solving process and any new intervention will inevitably reveal—in addition to individual and agency strengths—weaknesses in both past and current practices. The often dubious state of management and accountability within criminal justice agencies is well known; nothing, however, reveals it quite as sharply as trying to mount a fast-paced, fluid operation involving a multitude of moving parts drawn from a dozen or more agencies. The kinds of exercises in question are, basically, quite easy to describe—and a screaming nightmare to pull off. The skills and commitment necessary to see the process through—whether vested in an individual or a group, formally or informally—are simply essential.

A wide variety of incentives, disincentives, and moral voices. Much discussion about the homicide prevention effort in Boston has been devoted to essentially unanswerable questions about which of the strategy's elements—federal law enforcement agencies, probation and parole departments, church and community groups—played a dominant role and to equally unanswerable questions about which elements are indispensable in crafting similar strategies. The debate misses the point: Boston did what Boston did, working with what Boston had to work with—and there the matter should be mercifully allowed to rest. The real advantage, I think, is that there were so *many* elements—combining sanctions, incentives, services, and moral voices—and that they were applied in an explicitly normative fashion. When the menu is large, interventions can be tailored to what particular individuals and groups deserve—some merit severe federal sanctions, others do not. Interventions can be tailored to take advantage of the opportunities that present themselves—some individuals are on probation, others are not. They can be crafted from the different capacities of participating agencies—depending on the fact pattern and state law in different jurisdictions, firearms violations, for example, can be prosecuted most productively in state or federal courts. They can be crafted from what participating agencies are good at, depending on historical practice or on the special skills and dispositions of what may be just a few individuals; some police departments, for example, may be especially adept at mounting conspiracy cases, deploying confidential informants, or disrupting drug markets. They can pair sanctions—or the promise of sanctions—with help and services. When the risk of dealing drugs goes up, legitimate work becomes more attractive; when legitimate work is more readily available, a strategy based on raising risk becomes more effective. And, not least, all of those options can be pursued in a powerfully normative fashion: authorities, service providers, clerics, parents, and community spokespersons can stand together and treat offenders as at least potentially rational and responsible; speak to them respectfully; tell them that what they are doing is wrong and will not be tolerated; confront them with the pain and distress they cause; speak of the pain and distress of losing them to the streets, or prison, or the grave; engage them directly regarding their grievances. Boston's experience tells us, I think, what a powerful approach this mixing, matching, and engaging can be. What exactly to mix; how to match most effectively; and who should engage offenders, how, and on what grounds, is extraordinarily interesting and largely unexplored territory.

Frankness and transparency. The problem being addressed, the nature of the intervention, the discretion being exercised, and the principles guiding the exercise of authority and the provision of incentives should be made clear. Serious crime raises serious, often unpleasant issues. So too does serious crime control. In considerable part because of the efforts of the Ten Point Coalition, one could, in Boston, speak with relative safety about the painful realities of minority male offending and victimization, "gangs," chronic offending, and like matters. (Unlike, for example, in Minneapolis, where at an initial community meeting an activist said that she was glad somebody was finally taking violence seriously and that she did not want to hear anything about black males. In Minneapolis, nearly three-quarters of homicide arrestees and suspects and nearly two-thirds of victims were black males.) Ceasefire-style interventions require such conversations, about the problem and the intervention. The following points, to my mind, are essential to address.

—*The problem.* Much youth violence, and much adult violence, is concentrated in minority communities among highly active offenders and groups of highly active offenders. Those facts in and of themselves mean absolutely nothing more. They are not, in and of themselves, cause to criticize minority or majority communities, culture, and institutions; criminal justice practices; drug policies; or anything else. They absolutely will, however, raise such issues. In particular, focusing on these facts often causes minority communities to fear stigmatization and indiscriminate, scorched-earth policing and criminal justice practices.

—*The focus of the intervention.* Indiscriminate police practices are not acceptable, desirable, or necessary. We can, or so I am convinced, control violence (and perhaps much other crime) without them, in part because in even the most troubled communities relatively few people are part of the problem. We can influence their behavior and the criminogenic dynamics they create without wholesale or massive sanctions. In order to do so, however, we must focus on—or, less innocuously, target—those few. Even here, we need not employ massive sanctions; we can employ deterrence, assistance, moral suasion, and much else. But focus we must. Moreover, that we are focusing must be made explicit and be regarded as acceptable by the broader community. That process will most likely involve public discussion of the problem and the role of chronic offenders and groups of offenders; the intended workings of the deterrence strategy; and the means by which offending groups and participants in such groups are identified by the police and other authorities.

—*The exercise of discretion.* Ceasefire-style strategies involve the extensive exercise of discretion. Authorities may deploy the probation department against one group and the Drug Enforcement Agency against another; they may deal harshly with a group that has received previous warning while bypassing one that has not yet been put on notice. Such discretion is routinely exercised by criminal justice authorities, with little in the way of public knowledge or review. Ceasefire-style strategies, however, make the exercise of discretion a central and readily apparent operating principle. They also make readily apparent that there are virtually no mechanisms for governing the use of discretion. Traditional due process protections are of no use here. If the authorities deploy the probation department against one group and DEA against another, due process protections can tell us only whether the actions of the two agencies were or were not

allowable; they say nothing about the central question, which is why probation was pursued where DEA (or nothing) might have been, or vice
versa. Again, that discretion is being exercised, and how, must be made
explicit and be regarded as acceptable by the broader community. The same
is true with the provision of services, opportunities, and other incentives.
Should chronic offenders be given special access to—rewarded with, some
would say—drug treatment or job placement? These are not easy questions, and different communities are likely to have different feelings about
how to balance the crime control, equity, and other important public goals
that they entail. That, too, is likely to be the subject of a public, and possibly evolving, conversation.[62]

Conclusion

These are conversations worth having, I think, about work worth doing.
The largest lesson of the Boston Gun Project is that seemingly intractable
public safety problems may yield to serious, sustained, well-grounded, and
relentlessly pragmatic attention, and that criminal justice agencies can play
a role in solving them—in a way that will appeal to the agencies themselves, to the public, and even, in the oddest of ways, to those at the core
of the problems. I warned at the outset that this was a participant's account.
As a participant, I can say with some authority that the Boston Gun Project and Operation Ceasefire were uncertain, often frightening, and often
very creaky enterprises indeed. I am certain not only that others can do
what Boston did—I am certain that they can do better.

Notes

1. David M. Kennedy, Anne M. Piehl, and Anthony A. Braga, "Youth Violence in
Boston: Gun Markets, Serious Youth Offenders, and a Use-Reduction Strategy," *Law and
Contemporary Problems,* vol. 59, vol. 1 (Winter 1996), pp. 147–96; David M. Kennedy,
Anthony A. Braga, and Anne M. Piehl, "The (Un)Known Universe: Mapping Gangs and
Gang Violence in Boston," in David Weisburd and J. Thomas McEwen, eds., *Crime Map-
ping and Crime Prevention* (New York: Criminal Justice Press, 1997); David M. Kennedy,
"Pulling Levers: Chronic Offenders, High-Crime Settings, and a Theory of Prevention,"
Valparaiso University Law Review, vol. 31, no. 2 (Spring 1997), pp. 449–84; Anne M. Piehl
and others, "Testing for Structural Breaks in the Evaluation of Programs," Working Paper
7226 (Cambridge, Mass.: National Bureau of Economic Research, 1999); Anthony A.
Braga and others, "Problem-Oriented Policing, Deterrence, and Youth Violence: An Evaluation of Boston's Operation Ceasefire," working paper (John F. Kennedy School of Government, Harvard University, 1999).

2. On the traditional norms connected with scholarly research, see LaMar T. Empey, "Field Experimentation in Criminal Justice: Rationale and Design," in Malcolm Klein and Katherine Teilmann, eds., *Handbook of Criminal Justice Evaluation* (Beverly Hills, Calif.: Sage Publications, 1980); Lawrence Sherman, "Herman Goldstein: Problem-Oriented Policing," *Journal of Criminal Law and Criminology,* vol. 82 (1991), pp. 693–702. On academic research exercises that blend research, policy design, action, and evaluation, see Kurt Lewin, "Group Decision and Social Change," in Theodore M. Newcomb and Edward Hartley, eds., *Readings in Social Psychology* (Holt, 1947); David M. Kennedy and Mark H. Moore, "Underwriting the Risky Investment in Community Policing: What Social Science Should Be Doing to Evaluate Community Policing," *Justice System Journal,* vol. 17, no. 3 (1995), pp. 271–91; Mark H. Moore, "Learning While Doing: Linking Knowledge to Policy in the Development of Community Policing and Violence Prevention in the United States," in Per-Olof Wikstrom, ed., *Integrating Crime Prevention Strategies: Motivation and Opportunities* (Stockholm: National Council for Crime Prevention, 1995).

3. Other jurisdictions my colleague Anthony Braga and I have been involved with include Minneapolis; Stockton, California; Indianapolis; High Point, North Carolina; Winston-Salem, North Carolina; and Baltimore. See, for example, David M. Kennedy and Anthony A. Braga, "Homicide in Minneapolis: Research for Problem Solving," *Homicide Studies,* vol. 2 (1998), pp. 263–90; Veronica Coleman and others, "Using Knowledge and Teamwork to Reduce Crime," *National Institute of Justice Journal* (October 1999), pp. 17–23.

4. Kennedy, Piehl, and Braga, "Youth Violence in Boston," pp. 147–96; Kennedy, Braga, and Piehl, "The (Un)Known Universe," pp. 219–62; Kennedy, "Pulling Levers," pp. 449–84.

5. Braga and others, "Problem-Oriented Policing"; Piehl and others, "Testing for Structural Breaks."

6. Braga and others, "Problem-Oriented Policing."

7. The summer of 1997—the summer months typically are the city's most active homicide period—showed a sharp reduction in violence. Homicide figures for the ten months after the intervention began also were promising, although not as remarkable as the summer figures. See Kennedy and Braga, "Homicide in Minneapolis."

8. Personal communications between Edward McGarrell and Melinda Haag of the Indianapolis Violence Prevention Project and the author.

9. High Point was experiencing a peak homicide *rate* of some twenty-two per 100,000 population, a substantial figure roughly equivalent to Boston during its worst years. The homicide count in High Point was fourteen (five by firearm) in 1994; eleven (nine by firearm) in 1995; eleven (eight by firearm) in 1996; sixteen (eleven) in 1997; fourteen (fourteen) in 1998; and five (two) in 1999. Figures from Walter Holton, U.S. attorney for the middle district of North Carolina, January 14, 2000.

10. David M. Kennedy, Anthony A. Braga, and Anne M. Piehl, "Operation Ceasefire: Problem Solving and Youth Violence in Boston," final report to National Institute of Justice, U.S. Department of Justice (John F. Kennedy School of Government, Harvard University, 1999).

11. James Alan Fox, *Trends in Juvenile Violence: A Report to the United States Attorney General on Current and Future Rates of Juvenile Offending* (U.S. Department of Justice, Bureau of Justice Statistics, 1996).

12. See, for example, David M. Kennedy, "Can We Keep Guns Away From Kids?" *American Prospect*, vol. 18 (1994), pp. 74–80; Albert Reiss and Jeffery Roth, eds., *Understanding and Preventing Violence* (Washington: National Academy Press, 1993); Alfred Blumstein, "Youth Violence, Guns, and the Illicit-Drug Industry," *Journal of Criminal Law and Criminology*, vol. 86 (1995), pp. 10–36; Jeffrey Grogger and Michael Willis, "The Introduction of Crack Cocaine and the Rise in Urban Crime Rates," unpublished working paper (University of California–Los Angeles, 1997).

13. Philip Cook, "The Epidemic of Youth Gun Violence," paper presented at the Perspectives on Crime and Justice Lecture Series (National Institute of Justice, 1998); Philip Cook and John Laub, "The Unprecedented Epidemic of Youth Violence," in Michael Tonry and Mark H. Moore, eds., *Youth Violence* (University of Chicago Press, 1998).

14. Coramae Richey Mann, "We Don't Need More Wars," *Valparaiso University Law Review*, vol. 31 (1997), pp. 565–78.

15. William J. Bennett, John J. DiIulio, and John P. Walters, *Body Count: Moral Poverty and How to Win America's War Against Crime and Drugs* (Simon and Schuster, 1996).

16. See, for example, Deborah Prothrow-Stith, *Deadly Consequences* (Harper Collins, 1991).

17. Moore, "Learning While Doing," pp. 301–31.

18. Cook and Laub, "The Unprecedented Epidemic," pp. 27–64.

19. Cook, "The Epidemic of Youth Gun Violence," p. 112.

20. Bennett and others, *Body Count*.

21. Joseph Sheley and James Wright, "Gun Acquisition and Possession in Selected Juvenile Samples," *Research in Brief* (National Institute of Justice, 1993); Joseph Sheley and James Wright, *In the Line of Fire: Youth, Guns, and Delinquency* (New York: Aldine de Gruyter, 1995); Carl Taylor, *Dangerous Society* (Michigan State University Press, 1990); LH Research, *A Survey of American People on Guns as a Children's Health Issue*, Study 930018 (School of Public Health, Harvard University, 1993).

22. Jackson Toby, "The Schools," in James Q. Wilson and Joan Petersilia, eds., *Crime* (San Francisco: Institute for Contemporary Studies Press, 1995).

23. Cook, "The Epidemic of Youth Gun Violence," p. 108; Cook and Laub, "The Unprecedented Epidemic."

24. Cook and Laub, "The Unprecedented Epidemic," pp. 46–47.

25. See, for example, Reiss and Roth, *Understanding and Preventing Violence*; Franklin Zimring and Gordon Hawkins, *Crime Is Not the Problem: Lethal Violence in America* (Oxford University Press, 1997).

26. See, for example, Jonathan Caulkins, "Thinking About Displacement in Drug Markets: Why Observing Change of Venue Isn't Enough," *Journal of Drug Issues,* vol. 22 (1992), pp. 17–30. However, certain types of crackdowns and problem-oriented policing initiatives have been found to be effective in quelling violence and disorder problems associated with street-level drug markets. See David M. Kennedy, "Closing the Market: Controlling the Drug Trade in Tampa, Florida," *Program Focus* (National Institute of Justice, 1993); Mark A. R. Kleiman, "Crackdowns: The Effects of Intensive Enforcement on Retail Heroin Dealing," in Marcia Chaiken, ed., *Street-Level Drug Enforcement: Examining the Issues* (National Institute of Justice, 1988); David L. Weisburd and Lorraine Green, "Policing Drug Hot Spots: The Jersey City DMA Experiment," *Justice Quarterly*, vol. 12 (1995), pp. 711–36; Anthony A. Braga and others, "Problem-Oriented Policing in Vio-

lent Crime Places: A Randomized Controlled Experiment," *Criminology*, vol. 37 (1999), pp. 541–80.

27. On public health interventions, see Marc Posner, "Research Raises Troubling Questions about Violence Prevention Programs," *Harvard Education Letter*, vol. 10, no. 3 (1994); Alice Hausman, Glenn Pierce, and LeBaron Briggs, "Evaluation of Comprehensive Violence Prevention Education: Effects on Student Behavior," *Journal of Adolescent Health*, vol. 19 (1996), pp. 104–10. On gun buy-back programs, see David M. Kennedy, Anne M. Piehl, and Anthony A. Braga, "'Gun Buy-Backs' Where Do We Stand and Where Should We Go?" in Martha R. Plotkin, ed., *Under Fire: Gun Buy-Backs, Exchanges, and Amnesty Programs* (Washington: Police Executive Research Forum, 1996).

28. For a brief review, see Reiss and Roth, *Understanding and Preventing Violence*.

29. Kennedy, Piehl, and Braga, "Youth Violence in Boston"; Kennedy, Braga, and Piehl, "The (Un)Known Universe."

30. Kennedy, Braga, and Piehl, "The (Un)Known Universe"; Anthony A. Braga, Anne M. Piehl, and David M. Kennedy, "Youth Homicide in Boston: An Assessment of Supplementary Homicide Report Data," *Homicide Studies*, vol. 3 (1999), pp. 277–99.

31. Kennedy, Piehl, and Braga, "Youth Violence in Boston."

32. See, for example, Kennedy and Braga, "Homicide in Minneapolis"; Coleman and others, "Using Knowledge and Teamwork."

33. Marvin Wolfgang, *Patterns in Criminal Homicide* (University of Pennsylvania Press, 1958).

34. Marvin Wolfgang, Robert Figlio, and Thorsten Sellin, *Delinquency in a Birth Cohort* (University of Chicago Press, 1972).

35. Franklin Zimring, "Kids, Groups, and Crime: Some Implications of a Well-Known Secret," *Journal of Criminal Law and Criminology*, vol. 72 (1981), pp. 867–85; Albert J. Reiss, "Co-offending and Criminal Careers," in Michael Tonry and Norval Morris, eds., *Crime and Justice: A Review of Research*, vol. 10 (University of Chicago Press, 1988); Albert J. Reiss and David P. Farrington, "Advancing Knowledge about Co-offending: Results from a Prospective Longitudinal Survey of London Males," *Journal of Criminal Law and Criminology*, vol. 82 (1991), pp. 360–95.

36. For example, the Minneapolis police department follows a formal state of Minnesota protocol that requires that an individual both exhibit at least three of ten gang-related characteristics (such as admitted gang membership or having gang tattoos) and be involved in criminal activity. See Kennedy and Braga, "Homicide in Minneapolis," p. 277.

37. See Fox, *Trends in Juvenile Violence*; Mark Reidel, "Nationwide Homicide Datasets: An Evaluation of UCR and NCHS Data," in Doris MacKenzie, P. J. Baunach, and Roy Roberg, eds., *Measuring Crime: Large-Scale, Long-Range Efforts* (State University of New York Press, 1989); Mark Reidel and Margaret Zahn, *The Nature and Patterns of American Homicide* (Government Printing Office, 1985).

38. Braga, Piehl, and Kennedy, "Youth Homicide in Boston."

39. Zimring, "Kids, Groups, and Crime"; Reiss, "Co-offending and Criminal Careers"; Reiss and Farrington, "Advancing Knowledge about Co-offending"; Wolfgang, *Patterns in Criminal Homicide*; Wolfgang, Figlio, and Sellin, *Delinquency in a Birth Cohort*; Kennedy, Braga, and Piehl, "The (Un)Known Universe"; Kennedy, Piehl, and Braga, "Youth Violence in Boston"; Kennedy and Braga, "Homicide in Minneapolis"; Coleman and others, "Using Knowledge and Teamwork."

40. Kennedy, Piehl, and Braga, "Youth Violence in Boston"; Kennedy, Braga, and Piehl, "The (Un)Known Universe."

41. John Buntin, "A Community Responds: Boston Confronts an Upsurge in Youth Violence," case study C15-98-1428.0 (John F. Kennedy School of Government, Harvard University, 1998); David M. Kennedy, Anthony A. Braga, and Anne M. Piehl, "Operation Ceasefire: Problem Solving and Youth Violence in Boston," research report submitted to National Institute of Justice, U.S. Department of Justice (National Institute of Justice, 1999).

42. Youth Violence Strike Force, Boston Police Department, "Operation Scrap Iron," unpublished report on file with author, no date.

43. For more detailed accounts of the Scrap Iron operations, see ibid.

44. Unfortunately, we were not able to collect the necessary pretest and posttest data to shed light on any shifts in street-level dynamics that could be associated with the "pulling levers" deterrence strategy. Our research efforts during the pretest phase were focused on problem analysis and program development. We did not know beforehand what form the intervention would take and who our target audience would be. In this regard, our assessment is very much a "black box" evaluation. Additional ethnographic research is needed.

45. Malcolm Gladwell, "The Tipping Point," New Yorker, June 3, 1996, pp. 32–38; Colin Loftin, "Assaultive Violence as Contagious Process," Bulletin of the New York Academy of Medicine, vol. 62 (1984), pp. 550–55; Thomas Schelling, Micromotives and Macrobehavior (Norton, 1978); Jonathan Crane, "The Epidemic Theory of Ghettos and Neighborhood Effects on Dropping Out and Teenage Childbearing," American Journal of Sociology, vol. 96 (1991), pp. 1226–260.

46. The example is drawn from Philip Cook and Kristin Goss, "The Social Contagion of Youth Violence," unpublished report to the Sloan Youth Violence Working Group (Durham, N.C.: Sanford Institute of Public Policy, Duke University, 1996). Available on request from author.

47. The idea of mandatory arrest for domestic violence as a way to break an intergenerational cycle of violence is a clear exception. See Lawrence Sherman, Policing Domestic Violence (Free Press, 1992).

48. The "broken windows" approach is the signal exception to this. See James Q. Wilson and George Kelling, "Broken Windows: The Police and Neighborhood Safety," Atlantic Monthly, March 1982, pp. 29–38.

49. This is not to say that people in criminal justice are not in favor of prevention; in general, they are more given to supporting prevention than people in prevention are given to supporting criminal justice. It does mean that what criminal justice circles point out as prevention activities, like DARE, GREAT, police athletic leagues, and the like, almost invariably involve using criminal justice personnel to do things that are not core criminal justice activities.

50. See Coleman and others, "Using Knowledge and Teamwork"; "Reaching Violent Youth," Winston-Salem Journal, December 9, 1999; "Taking to the Streets," Winston-Salem Chronicle, December 10, 1999.

51. Mark A. R. Kleiman, "Coerced Abstinence: A Neopaternalist Drug Policy Initiative," in Lawrence M. Mead, The New Paternalism (Brookings, 1997).

52. Deborah Prothrow-Stith and Howard Spivak, "Turning the Tide on Violence" editorial, Boston Globe, November 24, 1996, p. D7; Deborah Prothrow-Stith and Howard

Spivak, "With Youth Crime Down in Boston, What Do We Do for an Encore?" editorial, *Boston Globe*, March 2, 1997, p. D7.

53. Christopher Winship and Jenny Berrien, "Boston Cops and Black Churches," *Public Interest* (Summer 1999), pp. 52–68; John Leland with Claudia Kalb, "Savior of the Streets," *Newsweek*, June 1, 1998, p. 20.

54. Fox Butterfield, "In Boston, Nothing Is Something," *New York Times*, November 21, 1996, p. A20.

55. See Anthony A. Braga, David M. Kennedy, and Anne M. Piehl. "Problem-Oriented Policing and Youth Violence: An Evaluation of the Boston Gun Project," final report to National Institute of Justice, U.S. Department of Justice (John F. Kennedy School of Government, Harvard University, 1999). Available on request from author.

56. Academics have taken principal roles in Boston, Indianapolis, and elsewhere.

57. See Coleman and others, "Using Knowledge and Teamwork."

58. Public health practitioner Gary Slutkin has played this role in Chicago.

59. Kennedy, Braga, and Piehl, "The (Un)Known Universe."

60. Kennedy and Braga, "Homicide in Minneapolis."

61. Coleman and others, "Using Knowledge and Teamwork."

62. This is a conversation well overdue in criminal justice, regardless of whether new crime control strategies are being pursued. As noted, such discretion is routinely exercised by all criminal justice agencies, without much public notice or guidance. One traditional response has been to deny that discretion is exercised, claiming that "we just enforce the law," which is a dangerous fiction. Another has been to explicitly restrict it, which has its place but also can lead to the curtailing of innovation, top-heavy supervisory structures, and other ills. Both open dialogue about agency discretion and meaningful accountability mechanisms are much to be desired, but nowhere are they well developed.

9

FRANCIS X. HARTMANN

Safety First: Partnership, the Powerful Neutral Convener, and Problem Solving

IN RECENT YEARS, criminal justice practitioners and researchers have begun to build on the growth of community policing to develop a number of promising "community" or "problem-solving" criminal justice strategies. Community prosecution, new probation practices, the Boston Ceasefire Project, and the New York City police department's Civil Enforcement Initiative and Comstat are just a few examples. Community-based approaches focus on fear, disorder, and serious crime, rather than just index crimes measured by the *Uniform Crime Reports*. They also emphasize the role of citizens in working closely with the police on behalf of their communities, and they promote decentralization and discretion in problem solving. Problem solving shifts the focus from reacting to individual cases to identifying and solving the larger problems of which individual cases are symptoms. There is mounting evidence that it is effective.[1]

The emergence of these strategies has motivated practitioners and researchers to explore ways to integrate strategies that might lead not only to further major reductions in crime but also to the revitalization of community life. Initiatives in Chicago, Las Vegas, Norfolk, Virginia, and Seattle as well other cities illustrate how the police can play a major part in solv-

Some sections of this chapter are derived from earlier pieces co-written with Stewart Wakeling, John Larivee, and Sara Stoutland.

ing the problems that contribute to crime, fear, and disorder by allying themselves with city agencies and community residents.[2] Their success has inspired other efforts.

One of the most important aspects of recent efforts is that they have engendered the sense that communities can be made safer, that the police can make a tangible difference in ensuring community safety, that prosecutors can think in terms of solving problems rather than processing cases, and that probation officers can help reduce criminal activity among probationers. This message is radically different from the conventional response of the criminal justice system to crime and fear. It has energized many people who, however well motivated, had been doing business as usual with the sense that their work did not make much difference. Now, there is the growing sense that together they—police and probation officers, prosecutors, and the community—can make a real difference.

Many criminal justice professionals now are operating this way. Their efforts are generally guided by the following principles:

—Geographic areas rather than political jurisdictions are the focus of analysis and problem solving.

—Specific, concrete problems, like a series of burglaries, domestic assaults, or homicides among young people, are targeted.

—Data are gathered and analyzed to get a handle on the targeted problems and then continuously analyzed in order to adjust tactics. The analytic process involves continuous learning and consequent adjusting, not just a change from one way of doing business to another, equally rigid way of operating.

—Many actors are likely to be included in the problem-solving process, not for the sake of including them but because the problem cannot be solved without their participation.

—The concept of deterrence is used creatively in the belief that it is possible to dissuade some criminals and would-be criminals from criminal behavior.[3]

—Both traditional and nontraditional performance measures are employed to manage the problem-solving process, evaluate progress toward goals, and assess the overall impact of the work of the partnership.[4]

Building these kinds of partnerships entails daunting challenges— mostly the pressure of having to take care of business as usual accompanied by political pressures to pursue traditional outcomes. The new partnerships require new ways of working: major changes in organizational culture, management structure, and training; meaningful ways of engaging communities as equal partners; and innovative combinations of traditional and nontraditional performance measures.

Often new ways of doing business are generated by creative, highly motivated practitioners; as they tire, the new effort recedes without lasting impact on traditional practices. The team policing initiative of the 1970s, an innovative and widespread strategy that attempted to decentralize policing by assigning teams of officers to neighborhoods, receded into ordinary practice after several years of initial enthusiasm. Community policing,[5] despite maximum attention, a clear win in terms of rhetoric, and substantial funding, will not be immune to the staying power of conventional ways of doing business.[6]

Despite the impressive results of many of the initiatives mentioned, the more important work is to use such examples of best practices to change institutionalized ways of doing business. Isolated improvements that leave no legacy affecting the way business is conducted or that do not bring and sustain powerful informing ideas about good practice are unhelpful and possibly even harmful. In the disillusioned aftermath of the Hartford police department's attempt at team policing in the 1970s, one of its proponents admitted saying to a police colleague, "Sarge, if I ever fall in love again, please kick me!"

Safety First

Safety First is a broad partnership of criminal justice agencies, city agencies, and community groups and residents in Lowell, Massachusetts, whose primary goals are to achieve significant and measurable reductions in crime, to institutionalize the everyday operations that produce those results, and to revitalize community life. However, there are many obstacles to building and maintaining partnerships that produce sustainable results because partners must change their ordinary ways of doing business to produce them. Safety First aims to overcome those obstacles in the following ways:

—By establishing a broad, nonhierarchical partnership of powerful criminal justice agencies (and non–criminal justice agencies) acting together. To do so, Safety First uses the concept of a "powerful neutral convener," a catalyst to hold players with conflicting or competing interests together.

—By designing and implementing strategies for preventing serious and persistent violence, particularly juvenile and domestic violence (both of which are significant problems in Lowell), and by developing a neighborhood-based crime prevention effort. Strategies include giving special attention to a variety of preventive measures, including sending the message to violent offenders that violence will not be tolerated; using sanctions creatively and productively; developing residents' sense of control over what goes on in their neighborhood; and maintaining a constant awareness of the importance of preventing the next crime.

—By concentrating on a core group of offenders—both violent youth and a separate group of men whose pattern of violence includes domestic violence—to convey the message that violent behavior will not be tolerated and to offer them support in finding productive alternatives. The core group is chosen for its potential impact not only on the behavior of group members themselves, but also on that of those whom they influence.

The ideas underlying Safety First were derived from a working group first convened in Boston in early December 1995 by the Crime and Justice Foundation,[7] a nonprofit organization whose mission includes demonstration-based research of ideas that promise to improve public safety.[8] (The author was then president of the foundation's board.) Energized by examples of successful crime reduction initiatives, particularly those in New York City and Boston's Operation Ceasefire, several people gathered to discuss the possibility of building on those efforts. Might it be possible to extend a successful crime prevention strategy to encompass a whole jurisdiction and create a new process that would become the established way of doing business? In the words of one member of the group, "It is possible for mobilized neighborhoods, backed by the authority of the state and completely consistent with constitutional liberty, to create conditions of almost complete safety for its citizens . . . through a comprehensive restructuring of our crime control efforts." After several working meetings, the group, consisting of a state corrections commissioner, a state legislator, the head of the Boston school board (and, at the same time, a prosecutor), a passionate public sector entrepreneur now in the private sector (quoted in the preceding sentence), the head of the foundation, and the author, decided on the following principles regarding the choice of a project site:

—The partnership must begin with the strong commitment of a wide range of criminal justice agencies, city agencies, elected officials, and the community to use the resources available to them to prevent and control crime in a genuinely collaborative relationship of all partners.

—The partnership must collect more and better data and information about criminals and criminal activity and to use that information strategically, for example, by sending the message to potential offenders that violence will not be tolerated.

—The partnership must be managed rigorously, using outcome measures that are at once practical, meaningful to the community, and politically robust.

—The partnership must organize its efforts around neighborhoods, rather than within conventional jurisdictional boundaries.

The effort differed from that of the New York City police department in that it proposed to include all essential parties in the criminal justice response, not only the police. And, unlike in Boston, one objective from the very beginning was to institutionalize the new management and accountability processes.

Not specifically enumerated among the basic principles was the idea that a powerful neutral convener is essential in establishing the working group/partnership process. There were many working groups in the collective experience of those convened at the Crime and Justice Foundation, and many had proven to be a waste of time. Often, the promise of the initial effort only faded later into business as usual. Parties of good will met, shared their problems and points of view, and agreed to work together toward a common vision of how things might be improved. Invariably, other demands, important on any particular day, interfered. Working meetings were missed or attended by persons of decreasing responsibility, deadlines were not met, work was not productive or was not energized by a sense of urgency, there was insufficient sense of accomplishment and momentum, and the process ground to a halt.

Given such discouraging experiences, how might the working group process be energized and managed so that it might achieve its goals? The first requirement was that the necessary people attend, do the hard work of thinking through the issues, agree on a set of goals, contribute the resources needed from their agency, and continue the working process with a sense of urgency, giving the work ongoing high priority. It was the author's sense that in almost every community of any size there is a person or a few people who have the informal authority, by reason of either institutional position or personal authority, to convene a group to work productively toward a community goal over time—a powerful neutral convener. Informal authority is necessary because although four different levels of government—local, county, state, and federal—and various nongovernmental institutions each play a role in ensuring public safety, no representative of any has the authority to convene and manage such a group—not the president of the United States, the governor of the state, the chief executive of the county, or the mayor or city manager. Each may call together a group for what often turns out to be a photo opportunity, but the actual work languishes. Using the bully pulpit, higher-level officials can demand attention and participation, but they invariably fall down on follow through, and lower-level officials have difficulty getting the real attention needed to produce and maintain effective effort.

The powerful neutral convener, on the other hand, is held in such high regard that no one ignores this person—or does so at the risk of alienating an essential local player. Such a person might be the head of a local foundation (from which everyone wants a grant, has a grant, or had a grant), CEO of a corporation so enmeshed with local interests that he or she plays an essential role in the distribution of a variety of necessities (the CEO of Aetna Insurance played such a role in Hartford at one time), or a politician of such status that everyone wants to be on his or her good side (the late U.S. senator Paul Tsongas had played this role in Lowell). A number of configurations might give a person such informal authority. Stated another way, this person's phone calls may be received with ambivalence, with wariness or welcome, but they are invariably returned quickly.

The task then was to find a jurisdiction in which this potential convener would be willing to pull together a working group, help them to choose goals that would make the community a better place in which to live and work, and manage the group so that it could achieve the desired results.

After the foundation had followed many leads, a chance and fruitful conversation about the concept of the neutral convener with Ed Davis, the superintendent of police in Lowell, Massachusetts, began the process of adopting the Safety First program in Lowell. Lowell is a mid-sized, urban city of 100,000—a manageable size for piloting Safety First—located forty miles northwest of Boston. The city, where per capita income ranks in the bottom 10th percentile in Massachusetts and nearly one-fifth of residents live in poverty, has experienced many of the problems typical of larger cities throughout the country. There are a significant number of empty storefronts downtown and uneasiness about what another recession would mean. Lowell's substantial and growing Hispanic and Asian communities give it a complex ethnic mix for a city of its size.

Lowell had already made the commitment to community policing under the chief's leadership, and the new strategy had begun to produce results—the city's crime problem was improving. Lowell had social capital; although the city had seen better days economically, there still were individuals, organizations, and institutions that were committed to making Lowell a good place in which to live and do business. Many criminal justice professionals seemed to be open to changing the ordinary ways of doing business, ranging from a judge who had lunch in ordinary city restaurants every day instead of having a sandwich in chambers so that he would know what was happening on the streets, to a district attorney who had already begun the process of including knowledgeable individuals in a weekly conversation about troublesome juveniles. Lowell was large enough to experience most typical urban problems, so any positive results there could not be dismissed as having been achieved in a hothouse; yet, it was defined and manageable enough to be suitable for attempting something new and determining whether it had an effect. It turned out that Lowell had other assets: a number of talented and dedicated professionals including a congressman (formerly a prosecutor) who was willing to use his personal and political capital to move the process along; a chief of police with immense credibility who was committed to increasing the effectiveness of law enforcement; and the publisher of the local newspaper, who was willing to convene a working group aimed at making Lowell a safer place.[9]

Safety First, as it unfolded in Lowell, was based on the initial principles described above and took them to another level:

—Start with a defined geographical area and learn just what is taking place there in terms of crime, public safety, and the public's sense of safety. In Lowell, there was a strong sense that, despite declining *Uniform Crime Report* (UCR) numbers,[10] the city was not generally viewed as a safe or desirable place in which to live or conduct business. Lowell's desire to improve safety and the sense of safety in the city as a whole was a strong motivation for its decision to take on the work of Safety First. Somewhat later in the working process, a specific neighborhood, the Lower Highlands, was chosen as the area in which to concentrate efforts to bring the community into the partnership.

—Establish a broad, dramatic goal ("Make Lowell the safest city of its size in the United States") in order to generate and motivate the working group.

—Convene a working group composed of all of the parties necessary to produce a dramatic public safety result. In Lowell, the idea of an initial open forum regarding crime was resisted. Instead, a working group was constituted in which membership was based on a member's capacity to bring to the table one or more necessary parts of a program to improve public safety.

—Choose a powerful neutral convener to initiate and maintain the working process. No formal governmental authority can constitute such a working group and keep it working together.

—Agree on a clearly defined problem to be addressed. In Lowell, after a lengthy conversation in the first meeting about troublesome young men, racial problems, and the need for federal grants, the Safety First working group chose an initial target of reducing aggravated assaults by 30 percent. This was concrete, measurable, and, if a stretch, within the realm of possibility.

—Gather and analyze information on an ongoing basis to identify those who contribute to the problem and under what circumstances (gender, age, type of crime, place, time, and so forth). In Lowell, the police department, aided by students from the Kennedy School of Government, did the initial information gathering and analysis and continued the analysis to inform the working group.

—Break the problem into manageable chunks or distinct targets. In Lowell, the target was a small group of twenty problem-generating juveniles and men whose violent acts included domestic violence. At the same time, given the geographical distribution of crime, a neighborhood effort involving residents and local stakeholders was undertaken.

—Send the message to the target group. A major aspect of the effort is based on "message sending," which is analogous to the Boston concept of "thick deterrence." The purpose in sending the message to the twenty young men was to convey that message to the much larger group that they influenced. Ongoing efforts were made to sustain the message.

—Establish a process of continuous learning. In Lowell, the working task forces (juvenile, domestic violence, neighborhood) "managed back" from criminal events. For example, when a youth committed a crime on Lane Street, members of the working group asked themselves how they might have anticipated and prevented it. As the task forces gained experience working together and produced valuable new outcomes, the enthusiasm and momentum necessary to continue the work were generated.

—Make successes public and build on them so that positive results will be so valued that it will be difficult to go back to business as usual. In Lowell, once there was a reasonable degree of success—29 percent reduction in assaults by juveniles on juveniles ("The high school has never been so quiet at this time of year")—the newspaper heralded that success and praised those who contributed. At a somewhat later stage, a major public event heralded the work of all involved.

—To promote public safety, empower the community. The goal of the Safety First effort is not community empowerment as such; it is public safety, with empowerment one of the means. Yet, until neighborhood residents have the sense that the public spaces around their homes belong to them, that they have reasonable control of those spaces, and that they are safe there, no overall reduction in the number of crimes will give residents a sense of safety. It must come from their own investment. In Lowell, the work with the Lower Highlands neighborhood emphasized the need to have residents realize and act on a sense of proprietary interest in the place where they live.

—Act first, and apply for grants later. Having the mindset that the first order of business is to obtain new grants can distract from the essential task of thinking through the issues and actually beginning productive work. While only additional resources can change some situations, we believe that convening the working group, choosing a goal, gathering and analyzing data, and undertaking tasks that might lead to the desired results are far more important than preparing grant applications. Waiting for grants to materialize often kills effective work because it subtly promotes the sense that without the grant, nothing is possible. In Lowell, this issue was addressed and resolved in the first meeting of the working group.

The Implementation of Safety First in Lowell

After substantial preliminary work, implementation of the initiative began in June 1996. The publisher of the *Lowell Sun*, Kendall Wallace, convened the inaugural meeting of the community safety working group. In attendance were the county district attorney, the Lowell chief of police, the county sheriff, a representative of the state department of youth services, the chief probation officer for the Lowell district court, the Lowell city manager, and the executive director of the Lowell Plan.[11] The discussion focused on the threat of crime to public safety and to the city's further economic development, on successful crime-control efforts to date, and on how much more could be done with greater cooperation. The meeting concluded with agreement among participants that their initial goal would be to reduce the incidence of serious assault in Lowell.

During the summer months, the police department and graduate students from Harvard University's Kennedy School of Government mapped the picture of assaults in Lowell: time and place, context, identity of the assailant, identity of the victim, and nature of their relationship. The analysis was presented at the group's October meeting.[12] In addition to the earlier attendees, the presiding justice of the Lowell district court and the headmaster of Lowell High School joined the group. The analysis led to a conversation about specific neighborhoods in Lowell and their quality of life and about local schools and students' experience within the schools. Members contributed additional information about assaults and other crimes, about recent efforts by their agencies to make the community safer, and about what more could be done through collaboration.

In December, the group looked more closely at the victims and assailants in the assaults—whether they were known to the criminal justice system at the time of the assault, what the disposition of the case was, and whether the assailants committed subsequent offenses—and the information was presented in a report.[13] At the conclusion of the session, the group turned its attention to specific strategies to coordinate resources and reduce serious assaults, which posed a significant crime problem in Lowell, by 30 percent. Although reducing serious assaults would be a major undertaking, it seemed feasible, and the Safety First group's initial efforts in that regard would allow it to build both the working relationships and the confidence it needed to pursue the broader, more ambitious goal of community revitalization.[14] The group decided to target three areas: juvenile assaults, domestic assaults, and neighborhood crime and disorder. In January 1997, the Safety First working group adopted agendas for initiatives targeting those three areas. Three task forces, with members drawn from local criminal justice agencies, city agencies, and the community, were established.

The Youth Violence Task Force

The behavior of youth was a top priority in Lowell not primarily because juveniles were responsible for a significant portion of the targeted crimes but because the negative behavior of some crime-prone youths dominated the very large city high school, causing parents of other children to protest or withdraw their children. In addition, there was agreement that crime-prone youths merited special attention because of the possibility that they would later engage in adult criminal behavior. If intervention was successful at this stage, it could spare the city and its residents future crime. Finally, one could detect in the working group's discussions the sense that Lowell was going to "hell in a handbasket" because of the number of juveniles who, in the minds of the adults, blatantly contravened social norms. The number actually was not disproportionate, and that sentiment seemed less prevalent among criminal justice professionals than those without direct everyday experience with youths.

The youth violence task force's strategy was driven by the police department and Kennedy School analysis of serious assaults involving youth in Lowell.[15] The analysis indicated that:

—In nondomestic violence incidents, approximately 25 percent of the victims and 20 percent of the offenders were under seventeen years of age. When youth under twenty-one were included, the figures rose to 41 percent of victims and 34 percent of offenders.

—In Lowell, schools were a hot spot; most serious assaults for those under seventeen occurred in or around schools between the hours of 2:00 p.m. and 3:00 p.m.

—Incident reports showed that after an assault, youth tended to be arrested less often than adults (53 percent versus 72 percent) and that most youth who were not arrested re-offended within a short period of time. In addition, when youths were arrested for serious assault and the court continued their case, there was a high likelihood that they would re-offend during the continuance. Finally, subsequent offenses were more likely to be violent than those of adults (43 percent versus 23 percent).

Those findings emphasized the importance of improving both the environment in and around schools and the criminal justice system's response to assaults by youth. The task force decided to focus on the core group of youth who were behind most serious assaults in Lowell—those who continually came to the attention of police and probation officers and who were readily identifiable by people familiar with the streets. Some of the youths had extensive criminal histories, but the most important reason for focusing on a particular youth was his or her ability to influence other youth to refrain from violence. Through record checking and long conversations about various individuals, the group arrived at a list that included twenty youths; by targeting them, the group hoped to have a "multiplier" effect on other youth in the community. The strategy was to prevent assaults by linking a rapid, well-coordinated criminal justice system response with support services, including employment and counseling—and advertising the strategy widely among youth. The last tactic was emphasized because an underlying premise of the initiative was that the criminal justice system and the community generally had not sent the message that violence would not be tolerated. Continuously reiterating that message is an important component of the Lowell effort.

The Lowell effort differed from Boston's Operation Ceasefire in its focus on individuals instead of gangs. Boston had the unhappy advantage of having multiple homicides to analyze. The analysis, combined with information and wisdom gathered from street-level workers, led to Boston's successful intervention. The data on aggravated assaults provided for Lowell's analysis were significantly more nebulous in terms of understanding the problems of Lowell youth and the problems generated by them, designing a response, and analyzing the results. It would have been worthwhile to attempt to learn more about the patterns of activities of young offenders and potential offenders; it might have generated a different response. The Boston team also had considerably more analytic capacity, developing and using its own analytic capacity as necessary rather than using that of partner agencies. While the Lowell effort did have the part-time assistance of two graduate students and their faculty supervisor in gathering and analyzing data, Lowell's capacity was considerably less than that of Boston.

The youth violence task force took a number of steps to coordinate its activities. Arrangements were made to ensure that criminal justice agencies shared information and worked closely to deliver rapid, targeted responses to violent offenses. Police computers were provided ready access to probation information. Probation officers were provided with reports describing police contacts with youth on probation. And police were frequently updated on the status of those youth at roll calls. Members of the task force also invited youth workers from local programs for at-risk youth, including the Streetworkers, YWCA, and Big Brother/Big Sister programs, to participate in order to ensure that youth who requested promised services would get them. In addition, those agencies served as effective conduits of the overall Safety First message.

Members of the task force then arranged individual meetings with each of the twenty most serious youth offenders/leaders. During those meetings, task force members presented a clear, forceful message: violence would not be tolerated. Youth workers met separately with the juveniles to offer them a variety of support services and access to educational and recreational programs. A few weeks later a carefully selected "second tier" of approximately thirty-five juveniles was brought together by school officials, probation officers, and youth workers and informed of the new enforcement effort and of the availability of services.

There was ongoing discussion in the task force of how to sanction negative behavior in untraditional ways. For example, one offender who might have been returned to jail for a probation violation was instead given a nightly 7:00 p.m. curfew and checked regularly to make sure that he complied with it. The idea behind the sanction was that a young macho juvenile was more likely to be bothered by a curfew that made him look like a little kid than by a sentence that sent him, predictably, to jail—just another small speed bump in his career. The attempt to sanction creatively encountered legal resistance to the practice of focusing on specific individuals; it also was hampered by an ongoing job action by probation officers that resulted in very few probation officers operating outside the confines of the court building.

The results, however, were worthwhile. High-school officials in Lowell reported a significant decrease in school-based violence, which traditionally marred the end of the school year as students attempted to settle scores before the summer break. Lowell also recorded a significant drop in serious assaults by and on youth (from 166 in the summer of 1996 to 118 in the summer of 1997, a reduction of 29 percent). And youth organizations reported an unusual increase in interest and participation in opportunities for employment and education. Just as important, the working group felt confident of its capacity to move forward on this and other problems.

As satisfying as those results were, the persistent nature of juvenile violence was evident when reports came in regarding a major, multiple gang melee planned for the evening of February 27, 1998. The task force mounted a quick, coordinated response: Probation officers met with each of their juvenile probationers and warned them not to be out beyond curfew. The department of youth services brought all of its juvenile parolees into its community center for an evening of pizza and movies. Police officers were strategically deployed and delivered a message of calm and caution. Street workers and youth service agencies scheduled additional events. And gang leaders were visited and reminded of the seriousness of the Safety First message. The weekend passed without incident. More important, the collaboration was successful and effective.

Equally important was experimenting with messages to potential offenders regarding violence. For example, in December 1997 the working group proposed reinforcing the message to the core group of youthful offenders that violence would not be tolerated. A proposal was made to publicly display posters that identified offenders and described the consequences of their actions. One member wisely observed that such posters might well enhance the status of the offenders on the street. The conversation then turned to how to send a message that diminished rather than raised the status of the offender because of his offense. Lowell is using the knowledge of front-line workers to develop more effective deterrent messages.

The task force continues to meet biweekly. It also has met for half-day brainstorming sessions, one of which was led by the local congressman. Forthcoming efforts dictate constant adjustment, particularly as the group "manages back" from events in which there was youth violence in order to learn how the violence might have been prevented. These events—a shooting, a homicide—have shaken the task force because each person knew the youths involved, but each time the primary question is how to learn from such tragedies to prevent others. The group continues to develop and deliver a range of both law enforcement and prevention strategies that share the goal of eradicating violence.

Perhaps most important, the practice of working together toward common goals and sharing information, resources, and responsibility is becoming institutionalized. As the sergeant who leads the task force says, it has changed the way that the police do business:

> Police work has always been about knowing what is going on in your sector and who is doing what, and this almost formalizes that. Police officers can look at who they want to stay in touch with and give them the option to get out of it. But if you're going to commit the crime anyway, I can work to bring everything I can down on you. I will also be able to solve the crime quickly because I now know who you hang around with, where you are going to be. It is also bringing in other agencies, and working with other agencies so that really everyone is paying attention not only to their needs but other needs in thinking about how to do the job right . . . . I look at that as the most beneficial thing from Safety First. Getting them to pay attention to certain things that we used to bitch about but not do anything about. Now, when we go to a meeting and raise the issue, it can change and get fixed. Everybody works together.

And, speculating about whether that might have been possible without Safety First, the sergeant continued,

> This would not have happened if we had just decided to do it on our own because all of us are too caught up in the things that are going on in our own space . . . . The importance of the Safety First working group is that everyone knows that there is a working group of supervisors watching. This makes them want to work to get things done. Otherwise they would say "I'm too busy doing my case load" or "I have too much going on and can't make that meeting" and then they wouldn't show up.
>
> The preventive piece is working. We're reaching the kids before they get into gangs and I've seen some kids want to get out of the gangs. We weren't seeing that before. Sometimes for kids already ganged up, we can give them an ultimatum and, at the same time, [say that] we are here for you.[16]

The Domestic Violence Task Force

The effort to combat domestic violence was driven by the fact that 52 percent of all aggravated assaults in Lowell were domestic in nature.[17] It is worth noting, moreover, that studies have shown that children exposed to domestic violence are more likely to become offenders as adults.[18] Since domestic violence is such a complex issue and has long resisted successful intervention, the task force developed a two-stage strategy. The tactics likely to be employed in both stages are quite similar, although the first stage is meant to provide an opportunity for the group to build its confidence and the working relationships it needs for more ambitious efforts. Both stages take note of the fact that a large group of domestic violence offenders are crossover offenders who commit numerous other offenses, which is important because domestic violence offenders can be targeted before they engage in non–domestic violence, and vice versa.

The first stage of the strategy focuses on the most serious domestic violence offenders in Lowell, and it follows the general outline of the youth violence task force's strategy—using multiple means of communicating to potential offenders the certainty of a rapid, targeted, well-coordinated law enforcement response to any offense. Careful coordination of efforts and joint "advertising" give the strategy credibility. While the strategies for communicating the message to domestic violence offenders and youths will be similar, the message is likely to travel through the groups differently.

The second part of the strategy begins with a detailed analysis of offenders and victims. The hope is to mine the data for a series of "levers" that can be used to develop a web of deterrents targeting potential offenders. As above, the goal is to build a proactive strategy, one that not only responds to incidents of domestic violence but also prevents them from occurring. This part of the overall strategy explicitly embraces the participation of city agencies and community groups as well as criminal justice agencies. It will benefit from an ambitious, complementary effort by the Lowell police to organize a comprehensive response to domestic violence.

Unlike the work of the youth violence task force, that of the domestic violence task force has been hampered by lack of agreement about the nature of the problem. Because the emphasis has been on protecting and supporting victims, strategies to deter domestic violence have not yet been adequately tested. Yet there is hope. Participants in the domestic violence task force report that the conversation is increasingly turning to the question of what works. Time will tell whether the Safety First approach will produce improved results.[19]

The Neighborhood Task Force

Reducing crime is necessary but insufficient to make a community feel safe. Efforts that help residents develop or maintain a sense of control of their own environment are important not only for their own sake, but because they help teach young people about acceptable behavior and the ramifications of behavior that violates social norms. A community that feels safe will take action to intervene when its norms are challenged and will do so in a way that conveys a message about what constitutes acceptable behavior. Criminal justice professionals are on the streets of the community an infinitely small amount of time compared with those who reside there. If potential criminals are to get the message regarding unacceptable behavior, residents must send it. For that reason, there is an essential interplay between the work of the youth violence task force and that of the group focusing on neighborhoods.

Despite significant recent decreases in crime in Lowell, many residents reported in police-sponsored quality-of-life surveys that they continued to feel vulnerable to crime. Police participating in neighborhood meetings reported hearing the same message. To address the persistent fear of crime, the working group chose, through its task force, to begin working with residents of the Lower Highlands, a diverse, transitional neighborhood in Lowell. The goal was to find out what types of crime and disorder troubled the community and to jointly develop strategies to address those problems. As noted, one important role of the neighborhood initiative was to provide a "testing ground" for mechanisms to meaningfully engage the community in Safety First.

At the first meeting, residents cited problems related to disorder and fear, including loitering youth, parking congestion, unsafe traffic, and graffiti. Residents also pointed out troublesome locations. A meeting was then held in which the police assigned to the neighborhood started thinking about the problem-solving strategies needed to address the problems that residents had identified. The neighborhood initiative of Safety First has met approximately twice monthly since August 1997. The group includes twelve ethnically diverse residents, the executive director of the Lowell Boys Club (which is located in the heart of the target neighborhood), several police officers, and other Lowell police department and Crime and Justice

Foundation staff. The group has routinely invited representatives from city agencies, local businesses, and the criminal justice system to provide input and assistance.

The group initially targeted three geographic areas because of the impact of conditions there on the daily lives of residents. The three areas—Cupples Square, Pailin Plaza and the intersection of Middlesex and Branch Streets, and the Clemente Park area—are heavily congested locations, all in the Lower Highlands section of the city. Residents in these areas expressed concern about the condition and number of parked cars, the number of traffic accidents, trash, graffiti, dumpsters, the poor condition of private property, and fear of gangs, youth, and crime.

Residents elected to work on Cupples Square first, where parking congestion prevented safe access to the area. Through the neighborhood intervention, police leafleted dozens of motor vehicles parked on the sidewalk with warning notices explaining the violation and the penalty. After three days of leafleting, only three cars were illegally parked, and each was ticketed. It was determined that the patrons of the post office located in the heart of the Cupples Square area were responsible for a significant amount of the congestion. A parking lot in close proximity was underused. Residents surveyed all the businesses in the area to ascertain where their employees and patrons park; changes made in response to the surveys, interviews, and discussions included having the post office add drop boxes in its rear parking lot, posting signs in the square indicating the location of free parking in the underused lot, and increasing the hourly rate of parking meters. Work on this project continues as residents assess the long-term effectiveness of the interventions and the level of satisfaction among residents.

Pailin Plaza, an indoor mall with several dozen, primarily Southeast Asian businesses, represents a myriad of concerns. An absentee landlord who employs an off-site property manager owns the plaza. The parking area is constantly full and overflowing while a lot behind the building is underused. The plaza is bordered on one side by an abandoned home that was the scene of an arson that resulted in the death of two children in June 1994; the other side is bordered by a multipurpose Asian market.

Participating residents invited the property manager to meetings to seek input and assistance; as a result, the property owner has installed new lighting, made improvements to the rear lot to encourage store owners and employees to park there, and ordered new doors and fencing to further improve the look and feel of the area. Code and building inspectors have attended the meetings to answer questions about the condition of the dumpsters, the residential property behind the plaza, and the burned abandoned building. Interventions by the code department have increased the regularity with which the market has the dumpster emptied and enforcement of the city's ordinances regarding graffiti and disposal of unregistered vehicles. In addition, residents have identified a vacant lot nearby that would be ideal for off-street parking and are working to ascertain ownership of the property and its intended future use.

The manner in which city departments conduct business has begun to change as a result of the direct contact with neighborhood residents in collaboration with the police. Many of the tasks related to the Pailin Plaza area are ongoing and incomplete; they are the subjects of future planned meetings.

The third area identified as a priority by the Safety First neighborhood task force was the Clemente Park area. This was the most ambitious of the three projects. Clemente Park had an undersized softball field, basketball courts, and a tot play yard. Neighbors included some light industry, the Boys Club, a culturally mixed low-to-mid-income residential area, and the Lowell police department Highlands precinct. In years past, the park was a hangout for active gang members, the scene of drive-by shootings, and a gathering spot for large numbers of Asian residents. It was targeted by Safety First because of more recent gambling and associated activities there that had created reluctance to use the park among residents of the neighborhood. Statistics show that a city free-lunch program offered at the park served 100 fewer meals in the summer of 1997 than in the summer of 1996.

Without input from residents or the police, the city parks department had removed debris and renovated makeshift lawn bowling courts that until then had been covered with tarps. Some speculate that thousands of dollars were bet on the games daily. The look and use of the area created a climate of fear among residents and businesses in the area, and many parents and children were so concerned for their safety that they did not walk to the nearby Boys Club. The problem was not only gambling, but also the problems associated with gambling, namely gang activity, drugs, and weapons.

The Safety First neighborhood initiative set preliminary goals to address the problems, including elimination of the gambling, community participation in planning future uses and changes at the park, and the creation of a safe, appropriate, and friendly place for city residents to enjoy. Letters of support for the goals came from citizen groups, the Safety First juvenile group, and parents of boys who attended the Boys Club. The group invited the commissioner of parks and recreation to its meeting in December 1997, and the somewhat surprised commissioner acceded to the views of the community and agreed to remove the renovated bowling courts. He also apparently learned not to act without consulting the local community. The broader lesson for Lowell officials is that they must reach out to the community and learn to think the way the community does about the issues that affect it. In Lowell, that meant that city inspectors joined residents and police officers in the Lower Highlands neighborhood to address problems identified by residents.

The police community liaison stated that in the first neighborhood meeting, a man said to her, with obvious skepticism, "Well, tell me girl, how you are going to change city hall?" That man has now become the biggest supporter of the process. According to the person who works most directly with the neighborhood effort, "People who on day one had a disbelief that they could impact the system a year later were enthralled, besides themselves about how they got people's attention . . . . At the last meeting they talked . . . [about the fact] that they felt that more than ever before, they were being listened to."[20]

The members of this group realized that they could affect their environment. The practical effects of that, one hopes, is that residents will become less passive when faced with situations that trouble them. Loitering youths are an example. Instead of avoiding contact, residents, together, should approach the youths to find out whether there is real cause for alarm or whether the loitering is in fact harmless. In the former case, the police are called, but residents also have a responsibility for ensuring safety in the community, even if they just watch from their windows to keep an eye on the street.

Outcomes

Safety First aimed to make Lowell safer, to reduce crime (specifically, serious assaults), to institutionalize an improved criminal justice approach to problems, and to help to revitalize the city. Lowell has continued its progress toward becoming the safest city of its size in the United States.[21] The 1997 UCR data indicate that Lowell was ranked in the top quarter (fifteenth place) of comparable United States cities. In 1993, it was in the bottom third, in forty-eighth place. Assaults listed as Part 1 crimes in the *Uniform Crime Reports* declined from 1,048 in 1997 to 916 in 1998.[22] We

have no data that attribute the results to Safety First but are currently working to measure the impact of the specific efforts aimed at changing the
negative behavior of young men. We are searching for surrogate measures
that will give us a handle on their behavior.[23] The question of causation is
made more challenging because other positive programs, such as the district
attorney's community-based justice initiative[24] and community policing and
internal police management processes,[25] have been at work in Lowell.

Ed Davis, the superintendent of police, believes that Safety First has
played a major role in changing the way that the Lowell criminal justice
response goes about its business.

> The [working] group has made the system a system. I cannot talk
> enough about how important that is to criminal justice, to our city,
> and for that ultimate feeling of safety. Because everyone is at the table,
> they look at the data, they make decisions based on the data, and also
> based on goals that have been set at the table . . . everybody is pulling
> in the same direction and . . . they feel empowered because of that.
> They feel that for the first time, this big monolith of a criminal justice
> system has a handle on it and that you can really do something.
>
> I was just interviewed by a reporter and he said to me, "Tell me
> what you are doing about this shooting." Almost everything I said to
> him came out of Safety First, because they don't want to hear that we
> responded to the scene and arrested the bad guy, they want to hear
> what we've done proactively to prevent this stuff from occurring.
> That conversation with the reporter made me think about my time
> on the governor's transition team for family and health issues. I did
> not realize what value I could add there until we started talking about
> the problems that DYS and DSS and other provider groups are deal-
> ing with. What we're doing in Safety First can be replicated in other
> areas. Most everything that I said had something to do with my expe-
> rience in either providing geographically focused services or in
> pulling together different people from different areas and overcoming
> the hurdles—hurdles like politics, like confidentiality that relates to
> the use of data in making decisions. It is a major win, and I know this
> sounds trite, to get outside the box, get outside your own agency,
> and think about what other people can bring to the table.[26]

Institutionalization of an improved way of doing business, the core goal
of Safety First, has been partially achieved; time will tell whether the gains
will be maintained.

Lessons Learned

In response to the demand for increased performance, managers of public institutions have begun to look to outcome measures as a way of focusing their agencies' efforts. It is useful to learn more about the ways in which outcome measures are identified and formulated and the ways in which outcomes drive the design of partnerships, the activities of partners, and the resources they bring to the partnership. The Safety First teams found that by constantly referring back to their goals—What are we trying to do? What do we care about?—the business of the day was centered, the working coalitions reestablished, and creativity regenerated regarding how goals might be met. At times the outcomes were traditional, for instance, to reduce assaults by 30 percent. At others, they were innovative: Let's measure and increase the number of lunches served to kids who ordinarily are afraid to go to this park in the summer. Regardless, focusing on the desired outcome enhanced the work.

The focus on and sense of accountability for results generated the concept of "managing back" from events. The juvenile task force in particular constantly worked to learn from unfortunate incidents that, once having taken place (for example, a shooting by a youth on Lane Street), provided a learning opportunity for the pertinent task force. "How could we have known about this? How could we have prevented this? Who should we have been talking/listening to? What should we have been doing? What will we do now to ensure that this does not happen again?" In contrast, the domestic violence task force has not been as productive as hoped because members have not yet been able to come to a sufficiently specific agreement about what they are trying to do. The process of regularly attending to the business of accomplishing what has been agreed upon, often termed managing by objective, was most evident in the New York City police department's Comstat process, and it was an essential part of Safety First.

Second, a working group composed of those necessary to make operational progress on an issue is a sine qua non. While it is possible for individuals and individual agencies to make marked contributions to enhancing public safety, Safety First confirmed our belief that only a working group can muster the necessary cross-cutting capacity and resources to successfully address issues like the negative behavior of young men. The working group process fueled the work of the task forces. As the chairperson of one task force said, "DYS for a while was not showing up . . . the actual case worker was not there on a regular basis. Then all of a sudden, there they were at every meeting . . . . Because of Bob Gittens (the DYS commissioner). Because they know that Bob Gittens is involved in the working group, they changed their feeling of how important this is."[27]

It is important to note the difference between the work of this group and the work of those who aim to make residents feel safe. The former group must think in terms of the transparency of its operations and its legitimacy in the eyes of citizens, and it must regularly take steps to reinforce its legitimacy. However, that does not mean that it must include citizens as members of the working group. On the other hand, no progress will be made toward establishing a sense of neighborhood safety—a different objective—unless it is the work of residents themselves. Residents must develop the sense that they are in charge of their neighborhood. Both the work and the membership of the working groups are different.

Third, the concept of the powerful neutral convener to chair the working group—someone whose professional status and personal reputation would make it difficult for local leadership to casually ignore his or her call—has been tested and proven effective. If one is going to reorganize the efforts of a wide range of criminal justice agencies to focus on outcomes, then it is necessary to secure cooperation across different jurisdictions and levels of government.[28] Formal political authority is not enough to manage such an effort. Mayors, for example, often cannot secure the cooperation of state agencies such as courts and probation and corrections departments, and state-level authorities often run into insurmountable obstacles in securing the cooperation of city agencies. The fact that the convener has only informal authority means that this person must be respected and must not have an obvious political or personal agenda. To some degree, his or her power is based on a sort of moral authority.

There is little doubt that the working group process would have drifted into ineffectiveness had Wallace, publisher and editor of the *Lowell Sun*, not been the person convening and chairing the meetings. As the local daily newspaper for Lowell and surrounding communities, the *Sun* is a powerful force in shaping public opinion and spurring economic development. Kendall had the stature to command the attendance and attention of key players, and the fact that the paper had no formal role in government improved the likelihood that participants saw it as having the broad interests of the community in mind.

Nonetheless, the concept might not have worked had the chief of police not been a particularly effective champion of change and of goal-oriented management. We found that the neutral convener needs reassurance from someone with professional (and perhaps personal) credibility to attest that the process of convening, choosing goals, and managing to achieve them is reasonable and worth doing. When the convener is not knowledgeable about the traditional workings of the criminal justice response, there also must be regular interaction between the architects of the process and the convener. The architects must act as if they are staffing the convener. In retrospect, we did not keep the neutral convener sufficiently informed about the process as it unfolded and occasionally had to use other people—usually the chief—to get results. We should have paid more attention to keeping the neutral convener informed and involved. On the other hand, one must assume that the neutral convener has a very full plate; it may be that we got as much of his time as was available. At least once, the congressman played the role of neutral convener. The lesson is that there is no formula for determining the working relationship of the convener, the person to whom he or she looks for assurance, and the architects of the process; it depends instead on the interaction of a set of relationships that require regular attention to remain productive.

Fourth, the role of the outsider, in this case the Crime and Justice Foundation, is in general to act as a catalyst. The outside organization knows that its own efforts are meaningless unless they inspire local officials and residents to bring new energy to the task of achieving agreed-upon goals. While the foundation sought out the Lowell opportunity, it cannot be overemphasized that if the city of Lowell had not been in a certain state of tension and readiness to do better, the foundation would have been whistling in the dark. But given the necessary receptiveness,[29] an outsider can offer a good deal: the ability to help local players realize that change is possible, to see their situation in terms that are meaningful to them but different from the way they saw it before, and to bring to the table a mosaic of independent parties to foster a conversation among them that leads them to act in concert to accomplish something that they value.

What would we do differently? Three things: first, provide more assistance to the chairs of each task force; second, provide analytic staff to the three task forces; and, third, staff the neutral convener more aggressively. Providing more assistance to each chair would have helped them move the issues more forcefully and find the balance between the analysis of information and the input of the practitioners needed to develop the momentum to overcome more of the institutional barriers. Working closely with each task force, analytic staff might have been able to undertake an ongoing parsing of the problem that, combined with the knowledge of the members, might have been more productive. And, if we had aggressively staffed the convener, he would have been in a stronger position to manage and push for the progress of the working group.

Nevertheless, we believe that real institutional change has begun in Lowell. While it could be reversed, it has an excellent chance to continue, to grow, and to reach a tipping point that will prevent those institutions from going back to business as usual.

Notes

1. See, for example, Fox Butterfield, "In Boston, Nothing Is Something: No Youths Slain by Guns in 16 Months; New Tactics Get Credit," *New York Times*, November 21, 1996; Fox Butterfield, "Homicides Plunge 11 Percent in U.S., FBI Report Says," *New York Times*, June 2, 1997.

2. For fuller descriptions, please see Kennedy School of Government case studies: "Community Development and Community Policing in Seattle's Chinatown," draft; "Policing St. Petersburg's Palmetto Park and Round Lake Neighborhoods," no. 1424.0; "The Las Vegas Metropolitan Police Department and the One Neighborhood for Everyone Collaborative," draft; "Norfolk's Police Assisted Community Enforcement (PACE): The Bay View and East Norfolk Neighborhoods," draft; "The Chicago Alternative Policing Strategy (CAPS): Activism and Apathy in Englewood," no. 1423.0 (Kennedy School of Government, Harvard University).

3. For an explanation of deterrence, or "pulling levers," see David M. Kennedy, "Pulling Levers: Chronic Offenders, High-Crime Settings, and a Theory of Prevention," *Valparaiso University Law Review*, vol. 31, no. 2 (Spring 1997), pp. 468–80.

4. A Milwaukee police lieutenant, when questioned by the author about how he knew that police work in a particular community was effective, replied, "Because more of the tenants are renewing their leases." See also Clyde Haberman, "A Security Shadowed by Caution," *New York Times*, December 29, 1998, p. B1.

5. Community policing is characterized by a focus on minor as well as major offenses in order to reduce crime and fear and to improve quality of life; by a problem-solving orientation; and by working partnerships with the community.

6. For example, in reference to community partnerships, one author writing in an important recent review of experience with community policing concluded that "successes in this regard are modest and that community policing initiatives have so far failed to tap the great wellspring of 'community' believed to lie waiting for the proper catalyst . . . community policing by and large remains a unilateral action on the part of the police." From Michael Brueger, "The Limits of Community," in Dennis P. Rosenbaum, ed., *The Challenge of Community Policing* (Thousand Oaks, Calif.: Sage, 1994), pp. 270–73.

7. Now named Community Resources for Justice, after merging with Mass Half Way House.

8. The foundation successfully demonstrated the usefulness of day reporting as a sentencing and postincarceration release option beginning in 1983.

9. An underlying assumption of this work is that practitioners are, overwhelmingly, competent. However, they often are caught up in institutions and systems that narrow the range of what is possible, that require them to do business as usual and reward them for it.

But, when given the opportunity to put their practical knowledge to work in addressing and solving a problem for which they have been given responsibility, they are remarkably creative and energetic. Lowell confirmed these beliefs.

10. Part I crimes totaled 9,981 in 1993; 8,654 in 1994; 8,659 in 1995; 5,166 in 1996; and 4,525 in 1997. Reductions continued until 2000: 4,055 in 1998; 3,399 in 1999; 3,999 in 2000; and 4,507 in 2001.

11. The Lowell Plan is a privately funded organization whose objective is to promote the economic development of Lowell.

12. "Identifying Opportunities for Reducing Aggravated Assaults in Lowell: An Analysis of Aggravated Assault Incidents, March–July 1996."

13 "Identifying Opportunities for Reducing Assaults in Lowell: A Preliminary Analysis of Criminal Histories." This was part of a Kennedy School of Government policy analysis exercise by Amy Solomon and Gillian Thomson, "Serious Assaults in Lowell: Opportunities for a Collaborative Crime Control Effort," January 22, 1997 (on file with author).

14. The number of assaults on youths in the summer of 1997 dropped 29 percent compared to the number during the previous summer.

15. Solomon and Thomson, "Serious Assaults in Lowell."

16. Sergeant Mark Buckley, Lowell police department, personal interview, December 29, 1998.

17. Solomon and Thomson, "Serious Assaults in Lowell," p. 9.

18. See Gary S. Katzmann, chapter 1 in this volume.

19. Community Resources for Justice (the former Crime and Justice Foundation) took the Safety First principles to Brockton and Lynn, Massachusetts. The Brockton work included, with much more success than Lowell, efforts to intervene in domestic violence.

20. Christine Cole, Lowell police department community liaison, personal interview, January 11, 1999.

21. Eli Lehrer, "Lowell on the Rise as Crime Falls," *Boston Herald,* July 2, 2000, p. 25.

22. Assaults continued to decline in Lowell until 2001: 753 in 1999; 555 in 2000; and 682 in 2001.

23. An example of a surrogate measure is the quote in note 5 from the police lieutenant who observed that more tenants were renewing their leases in a particular neighborhood.

24. See Catherine Coles and George Kelling, chapter 2 in this volume.

25. Edward F. Davis III, "Turning a Dangerous City into a Safe One," Heritage Foundation Lecture, Washington, August 8, 2000.

26. Superintendent Edward F. Davis, Lowell police department, personal interview, January 6, 1999.

27. Sergeant Mark Buckley, personal interview, December 29, 1998.

28. This would apply to noncriminal justice agencies as well and to any partnership that reaches across jurisdictions and disciplines.

29. While much more can be written about "ripeness," it certainly consists of competent practitioners who already have the sense that they can and would like to be more effective, who are ready to rethink their operations and who are authorized by their superiors to do so, and who will use that opportunity creatively. It is the first characteristic—that current operations are unsatisfactory—that produces the necessary tension.

10

AMALIA V. BETANZOS

Youth Violence, Schools, and Management: A Personal Reflection across the Sectors

NEARLY FORTY YEARS SPENT addressing the challenges of youth and education perhaps permits one to reflect on the lessons of those experiences. From a career that has involved the nonprofit, government, and private sectors, I know that while there are no magic panaceas to the problems of youth violence, an understanding of the diversity of environments in which solutions are attempted is essential if we are to improve the lives of the young.

Beginnings

When I first started working with issues of youth and poverty in 1965, I was very much involved in the Puerto Rican Community Development Project, a nonprofit organization, where I was chief executive officer and administrator. One of our goals was to organize the Puerto Rican community so that it would be more effective in dealing with the challenges it confronted. Youth and their problems, particularly those relating to gang involvement, were a large concern. What we tried to do was to get community organizations to involve youth in more productive endeavors and to promote conflict mediation and the like in order to reduce violence.

I next worked as vice president for membership of the United Parents' Association (UPA), a federation of parents' associations throughout New

York City that sought to promote public education through a range of legislative and programmatic initiatives. We tried, for example, to encourage greater school involvement in students' lives and to generate after-school programs—educational or recreational—in order to get kids off the street. Again, providing an alternative to mischief was an important component.

Subsequently I went to city hall, working successively as an assistant to the mayor, as commissioner of youth services, and as commissioner of the housing authority. In the youth services agency, the issue of youth gangs was paramount. We had a division of gang outreach workers, young men who were assigned to work with various gangs to try to turn their violent behavior into nonviolent, productive activity. These young men, who were quite brave, often found themselves in the position of mediating between the gangs and the police. Theirs was a very dangerous job, and a number of them got seriously hurt. The gang workers were community workers, twenty-five to thirty years old, who knew their communities well. Some of them had been gang members in their early youth. Some of them had a real desire to do social work; some even eventually became policemen and youth officers in the police department. They wanted to better the community.

We felt very strongly that many kids were gang members because the gangs served as a substitute family.[1] The kids who had come up from Puerto Rico and the South were beset by real feelings of loneliness within a large community, and the youth gangs provided a family structure for them. We tried to provide alternative structures. The youth services agency set up city-financed youth centers in various communities that would stay open until ten o'clock at night or midnight so that the kids would have a safe, legal place to spend their time, whether doing homework or watching television. The youth centers were a good alternative to gangs in providing some emotional support to kids in an environment where their families, which very often were disjointed or dysfunctional, might fail to do so. In my subsequent work as commissioner of the housing authority, we also promoted the development of youth centers.

The Wildcat Services Corporation

Following my work at city hall, I came to the Wildcat Services Corporation, where I have been president and chief executive officer for twenty-three years. The Wildcat Services Corporation is a nonprofit organization started in 1972 by a group of businessmen who wanted to offer ex-offenders and ex-addicts an opportunity to work in their companies. However, the business community found that this population was failing, not because of lack of work skills—most companies will train workers to do the job they want done—but because of lack of good work habits. Wildcat was started primarily to address that problem.

Wildcat provided an opportunity for supported work, through which participants developed work skills and good work habits while receiving subsidized pay; I believe we were the first supported work program in the nation. Wildcat would contract with the city and some corporations to provide labor, in return for which Wildcat would be paid on an hourly basis. Employees would learn to come to work every day on time, learn that there were monetary rewards for excellence in work, and learn how to deal with supervision. While our source of funding and our client population have changed over the years, our mission—which has been to take people who are among the structurally unemployed and turn them into wage earners and taxpayers—has remained constant. Wildcat was formed on the premise that we would be prospecting for human potential on unlikely ground, and we are still doing that. Today, Wildcat runs the largest supported work program in the country, with another 3,000 participants enrolled in our various training programs throughout the year. Program participants include welfare recipients, former substance abusers, ex-offenders, prisoners in work-release programs, crime victims, juvenile dropouts and delinquents, noncustodial parents who are delinquent in child support payments, and Hispanics with limited English proficiency.

It is my responsibility to run the organization—that is, to raise money, make sure that we get contracts with city and other agencies, and promote legislation that favors the work that we do. I am required to run a tight ship, making sure that we do not overspend our budget; we even achieve a surplus when possible. Although we are nonprofit, because we were started by businessmen we are expected to watch the bottom line, not only in fiscal but also in programmatic terms. In short, we are a social service agency, but we are run like a business. That is one of the strengths of Wildcat.

When I came to Wildcat, only 20 percent of our income was derived from fees for services performed by program participants; now, appropriately, that figure has risen to 55 percent. We like to say that, with the exception of the licensed trades, our people do everything from maintenance to microfilming. The clerical division is our largest, with increasing emphasis on computer training. Not only do our people learn how to work, they also learn job skills.

Wildcat's partnership with the private sector is an ongoing one, reinforced by open channels of communication, that seeks to respond to our mutual needs. For example, in July 1995, Wildcat and Salomon Smith Barney established the Private Industry Partnership (PIP), an innovative employment program that offers career opportunities to single mothers receiving welfare. Wildcat trains entry-level clerical workers according to Salomon Smith Barney's specifications, thereby providing industry- and job-specific training. (Other PIP partners include Chase Manhattan Bank, McCann-Ericson, and Morgan Stanley Dean Witter, with future partnerships planned for other Travelers Group subsidiaries.) Moreover, as a member of the board of directors of the Private Industry Council of New York City, Inc. (which is composed of representatives from industry, the public sector, and education, labor, and community-based organizations), we are always striving to nurture effective partnerships with the business community.

In addition to fees for services, Wildcat receives some foundation grants for innovative programs. City and state contracts also are sources of income. For example, we have contracts with the city's human resources administration and probation departments and with the state's social service agencies and departments of corrections and parole. We also receive money from the U.S. Department of Labor and welfare-to-work funds. Often we respond to RFPs (requests for proposals) with innovative ways of approaching a problem.

While Wildcat's mission has been constant, over the years the populations we have trained have varied. We began with ex-offenders and ex-addicts and then expanded to include welfare recipients; today, more than half of our participants are welfare recipients. For a time, when Haitians were coming to the United States in large numbers, we conducted a refugee program for both Haitians and Cubans from the Mariel boat lift. When we found that Haitian organizations were competing for the same grants that we were getting to serve them, we decided not to bid on those contracts any longer. In short, we got out of the refugee business and began to focus increasingly on our youth programs. For example, we developed a program for violent juvenile offenders who had dropped out of school to try to help them get their GEDs as well as jobs. Because we had experience doing programs for out-of-school youth, when the board of education called on us to develop a new concept school for kids with violent backgrounds, we were ready. That school, the Wildcat Academy, is one of the great successes of the Wildcat Services Corporation.

The Wildcat Academy

From 1987 to 1990, I was a member of the New York City board of education. Largely because of my experiences as a vice president of the United Parents' Association, it was enlightening to sit on the other side of the table and see the frustrations of being a member of the board of education.

One issue that concerned me tremendously was the problem of what to do with students who misbehave in school, including engaging in such serious behavior as hurting another student or hitting a teacher. All too often the penalty was suspension, which I thought to be an absolutely ridiculous "solution." Here you have a troubled youngster who probably does not find school too agreeable, and how do you punish him? You tell him "You can't come to school." I would complain bitterly when members of the board were asked to approve such suspensions or penalties.

About the time that I was leaving the board of education, I was approached by Joseph Fernandez, then the chancellor of schools, who knew of my concerns about counterproductive suspension policies. He had had a meeting with the principals of the twelve city high schools with the worst student violence problems, and he called to ask whether I would be interested in starting a school for the kind of kids involved. And I said, "Sure, I'd love to do that." He continued, "I know you've had experience dealing with tough kids and have done well in out-of-school programs, but these kids are still in school. And I know how you felt about suspension here, so come up with a plan."

So it was that over two weeks, the head of our youth program at the Wildcat Services Corporation, the very able Ronald Tabano—who had been an assistant principal at a Catholic high school before he came to Wildcat—worked with me to develop a plan. The Manhattan Institute, a New York–based think tank that has given serious thought to educational innovation, reviewed the plan, which resulted in the establishment of the Wildcat Academy, an alternative high school for at-risk teens sponsored by the Wildcat Services Corporation and the New York City public school system. Tabano is now in charge of the academy.

The Wildcat Academy opened its doors in the fall of 1992, housed on one floor of a converted warehouse in Manhattan; it remained there until 1999, when it moved to a new facility in Battery Place. Created for students identified by the board of education as being at risk of failure because of behavioral problems, criminal activity, poor attendance, or poor academic achievement, the academy is the educator of "last resort." All of the doors are locked during classes, all of the staircases are alarmed, and students are not permitted to leave the building for lunch. Students come from the toughest backgrounds: one-third are on probation or parole, often for serious, violent offenses; one-third of the young women have children; most are from single-parent families; the majority have a history of welfare dependence; and 15 percent are living in group homes or foster care. As an alternative school funded first by the city board of education and since September 1999 as a charter school subject to state regulation, the academy gets students who have been suspended from other schools for carrying guns and knives, who are otherwise "in trouble with the law," or who attended classes so seldom that they were "in-school truants." Our students are generally sent to us by guidance counselors from the regular high schools. The academy operates under a five-year contract with the state board of regents and receives a budget based on an annual allocation of $6,400 per student. We supplement that budget with grants from private foundations, such as the Robin Hood Foundation.

The original plan had several key elements, discussed below, which remain pillars of the academy today: small class size; a staff prepared to meet the challenges of the student body; a "conspiracy of adults"; a longer school day; discipline; work opportunities for students; and organizational autonomy.[2]

—*Small class size and staffing requirements.* We have a current enrollment of 160 students. The school is deliberately kept small because our students require personal attention and an environment in which they cannot become anonymous. We have a staff of eighteen: seven full-time and three part-time teachers, three case managers, one attendance monitor, one work-site monitor, one peer mentor, one maintenance man, and a headmaster. The teachers are chosen by Wildcat; while they must have the same qualifications as other New York City school teachers, they also must satisfy us that they really want to teach—and that they believe that our students can learn. We have maintained a ratio of about twenty students per teacher because we want to promote opportunities for intensive one-on-one learning.

We have been able to recruit truly dedicated teachers. For example, we found an art teacher who thought that it would be the best thing in her life to be able to teach a Wildcat student. She is a talented person who not only can teach art, but also is licensed to teach Spanish, English, and anthropology. She determined that many of our youngsters are dyslexic, and she knew that many great artists also were dyslexic. After she inspired one of our dyslexic youngsters to develop his artistic gifts, he won the *National Scholastic Magazine* prize for oil painting and his painting was hung in the Corcoran Gallery in Washington, D.C.

We have case managers on our staff because we insist on a very strict attendance policy. If a youngster is absent one day, a case manager will call the home or group home; if a student is absent three days, the case manager will make a home or facility visit. We make it clear to students that attendance is very important, that they cannot learn unless they attend. Case managers also accompany students to court when they have cases pending or are under court supervision, and they advocate on behalf of students as appropriate. Case managers try to teach students how to dress for court and can buy them appropriate clothing—a white shirt, or shoes instead of sneakers—out of Wildcat funds. Sometimes, if the court matter is particularly serious, the case manager can arrange for legal assistance from one of the lawyers on the Wildcat board. We also have a case manager who is a college guidance specialist and can help match students to the right college. We rent a van four or five times a year to tour schools outside of New York City because we want our students to expand their horizons.

—*Conspiracy of adults.* Related to the emphasis on small class size and the recruitment of a staff committed to the school's mission is the phenomenon of what has been called "a conspiracy of adults." Our staff envelop the students with a dedication and concern that reduces the possibility that they will fail or misbehave. One nice aspect of having a school of only 160 youngsters is that all the students recognize that they are known. We have asked kids why they like the school; a common answer is, "Well, everybody knows my name." I think that in addition, although they may not say it, students believe that they have a special friend, all the way from the maintenance man to the principal—that somebody in the school really cares. That genuine concern is tremendously important for youngsters who sometimes have never had anybody who overtly cared for them.

I think one of the happiest days of my life occurred in the second year of school. A new student was pushing the person in front of him in the lunch line. The president of our student organization, an imposing fellow, came up to the new student and said, "We don't do that kind of thing at Wildcat. That's not the Wildcat way. If you have a problem, go see a counselor." In short, the students themselves have developed a culture that is very protective of the school, and they want to make sure that nothing happens that would interfere with their ability to attend.

—Longer school day. We also require a longer day for our students, running from 9:00 a.m. to 5:00 p.m., because we know that many students wasted or misspent their time when they were in regular public schools and that they need to make up for it. The longer day allows us to provide students with an enriched curriculum that includes subjects such as art, music, and drama, as well as computer-assisted learning.

—Work opportunities. We also wanted to give our students an opportunity to work. The Wildcat Services Corporation has always believed that work was tremendously important; it also is important for school kids. If a student is with us for at least a month and demonstrates true effort—academic ability is not as important as effort—then the student is given an opportunity to work. Our internship program allows students to attend school one week and to work the next, at work sites selected by Wildcat. We pay the salaries so that we can take a youngster out of a site if we do not like what he is learning and transfer him to another. The work schedule is one week on, one week off, as it is in the regular school co-op programs, but there is a difference. Wildcat students are required to do twelve hours of homework the week that they are working; if they do not turn in their homework on the Monday after the week that they worked, they are not permitted to return to work during the next cycle. They must bring their academic work up to date before they can return to their job.

The work sites that we have found for our students—ranging from the medical examiner's office to the Brooklyn Aquarium, stock brokerages, and law firms—have broadened their horizons. And the success stories have been great. One young lady so impressed a stockbroker during her internship that the stockbroker gave her a four-year scholarship to Marymount College. Another student worked first as a bursar messenger for a law firm, then became a paralegal, and now is starting law school at night. Quite apart from broadening their horizons, the work assignments have taught students the importance of discipline, the connection between effort and reward, and the value of education.

—Discipline. Self-discipline and self-respect are important elements of the culture we seek to develop at the Wildcat Academy. Our small size and conspiracy of adults have enabled us to make clear to our students that they are expected to maintain the highest standards of comportment and that any misconduct, ranging from verbal disrespect to bullying or violent behavior, will not be tolerated and will bring swift sanction. On Wednesdays, all students are required to wear their Wildcat Academy blazers;

indeed, whenever they go out, whether to a museum or a basketball game, they are required to wear the blazers—which they wear with pride.

We also have sought to teach our students through example that society rests on a social contract. We care deeply about our students, and we will make every effort to help them, but they must justify our trust and respect. Early on, the school's metal detectors revealed that students were attempting to bring knives into the building. I addressed the students in assembly, telling them that I would make a deal with them: "If you can get a letter from your mother saying that it's ok for you to carry a knife," I said, "I'll take the letter to the First Precinct, which is only a block away, and show it to the police so that they'll know that you're carrying a knife because your mother says it's ok." Not surprisingly, we did not receive a single letter—nor did we detect a single knife. I am pleased that we have not experienced any fighting or violence in the Wildcat Academy. We respect our students, and we expect respect from them.

—*Autonomy.* Because we are able to operate with relative autonomy from the school system, we can hire staff who are committed to our mission and apply for foundation grants to foster innovation in the classroom. The grants allow us to provide students with "extras" that other schools do not provide. For example, we give students special SAT preparation classes. We take them to visit colleges. We buy them class rings when they are graduating, and we give them a magnificent graduation at Manhattan Community College.

Results

What have been the results of the Wildcat Academy?[3] They can be seen in the wonderful student art work on the school walls. They can be found in the writing done by our students, on which we place great emphasis. The students write short stories and poetry, and they are required to produce both junior and senior papers—regular academic papers with footnotes. Their topics are fascinating: "Why Hispanics Choose Alternative Medicines"; "The History of Army Officers from the African American Community"; "What Do Hispanic Politicians Feel About Certain Issues?" Our students choose meaty subjects and then do a good job of researching them using the Internet or the library.

Quite apart from such measures, statistics confirm the Wildcat Academy's success. For example, of the 151 students attending Wildcat during the 1999 school year, 93 percent were graduating or continuing their education; of the 2001 Wildcat graduates, almost 80 percent enrolled in college, 9 percent entered the military, and 11 percent took a full-time job.[4] Our students have gone on to such schools as Georgia Tech, Morgan State, Howard, and Syracuse.

Perhaps the most graphic proof of our success is the fact that although many of our students came to us with behavior problems or a history of criminal activity, the academy has never experienced a riot or even a fight. Moreover, the Wildcat model has served as the blueprint for two other schools in the Bronx—the Second Opportunity School and Wildcat Academy III—operating under our direction.[5] We might also note that three schools in Chile—including El Colegio La Puerta, a school for at-risk and disruptive teenagers—as well as a school for teenage pregnant women were based on Wildcat and created in consultation with us.[6]

The Mayor's Commission on School Safety

During many years of working with the public school system, I had become distressed by the rising violence and lack of security in our schools. Some parents were literally afraid to send their children to school because of the physical harm that could befall them there. One particularly compelling comment came from the mother of a Wildcat Academy student who told me that for the first time in her child's life, he was not afraid to go to school. The notion that one had to attend an alternative school for youngsters with a history of violence in order to feel safe only reinforced my sense that some of the "regular" schools were in poor shape. In the same way that the school system's policy on suspension of students seemed to me ineffectual and counterproductive, school safety seemed to be poorly and irrationally managed. For example, it seemed to me that school security varied very much from school to school and by individual principal. A youngster who brought a knife to one school would be arrested; a youngster who brought a knife to another school would get the weapon back at the end of the school day; in still another school, the knife could be confiscated. Some security guards were much too friendly with the students; others were martinets. There was no real feeling of overall control. I wanted to see some sort of standardization regarding the security function, and I was pleased to examine the issue as a member of the mayor's commission on school safety.

The commission was appointed to investigate and report on the level of crime and misconduct in city public schools and on the ability of the board of education's division of school safety to ensure the safety of the city's school children. The commission found that that there was no accurate, reliable, and consistent system of gathering data on the level of crime and misconduct in the public schools; that school principals consistently under-reported crime and misconduct in school; that there was no rational system in place for allocating safety resources; that the role of school safety officers was not clearly defined; and that school safety officers were inadequately recruited, screened, and trained.[7] The commission's report concluded:

> For too long, the principals in our City's schools, as well as [the Division of School Safety] and the Board [of Education] . . . have clung to the view . . . that the schoolhouse is like a "ship at sea"—with the principal at its helm—separated from the community that surrounds it. Under this view, the school principals—like the ship captains—should manage and direct the school safety officers assigned to them and together, they should approach school safety as if it were disconnected from the surrounding neighborhood and community.
>
> The commission emphatically rejects that view. Overwhelming evidence shows that the problem of crime and misconduct in the schools is intimately connected to the violence and physical threats that students face every day in their streets and neighborhoods. A coordinated, integrated approach to these interconnected and interdependent safety problems, managed by law enforcement professionals, that attempts to link what goes on in our schools to the events outside is, in the commission's view, the only way that we can hope to reduce crime and misconduct in the school forcefully and effectively. Only then can our schools once again be the safe havens for learning that they once were.[8]

After the commission issued its report, the board of education entered into a sensible arrangement to transfer day-to-day operation of the division of school safety to the New York City police department. Under the compromise, which does not cede complete control to the police, the board contracts for services with the NYPD for a four-year period during which the police department will recruit, hire, train, and supervise school safety officers. Although they will be police department employees, the 3,200 school safety officers will remain unarmed and will not be sworn police officers.[9]

Concluding Reflections

After grappling with the challenges confronting young people for more than thirty-seven years, what broader observations might I attempt to make about the role of government, nonprofit organizations, and the private sector in the same endeavor?[10] Herewith some thoughts, concluding with reflections about schools and youth violence.

—*Mission*. Much has been discussed, often in rather esoteric terms, about the various missions of the public, nonprofit, and private sectors. In my view, the public sector mission is to govern and provide services in such a way that the person who was elected to govern gets reelected. The private sector, in comparison, has a bottom line—and that bottom line is to do as good a job as possible in order to make as much money as possible. Hopefully, those goals do not conflict. Some private sector companies do a lot of public good, and while it is wonderful that they are using their resources to further the public interest, that is not their main purpose. If they can both work for the public good and increase their bottom line, that is a double good. In contrast to the private sector, the nonprofit sector has been set up precisely to do the public good. Yet, nonprofits still have to worry about the bottom line, and they have to worry about their reputation.[11]

In sum, each of the sectors is defined and may be limited by its mission. But at the same time, each has a different role to play and can play it extremely well. If you can manage to do as much public good as possible while covering your private back, you are probably way ahead of the game.

—*Management and organization*. The managerial challenges in running an organization—public, private, or nonprofit—can differ among organizations, yet it is generally true that those challenges are strongly influenced by the person or forces that control the manager.

Thus, in public service, where you often report to elected officials, you may be restrained to some extent by their political aspirations or they may encourage you and give you a lot of leeway. Some administrations may not give you the kind of leeway that you have in others. A department commissioner may be extraordinarily talented and competent, but if that commissioner does not do well with a particular deputy mayor or mayor, he or she may be removed. The same thing can occur if a public manager becomes embroiled in a controversy in which he or she is "right," but the public perception is to the contrary. In the private sector, the bottom line must be a primary consideration if the manager is going to survive. In nonprofit organizations, the bottom line may also be an important consideration. Certainly, the nonprofit chief executive must answer to a board of directors, and the managerial environment can be very heavily affected by power struggles within the board. In community-based organizations, there are sometimes very damaging political forces driven by parochial power impulses and not by the best interests of the organization. At the same time, however, community-based organizations can offer the open channels of communication and informal structural arrangements that are most conducive to successful interventions. Community-based organizations often are "closer to the problem" and members may have a feeling of personal involvement and responsibility arising from their grassroots relationships. The manager or leader of a community-based organization can act on the basis of information that has not been filtered or distorted by layers of bureaucracy, in contrast to managers in government and large nonprofit organizations, where there is a real danger of information distortion.

—*Measures of success.* As I think about my various experiences, I realize that for me the best and most rewarding measure of success is to see that I changed somebody's life. In government, it is more difficult to gauge that change. The things that you can do through government may ultimately change more peoples' lives, but generally you do not get to see it. Even if you go out in the field a lot, you usually do not get to know the people that you are serving well enough to know that you really made a difference. One of the wonderful aspects about working in a small nonprofit or for a favored program such as the Wildcat Academy is that one gets to know the people and to follow their progress, whether it is a student who is now a Navy Seal in Alaska or one who is a pharmacist in Japan. Such personal relationships are probably the most rewarding measurement of impact one can experience.

At the same time, the nature of nonprofits and the incentives sometimes used for rewarding nonprofits can create frustration. As I have stated, an important goal of nonprofits is doing good for the public, while also, quite appropriately, being concerned on a certain level with the bottom line. Because the bottom line often is related to outcomes, there is a danger of "creaming," whereby organizations select clients who are most likely to succeed, while avoiding those who are most in need of help.[12] Creaming is to be deplored. In my view, people who cream really do not have any right to run programs. While even in our private industry program one might say that we cream because only some participants can absorb successfully the kind of training needed for particular jobs, we do have programs for people who do not fit into those categories. Ideally, everybody who comes in the door should be served. One must recognize that everybody is not alike; different people have different strengths and weaknesses. Nonprofits have an obligation to provide services to meet a variety of needs.

By and large, I do not believe that profit-based organizations should provide services for needy people. They generally have proven to be less desirable than nonprofits because they are too concerned with the bottom line; unfortunately, as a result, some very good and necessary services are cut. At the same time, I do not believe that organizations can be allowed to function with fuzzy funding bases and no proven measures of whether they are doing a good job. People should not be funded "just because they did it last year." Nonprofits should be reviewed every year to determine whether they deserve funding.

The Wildcat Academy is evaluated every year by the state board of regents; we also are evaluated by the Robin Hood Foundation, which is a source of our funding. One of the most useful functions a foundation can perform is to evaluate how its money is being used. Indeed, such assessments are important for both government and nonprofit organizations.

—*Funding.* In a world of scarce and finite resources, the executive who seeks support for initiatives, whether in the area of youth violence or other areas, must necessarily be alert to funding possibilities—public, private, or nonprofit. Depending on the source, funding may come subject to varying degrees of control. This is a reality, but not a condition to be feared. The fact that there may be greater control of purse strings from government sources should not be bothersome. If managers are honorable, they will act in good faith in accordance with their representations when they sought funding and should not be concerned about restrictions.

The value of a funding source is not determined solely by its monetary dimension. For example, foundations provide a small yet a very important component of the funding of the Wildcat Academy, allowing us to offer services and programs that are not funded by government or other sources. As noted, we have consistently gotten a grant from the Robin Hood Foundation that has permitted us to provide SAT prep courses, to hire a special reading teacher, and to help pay the youngsters for the jobs that they perform. Such is the value of foundation support that at Wildcat our vice-president is a development specialist who works with me very closely in trying to attract the foundation dollars that allow us to achieve excellence.

Indeed, if one could imagine a situation in which funding was equally and fully available from every possible source—from the public and private sectors and foundations—one would opt for funding from foundations, simply because foundation funding is the most direct source of support. It does not produce the terrible cash flow problems that arise from other sources, particularly government, when an organization may perform a service and then have to wait a substantial time to be paid.

—*Partnership, innovation, and competition.* Clear objectives, trust, and flexibility all make for a good partnership. As noted earlier, the Wildcat Services Corporation has enjoyed a great relationship with Salomon Smith Barney, for whom we train entry-level clerical workers. The value of partnership may present itself in subtle ways. While most innovative initiatives occcur in the nonprofit world, they could not be realized without the financial support of government.[13] Some requests for proposals from municipal, state, and federal agencies have stimulated great innovations. For example, the nonprofit world, in conjunction with government, has developed some outstanding examples of effective programs in the area of youth violence prevention. One such program is the Beacon Schools, which allows public schools to stay open in the evening;[14] another is the After-School Corporation—a nonprofit organization funded by the Soros Open Society Institute and by government—which supports in-school after-school programs. Such initiatives exemplify how the combination of nonprofit and government funding has been used to provide young people with an alternative to violent or criminal activities.

While partnership among the sectors is to be encouraged, competition also can be constructive when it promotes creative ways of looking at a problem. Competition within sectors, such as among nonprofits, can similarly be productive when it produces alternative approaches. In a world of finite resources, however, it is perhaps an inevitable fact of life that cutthroat competition can inhibit the sharing of information, to the detriment of sound policy.

—*Schools and violence.* As we have become increasingly concerned as a society with youth violence, we have come to realize that there is no single solution. For the school administrator and educator, managing youth violence has taken a variety of forms[15]—for example, enriching curricula and teaching conflict resolution and gang aversion skills.[16] Initiatives such as the "resolving conflict creatively" program in New York City public schools—which trains teachers, administrators, parents, and students how to mediate disputes without violence—come to mind.[17] Other programs teach students how to deal with peer pressure, including gang pressure. Still other efforts have involved creating partnerships with other professionals, such as mental health providers,[18] while also sensitizing school personnel to the early warning signs of potential violence in a student.[19] Some efforts have involved promoting the physical security of schools—for example, by using metal detectors and trained security personnel as well as school resources officers.[20] Some school systems have created new partnerships with prosecutors[21] and probation officers to help control youth violence.[22] Other initiatives, such as the Safe Passage program in New York, which coordinates school dismissal times with train schedules and places police officers on subway cars to ensure the safe passage of students, and the Safety Corridors program in Philadelphia are further indications of new links between law enforcement and schools.[23]

What many of these recent efforts have shown is that to address youth violence in schools, we need to be hardheaded pragmatists. The Wildcat Academy—based on notions of small size, intensive supervision, a longer school day, discipline, work experience, autonomy, and genuine concern— has demonstrated, I think, that to deal with school violence we must be prepared to tackle the chaotic conditions that have undermined the school experience. As an outgrowth of the Wildcat Services Corporation, the academy quite appropriately bears witness to the notion that human potential must be developed and that efforts to attain that goal constitute a worthy investment of time and money. Beyond that, in our vigorous pursuit of partnerships among sectors and within sectors, we must create alternatives to the violence that is so detrimental to our youth. We must demonstrate by our actions that we care about our young people.

Notes

1. On gangs, see Irving A. Spergel, *The Youth Gang Problem: A Community Approach* (Oxford University Press, 1995), pp. 90–109; Malcolm W. Klein, *The American Street Gang: Its Nature, Prevalence, and Control* (Oxford University Press, 1995), pp. 82–85.

2. Kay S. Hymowitz, "Up the Up Staircase: A Place to Unlearn the Lessons of the Street," *City Journal*, vol. 4, no. 2 (Spring 1994), pp. 31–39.

3. Laura A. Siegel, "Tough Kids Learn to Meet Tough Standards: Wildcat Academy Makes High School Graduates of Students No One Could Reach," *Christian Science Monitor*, July 3, 1997, p. 12.

4. Philliber Research Associates, *Achievements of Students Attending John V. Lindsay Wildcat Academy* (New York: Accord, 2001), on file with author.

5. The Second Opportunity School, with an enrollment of seventy-five to 100 students, is funded by the board of education. It enrolls students suspended from public schools throughout the city for carrying guns or for other violent conduct. Students attend

the school during their one-year suspension. Wildcat Academy III, with an enrollment of 240 students, is funded by the state human resources agency and is patterned in all significant respects after Wildcat I.

6. *El Colegio La Puerta* was created with the active involvement of the Manhattan Institute's Inter-American Policy Exchange. "Inter-American Policy Exchange at the Manhattan Institute" (www.manhattan-institute.org/html/iape/htm [February 5, 2002]).

7. *Report of the Mayor's Investigatory Commission on School Safety* (January 4, 1996), pp. 1–2.

8. Ibid., pp. 4–5.

9. New York City Board of Education, "Board of Education Votes to Enter into an Agreement with the City of New York on the Performance of School Security Functions by the New York City Police Department," press release (September 17, 1998).

10. For a discussion of the exercise of drawing from experience, see Ellen Schall, "Notes from a Reflective Practitioner of Innovation," in Alan A. Altshuler and Robert D. Behn, eds., *Innovation in American Government: Challenges, Opportunities, and Dilemmas* (Brookings, 1997), pp. 360–77.

11. See Paul C. Light, *Making Nonprofits Work: A Report on the Tides of Nonprofit Management Reform* (Brookings, 2000); Peter Frumkin and Alice Andre-Clark, "When Missions, Markets, and Politics Collide: Values and Strategy in the Nonprofit Human Services," *Nonprofit and Voluntary Sector Quarterly*, vol. 29, supplement (2000), pp. 141–63.

12. On "creaming," see Peter Frumkin, *Managing for Outcomes: Milestone Contracting in Oklahoma* (PricewaterhouseCoopers Endowment for the Business of Government, January 2001), p. 9 (www.endowment.pwcglobal.com/pdfs/Frumkin.Report.pdf [January 2002]).

13. On the relationship between nonprofits and the public sector, see Peter B. Goldberg, "Nonprofits and the Public Sector: An Evolving Relationship," in Nonprofit Sector Research Fund, *Competing Visions: The Nonprofit Sector in the Twenty-First Century* (Aspen Institute, 1997), pp. 83–91. See, generally, Peter Frumkin, *On Being Nonprofit: A Conceptual and Policy Primer* (Harvard University Press, 2002).

14. On the Beacon Schools, see Geoffrey Canada, *Fist Stick Knife Gun* (Boston: Beacon Press, 1995); Lisbeth B. Schorr, *Common Purposes: Strengthing Families and Neighborhoods to Rebuild America* (Anchor Books, 1997), pp. 47–55.

15. Delbert S. Elliott, Beatrix A. Hamburg, and Kirk R. Williams, *Violence in American Schools* (Cambridge University Press, 1998).

16. David C. Anderson, "Curriculum, Culture, and Community: The Challenge of School Violence," in Michael Tonry and Mark H. Moore, eds. *Youth Violence* (University of Chicago Press, 1998), pp. 317–63.

17. Linda Lantieri and Janet Patti, *Waging Peace in Our Schools* (Boston: Beacon Press, 1996).

18. Stephen Marans and Mark Schaefer, "Community Policing, Schools, and Mental Health: The Challenge of Collaboration," in Elliott, Hamburg, and Williams, *Violence in American Schools*, pp. 312–47.

19. U. S. Department of Education, *Early Warning, Timely Response: A Guide to Safe Schools* (1998).

20. Dennis J. Kenney and T. Steuart Watson, *Crime in the Schools* (Washington: Police Executive Research Forum, 1998); Pamela L. Riley, *Meeting the Challenge of School Violence:*

School Resource Officers (Raleigh, N.C.: Center for the Prevention of School Violence, 1997).

21. See Catherine Coles and George Kelling, chapter 2 in this volume.

22. See Ronald P. Corbett Jr., chapter 6 in this volume.

23. General Accounting Office, *School Safety: Promising Initiatives for Addressing School Violence*, HEHS-95-106 (April 1995).

11

RONALD G. SLABY

Media Violence:
Effects and Potential Remedies

I believe television is going to be the test of the modern world, and that in this new opportunity to see beyond the range of our vision we shall discover either a new and unbearable disturbance of the general peace, or a soaring radiance in the sky. We shall stand or fall by television—of that I am quite sure.

THESE ARE THE prophetic words of E. B. White, author of the classic children's story *Charlotte's Web*, describing his thoughts in 1938 as he sat in a darkened room transfixed by the shimmering images being projected from a primitive electronic box called a "television."[1] For nearly sixty-five years, television and other electronic media have indeed presented the modern world with a continuing series of tests. None is greater than the test of how we deal with the effects of, and potential remedies for, media violence.

Television and other electronic media have now become permanent residents in our homes. Each brings with it the capacity to deliver to our family either an "unbearable disturbance" or a "soaring radiance." Most often, however, they deliver *both* of these effects, mixed together in a tangled web of potentially harmful and helpful messages. The electronic messages, delivered through television, videos, interactive video games, and the Internet, fiercely compete for our hearts and minds, as well as our precious time and money. These media now present us with what is both a fundamental problem and a momentous opportunity: the task of untangling this complex web and enabling the media's "soaring radiance" to prevail.

To manage youth violence effectively, we must ultimately understand how media violence contributes to real-life violence and what can be done to remedy its effects. This chapter first describes how a long-standing education gap regarding the effects of media violence is beginning to close—myths are slowly being replaced by a broad public understanding of the research evidence and the key policy issues. It then presents a brief history of research on media violence and some of its documented effects. Next it discusses how media violence effects may be altered depending on the context in which violence is presented and the susceptibility of the viewer, thereby providing clues to what can be done to develop remedies for the effects. Finally, it presents several potential remedies for media violence. Although some publicly proposed remedies would fail or irresponsibly restrict social or personal freedoms, there are many sound proposals that call for greater education, innovation, and responsible action on the part of both the media industry and the viewer.

Closing the Education Gap

The potential harmful effects of media violence on youth have been a continuing source of concern to parents, educators, policymakers, and various professional organizations during the last half of the twentieth century to the present. Stimulated by that concern, behavioral scientists have generated a large and cohesive body of evidence that documents the effects of media violence and how to minimize or prevent them.[2] Throughout much of this time, however, a large education gap has existed regarding the topic of media violence. The general public has been largely unaware, confused, or misinformed about its documented effects and about potentially effective remedies.

Television has become a major source of public knowledge and concern about many important social issues. The medium often plays a major role in educating the public on many topics related to public health, education, and safety by presenting new scientific evidence and its practical applications. Yet, the research evidence regarding the harmful effects of media violence has generally been treated by the television industry as a direct threat to its business. Rather than providing accurate coverage, the television industry has generally ignored, denied, attacked, or even misrepresented the evidence in its reports to Congress and presentations to the general public.[3] Decades of denial and distortion by television, motion picture, music recording, and electronic game industries have taken their toll on the American public. For many parents, educators, and policymakers who had been misled and desensitized for decades, media violence was perceived to be an invisible, trivial, or harmless issue, while actual youth exposure to media violence became more extensive, pervasive, graphic, and glorified.

Now this once enormous education gap is beginning to close. Growing national concern over youth violence, combined with the recent series of student shootings in American schools and their reported links to media violence, has reawakened the American public to the real-life consequences of media violence. In profiles of nine youths involved in seven school shootings from 1996 to 1999, movies, video games, and music with violent content turned up repeatedly as key influences.[4] As public discourse on media violence has reopened, Americans have begun to replace myths and misinformation with a deeper and more accurate understanding of well-documented scientific evidence of media violence effects. They have also begun to call for sensible and effective remedies for media violence based on educated and responsible action by both the media industry and media users.

In a recent Gallup Poll, 62 percent of adults said violence in popular entertainment was one of the major causes of violence among young people. In a CNN/*USA Today* poll, 76 percent said that television and movies were a negative influence on children and 81 percent thought that stricter regulation of violence would be effective.[5] Even television programmers are becoming alarmed by the growing public concern. Several years ago, CBS deleted an especially violent program about the Mafia from its broadcast schedule. "This is not the time to have people being whacked on the streets of New York," explained network chief Leslie Moonves.[6] The American public—frustrated by feelings of powerlessness to control the flood of media violence invading American homes, movie theaters, marketplaces, and communities—has raised an outcry. As media violence has become a topic of national debate, policymakers have proposed new ways to address the issue and particular segments of the media industry have slowly and reluctantly begun to respond.

History of Research on Media Violence

In 1951, the National Association of Educational Broadcasters surveyed television programming in four large American cities and reported that crime and horror programs accounted for 10 percent of program time. Several years later the U.S. Senate Subcommittee on Juvenile Delinquency initiated the first in what was to become a long series of public inquiries into the effects of televised violence. The subcommittee issued a series of reports based on testimony and findings from those hearings that indicated that

—television could potentially be harmful to young children (in 1956).

—the amount of televised violence had increased and much of it was shown when young children were heavily viewing (in 1961 and 1964).

—televised crime and violence was related to antisocial behavior among juvenile viewers (in 1965).

In 1968, President Lyndon Johnson established a National Commission on the Causes and Prevention of Violence, headed by Milton Eisenhower, the brother of former president Dwight Eisenhower. On the basis of a large-scale content analysis of television violence and a review of the scientific evidence, the Eisenhower Commission in 1969 concluded that viewers learned from televised violence how to engage in violent behavior, and it presented recommendations for reducing the harmful effects.

Before the Eisenhower Commission had issued its final report, the Senate Subcommittee on Communications requested the U.S. surgeon general to commission a series of original studies designed to establish definitively whether a causal connection existed between televised crime and violent and antisocial behavior of viewers, particularly children and youth. The National Institute of Mental Health (NIMH) received $1 million to fund twenty-three independent research investigations and to convene a scientific advisory committee to review, evaluate, and develop conclusions regarding the findings.[7] Although the collective evidence generated by those empirical studies is generally regarded as a major scientific achievement, the advisory committee's summary and conclusions were criticized.[8] Critics began by pointing out that advisory committee members were selected through a political process that permitted television executives to blackball noted scientists while allowing individuals with financial ties to the television industry to participate. Critics also faulted the advisory committee for understating the strength and scope of the relationship between televised violence and antisocial behavior. Despite the political influences, the summary report concluded that television entertainment offerings may contribute, in some measure, to the aggressive behavior of many children and that such an effect had been found in a wide variety of situations.[9]

In the decade following the Surgeon General's report in 1972, several hundred research publications addressed the influence of television on viewers, many focusing on the specific nature, conditions, and effects of various types of televised violence on different viewers. Recognizing the growing need to review, evaluate, and make recommendations based on the new surge of research evidence, the National Institute of Mental Health was encouraged by the Surgeon General to prepare a summary report[10] as well as twenty-four integrative reviews.[11] The reports, issued in 1982, concluded that a *causal* link between televised violence and aggressive behavior had been established and that the major remaining research task was to seek explanations for the effect. The reports also indicated that

—violence on television had increased since the Surgeon General's report a decade earlier.

—the effects of televised violence could be applied confidently to girls as well as boys and to children from preschool age through adolescence.

—in magnitude, television violence was as strongly correlated with aggressive behavior as any other behavior variable measured.

—televised violence may lead not only to increased aggression but also to increased fear of being a victim of violence.

In 1985, the American Psychological Association (APA) released a position paper declaring that, because viewing televised violence may lead to an increase in aggressive attitudes, values, and behaviors, particularly in children, responsible actions were needed.[12] Specifically, the APA

—encouraged parents to monitor and control television viewing by children.

—requested industry representatives to reduce direct imitable violence in children's programming and to provide more programming designed to mitigate the effects of television violence, consistent with the guarantees of the First Amendment.

—urged industry, government agencies, and private foundations to support research activities aimed at ameliorating the effects of televised violence on children.

To follow up its call for action, the APA established a task force to review the existing literature on television's effects and to make recommendations on mitigating the negative and strengthening the positive influences. After examining hundreds of experimental and longitudinal studies, the APA task force report in 1992 supported the conclusion reached a decade earlier by the NIMH that viewing televised violence was *causally* related to aggressive behavior. Furthermore, examination of naturalistic field studies and cross-national studies suggested that when viewing televised violence led to increased aggression during childhood and early adolescence, a life-long pattern of behavior could be established that could manifest itself in serious adult antisocial behavior.[13]

While the APA task force was meeting, a study group was convened following a major conference of media researchers and industry representatives on television and adolescent health held in Los Angeles in 1988. The group's report concluded that exposure to media violence presented a major concern for adolescent health because

—media violence can teach adolescents social scripts (approaches to solving social problems) about violence.

—it can create and maintain attitudes in society that condone violence.

—constant exposure to media violence can lead to emotional desensitization in regard to violence in real life.

—the social, political, and economic roots of violence are rarely explored, giving the impression that violence is mainly an interpersonal issue.[14]

In a national plan for the prevention of violence released by the Centers for Disease Control (CDC) in 1992, concern was again raised over children's exposure to particular forms of media violence. Parents were urged to avoid exposing their children to mass media depictions that "aggrandize" violence and to search out alternative programs that educate families in the use of nonviolent solutions.[15]

Throughout the last several decades, many professional organizations, including the American Academy of Pediatrics, the American Medical Association, the American Psychological Association, the National Association for the Education of Young Children, and the National Parent Teachers Association, have reviewed the large body of research evidence on the effects of media violence, adopted resolutions, and presented recommendations for policymakers, practitioners, and the general public. For example, more than two decades ago, the National Parent Teachers Association (PTA) made the issue of how to control television violence effects a top national priority.[16] The PTA leadership realized the seriousness of the problem, the strength of the research evidence, and the potential for teachers and parents to work together to contribute to a solution. The National Association for the Education of Young Children has also identified an important role for early childhood educators in helping to remedy television violence effects.[17]

A half-century of research evidence on television violence has conclusively documented its potential harm. Meanwhile, major changes in the extent and nature of television portrayals of violence have produced increasing cause for concern. As Newton Minow, chairman of the Federal Communications Commission (FCC) during the Kennedy administration, more recently stated:

> I think the most troubling change over the past 30 years is the rise in the quantity and quality of violence on television. In 1961 I worried that my children would not benefit much from television, but in 1991 I worry that my grandchildren will actually be harmed by it.[18]

Recent changes in technology and program access have also resulted in an explosive increase in youth access to violent programming and related materials beyond traditional television. Today youth may be regularly exposed to
—violent programming on broadcast TV, cable TV, and satellite TV.
—violent programming in motion pictures and on videocassettes, digital video disks, and Internet websites.
—violent audio programming delivered through traditional radios, Walkman radios, compact disk players, and Internet websites.
—violent interactive video games delivered through television monitors, computer monitors, portable devices, Internet web sites, and arcade games.
—violent toys, games, and other devices directly related to violent media programming.
A large body of evidence on the effects of televised violence provides a great deal of guidance, and we are beginning to learn about the effects of exposure to violence delivered through video games and other electronic media.[19] Interactivity, realistic simulation, and rehearsal of simulated violent activities by the user would be expected to increase media violence effects. More extensive and broader-based exposure to violence would be expected to lead to increased levels of violence and more widely generalized effects.

Effects of Media Violence

Television violence can and does affect the thoughts, feelings, and actions of viewers. Several major effects of viewing violence have been established,[20] but, as with the effects of smoking, a given individual may or may not exhibit them.[21] Some people who smoke never get lung cancer, and some people who get lung cancer never smoked. Nevertheless, we know that smoking is a contributing cause of lung cancer. We also know that lung cancer is only the tip of an iceberg of broader health effects of smoking. Even though an individual smoker may not contract lung cancer in his or her lifetime, is it still likely that smoking has contributed to a variety of other health problems that are perhaps more prevalent but less extreme, such as emphysema, heart disease, and skin damage.

Similarly, media violence appears to serve as a contributing cause of several major effects, and additional hypothesized effects are being explored. Media violence effects are neither inevitable, nor determined solely by media exposure, nor unchangeable, nor equally probable for all depictions of violence and viewing conditions. Media violence effects appear to interact with other contributing causes of violence (for example, an individual's personal real-life experience with violence), and they vary considerably depending on the context in which violence is presented and the viewer's susceptibility, discussed below. Nevertheless, the following major effects of media violence have been found to occur reliably across a broad variety of portrayals, viewing conditions, and viewers.

—*Aggression effect.* The aggression effect consists of increased meanness, aggressive behavior, and even serious violence toward others. This effect can occur during or immediately after viewing a single exposure, or it can produce long-term cumulative effects from repeated or multiple exposures. The amount of televised violence children view has been found to be one of the best predictors of their likelihood to engage in serious and criminal acts of violence as adults, even when the effects of major background factors are statistically controlled.[22] It appears that viewing violence on television during childhood can inculcate aggressive habits in the young that, unless changed, may continue to affect their behavior for many years.

Despite consistent claims by top television industry executives from the 1960s through the early 1980s, there is virtually no evidence of the so-called "catharsis effect"—that viewing televised violence enables children to release "pent up" hostility, anger, or rage that otherwise might result in aggressive behavior. To the contrary, viewing violence generally increases children's knowledge of how to perform aggressive acts and decreases their inhibitions against behaving aggressively.[23]

—*Fear effect.* The fear effect consists of increased fearfulness, mistrust of others, and self-protective behavior. After viewing media violence, some young children have recurrent nightmares or daytime fears of becoming a victim of violence. Those who view a great deal of media violence, especially children, are more likely than others to exhibit distorted perceptions of the real world, referred to as "the mean world syndrome."[24] Those who display this syndrome generally believe that the world is a mean and dangerous place in which violence is everywhere and others are generally untrustworthy and ready to harm them. Those distorted beliefs are consistent with the distorted ways in which the media commonly presents violence as prevalent, extensive, and rewarded.

—*Callousness effect.* The callousness effect consists of increased callousness, desensitization, and behavioral indifference in regard to real-life violence among others. Individuals who view a great deal of violence show decreased levels of physiological arousal to portrayals of violence and become less likely to respond responsibly to real-life violence.[25] Instead, they often become bystanders who passively accept violence among others. For example, children who were experimentally exposed to a violent program were found to be less likely than children exposed to a neutral program to intervene or to seek help when younger children for whom they were "babysitting" began to fight.[26] Particularly when violence is portrayed as commonplace, acceptable, and justifiable, the viewing of violence appears to undermine the viewer's feelings of concern, empathy, or sympathy toward real-life victims.

—*Appetite for violence effect.* The appetite for violence effect consists of a learned desire for further violent involvement of greater frequency and intensity than previously experienced. In particular, viewers who repeatedly view and uncritically accept violence depicted in glorified, glamorized, and heroic ways may be motivated to view violence more often, play violent games more often, and engage more often in potentially violent activities.[27] Viewers' appetites for media violence do not seem to derive from any preexisting human need to view real violence; they appear instead to be learned and cultivated through the media's own typically unrealistic and glorified presentations of violence. To paraphrase former Senator Paul Simon (D-Illinois):

> Glorify soap for thirty seconds and people will buy it. Glorify violence in program after program from the time young children first watch television and throughout their childhood and youth, and it should come as no surprise that some children and youth will buy this glorified version of violence.[28]

By seeking out and exposing themselves to more media violence, individuals may build their own cycle of increasingly greater media violence effects. By engaging in potentially violent situations, individuals may expose themselves and others to greater risks of becoming involved in real-life violent encounters.

Presentation and Susceptibility Factors

Each of the major media violence effects described generally contributes in its own way to greater viewer acceptance of violence in real life. Although those effects are reliably manifested, on average, across a wide range of viewing conditions and individuals, they are clearly mediated by certain external presentation and internal susceptibility factors. Thus, the overall probability and extent of each effect varies greatly with both the way violence is presented and the susceptibility of individual viewers. Factors that increase or decrease media violence effects provide valuable clues to understanding how to develop potential remedies for those effects.

Presentation Factors

Much of the television programming that children view contains violence, and programming designed for children has consistently been found to contain higher levels of violence than any other category of programming.[29] Although children typically watch some television in their first two years, it is between usually the ages of two and three that children first acquire the habit of watching their favorite television programs.[30] By six years of age, more than 90 percent of American children watch television as a steady habit.[31] The typical child between the ages of two and eighteen currently consumes an average of 5.5 hours of media daily outside of school. Television (2 hours, 46 minutes) is the clear favorite, followed by computer games and other computer uses (49 minutes), recorded music (48 minutes), reading (44 minutes), and radio (39 minutes).[32]

Even more important than the sheer amount of violence contained in television programming may be the ways in which violence is commonly presented. Rather than presenting valuable insight into the true nature of violence and how to deal effectively with it in real life, television programming and other electronic media commonly present violence in a misleading, unrealistic, and glorified manner. Fictional television programs commonly present violence as highly prevalent, justified, socially approved, rewarded, effective, sanitized of blood and gore, and inconsequential.

Sometimes violence is also portrayed as heroic, manly, funny, and even pleasurable.[33] Each of those factors typically enhances the potential influence of the portrayal.[34] Many news and other nonfiction programs overrepresent and sensationalize violence while failing to provide accurate presentations of violence and the context in which it occurred.[35]

Violence presented in accurate, realistic, and unglorified ways could be expected to reduce the risk that viewers would imitate such portrayals. Programs that place strong emphasis on an antiviolence message—that violence is destructive and wrong—might even be expected to produce aggression-reducing effects. But accurate and socially responsible presentations of violence are all too rare in American television programming. In a broad national study, only 4 percent of American television programs containing violence were found to fit one of the following antiviolence patterns:

—Alternatives to violent actions are presented throughout the program.

—Main characters repeatedly discuss the negative consequences of violence.

—The physical pain and emotional suffering that results from violence are emphasized.

—Punishments for violence clearly and consistently outweigh rewards.[36]

Susceptibility Factors

Some viewers are especially susceptible to media violence effects because they view the usual glorified depiction of media violence uncritically. For example, young children are generally more susceptible to the effects of media violence than adolescents or adults, for several reasons. First, children often are heavy viewers of media violence. Second, children are quite likely to identify themselves with characters portrayed as powerful, effective, and rewarded, such as superheroes, who often solve their problems by the use of violence. Third, children often have relatively little experience through which to fully distinguish presentations that are real, realistic, or probable from those that are fictional, unrealistic, or improbable. Finally, they often lack the media literacy skills to critically evaluate the production techniques, values, and agendas underlying media glorifications of violence. Lacking these skills, children are susceptible to believing that violence is widely prevalent, does not entail real pain and suffering, and provides an effective solution to problems.[37]

Two significant and reliable mediators of viewer susceptibility to media violence effects are the extent to which the viewer identifies with the characters and believes that the portrayal is realistic and relevant to his or her own life.[38] Viewers who are most susceptible to the aggression effect are often those who identify most strongly with the aggressive characters. On the other hand, viewers who are most susceptible to the fear effect are often those who identify most strongly with the victimized characters. Although males and females are generally equally susceptible to media violence effects, the disproportionate presentation of male characters as aggressors and female characters as victims, combined with the tendency of children to identify with characters of their own sex, often lead to different outcomes for male and female viewers.[39]

During the preschool years, boys and girls develop the understanding that gender is an identifiable, stable, and consistent social category that has important implications for everyone in society.[40] As children develop a fuller understanding of the gender concept, they become highly motivated both to learn what it means to be a male or a female and to use that information to guide their own lives. During this period, children begin to seek out, pay greater attention to, and become increasingly influenced by characters of their own sex because those characters provide models relevant to their own gender role.[41] As a result, boys often view male characters whose power comes from their superior strength and aggressive behavior, while girls often view female characters who are either victimized or rescued by male characters or whose strength lies in their magical powers. When boys and girls view the same program, boys may show an aggression effect because they identify with a typically aggressive male character, while girls may show a fear effect because they identify with a typically victimized female character.[42]

Minority and nonminority children appear to be equally susceptible to the effects of media violence. However, the manifestation of the effects may differ because of different levels of viewing, different media portrayals of minority and nonminority characters, and children's developing tendency to identify with characters of their own ethnic group.[43] African American children commonly have been found to watch more television than white children. In much of television programming, minority characters are either nonexistent or presented in a negative manner or context. When African American, Hispanic, Asian American, or Native American characters appear, they are often stereotyped as either dangerous aggressors or victims of violence. Thus, when minority children identify with media characters of similar race and ethnicity, as they begin to do during the preschool and elementary school years, they are likely to selectively view programs containing characters of similar race or ethnicity, selectively attend to those characters in the programs they view, and selectively remember and become influenced by those characters' actions in regard to violence.

Remedies for Media Violence

While television and other media commonly contribute to a general acceptance of the use of violence in real life, the same media can be used to reverse the effects of media violence and to help develop solutions to real-life violence.[44] Although no single approach is likely to provide a complete solution, a variety of potential remedies currently offer partial solutions. Several sound initiatives involve greater education, innovation, and responsible action on the part of both the media industry and the viewer.

A key obstacle has been the use of particular rationales to dismiss or foreshorten debate about media violence effects and remedies. Sissela Bok presents the following eight rationales that serve the double function of offering both a "simplistic reason for not entering into serious debate" and "rationalizations for ignoring or shielding ongoing practices from outside scrutiny or interference:" [45]

1. America has always been a violent nation and always will be: violence is as American as cherry pie.

2. Why focus the policy debate on TV violence when there are other more important factors that contribute to violence?

3. How can you definitively pinpoint, and thus prove, the link between viewing TV violence and acts of real-life violence?

4. Television programs reflect existing violence in the "real world." It would be unrealistic and a disservice to viewers as well as to society to attempt to wipe violence off the screen.

5. People can't even agree on how to define "violence." How, then, can they go on to discuss what to do about it?

6. It is too late to take action against violence on television, considering the plethora of video channels by which entertainment violence will soon be available in homes.

7. It should be up to parents, not to the television industry, to monitor the programs that their children watch.

8. Any public policy to decrease TV violence constitutes censorship and represents an intolerable interference with free speech.

Although those rationales raise points worth considering and represent natural points of inquiry, they should not be permitted to block discussion and impede progress in developing and implementing effective remedies for media violence. The need to deal effectively with the risks that media violence poses to children and youth is far too critical. In fact, when dealt with directly, media violence effects, while complex, may be more controllable than many other risk factors that contribute to youth violence. A conference, Remedies for Media Violence, was held in Boston in 1996 to engage prominent members of the community in the search for potential solutions to the problem. To stimulate participation and discussion around particular themes, background materials and exemplary initiatives were presented in each of the following categories: media/business remedies; policy/regulatory remedies; public health/education remedies; parent/teacher remedies; and action group/community remedies.

Media/Business Remedies

The most direct remedy for media violence is for the media industry voluntarily to produce and disseminate new programming designed to prevent and reduce violence and promote prosocial behavior among viewers, presumably by teaching them effective alternative ways to resolve conflict nonviolently.[46] Viewing programs that stress positive and socially valued interaction among people can increase a wide range of prosocial behaviors, including helping, sharing, cooperating, playing imaginatively, and showing empathy.[47] The positive effects of television programming can be greatly enhanced when it is supplemented with coordinated community education activities.[48]

This somewhat obvious but often overlooked remedy would require no act of Congress, no new regulations, no overt structural changes in business practices, and no adversarial community action against the media. The same freedoms and resources that have permitted the media industry to generate violent programming provide it the opportunity to produce programming that could reduce societal violence. This media remedy might lay a foundation for additional remedies involving public education, support from businesses interested in serving the public interest (for example, through advertising or underwriting), and participation of parents, teachers, and community organizations.

Of course, a media remedy will become broadly probable and sustainable only when the incentives and disincentives begin to favor programming with socially helpful rather than harmful effects. Although media businesses often are "more interested in making dollars than in making sense,"[49] profits are not their only motivation. Incentives and disincentives that favor socially beneficial programming may come in different forms for individuals, program producers, public television stations, commercially operated television stations and networks, cable television companies, and other media businesses. They include responding to the marketplace; projecting a favorable public image; generating public satisfaction and loyalty; responding to public pressure for change; responding to advertisers' concerns; providing competitive positioning (for example, by attracting family viewers with "family friendly" programming); winning awards, recognition, and promotions; gaining the respect of one's colleagues; serving personal and societal concerns; avoiding public embarrassment, community opposition, and lawsuits; and preempting anticipated regulation or legislation.

Understandably, the Public Broadcasting Service (PBS), with its higher priority on serving the public, has led the way toward remedying media violence effects by producing and airing programming designed to prevent violence and foster prosocial behavior. In 1995, the producers of all major PBS children's television series attended a forum in Washington, D.C., cosponsored by the Corporation for Public Broadcasting and the American Center for Children's Television to learn about the latest research evidence on media violence effects, hear children's own views on media violence, review past successes, and consider future strategies and incentives for remedying the effects of media violence.[50]

PBS has addressed the issue of youth violence in two distinct ways: through programming that addresses media violence as a specific factor related to youth violence and through programming that addresses non-media factors related to violence. PBS launched several programs as part of the National Campaign to Reduce Youth Violence, which was funded by the Corporation for Public Broadcasting, including a series produced by Bill Moyers entitled *What Can We Do about Youth Violence?* that included a program that focused on media violence effects and remedies.[51] In a separate initiative, KQED produced a one-hour PBS television special, "The Smart Parent's Guide to TV Violence," hosted by their education director, Milton Chen. The program, also available in videotape, presented a town meeting, children's interviews, a panel discussion (involving panelists First Lady Hillary Rodham Clinton; Rachelle Chong, commissioner for the Federal Communications Commission; and Donald Roberts, professor at Stanford), and recommendations. It was supplemented with a book for parents, *The Smart Parent's Guide to Kid's TV.*[52]

For commercial television stations and privately owned media businesses, the dominant factor is usually profit, although other incentives also play a role. One station manager for a network-affiliated television station serving a major urban area in the mid-1990s succinctly stated her dilemma. After an hour-long private conversation on the topic of how media violence affects youth, she said that she was aware of growing concerns among the station's audience and advertisers. She also revealed personal concerns about the effects of media violence on her family members and on the youth in her community, but noted that as station manager she needed to ask herself what would it cost her station to make a change. I replied that if I were in her position, I would be asking myself, "What are the new markets?" I pointed out that the tide of public demand was rapidly turning on this issue, led by those most concerned about the welfare of children and youth. On any given evening, hundreds of viewers might turn off her station's programming to attend a meeting of the parent-teacher organization to find out what they could do to remedy the effects of media violence.

Within several months, the station manager had initiated a major public awareness campaign, Stop the Violence. It involved public service announcements, community outreach programs, and statements by the station's most prominent newscasters, as well as walkathons and telethons to raise money for shelters for abused women. The campaign has served the station well, winning industry awards, public accolades, and goodwill among the station's viewers and advertisers. The station has also collaborated with a major health foundation to produce, broadcast, and distribute a series of one-minute public service announcements, entitled "Think: Violence is for People Who Don't."[53] A video also was prepared for community outreach programs that featured the spots presented in a format designed to stimulate further discussion between youth and adults about changing personal habits of thought and action that would lead to violence. The video and accompanying print materials are available in the Violence Prevention Kit, distributed by the Harvard/Pilgrim Foundation in Boston. Although the campaign effectively used the various resources of the commercial media to address several important factors related to violence in society, it explicitly avoided the topic of media violence.

Recently "emerging markets" of media users who favor nonviolent or even antiviolent programming are being identified and pursued by the media industry through new forms of programming (for example, the award-winning *Touched by an Angel*) and even new stations and a new network (for example, the Fox Family Station; Home Box Office for Families; PAX-TV Network). Although viewer demand for nonviolent programming appears to be growing, new and engaging formats for presenting action and suspense without gratuitous violence will need to be developed in order to attract young viewers, many of whom have already developed an appetite for graphically violent programs. Research evidence on children's interest in, comprehension of, and behavioral response to various types of television content and presentation features offers valuable information to guide the development of new forms of programming.[54]

One often proposed strategy for addressing television violence is for viewers to pressure companies that advertise on television (for example, through letter-writing campaigns or threatened boycotts) to refuse to "sponsor" violent programs and to advertise only on violence-free programs. Research linking the level of violence in television programs to its "sponsors" was initiated in the mid-1970s.[55] Although consumer pressure has led some companies to declare publicly that they will no longer advertise on programs that contain gratuitous violence and others to use their advertising dollars more selectively, the strategy is circuitous and potentially hazardous.

This strategy would put power in the hands of advertisers and special interest groups that may misuse it to promote private agendas that would not necessarily serve the public interest. Ultimately, the strategy defines the power of the American people primarily in terms of their value as consumers rather than their rights as owners of the airwaves. It calls on the broadcast television industry to shape program content based on market pressures from advertisers, rather than from its direct responsibility to the public. It attempts to transfer some of the power (and none of the responsibility) for shaping program content from the large corporations that operate television stations to the large corporations that advertise on them.

Corporations have their own agendas, which will always differ to some degree from those of the American public. Some corporations air ads that contain violence (usually promoting violent movies, television series, or forthcoming news reports), and others advertise products that support violence (for example, violent games and toys). Some companies even find ways to exploit public concern over violence for their own interests. For example, the Philip Morris Company recently initiated a series of television ads designed to repair its public image, which was badly damaged when it was revealed that the company deliberately misrepresented the health risks of smoking and targeted the youth market to sell cigarettes. The ads portray families that have been saved from domestic violence because they had access to shelters for battered women and present Philip Morris as a major contributor to abused women's shelters.

Companies that declare they will not "sponsor" television programs containing gratuitous violence may face limited accountability for their claims. Corporate decisions about how and why they spend their advertising dollars do not have to conform to stated policy or enduring principles, only to corporate self-interest, which could diverge at any time from the public's concern over media violence. A better way to involve businesses in the issue of media violence may be to call on them to support needed programming, public service announcements, and public education campaigns.

Policy/Regulatory Remedies

Because the media industry has been largely unresponsive to calls for voluntary changes to remedy media violence, many policy/regulatory remedies have been proposed and some have been implemented. When a credible threat of legislation or regulation develops, the industry often responds preemptively by making smaller changes voluntarily. Some media businesses state that they would support legislative or regulatory changes as long as they create a level playing field among competitors. Current policies guiding the media industry derive primarily from several key sources, including the First Amendment, the Federal Communications Act of 1934, the Children's Television Act of 1990, and the Telecommunications Act of 1996.

The First Amendment to the U.S. Constitution states that "Congress shall pass no law respecting the establishment of religion or prohibiting the free exercise thereof, or abridging the freedom of speech or of the press, or the right of people peaceably to assemble and petition the government for a redress of grievances." The First Amendment, which was designed, in part, to guarantee that the voice of criticism would be heard, ironically has often been used by the television industry to redirect or stifle criticism of the industry itself. For example, many Americans have a visual image of what their brain looks like when they take drugs, because an effective series of public service announcements on drug abuse aired on television about a decade ago. Yet, the American public has not seen even a single public service announcement on commercial television that addresses the harmful effects of media violence, even though several U.S. surgeons general and many professional organizations have repeatedly warned us over the last two decades of potentially harmful effects of media violence.

The Federal Communications Act of 1934 was designed to protect the freedoms guaranteed by the First Amendment from potential abuse by broadcasters. This act states that the airwaves belong in the public domain and that they are not privately owned by the commercial entities that use them. In order for broadcasters to receive or renew a license to operate over the public airwaves (one of the most influential, potentially lucrative, and scarce commodities in our society), the act requires them to "serve the public interest, convenience, and necessity." The FCC has tried to put that requirement into practice in a variety of ways. For example, to help ensure that broadcasters were indeed serving the public interest, the FCC required broadcasters petitioning for an original license or a renewal to ascertain what constituted the public interest in their community by seeking out, meeting with, and inviting comment from community leaders, diverse groups, and minority representatives. Once the current public interest had been ascertained, broadcasters needed to demonstrate specifically how they had responded to the public interest. Although the FCC appointed during the Reagan administration dropped the ascertainment requirement, nothing but lack of political will prevents it from being reinstated.

The Children's Television Act of 1990 requires television broadcasters, as a condition for license renewal, to serve the "educational and informational needs of children," both through programming and through non-broadcast outreach efforts that "enhance the educational and informational value of such programming." The law offers educators and the general public an opportunity to help change the way that the media deals with media violence effects. The American Psychological Association's Commission on Violence and Youth took advantage of the opportunity in presenting its policy recommendations: "We call upon the Federal Communications Commission (FCC) to review, as a condition for license renewal, the programming and outreach efforts and accomplishments of television stations in helping to solve the problem of youth violence."[56]

The Telecommunications Act of 1996 includes a specific provision introduced by Representative Edward Markey (D-Massachusetts) to address the issue of media violence. It requires television manufacturers to implant in every new TV set a "v-chip" (violence chip) to allow viewers the option of blocking transmission of programs rated as violent, and it encourages the television industry to adopt a standard rating system to designate violent programs. As of January 2000, all manufacturers had begun to include a v-chip in TV sets thirteen inches and larger. V-chip boxes that can be attached to many old TV sets also will be available.[57]

Unfortunately, the television industry has responded to this legislation with great reluctance and obfuscation, leading some critics to claim that the "v" in "v-chip" may end up standing for "vague." The industry began by proposing an age-based, rather than a content-based rating system, modeled after the system used by Motion Picture Association of America (MPAA). That system, designed primarily to protect the motion picture industry against scrutiny of the content of films, is virtually worthless for informing viewers about specific types of content. It intentionally mixes its evaluation of violent content with evaluation of sex, nudity, profanity, and adult themes. It arbitrarily designates particular indecipherable mixes of these types of content as inappropriate for children and youth of specific ages. The television industry's original proposal in 1997 met with a resounding rejection by parents and professional groups. For example, Parent Teacher Association president Joan Dykstra said:

> The television industry had an opportunity to show itself as respon-
> sive and responsible to American consumers, and today it failed to do
> so . . . . We're concerned that only the letter rating will be broadcast
> with the programs and that age information alone isn't enough to
> help parents make informed decisions about what their children are
> watching.[58]

In a comprehensive national study on television ratings conducted by the National PTA in collaboration with the Institute for Mental Health Initiatives and Dr. Joanne Cantor, the findings were compelling and clear. Eighty percent of parents preferred ratings that tell them specifically what a program's content is to those that tell them whether children of a certain age should be shielded from seeing it.[59]

The current rating system of the television industry uses a complicated set of labels for many TV programs that include both an age-based and a content-based rating. If they can understand and apply this complicated system, parents can set the so-called v-chip to block out many television programs on the basis of age (TV-Y = all children; TV-Y7 = older children; TV-G = general audience; TV-PG = parental guidance suggested; TV-14 = parents strongly cautioned that it may be unsuitable for children under fourteen; and TV-MA = mature audience only) and content (V = violence;

FV = fantasy violence; S = sexual situations; L = coarse or crude indecent language; and D = suggestive dialogue, usually about sex). What is meant by the label FV (fantasy violence) is unclear and perhaps misleading. It refers to a program that may contain some or all of the following characteristics: "violence as a prevalent feature of the program; fighting presented in an exciting—even thrilling—way; villains and superheroes valued for their combat abilities; violent acts glorified; and violence depicted as an acceptable and effective solution to a problem."[60]

Besides being complicated and unclear, those industry (self) ratings are unlikely to be applied consistently or completely because they will be the responsibility of each producer of a television program or each network that broadcasts it. No ratings of any kind will be applied to news programs or sports programs. Unedited movies shown on cable television will display only the original MPAA age-based rating and not the new age-based and content-based rating. The rating system is entirely voluntary, and some programmers have refused to follow a single standard. For example, NBC uses its own age-based rating system instead of the more standardized content-based system. Thus, it remains to be seen whether the new rating system and block-out technology will be of much value as even a partial remedy for American viewers concerned about media violence effects.

A wide range of additional media violence legislation was advanced in the 1990s. For example, Senator Ernest F. Hollings (D–South Carolina) introduced a bill that would prohibit the public distribution of violent video programming during hours when children are likely to comprise a substantial portion of the viewing audience. Senator David Durenberger (R–Minnesota) introduced a bill that would require the FCC to establish rules on audio and visual warnings for television programming depicting violence or unsafe gun practices shown between the hours of 6:00 a.m. and 11:00 p.m. Senator Carl Levin (D–Michigan) introduced a bill that would prohibit promotions or commercials for violent television movies and require broadcasters to preserve copies of the advertising they air and provide copies to the public upon request. Senator Byron Dorgan (D–North Dakota) introduced a bill that would require the FCC to periodically issue reports listing TV programs that contain the most violence, as well as their sponsors. Representative Charles E. Schumer, now Senator Schumer, (D–New York) introduced a bill that would establish a presidential commission to investigate and propose solutions to reduce the amount of violence broadcast on television.

The proposed legislation has had the effect of stimulating public debate on potential remedies for media violence and sometimes pressuring the television industry to respond preemptively. For example, Senator Paul Simon (D–Illinois) was concerned with a broad industrywide denial of media violence effects and the industry's failure to monitor its own programs and take responsible action. He first supported passage of the Television Violence Act of 1990/91, which provided a three-year moratorium on antitrust barriers to permit all producers of television programming (including broadcasters and cable, video, and movie producers) to work together on remedies for media violence. He then persuaded the heads of the major television networks to affirm in a public press conference in 1993 that the scientific evidence indicated that televised violence contributed to real-life violence and that the television industry needed to take responsible corrective action. A seemingly small step, this joint public statement came at a time when the heads of tobacco companies were still denying scientific evidence for the harmful health effects of smoking. Finally, Simon persuaded the television industry to support independent research designed to monitor the portrayal of media violence on television. This led to the most comprehensive and informative content analysis of television programming, the National Television Monitoring Study, supported by the National Cable Television Association.[61]

Representative Joseph Kennedy (D–Massachusetts), working with this author, introduced a noteworthy bill in 1993 designed to amend the 1934 Federal Communications Act to strengthen the voice of the American public and to stimulate greater responsiveness on the part of the television industry. The proposed amendment would provide a toll-free number to allow the American public to phone the FCC with their comments, recommendations, and new ideas regarding media violence. Those comments would be summarized, analyzed, and published on a quarterly basis and reported to Congress each year. The FCC would send each licensee any comments regarding media violence made with respect to its station. It would then evaluate whether the stations had effectively responded to the comments, consistent with the station's legal obligations to "serve the public interest" and to "serve the educational and informational needs of children." Although the bill did not come to a vote, it stimulated preemptive moves by the industry to set up its own temporary toll-free numbers, such as ABC's short-lived 800-VIOLENT.

In 1999 Senator Joseph Lieberman (D–Connecticut) introduced new legislation designed to protect children from the threat of media violence and encourage greater responsibility in the entertainment industry. The legislation called for the Federal Trade Commission and the U.S. Department of Justice to investigate the marketing practices of major media companies to determine whether they are targeting children to sell extremely violent products. Senator Lieberman presented anecdotal evidence at a Senate hearing indicating that the movie and video game industries were using tactics similar to those of the tobacco industry to sell graphic murder and mayhem to young teenagers. The legislation also called on the various entertainment media to collaborate on developing stronger industry codes to improve content standards and to better shield children from harmful products. In addition, it directed the National Institutes of Health to conduct a comprehensive study of the effects of violent entertainment on children aimed at raising public awareness of the influence the media can have. Lieberman said:

> I hope the entertainment industry will see this legislation as an urgent plea to stop the denials and the excuses and to start working with us in addressing the toxic mix that is turning our kids into killers. At a minimum, I hope they will take it as a stern warning that we will not tolerate the marketing of ultraviolent, adult-rated products to children. [62]

The Lieberman legislation has served as a catalyst for further action. After it was passed unanimously by the Senate but stalled in joint committee, President Clinton ordered the Federal Trade Commission to launch an investigation of the media industry's marketing of violent products to children. The FTC's investigative reports have raised public concern and led the media industry to take strong steps to strengthen its marketing codes and practices.

In a follow-up initiative Senators Lieberman and John McCain (R–Arizona) introduced legislation to create a uniform rating system for all entertainment media violence. The 21st Century Media Responsibility Act would amend the Cigarette Labeling and Advertising Act to apply that law's warning label requirements to violent media products. It would give the various entertainment media industries six months to work together to develop a common rating system for motion pictures, television programs, interactive video games, and recorded music. The standard warning labels would have to reflect the nature, context, intensity of violent content, and age appropriateness of the media product. Retail outlets would be responsible for enforcing age restrictions in accordance with the new system. The

Federal Trade Commission would be given the authority to accept, reject, or modify the proposed industry rating system to reflect the intent of the law. Labels would have to be conspicuously displayed and identical, regardless of product or service.

In an appeal to Hollywood released by Lieberman and McCain at a Capitol Hill press conference, American parents were described as "deeply worried about their children's exposure to an increasingly toxic popular culture." While acknowledging parents' share of the responsibility for attempting to shield their own children from harmful media exposure, the appeal argues that "even the most conscientious parent cries out for help" from an industry it says "too often abdicates its responsibility for its powerful impact on the young."[63]

Public Health/Education Remedies

Public education campaigns can be effective in changing the attitudes, beliefs, and behaviors of viewers, particularly when they are combined with coordinated educational outreach activities.[64] The American Psychological Association has led the way in recommending and developing public education campaigns as a remedy for media violence. In 1993 the APA Commission on Violence and Youth stated:

> We ask Congress to support a national educational violence prevention campaign involving television programming and related educational outreach activities to address the dire need for public education to help prevent youth violence in America. This campaign would be based on our best available scientific evidence about which changes will be most effective in helping to prevent violence, and our best educational and media strategies for fostering such change.[65]

In 1999 APA joined resources with the National Association for the Education of Young Children and the Ad Council to develop a national education campaign, ACT (Adults and Children Together) against Violence, designed to educate parents, teachers, and other caregivers about effective early violence prevention strategies for children up to the age of eight. One part of the campaign focuses specifically on media violence effects and remedies. Launched in 2000, the campaign is funded primarily by grants from private foundations, and it features an initial mass media component followed by a community education component. It presents a series of public service announcements to educate viewers and lead them to useful community education resources, including print materials and workshops with psychologists and early childhood educators trained in early violence prevention techniques.

Parent/Teacher Remedies

Parents, teachers, and other adults can directly alter the effects of media violence on children and youth when they watch programs and movies with them while commenting critically on the depiction of violence and discussing nonviolent alternatives;[66] they also can teach media literacy skills that permit young viewers to "see through" the falseness of particular media presentations. Adults need to become aware of children's viewing habits, the types of programs they view, and what they think about the characters and the behaviors depicted in those programs. Since children have relatively little real-world experience by which to evaluate the many ways that the media often exaggerate, falsify, and glorify violence, they stand to benefit greatly from hearing adult comments and from discussing with adults the differences between media violence and real-life violence.

Important topics for discussion include the unrealistic ways that violence is portrayed in the media, the problems of applying media portrayals of violence in real life, and using effective nonviolent solutions for problems in real life. Ideal times for making comments, asking questions, listening to children's comments, and discussing key issues often occur while viewing programs with children, during commercial breaks or videotape pauses, or immediately after viewing. Young children often fail to connect a violent act, the motives that precede it, and the consequences that follow, particularly when there is a time lapse in between. Explanatory comments and questions at key points during the program can help young children understand the connections and think about alternatives. Coviewing adults can also guide children in forming their own evaluations and critical judgments about both the violent and the prosocial behaviors they view.

Several media literacy programs have been developed in the hope of providing a partial remedy for the effects of media violence. These initiatives stem from research indicating that individuals who view media violence with a critical understanding of its purposeful fabrications and its potential effects are often less susceptible to its effects.[67] For example, a program, Flashpoint: Life Skills through the Lens of Media Literacy, was designed specifically to help youth who are involved in the juvenile justice system to develop the media literacy skills they need to "see through" the media's glorification of violence and drug abuse and stereotyping of characters. Developed by Kevin Burke, district attorney for eastern Massachusetts, and his staff, the Flashpoint program engages youth in interactive exercises to help them deconstruct the codes, agendas, values, and attributed meanings that underlie media programming. The exercises prepare youth to build a critical understanding of potentially harmful media messages, to interpret media messages realistically, and to make more responsible choices in the ways that they apply those messages in their own lives.[68]

Because the amount and specific content of the programming children view make a critical difference in its likely effects, adults may need to put limits on children's television viewing. Although parental restrictions can be effective, particularly for young children, all children ultimately need to learn how to regulate their own viewing. With guidance and initial incentives from both families and teachers, even young children can be taught to select their favorite prosocial programs in advance, turn the television set off after viewing those programs, and substitute interesting prosocial programs for violent ones. Recording favorite prosocial programs can make it easier to offer children a substitute for violence, particularly since young children are often interested in watching their favorite programs repeatedly. Providing children with fundamental guidance in making thoughtful program selections is an important first step in developing youth who take responsibility for regulating their own healthful media diets.

The following "See No Evil Pledge" was written by a twelve-year-old girl and her ten-year-old brother in Massachusetts and posted on the Internet by the American Academy of Pediatrics (AAP) Task Force on the Media. It provides a good example of how youth can become actively involved in making important choices for themselves, while also having a positive influence on others:

> Out of respect for the young people killed at Columbine High School in Littleton, Colorado, and to show that we have learned from their deaths, we pledge that we will, from this point forward, avoid all movies containing violence as entertainment. We will read advertising and newspaper "mini-reviews" as our guides. If, despite this research, we end up viewing a violent film, we pledge to leave the theatre immediately and demand a refund due to false advertising. We shall learn war no more.[69]

Advocacy Group/Community Remedies

A number of public interest advocacy groups are committed to developing and promoting effective remedies for media violence, including the Center for Media Education, the Center for Media Literacy, Children Now, Mediascope, Mediawatch, National Institute on Media and the Family, National PTA, the National Alliance for Nonviolent Programming, the National Coalition on Television Violence, and the National Foundation to Improve Television.

As noted, a community-wide strategic planning conference, Remedies for Media Violence, was held in Boston in 1996, organized by the Massachusetts Medical Society and its Alliance in cooperation with the Harvard Community Health Plan Foundation, the National Foundation to Improve Television, and the Education Development Center. Its purpose was to provide a forum for a broad group of community leaders, including health professionals, educators, parents, civic leaders, and media representatives, to generate, disseminate, and advance specific remedies for media violence. Perhaps the most important contribution of the conference, according to Jeanne Gaz, president of the Massachusetts Medical Society Alliance, was that it "brought together a diverse group of people and organizations to develop a concrete plan of action."[70]

As a follow-up to the conference, an educational campaign was developed for the greater Boston area to build community partnerships and advance community education on media violence. The campaign, Seeing through Media Violence, was cosponsored by the Massachusetts Medical Society and its Alliance, the United Nations Children's Fund (UNICEF), the Children's Hospital, the Massachusetts Department of Public Health, the Education Development Center, the National Foundation to Improve Television, and Wheelock College. Carol Bellamy, executive director of UNICEF, called on the television industry worldwide to initiate a campaign against violence on December 15, 1996, UNICEF's International Children's Day of Broadcasting.[71] The following message was sent to several thousand television stations worldwide that participated in the International Children's Day of Broadcasting, including several stations in the Boston area:

Television is a persistent and effective teacher—whether the lessons are taught by design or default. Television can continue to teach our children the unrealistic, misleading, and deadly lessons that have for decades fostered violence, fear, and desensitization—as research evidence has clearly confirmed. Or this teacher can design a new lesson plan that will serve the educational and informational needs of children throughout the world by teaching a broad variety of accurate, effective, and life-saving solutions to the problems of violence.

Which television teacher will we choose for our children? The time to decide is upon us.[72]

The New Hampshire Coalition on Media Violence illustrates a growing national trend toward developing broad community-based coalitions focused on media violence. Its partners include the New Hampshire Medical Society, the state department of health and human services, the state department of education, the University of New Hampshire, the Injury Prevention Center at Dartmouth Medical School, the New Hampshire Coalition against Domestic and Sexual Violence, Educators for Social Responsibility, Dartmouth Hitchcock, the Children and the Living Earth Initiative, Alvine High School, MediaOne (the cable service provider), and many parents, teachers, public television executives, youth organizations, and law enforcement officials. In a recent Seeing though Media Violence initiative, MediaOne supported a poster and video contest for New Hampshire's school children. The posters expressed a variety of concepts, including "Media Violence Is: Not Fun"; "Prevention: Watch Less TV"; "Watch Nonviolent Programs"; "Watch/Read with Parents"; and "Be Aware That It's Not Real." Community-based initiatives such as these are certainly steps in the right direction.

Conclusion

Media violence has been established as a contributing cause of youth violence in our society. The media industry has for decades contributed to the problem of violence and for the most part denied proven effects and failed to take responsible action to contribute to solutions. Recent public reawakening to the problem of media violence has increased the stakes for both the industry and the public. Growing public concern has stimulated a flurry of media initiatives, proposed policies, public health initiatives, parent-teacher strategies, and community actions—all designed to help remedy the problem of media violence. The best of these initiatives have begun to produce higher levels of understanding and responsible action by both the media industry and the media user. They are designed to build on rather than to limit the guarantees of the First Amendment as well as assume the responsibilities outlined in the Federal Communications Act, the Children's Television Act, and the Telecommunications Act.

To date, no single initiative has achieved overwhelming success in producing comprehensive and sustained change. Taken together, however, these initiatives signal the beginning of a growing movement in the United States that may very well lead to fundamental change in our society's relationship to media violence. In reference to E. B. White's statement at the opening of this chapter, we have at long last begun to prepare ourselves for this important test of our modern world.

Nearly forty years ago, Newton Minow made his first speech as the newly appointed chairman of the FCC, addressing the nation's television broadcasters. His speech will always be remembered for two words that he used to characterize television programming: "vast wasteland." He had intended instead to have it remembered for two different words: "public interest." Once again, Minow has called on the television industry to fully serve the public interest by raising its vision and its standards for responsible action:

> To me, the public interest meant, and still means, that we should constantly ask: What can television do for our country? For the common good? For the American people?
>
> What you gentlemen broadcast through the people's air affects the people's taste, their knowledge, their opinions, their understanding of themselves and of their world. And their future . . . . The power of instantaneous sight and sound is without precedent in mankind's history. This is an awesome power. It has limitless capabilities for good—and for evil. And it carries with it awesome responsibilities—responsibilities which you and I cannot escape . . . . I urge you to put the people's airwaves to the service of the people and the cause of freedom. You must help prepare a generation for great decisions. You must help a great nation fulfill its future.[73]

Notes

1. E. B. White, quoted in Ernest Boyer, "Opening Remarks," in John Y. Cole, ed., *Television, the Book, and the Classroom* (Library of Congress, 1978), pp. 11–13.

2. Brad J. Bushman and L. Rowell Huesmann, "Effects of Television Violence on Agression," in Dorothy G. Singer and Jerome L. Singer, eds., *Handbook of Children and the Media* (Thousand Oaks, Calif.: Sage, 2001), pp. 223–54; Edward Donnerstein, Ronald G. Slaby, and Leonard D. Eron, "The Mass Media and Youth Aggression," in Leonard D. Eron, Jacqueline Gentry, and Peggy Schlegel, eds., *Reason to Hope: A Psychological Perspective on Violence and Youth* (Washington: American Psychological Association, 1994), pp. 219-50; Aletha C. Huston and others, *Big World, Small Screen: The Role of Television in American Society* (University of Nebraska Press, 1992); Robert M. Liebert and Joyce

Sprafkin, *The Early Window: Effects of Television on Children and Youth* (Pergamon Press, 1988); National Institute of Mental Health, *Television and Behavior: Ten Years of Scientific Progress and Implications for the Eighties*, vol. 1, *Summary Report* (U.S. Department of Health and Human Services, 1982); National Institute of Mental Health, *Television and Behavior: Ten Years of Scientific Progress and Implications for the Eighties*, vol. 2, *Technical Reviews* (Washington: U.S. Department of Health and Human Services, 1982); Ross D. Parke and Ronald G. Slaby, "The Development of Aggression," in Paul H. Mussen, ed., *Handbook of Child Psychology*, vol. 4, 4th ed. (Wiley, 1983), pp. 547–641.

3. Brad J. Bushman and Craig A. Anderson, "Media Violence and the American Public: Scientific Facts versus Media Misinformation," *American Psychologist*, vol. 56 (2001), pp. 477–89; Ronald G. Slaby, "Combating Television Violence," *Chronicle of Higher Education*, vol. XL, no. 18 (1994), pp. 1–2; Donnerstein, Slaby, and Eron, "The Mass Media and Youth Aggression," pp. 219–50.

4. John Cloud, "Special Report: School Violence; Just a Routine School Shooting," *Time*, May 31, 1999, pp. 34–39.

5. Kenneth Turan, "Time for a Cease-Fire before the Hellfire," *Los Angeles Times*, August 22, 1999, p. 8, calendar section.

6. "Special Report: School Violence," p. 33.

7. Surgeon General's Scientific Advisory Committee on Television and Social Behavior, *Television and Growing Up: The Impact of Televised Violence* (Government Printing Office, 1972).

8. P. M. Boffey and J. Walsh, "Study of TV Violence: Seven Top Researchers Blackballed from Panel," *Science*, vol. 168 (1970), pp. 949–52; D. Cater and S. Strickland, *TV Violence and the Child: The Evolution and Fate of the Surgeon General's Report* (New York: Russell Sage Foundation, 1975).

9. Surgeon General's Scientific Advisory Committee, *Television and Growing Up*.

10. National Institute of Mental Health, *Television and Behavior*, vol. 1.

11. National Institute of Mental Health, *Television and Behavior*, vol. 2.

12. N. Abeles, "Proceedings of the American Psychological Association for the Year 1984," *American Psychologist*, vol. 40 (1985), pp. 621–53.

13. Huston and others, *Big World, Small Screen*.

14. H. M. Hoberman, "Study Group Report on the Impact of Television Violence on Adolescents," *Journal of Adolescent Health Care*, vol. 11 (1980), pp. 45–49.

15. Centers for Disease Control and Prevention, "Prevention of Violence and Injuries due to Violence," in *Injury Control: Position Papers from the Third National Injury Control Conference: Setting the National Agenda for Injury Control in the 1990s* (Atlanta, Ga.: Centers for Disease Control, 1992).

16. Ronald G. Slaby, "The Lessons Children Learn from Televised Violence," National Parent-Teacher Association Hearing on Television Violence, Portland, Oregon, February 1977.

17. National Association for the Education of Young Children, "NAEYC's Position Statement on Violence in the Lives of Children," *Young Children*, vol. 48 (1993), pp. 80–84; Ronald G. Slaby and others, *Early Violence Prevention: Tools for Teachers of Young Children* (Washington: National Association for the Education of Young Children, 1995).

18. Newton N. Minow, "How Vast the Wasteland Now?" (Columbia University, May 9, 1991), p. 12.

19. Craig A. Anderson and Karen E. Dill, "Video Games and Aggressive Thoughts, Feelings, and Behavior in the Laboratory and in Life," *Journal of Personality and Social Psychology*, vol. 78 (2000), pp. 772–90.

20. Donnerstein, Slaby, and Eron, "The Mass Media and Youth Aggression," pp. 219–50.

21. L. D. Eron, testimony before the Senate Committee on Governmental Affairs, 102 Congress, 2 sess., *Congressional Record*, vol. 138, no. 88 (June 18, 1992), S8538.

22. Bushman and Huesmann, "Effects of Television Violence on Aggression," pp. 223–54; L. Rowell Huesmann and others, "Stability of Aggression over Time and Generations," *Developmental Psychology*, vol. 20 (1984), pp. 1120–34.

23. Bushman and Huesmann, "Effects of Television Violence on Aggression," pp. 223–54; Huston and others, *Big World, Small Screen;* Parke and Slaby, "The Development of Aggression," pp. 547–641.

24. George Gerbner and others, "TV Violence Profile No. 8: The Highlights," *Journal of Communication*, vol. 27 (1977), pp. 171–80.

25. D. K. Osborn and R. C. Endsley, "Emotional Reactions of Young Children to TV Violence," *Child Development*, vol. 42 (1971), pp. 321–31.

26. Margaret H. Thomas and others, "Desensitization to Portrayals of Real-Life Aggression as a Function of Exposure to Television Violence," *Journal of Personality and Social Psychology*, vol. 35 (1977), pp. 450–58.

27. Donnerstein, Slaby, and Eron, "The Mass Media and Youth Aggression," pp. 219–50.

28. Senator Paul Simon, "Family Violence and the Media," National Conference on Family Violence, Health and Justice, Washington, D.C., March 1994.

29. "Is TV Violence Battering Our Kids? New Study, New Answers," *TV Guide,* August 22, 1992.

30. Daniel R. Anderson and others, "Watching Children Watch Television," in G. Hale and M. Lewis, eds., *Attention and Cognitive Development* (Plenum Press, 1979), pp. 331–61.

31. John Condry, *The Psychology of Television* (Hillsdale, N.J.: Lawrence Erlbaum Associates, 1989).

32. "TV Is Top Medium for Children," *Boston Globe,* November 18, 1999, p. C20.

33. Ronald G. Slaby, "Combating Television Violence,"*Chronicle of Higher Education*, vol. 40, no. 18 (1994), pp. B1–2.

34. George Comstock and H. Paik, "The Effects of Television Violence on Antisocial Behavior: A Meta-Analysis," *Communication Research*, vol. 21 (1994), pp. 360–65.

35. Roger N. Johnson and Gordon W. Russell, "Violence and Suffering on Canadian versus American Network Television News." Conference presentation, International Society for Research on Aggression, Banff, Canada, June 1990.

36. *National Television Violence Study: Executive Summary, 1994–1995* (Studio City, Calif.: Mediascope, 1995).

37. Slaby and others, *Early Violence Prevention.*

38. L. Rowell Huesmann and others, "Longitudinal Relations between Children's Exposure to Television Violence and Their Later Aggressive and Violent Behavior in Young Adulthood: 1977–1992," Conference of the International Society for Research on Aggression, Mahwah, New Jersey, July 1998.

39. Kate Hendrix and Ronald G. Slaby, "Cognitive Mediation of Television Violence in Adolescents," Conference of the Society for Research in Child Development, Seattle, Washington, April 1991.

40. Ronald G. Slaby, "The Gender Concept Development Legacy," in Dawn Schrader, ed., *New Directions for Child Development: The Legacy of Lawrence Kohlberg,* vol. 47 (San Francisco: Jossey-Bass, 1990), pp. 21–29.

41. D. B. Luecke-Aleska and others, "Gender Constancy and Television Viewing," *Developmental Psychology,* vol. 31 (1995), pp. 773–80; Diane Ruble, Theresa Balaban, and Joel Cooper, "Gender Constancy and the Effect of Televised Toy Commercials," *Child Development,* vol. 52 (1981), pp. 667–73; Ronald G. Slaby and Karin S. Frey, "Development of Gender Constancy and Selective Attention to Same-Sex Models," *Child Development,* vol. 46 (1975), pp. 849–56.

42. Katrina G. Henchman, "Sex-Typing as a Predictor of Adolescent Responses to Television Violence," Ed.D. dissertation, Harvard University, 1994; Hendrix and Slaby, "Cognitive Mediation of Television Violence in Adolescents."

43. Rita M. Triviz, "Gender Salience over Ethnicity in First Graders' Identifications," Ed.D. dissertation, Harvard University, 1987.

44. Slaby, "Combating Television Violence," pp. 1–2.

45. Sissela Bok, "TV Violence, Children, and the Press: Eight Rationales Inhibiting Public Policy Debates," discussion paper D-16 (John F. Kennedy School of Government, Harvard University, April 1994), pp. 201–24.

46. S. Hearold, "A Synthesis of 1,043 Effects of Television on Social Behavior," in George Comstock, ed., *Public Communication and Behavior,* vol. 1 (San Diego, Calif.: Academic Press 1986), pp. 65–113; Marie-Louise Mares, *Positive Effects of Television on Social Behavior: A Meta-Analysis,* report series no. 3 (Philadelphia: Annenberg Public Policy Center of the University of Pennsylvania, June 17, 1994); Comstock and Paik, "The Effects of Television Violence on Antisocial Behavior," pp. 360–65.

47. Ronald G. Slaby and Gary R. Quarfoth, "Effects of Television on the Developing Child," in Bonnie W. Camp, ed., *Advances in Behavioral Pediatrics,* vol. 1 (Greenwich, Conn.: Johnson Associates, 1980), pp. 225–66.

48. Brian S. Flynn and others, "Prevention of Cigarette Smoking through Mass Media Intervention and School Programs," *American Journal of Public Health,* vol. 82 (1992), pp. 827–34.

49. Slaby, "Combating Television Violence," pp. 1–2.

50. Ronald G. Slaby, "This We Know: Media Violence Effects and Remedies," Public Television Producers' Forum, Corporation for Public Broadcasting, Washington, D.C., February 1995.

51. Bill Moyers, *What Can We Do about Violence?* Public Broadcasting Service series (New York: Public Affairs Television/WNET, 1995).

52. Milton Chen, *The Smart Parent's Guide to TV Violence* (San Francisco: KQED, 1997).

53. Harvard Community Health Plan Foundation, *Think: Violence Is for People Who Don't* (Boston: WBZ-TV and Radio, 1995).

54. Daniel R. Anderson and Patricia A. Collins, *The Impact on Children's Education: Television's Influence on Cognitive Development,* Working Paper 2, OR-55-507 (U.S. Department of Education, Office of Educational Research and Improvement, 1988).

55. Ronald G. Slaby, Gary R. Quarfoth, and Gene A. McConnachie, "Television Violence and Its Sponsors," *Journal of Communication*, vol. 26 (1976), pp. 88–96.

56. American Psychological Association, *Violence and Youth: Psychology's Response*, vol. 1, *Summary of the American Psychological Association Commission on Violence and Youth* (Washington: 1993), p. 77.

57. For useful and detailed information about how to use the new system, see Bobbie Eisenstock and Cathryn D. Borum, *A Parent's Guide to the TV Ratings and V-Chip* (Washington: Center for Media Education and the Henry J. Kaiser Family Foundation, 1999).

58. Joan Dykstra, "TV Rating System Doesn't Go Far Enough, PTA Says," *Colorado PTA Bulletin* (February/March 1997), p. 2.

59. Ibid.

60. Eisenstock and Borum, *A Parent's Guide to the TV Ratings and V-Chip*, p. 3.

61. *National Television Violence Study: Executive Summary.*

62. Joseph Lieberman, "Senate Unanimously Passes Lieberman Plan to Protect Kids from Media Violence," May 12, 1999 (www.senate.gov/member/ct/lieberman/general/r051399a.html [March 6, 2002]).

63. Joseph Lieberman, "Lieberman, Leading Public Figures Issue 'Appeal to Hollywood' for Higher Media Standards," July 21, 1999 (www.senate.gov/member/ct/lieberman/general/r072199b.html [March 6, 2002]).

64. See National Institute of Mental Health, *Television and Behavior*, vol. 2, and especially Daniel S. Solomon, "Health Campaigns on Television," pp. 308–21.

65. American Psychological Association, *Violence and Youth*, p. 78.

66. W. Andrew Collins, B. L. Sobol, and S. Westby, "Effects of Adult Commentary on Children's Comprehension and Inferences about a Televised Aggressive Portrayal," *Child Development*, vol. 52 (1981), pp. 158–63; Joan E. Grusec, "Effects of Co-Observer Evaluations on Imitation: A Developmental Study," *Developmental Psychology*, vol. 8 (1973), p. 141; David I. Hicks, "Effects of Co-Observer's Sanctions and Adult Presence on Imitative Aggression," *Child Development*, vol. 39 (1968), pp. 303–09.

67. Leonard D. Eron, "Interventions to Mitigate the Psychological Effects of Media Violence on Aggressive Behavior," *Journal of Social Issues*, vol. 42 (1986), pp. 155–69.

68. Kevin M. Burke, *Flashpoint: Life Skills through the Lens of Media Literacy* (Salem, Mass.: Eastern District Attorney's Office, Commonwealth of Massachusetts, 1997).

69. American Academy of Pediatrics. "See No Evil Pledge," April 26, 1999 (mm-team@listesrv.aap.org [March 6, 2002]).

70. Jeanne Gaz, "Tackling TV Violence," *American Medical Association Alliance Today* (March/April 1996), pp. 4–7.

71. Carol Bellamy, "Address to the International Conference on Violence on the Screen and the Rights of Children," Lund, Sweden, September 26, 1995.

72. Ronald G. Slaby, "Statement to UNICEF: International Children's Day of Broadcasting" (Newton, Mass.: Education Development Center, 1996).

73. Minow, "How Vast the Wasteland Now?" pp. 9, 33.

12

MARK H. MOORE

Creating Networks of Capacity: The Challenge of Managing Society's Response to Youth Violence

THE RECENT EPIDEMIC of youth violence has created a crisis in many of the nation's communities. The problem is both frightening and disheartening.[1] The drive-by shootings that have become emblematic of the problem have frightened those living near the epicenter of the violence. Repeated funerals of fifteen-year-old gang members have made many others despair of the kind of country ours has become. What makes the crisis feel especially urgent, however, is not just that the problem itself is bad; it is also that the institutions we rely on to deal with the problem do not seem up to the task. Their failure may stem from the fact that, as a society, we have failed to invest enough in efforts to raise our children—that, in an important sense, "America hates its children."[2] How else could we tolerate the conditions in which children are now being raised? Yet, a fair appraisal would reveal a wide array of institutions—some private, some public; some federal, some local; some dedicated to social service, some to criminal justice—that are now helping children navigate the transition from infancy to adulthood without being victimized or victimizing others.[3]

That array of institutions begins with the family—with parents who naturally assume (or guardians who are assigned) the responsibility for raising children. It includes the admittedly imperfect network of welfare support, including prenatal care and early childhood education, that helps the nation's neediest children to get off to a reasonably healthy start.[4] It includes an array of laws and institutions designed to guard children from abuse and neglect.[5] It includes publicly financed educational and recreational opportunities. And when all else fails, it includes the agencies of the criminal justice system—the police, prosecutors, defense attorneys, courts, and correctional agencies, including the specialized parts of that system that deal with juvenile offenders and with abuse and neglect of children.

So there is at least a wide if not a dense network of institutions in which society has invested a substantial amount of hope, public money, and state authority to guide children toward responsible citizenship. That network can fail to produce satisfactory results, of course. And when it fails, one reason for the failure may be that the overall social investment in the institutions is too small or is badly allocated across the network, with too much going to reactive criminal justice interventions and too little to preventive social service investments. But there may also be a problem in the *performance* of those institutions.

The performance problem comes in two different forms. On one hand, each institution may be failing in its own sphere of operations and on its own terms. Faced with today's economic pressures, parents and guardians may not be giving their children consistent enough attention and guidance to make sure that they develop properly. The welfare system may not have figured out how to combine assistance with incentives to enable poor but competent parents to give their children the time and attention they need.[6] Prenatal care may fail to reach enough young mothers to ensure that their children are born with a reasonable chance for success.[7] The child protection system may not only fail to respond appropriately to children who have been abused and neglected, but it may also fail to do what is necessary to prevent abuse and neglect in the first place.[8] Preschool programs may fall short of preparing kids for learning in school.[9] The schools themselves may be bad.[10] The criminal justice system may respond both ineffectively and unjustly to crimes committed by and against children.[11] And so on.

On the other hand, the institutions may not be coordinating and combining their efforts in ways that could magnify their separate effects. It may be that public agencies are not intervening in the lives of children in ways that support rather than erode the competence of caretakers and their motivation to do their work. It may be that service gaps yawn wide along the path of child development, with the result that investments at both early and later stages of development are lost because nothing is available at some particular stage—say, the ages between one and four or between ten and fifteen. It may be that instead of working collaboratively to both prevent and respond to youth violence, social service, public health, and criminal justice agencies are struggling with one another to establish their separate approaches as the only effective and just responses to the epidemic of violence.[12]

All is not lost, however. In the tradition of Americans facing a serious national problem, individuals, associations, governments, and agencies have made efforts to respond to the challenge of escalating youth violence.[13] Many communities have rededicated themselves to the effective care and guidance of their children. Many government agencies—federal and local, social service and criminal justice—have begun the painful process of searching for more effective responses to youth violence.[14] Throughout the country, individuals and groups, acting on their own or prompted by political and public sector leaders, have sought to build "networks of capacity" that can respond effectively to youth violence precisely because they cross the boundaries of existing organizations. Assembled in these networks of capacity are

—public-private partnerships that link community-based and government organizations in new ways;

—interagency collaborations that restructure working relationships among government agencies at a given level of government; and

—federal/state/local government partnerships that seek to create more effective partnerships vertically across levels of government.

The aim of these networks is not just to create a broader response to youth violence, but a more considered and effective one—one that uses all the capacities at hand more effectively and that meets the distinctive needs of particular clients in particular contexts.

The purpose of this chapter is not to answer the question of whether these new networks and the strategies they adopt are more or less effective in dealing with youth violence than those that came before. We will assume that they are, and point to the many examples offered in the other chapters of this book as plausible evidence, if not proof, of that claim. The aim, instead, is to explore the managerial challenges in creating and using these networks as either a supplement or an alternative to more traditional aggregations of single-agency responses. Those challenges are significant. As one wag commented, "Interagency collaboration is an unnatural act undertaken by nonconsenting adults." In the case of youth violence prevention, the difficulty of acting across agency boundaries is compounded by the difficulty of operating across the boundaries that divide community groups from government and one level of government from another.

Yet, a body of literature and some accumulating experience offers guidance on how to meet those challenges. This chapter reviews that literature and experience, beginning with a more analytic approach to the problem: why it is that we are now trying to address youth violence through networks of capacity rather than single organizations? The chapter next reviews literature on cross-functional teams in business organizations and experience with community-based crime prevention efforts here and abroad; it then concludes with suggestions on how to maximize the effectiveness of the emerging networks.

Youth Violence as a Managerial Challenge

To size up the managerial challenge posed by animating and sustaining an effective social response to youth violence, one has to understand what makes the problem of youth violence so difficult. The answer is straightforward, I think: both the problem and the institutional arrangements through which we try to address it are complex. The problem is complex because it has many different parts that interact in unknown and unpredictable ways. As a result, it is hard to know which part of the problem offers significant leverage to those trying to solve it. The institutional arrangements are complex because many different agencies feel that they have sole or primary responsibility and capacity to deal with the problem of youth violence. That may be valuable insofar as it means that many different actors are committed to making a contribution. Yet, problems can arise if the efforts they make are so uncoordinated that the ultimate impact is less than the sum of its parts. And the price of coordinating the efforts can be very high—particularly when, as is often the case, the actors come to the problem with widely varying values and ideas about what constitutes a humane, effective, and just response.[15]

The Complexity of the Problem

Both natural intuition and social science investigations tell us that youth violence is a complex problem that arises from varied causes at many different levels. For example, when one gang member kills another in a drive-by shooting, we can see the causes of that event in

—the individual propensities of the "shooter" (including psychological attributes that make him particularly aggressive or leave him numb to the consequences of his actions).

—the family and social background of the youth, which may have contributed to that that propensity. For example, the youth may have been a victim or witness of violence in his own family, or he may have experienced with his parents the painful and shameful experience of being poor and unemployed and discriminated against.

—the influences of a gang culture that makes such violence a virtue and sets up powerful norms that require gang members to play out particular roles on pain of excommunication if they fail to do their "duty."

—the past failures of social service agencies to transform the conditions in which families are living, working, and raising children by providing both economic opportunities and protection from abuse and neglect.

—the present failures of criminal justice agencies to deal effectively with recurrent disputes among gangs, to make themselves a reliable instrument of justice for gang members who feel that they have been wrongly victimized by others, or to establish a powerful normative order that is intolerant of violence and imposes just punishment if its norms are broken.

We can also sense that the causes operate not only at different levels of society but also with varying degrees of force and generality. The "root causes" of youth violence might lie in economic and educational factors, such as the lack of prospects for economic advancement in unskilled jobs; in a national culture that exalts competition and violence as a means for achieving one's ends; or in the rage engendered by relentless racial discrimination. Yet, a particular violent incident may have been triggered by far more local and temporary events: a chance meeting of two rival gang members at a time when tensions were high because of an unavenged attack by one gang on another.

The fact that different causes are operating at different levels with different degrees of force and generality raises the important question of which of those causes is the "best" target for intervention. Note that in this context "best" has a complex meaning. By "best" we often mean "most effective"—the intervention that is likely to produce the most and the most enduring effect, regardless of the cost of mounting the intervention. But "best" could also mean the response that is fairest, or most just, or most humane. It could also mean the response that produces the most value for the money—the biggest "bang for the buck." The cost, in turn, could be measured in terms of either money or state intrusiveness in citizens' private affairs.

To many, it seems obvious that the best responses to youth violence are those that focus on the root causes of the problem because such responses lead to the broadest and most enduring effects. Those effects, in turn, constitute a "real solution" to the problem rather than a "mere palliative," and a "real solution" relieves society of the necessity of maintaining the capacity to cope with the problem in the future. Yet, it is at least logically possible (and, given recent experience, it seems increasingly plausible as an empirical reality) that interventions that focus on less fundamental causes can also have an important effect. For example, a community-based or criminal justice intervention that focused specifically on the immediate circumstances of a gang shooting might have been effective in preventing that particular shooting. Enough of such microinterventions in minor occasions for violence could well produce, in the aggregate, a level of violence far below the level expected given the broader social factors that shaped the aggregate propensity for violence.[16]

The difficulty is that we really do not know enough about the interactions of these variables. It is natural to make a simplifying assumption— that the causes of violence are independent and additive, with each variable contributing its particular influence to the overall level of violence. It is also natural to assume that some of the variables will have bigger effects than others and that those constitute the best target for intervention. But however satisfying those assumptions might be to William of Occam—and to social scientists who would like to rely on the techniques of multiple regression to understand the root causes of crime—the reality may be quite different. It may be that the causal variables interact in complex rather than simple ways, so that the effects of a change in one variable may be either significantly reduced or exaggerated by changes in other variables. For example, a community could get a lot poorer but still have less violence if its members shared a strong cultural commitment to nonviolence sustained by a strong partnership among community groups, faith-based organizations, schools, and criminal justice agencies. In contrast, a few violent incidents, occurring almost accidentally within a short period of time, could so traumatize a community that violence could temporarily spin out of control despite the fact that nothing much had changed in the overall socioeconomic condition of the community.

If youth violence has many causes, operating at different levels in society and interacting in complex and nonlinear ways, then it becomes apparent why a "portfolio" of interventions becomes the favored social response. First, if it is true that the causal variables interact in complex ways, then the effects of combinations of interventions—of strategies consisting of bundles of programs—may be quite different from the effects of single programs. For example, while a school-based program for teaching children techniques of nonviolent conflict resolution may have little impact if the children are continually exposed to violence in their homes, it could have a large impact if it was paired with programs to reduce domestic violence. In a similar manner, a program designed to protect infants from violence in their homes may have little impact if they are later exposed to violence in schools, but programs that work to control violence in both places throughout childhood could have a significant cumulative effect.

Second, because we cannot be sure which programs will actually reduce violence, it may be prudent for a community not to put all its eggs in one basket. Uncertainty about future economic returns motivates many investors to accumulate a portfolio of diverse investments rather than invest in a single stock or economic sector. Similarly, uncertainty about the effectiveness of different youth violence interventions leads communities to invest in portfolios as well. There is a price to be paid for depending on a portfolio, of course. Just as some stocks will not perform, so some programs will not work, and we will regret having spent money on the things that did not pay off. Moreover, if a portfolio of interventions seems to produce a result, it may be difficult to determine which of the interventions did the job. But, given the state of uncertainty about what would actually succeed and the belief that the system is a complex one, it is probably wise for communities to invest in portfolios despite those costs.

Third, portfolios of responses are valuable because they allow many different people and agencies to contribute. A broad strategy consisting of many different components has the desirable effect of increasing the overall scale of the effort. Variety also guarantees that many potentially promising avenues of attack will be explored. It also tends to increase the overall legitimacy of and political enthusiasm for an intervention. All that is to the good. But many people worry that broad responses to a problem are potentially wasteful and run the risk of losing their focus. The alternative they imagine is one in which, instead of attacking a problem scatter-shot, we commit our main force to an approach that we know will work. In their view, what is missing from many social interventions is precise knowledge of "what works" and, rather than try many things, we should wait until we have a great deal of knowledge.

That idea, too, makes sense. But it makes sense in a context in which we view resources and knowledge as the factors limiting our ability to effect social change. From that point of view, because resources are scarce, we have to develop knowledge about what works to ensure that our limited resources are used most effectively. But one can also imagine a context in which the scarce resource is not knowledge of what works, let alone what works best. Instead, what is scarce is the will and capacity to act. In this view, if there is enough will and capacity to act, limitations on both resources and knowledge might be overcome. In effect, we can solve the problem with the scale and urgency of our action—doing lots of things that do not work, but also many things that do.

Obviously, if many people are willing and able to act on a problem but want to act on the problem in different ways, then a framework that authorizes and enables them to act in a more or less coherent way is more valuable than one that discourages them from making the contribution they want to make. Their contribution to the scale and development of an intervention that targets a previously neglected variable might be just what is needed to tip the system toward a significant reduction in violence. In the country of the blind, a one-eyed person might be king, but that king might be enormously aided by many others groping with their hands.

The Complexity of Institutional Arrangements

The institutional arrangements through which society addresses the problem of violence are equally complex. One must recognize at the outset that much of the work of raising children is done by the private institutions of family, community, and church. Indeed, so much of that work is performed by those institutions that very small decreases in their productive capacity could result in very large increases in the portion of work done by public agencies. The work of public agencies therefore must be to ensure that the work of keeping children free from violence remains primarily within private institutions, while strengthening those institutions when they falter and substituting for them in the small number of cases in which they fail completely.[17] This is no mean feat. Efforts to aid struggling families may end up either strengthening the family by providing additional assistance or weakening the family by relieving them of the full responsibility for the care of their children.

The public agencies that have a role to play are distributed across all levels of government. At the federal level, money raised through income taxes is spent on both direct operations and transfers of funds to different levels of government. Direct operations sometimes focus on altering national conditions that create the context for local problems, such as federal efforts to control the national supply of drugs and guns, and sometimes they attack local problems directly, such as through federally supported enforcement programs that target serious, habitual youthful offenders. Transfers sometimes come in the form of block grants allocated by formula, some-times in the form of discretionary grants allocated according to the merits of the proposals received. The state and local levels of government have their own revenue sources, and they can tap voluntary contributions of time and money from foundations, corporations, and individuals. With those funds, they pay agencies to do work that has an effect on youth vio-lence, whether or not that is its primary purpose. They also support net-works of community-based organizations (and, increasingly, church groups) that also contribute to the prevention and control of youth violence.

Public agencies also are distributed across the functions of government. One way to think about the functions of government is to consider their purpose and target populations. Some government programs focus on the economic development of poor neighborhoods, some on preparing work-ers for employment, some on providing income support to those who are temporarily or permanently out of the job market, some on preventing domestic violence and spouse abuse, some on maternal and child health, some on guarding against child abuse and neglect, some on preschool readiness, some on schooling, some on prevention and control of juvenile delinquency, some on providing recreational opportunities to young peo-ple and teenagers, some on managing the transition from school to work, and some on dealing with gang violence. Obviously, some of those func-tions focus much more directly on the problem of youth violence than others, and some are more closely tied to the individuals who become involved in youth violence, either as victims or perpetrators. But all might play an important role in preventing as well as responding to instances of youth violence.

A slightly different way to think about the functions of government, however, is to divide programs into those that deliver *services* to clients and those that impose *obligations*. Much of government is involved in the deliv-ery of services to particular clients whose needs are considered important to fulfill. We provide low-interest loans to community-based organizations that want to start businesses or build housing in poor neighborhoods. We provide employment training to those who are unemployed. We provide income support to those who are unemployed or unemployable. And so on.

But another part of government is involved in imposing duties on citi-zens.[18] Through the child protection system, we remind parents and care-takers that they must refrain from abusing and neglecting their children or lose their parental and custodial rights or even face jail terms if they fail to perform their duties. Through the juvenile justice system, we remind both

children and their parents that it is wrong for children to attack the lives
and property of others and to engage in conduct, such as truancy or
promiscuity, that threatens their future as independent and resourceful citizens.[19] Through the adult criminal justice system, we respond to acts of
violence committed by young people as crimes and impose significant jail
terms on those who commit such crimes.

In one tempting conception of government crime control programs,
one approach to youth violence is primarily social science oriented; it both
provides services and prevents violence. A second approach, more law
enforcement oriented, both imposes obligations and reacts to violations of
them. A little reflection suggests that this is not quite accurate or useful,
however. After all, imposing obligations has a potentially important *preventive* effect—not only on the person who becomes the subject of state
attention, but also on others, through the example set. The "thin" version
of this preventive effect is "deterrence," the altering of the behavior of an
individual by threatening punishment for misconduct.[20] The "thick" version of the effect includes "norm creation" and "informal social control."
The idea of "thick deterrence" comprises a determined effort to rationalize
and legitimize the principles behind the threats that constitute the thin
form of deterrence. "Thick deterrence" also seeks to engage many others in
the community in imposing more frequent, milder, and more informal
sanctions against those who are edging toward serious offending.[21]

There might also be an important role for "service delivery" in *reacting* to
instances where misconduct has occurred. The response to a family that has
abused and neglected its children might well include significant service
components: alcohol treatment for dad, treatment for depression for mom,
baby-sitting to provide parents some relief from the rigors of raising children, and special after-school education programs for the kids. The response
to a juvenile offender can and usually does involve services as well as jail sentences. Although such interventions come only after at least one offense has
occurred (and in that sense have failed to be fully preventive, even with
respect to the particular individuals involved, to say nothing of society as a
whole), they are nonetheless capable of preventing future offending.

The public health community has a useful way of classifying programs
that points up the idea that some programs are preventive and some reactive. They distinguish among "primary," "secondary," and "tertiary" prevention programs. Primary prevention programs target the broad social
conditions that enable but do not directly or automatically cause a particular problem. Secondary programs focus on individuals who are at

particularly high risk of being affected by some social or health problem. Tertiary prevention programs come into play after an event has occurred or a condition has emerged, and they seek to both minimize losses and guard against recurrence of the problem.

In the context of youth violence, a primary prevention program might be one that reduces social disadvantages in communities, strengthens maternal and child health services, transforms a culture that favors violence, or reduces the general availability of guns. A secondary program might be one that seeks to reduce the level of violence in families that have a history of violence between spouses or between parents and children or one that works to mediate emerging conflicts among gangs. A tertiary prevention program might be one that responds to gang conflict with a sustained effort to incarcerate the "shooters" and engage the community in counseling the others to refrain from future acts of violence, in their own and the community's interest.

So one can usefully think about the array of government programs along several different dimensions: which level of government finances or operates them, what their focus is and who their client populations are, whether they deliver services or impose obligations or do both in some combination, and where they stand in the chain of prevention. Given the complexity of the problem of youth violence and the virtue of having a portfolio of approaches to deal with it, the complexity of the government structure is a potential aid rather than a hindrance. There are different platforms and approaches that will inevitably produce a portfolio of responses in any given locale. The challenge, of course, is to find some way to use the capabilities of different government programs, in conjunction with those of private institutions, to mount the most effective social response to youth violence.

Building and Deploying Networks of Capacity

The challenge of developing the most effective response to youth violence becomes in turn the challenge of building self-conscious "networks of capacity" that can take the uncoordinated operations of different agencies and turn them into a more or less coherent and well-understood strategy for action that can be implemented successfully. Of course, one can have different degrees of ambition in building a network. The degree of ambition can be measured in terms of the *scope* of the effort and the *depth* and *intensity* of the coordination achieved across agencies.

With respect to scope, for example, one could, at one end of the continuum, try to coordinate the full array of programs that have any impact on youth violence in a city. Somewhere in the middle, one might try to coordinate the activities of community groups, school officials, and criminal justice officials in responding to violence among junior high school and high school students. At the opposite extreme, perhaps, one might try to coordinate the activities of criminal justice agencies responding to emergent gang violence. While these conceptions involve some degree of cross-boundary coordination, the first idea involves a far greater need for coordination than the second, and the second is probably much more demanding than the third. In general, the greater the number of agencies involved, the more distant their relationship to the problem of youth violence, the more ideologically diverse their commitments and professionally diverse their approaches to the problem, and the greater the challenge of coordinating the efforts.

With respect to the depth and intensity of the coordination desired, one can rely on a framework developed by Steven C. Wheelwright and Kim B. Clark that distinguishes four different levels of integration in team structures designed to cross organizational boundaries.[22] Level 1 is the status quo: independent agencies act alone, without explicit or self-conscious coordination, affecting observed levels of youth violence. Level 2 is the "lightweight team structure": a project manager emerges who is responsible for some kind of coordination across agency boundaries but has influence with only a few of the agencies that are supposed to be part of the network. Level 3 is the "heavyweight team structure": the project manager has effective working relationships with all agencies that are defined as important in the network. Level 4 is the "autonomous team structure": the parts of the independent agencies that are particularly important to the amelioration of the problem are essentially independent of the explicit control of their agency and fully integrated in a coherent operation led by the project manager.

Obviously, there is a huge difference in the leadership and management required to create the kind of "parallel play" that occurs at level 1 and that required to create the kind of focused, sustained, and largely autonomous effort that characterizes level 4. One might assume that the goal is always to reach level 4, and once having reached level 4, never again to retreat to level 1. But that need not be true. How closely a cross-boundary enterprise needs to collaborate depends crucially on how much synergy exists among the components of the network. If much of the desired effect on youth violence comes from having a certain number of programs operating at about the right scale—with little need to make fine adjustments in how each component operates or to integrate their operations at particular times or in the lives of particular clients—then one can get away with the loosest forms of coordination. On the other hand, if the desired effects can be achieved only by integrating the diverse components tightly with one another, then higher levels of coordination are required. If one needs high levels of coordination for a long time, then it might make sense to create a new organization that combines the various components under one unified authority.

For purposes of this analysis, we will assume that the scope of the effort and the depth and intensity of the coordination needed to deal effectively with youth violence lie somewhere between the extremes outlined above. This means that we are squarely in the realm of looking for some of the benefits of cross-agency collaboration, for a long enough time to make a difference in the problem, but we are not committed to creating a special new office for youth violence prevention and control. It is the managerial challenge of constructing this kind of coordination that we need to address.

The Management Literature on Networks of Capacity

Fortunately, over the last several decades, some literature has developed on managing networks of capacity. It has come from the business world, from the world of public administration and management, and from the more specialized world of crime prevention.

The Business Literature: Cross-Functional Project Teams

In concept and perhaps in operation, private sector management has always been a bit simpler than public sector management. In the private sector, we know what is to be managed: the assets of a particular firm. We know who is to manage those assets: the chief executive officer. We also know the purposes for which those assets are to be managed: to maximize the wealth of those who own the assets. And, although uncertain judgments have to be made about the specific products or market strategy that would best achieve that goal, the private sector has always had the advantage of being able to rely on its bottom line to tell it relatively quickly whether the bets it made paid off.

In contrast, the object of management in the public sector is much less clear. Public sector organizations exist, of course. And, to some degree, they look like bundles of assets to be managed just like those in the private sector. In the public sector, however, we tend to think that the focus of management should not be on how best to use an organization but instead on how best to deal with particular problems. We focus on the management of *policies* to deal with problems, rather than on the management of *organizations* to get the most value from them.

It is significant, I think, that the relationship between managing organizations and managing policies is not entirely clear. Sometimes, we think of public sector organizations as nothing but bundles of policies and programs initiated to solve particular problems. In this view, public sector organizations have no life, no reason to exist apart from their role as implementers of the policies and programs they were created to implement. They are not pieces of capital built up over time that might serve purposes other than those for which they were originally created. They are simply the means to certain ends. Other times, we think of policies and programs as activities that cut across the boundaries of organizations. Indeed, to the extent that this is true, one can understand immediately why cross-boundary partnerships might be important in government.

Not only is it unclear what is to be managed in the public sector, it also is unclear who is in charge of managing. Again, there are people who are designated as "managers" of public sector organizations. But their grip on their organization is far looser—and the amount of discretion they are granted in managing it much less broad—than that of their counterparts in the private sector. They expect to be "micromanaged" by elected officials, who may be motivated to interfere in their affairs by stories in the press.[23] Since often the terms of appointed public sector managers are short, they expect their organizations to be a little less responsive to them, and their employees have many ways of resisting their leadership.[24]

It is also unclear for what purposes public sector organizations are to be managed. Their purposes are supposed to be set out in the legislative mandates that define the policies and programs to be administered by the agency. But legislative mandates typically leave important conflicts about the purposes of the organization unresolved and hand them over to the manager to solve as best he or she can.[25] But because the resolution will always be imperfect, the manager will always be vulnerable to criticism from one quarter or another that weakens his or her control over agency operations. Finally, while it is possible to construct measures to evaluate the performance of public sector organizations, typically those measures are less precise and the evaluations less persuasive and far more expensive to arrive at than the private sector's bottom line.[26] As a result, public sector managers learn later and less perfectly about what they have accomplished than private sector managers do.

Given the relative simplicity of private sector managers' job, it is particularly significant that one of the problems they have found difficult to handle is that of the cross-boundary team. Paul Lawrence and Jay Lorsch heralded the problem in an article in the *Harvard Business Review* in 1967.[27] In a study of ten firms, they discovered that the firms were having a hard time coping with the need to respond quickly to changing market conditions and to exploit new technologies. The firms had committed themselves in the past to developing and refining specialized capabilities used to achieve economies of scale; when it became necessary to adapt the old processes to exploit new opportunities, the firms were sluggish and slow. Since the typical problem was to bring a new product on line in a functionally based organization, the authors described the problem as one of "integrating" the different functional units to develop new products or to exploit new production technologies. They defined "integration" as

> the achievement of unity of effort among the major functional specialists in a business. The integrator's role involves handling the non-routine, un-programmed problems that arise among the traditional functions as each strives to do its own job. It involves resolving interdepartmental conflicts and facilitating decisions, including not only such major decisions as large capital investments, but also the thousands of smaller ones regarding product features, quality standards, output, cost targets, schedules and so on.[28]

They also noted that the integrator's role was being performed by individuals with many different titles, and they took the proliferation of titles as a clear indication of the need for this particular function to be performed:

> In recent years there has been a rapid proliferation of such roles as product manager, brand manager, program coordinator, project leader, business manager, planning director, systems designer, task force chairman, and so forth. The fine print in the descriptions of these jobs almost invariably describes the core function as that of integration as we define it.[29]

Other business writers picked up the theme, focusing not only on the function but also on the techniques that managers were using to perform the function. One technique that attracted a great deal of attention at that time was "project management," an elaborate method of planning and scheduling the steps required to execute a project. John Stewart, a McKinsey consultant, describes the problem to which "project management" was the solution:

> The essence of project management is that it cuts across and in a sense conflicts with the normal organizational structure. Throughout the project, personnel at various levels in many functions of the business contribute to it. Because a project usually requires decisions and actions from a number of functional areas at once, the main interdependencies and flows of information in a project are not vertical, but lateral.[30]

He also noted that while some private sector organizations operated wholly in a traditional functional mode, there were others—specifically, in the construction and aerospace industries—that operated entirely in the project mode.[31] Stewart then went on to define three guidelines for successfully managing projects that cut across the functional boundaries of private firms:

—*Guideline 1*. Define the objective: characterize the intent, scope, and desired end result of the project.

—*Guideline 2*. Establish the project organization: Identify and authorize the project manager; limit the team to work with the manager to the smallest number needed to accomplish the task.

—*Guideline 3*. Install project controls: Develop a detailed schedule of activities with assigned responsibilities and deadlines.

Both articles noted the difficulty that the designated project manager would have in carrying out the project successfully in organizations dominated by functional organizational structures. The managers would be temporarily outside the ordinary lines of organizational authority; they also would take themselves off the established career track in the organizations for which they worked. They would be held accountable for achieving a result without exclusive control over the resources needed to achieve it. They would be in a position to make trouble for their colleagues who remained in charge of functional units by taking resources from them, interfering in their operations, or complaining to top management about their unwillingness to cooperate on the project. All those factors made the job somewhat risky and the individual who took it vulnerable to internal attack.

Lawrence and Lorsch then examined some of the temperamental attributes and interpersonal skills that distinguished successful from less successful project managers. They concluded that successful "integrators" were
those who were seen as "contributing to important decisions on the basis
of their competence and knowledge rather than on their positional authority" and who demonstrated a well-developed "capacity for resolving inter-
departmental conflicts and disputes."[32] They thought that the key personality traits of successful integrators included a higher need for affiliation
than for achievement but a high need for both. They were people who
liked working with others and were willing to share the credit for the team's
accomplishments. They took the initiative and were aggressive and confident, but they also were persuasive and verbally fluent, flexible, and
humorous.[33]

The authors also identified three distinct modes of behavior in resolving
the inevitable conflicts that arose in executing a project.[34] One was "confrontation." In this mode, the integrator put all the facts on the table and
kept the team working until members reached an agreement about how
they were going to proceed. The second was "smoothing." In this mode,
the integrators emphasized the importance of maintaining friendly relationships among team members and avoiding conflict. The third mode
was "forcing." In this mode, the project integrator used all his formal and
informal authority to decide the matter. In the authors' view, "confrontation" seemed to work best.

Subsequent authors have examined the development of project teams
that cut across organizational boundaries in private companies and come to
similar conclusions about the importance of project teams to the success of
organizations, the difficulties of creating and sustaining such teams, and
the personal styles of leadership and collaboration that make the teams
successful. Richard Hackman, reviewing the literature on project teams in
business, identified the following conditions as important in ensuring their
success:[35]

—A *real team* whose task and composition remains bounded and stable
over time, that understands that it is working interdependently for a common goal, and that has the authority to manage its own work and internal
processes.

—A *clear, engaging direction* that focuses on ends to be achieved rather
than the means to achieve them.

—An *enabling team structure* that includes a motivating team task; a
small number of people with the right combination of knowledge and

skills for the task and demonstrated interpersonal skills; and clear norms of conduct that keep attention focused on the work and promote the accountability of team members to one another.

—A *supportive organizational context* that includes a reward system for performance; an educational system that provides for training and assistance; an information system that supports planning and performance; and sufficient material resources to perform well.

One last thing to note about the literature on teams in business enterprises: teams have been used to manage many different kinds of projects. Most commonly, they have been used to overcome the weaknesses of functional organizations in making the investments necessary to bring new products to markets quickly.[36] As that need has become more widespread, organizations have changed their structures: they have shifted from *functional* organizational structures to organizational structures focused on *products* and *customers*. Currently, teams are used most often to improve production processes in order to guarantee quality in existing products and services. Less common is the need for a project team to ensure the quality of an individual product or transaction. The image here might be that of a hospital in treating a patient. The team is required to ensure not only the quality of an individual service (say, coronary bypass surgery) but also that of a stream of subsequent services to the patient (drug therapy, exercise regimen, instruction of the family in the care and support of the patient, and so forth). To do that, sometimes a manager of the capabilities of the hospital as a whole is needed to ensure the quality of the product to the individual consumer.

The Public Management Literature: Cross-Boundary Management

A large and eclectic literature on "cross-boundary management" in the public sector has grown up alongside the literature on "cross-functional teams" in the private sector. While the literatures are similar in many respects, an important difference lies in the nature of the organizational boundary to be crossed. As noted above, the literature on private sector project teams begins with a *firm* as the unit of analysis. The firm may be smaller or larger; it may be a start-up or a well-established enterprise; it may be operated as a "production line" or a "job shop"; it may be highly centralized with tight controls or decentralized with independent profit and loss centers; it may produce a single product or be a multiproduct conglomerate. Nevertheless, the unit of analysis is usually the same—the firm. And one important characteristic of a firm is that somebody is in charge:

somebody with the accountability and authority to manage all the firm's assets.[38]

In the private sector, the key boundaries to be crossed are usually those that divide functionally defined subunits within the organization. Those boundaries typically are crossed when, first, top management recognizes the need to do so and then acts on that need by appointing project managers, providing fungible resources to the project team, and pledging its support of the project manager's efforts to enlist the efforts of subunits within the firm.

In the public sector, however, the unit of analysis is not necessarily a single organization. More commonly it is a social problem to be solved or a policy to be enacted. The work to be done to solve the problem or enact the policy is not the responsibility of a single organization, but of multiple organizations, including private and public entities. Here, three different types of organizational boundaries must be spanned: the boundaries that divide different levels of government, those that divide government from the private sector, and those that divide agencies of government at the same level. Those entities usually do not have a common superior; no coherent hierarchy of authority spans them; and no single person can command or authorize their joint effort. In principle, I think, that presents a harder management problem than the one faced by private enterprises trying to get new products to markets.

The managerial problem posed by the fact that many social problems cut across organizational boundaries became manifest in the late 1960s and early 1970s as the federal government undertook major initiatives to "keep the world safe for democracy" in the international sphere and to produce the "Great Society" at home. That problem continues to bedevil the successful management of large public sector enterprises, including efforts to respond to youth violence.

THE FEDERAL STRUCTURE AND IMPLEMENTATION ANALYSIS. The first important boundaries are those that divide different *levels* of government from one another: the federal from the state, the state from the local. Those boundaries, of course, were created in the Constitution, and they are more important in domestic policy (where the federal government typically is only one player on the field) than in foreign policy (where the federal government has more of a monopoly). But in the late 1960s, as the federal government sought to create the Great Society, its inability to operate successfully across these boundaries came to be seen as a major impediment to social progress.[39]

That, at least, was the major finding of a series of studies that examined the success of federal agencies in "implementing" national policies through state and local governments.[40] In studies of crime control, education, employment training, and welfare policies, it became clear that policies conceived and funded at the federal level looked very different when they emerged at the local level after crossing the many boundaries that divided the federal government from the state and local implementing agencies. The reason was simply that the federal managers of those programs had relatively little formal or informal power to insist on compliance with federal policies. Nor was there enough time and money to monitor implementation. Even when monitoring occurred and "problems" were found, lower-level governments could successfully resist federal intervention through both political and legal means. In essence, federal policy did not survive the passage from federal funding and policysetting agencies to state and local implementing agencies.

Analysts who studied the process of implementing federal polices searched for ways to ensure their more faithful execution. Some recommendations called for simplifying and clarifying policies that were to be implemented so that there was less room for confusion and obfuscation.[41] Others focused on closer monitoring and on the imposition of rewards for compliance and penalties for noncompliance. But the analysts gradually realized that their premise might have been false—that "success" in the implementation of a federal program did not necessarily mean faithful compliance with federal intentions and directives. Instead, success meant pushing things at the state and local levels in the direction that the federal government wanted to move, while negotiating with lower-level governments on what they thought was important to achieve and taking into account their judgment about the best means of accomplishing the desired ends.[42] In effect, the relationship between the federal government and the lower-level governments was not one of superior and subordinate; it was instead a relationship among partners in which each partner had its own purposes and each had its own resources and capabilities.

The challenge, then, was for federal, state, and local managers to figure out how far they were prepared to go in accommodating the others' interests and commitments. They learned to talk in terms of federal-state-local partnerships rather than in terms of the implementation of federal mandates. The inevitable result was a much more varied approach to a problem than the federal government first imagined. That variability strained the federal government's sense of propriety and accountability, and with that, its confidence that the states and localities were performing well. At the same time, it accommodated the constitutional reality that the states and localities were independent entities. It may also have produced local policies and programs that reflected local priorities better, took greater advantage of local capabilities, and responded more precisely to local needs. In effect, the different levels of government rediscovered the virtues of the "loosely-coupled" structures of federalism.[43]

MAXIMUM FEASIBLE PARTICIPATION, COMMUNITY ENGAGEMENT, AND PUBLIC-PRIVATE PARTNERSHIPS. The second boundary is the one that divides government from the private sector, including both community groups and businesses. Private partners are key to the success of public sector initiatives for several different reasons. First, to some degree, private partners often are the ones who are supposed to benefit from government efforts. When, as a matter of public policy, we decide that we would like to promote the economic or political development of a poor community or that we would like to help private enterprise maintain its competitive edge, we make private sector entities important "customers" and "intended beneficiaries" of government programs. It makes sense, then, for public sector organizations to attend to the private sector's needs and respond to its demands—in effect, to let its demands flow across the boundaries of public sector organizations. In this case, the satisfaction of the private sector is the public sector's goal.

Second, private sector agencies often are important "coproducers" of the results that government agencies are trying to achieve. If the government is trying to make communities safer, for example, its policing efforts will be magnified if it can partner successfully with community groups that are willing to accept some of the responsibility for defending their own communities against crime.[44] If the government is trying to educate children, it benefits from the cooperation of PTAs in mobilizing parents to commit themselves to supplementing classroom instruction at home. If the government is trying to reduce pollution without paying too high a price in terms of economic development, it needs to engage private sector firms in finding and implementing ways to do so.[45] To take advantage of opportunities for coproduction of desired results, public sector organizations have to find ways to develop formal and informal partnerships with the private sector.

Third, private sector entities are important in providing the legitimacy and financial support that government enterprises need to stay in business.[46] If citizens, acting as individuals or in groups, do not believe that the public enterprises they support create value, they will stop supporting them. With that, public organizations will become less effective. They will lack the money they need. They will fail to get the cooperation they need from citizens in pursuing their goals. And they will fail to enjoy the popularity that comes from being responsive to the needs of their "customers"— citizens who would like to use government enterprises for their individual and collective purposes.

In the late 1960s and early 1970s, those ideas were embodied in the notion of "maximum feasible participation" by poor communities in the design and execution of policies that affected them.[47] Putting that notion into practice turned out to be a struggle for local government agencies as they tried to learn how to simultaneously evoke an authentic community voice and respond to it. More recently, the idea has emerged that government should form "public-private partnerships" for everything, from child protection services, to education, to environmental protection.[48] Sometimes partnerships are structured as consulting groups of interested citizens attached to single- or multiple-agency initiatives. Other times, government agencies explicitly contract with private entities to accomplish public purposes through the process of privatization.[49]

INTERAGENCY COLLABORATIONS: MODEL CITIES AND SERVICES INTEGRATION. The third boundary to be managed successfully in public sector enterprises is the one that divides agencies of government at the same level from one another: for example, the gap that yawns wide between diplomatic, intelligence, and military organizations in the foreign policy domain; or the one that separates police departments, schools, and recreation departments at the local level. In many ways, the problem of interagency cooperation within the same level of government most resembles the problem faced by private sector managers. The fact that these agencies operate at one level of government suggests that they can be viewed as part of the same organization. Presumably, the state department, the CIA, and the defense department all work for the president, the "CEO" of the federal government. Similarly, the police department, the school department, and the recreation department all work for the mayor. Yet, even here there are important differences. For example, at the federal level, the president's command often is threatened by Congress, aided and abetted by agency interests of one kind or another. At the local level, mayors have their own struggles with city councils. In addition, however, they may not even have direct control over local schools, which often are guided by separately constituted and elected independent school boards.

Again, the difficulty created by the lack of interagency coordination was
first identified in the late 1960s and early 1970s, when discussions began
regarding the complexities of the "interagency process" in formulating and
executing foreign policy and the role of the National Security Council in
managing (as opposed to advising) foreign policy operations.[50] Foreign policy increasingly consisted of more than maintaining diplomatic relationships with individual countries on one hand and fighting declared, conventional wars on the other. Instead, in the diplomatic sphere, foreign
policy consisted of trying to accomplish U.S. purposes overseas through
increasingly complex multilateral agreements. In the military sphere, foreign policy increasingly relied on operations that were less than all-out,
declared wars and that seemed to require a demanding blend of diplomacy,
intelligence, and diverse military capabilities to succeed. In short, foreign
policy initiatives increasingly combined diplomatic, intelligence, and military capabilities, and each initiative required significant cross-boundary
coordination. The whole set of initiatives taken together also had to be
coordinated across the boundaries of the state department, the CIA, and
the defense department. No wonder the National Security Council became
active as the "integrator" of U.S. foreign policy.[51]

At the state and local level, two different concerns animated efforts to
encourage interagency coordination. One, closely associated with the
Model Cities program, was the idea that resources were misallocated across
agencies at the city or neighborhood level.[52] In this view, some problems
were more urgent than others, yet funding decisions failed to reflect their
urgency. Another view was that the productive synergy that could result if
government agencies interacted was being ignored. For example, the provision of new public housing required development of new social service
programs to ensure that the full benefits of the housing would be experienced and maintained over time. Yet, such important technical relationships were not captured in budgeting decisions. A housing program would
be undertaken without necessarily providing for the social services needed
to ensure that the families occupying the housing would be able to build a
social as well as a physical community. Efforts were therefore made (often
in conjunction with efforts to engage community groups) to improve the
allocation of resources.

A second concern was that services were not well integrated at the level
of the individual client, whether the client was an individual or a family.
The lack of integrated social services could be viewed from the client's perspective as a "service delivery" problem; in that view, it was needlessly
expensive and degrading for clients to have to find their way from one

office to another and to submit multiple applications for different programs. But it also could be viewed from the government's perspective as a
performance problem. Costs could be reduced if space costs could be
shared, application processes could be consolidated, and so forth. Performance in achieving social purposes could be improved if, instead of receiving separate, unnecessary services, clients could get the specific set of services they needed most to improve their social functioning.

To take advantage of opportunities to improve services to clients, lower
costs, and improve outcomes valued by society, social service agencies
sought to "co-locate" their services in the same building and to institute
"one-stop shopping" for their clients. They also sought to simplify the
application process for individual programs and to see the individual client
not simply as a client of a single program, but as a recipient of benefits
from many different programs who had a history with different government organizations. In many respects, the challenge of producing integrated social services by assembling services from many different agencies
is analogous to the problem that hospitals face in delivering high-quality
care to individual patients. It also is similar to the problem that the foreign
policy apparatus faces in trying to mount a successful foreign policy initiative. To succeed, they both have to integrate capacities distributed across
different organizational units to deliver a particular product that serves a
unique purpose. In this, they can also be likened to the "assembler" in a
McDonald's restaurant who moves across the separate production lines to
select the drinks, french fries, and sandwiches that constitute a particular
customer's order.[53]

Eugene Bardach completed a significant research project examining
nineteen cases of interagency collaboration in the public sector in order to
determine to what extent interagency collaborations were necessary to the
effective performance of government; what conditions favored the creation
and operation of successful interagency collaborations; and what kinds of
"craftsmanship" went into creating them.[54] Bardach found that such collaborations were often undertaken by government agencies, but he worried
that the emphasis on collaboration was animated by general enthusiasm for
that particular style of management, not necessarily by its value in improving performance.[55] Still, on reflection, he concluded that it was likely that
interagency collaborations were, in fact, much needed in government.[56]

Given that interagency collaborations were needed, it became important
to think about how they might be created and sustained and about what
would constitute a successful collaboration. Here, Bardach departed from
conventional thinking, focusing his attention not only on the specific

activities undertaken by the collaboration but also on its continuing capacity to mount initiatives of one kind or another. He called this the development of "interagency collaborative capacity" (ICC).[57] An enterprise with that capacity was in many ways like an organization in that it had a mission and might even have tangible resources such as personnel and money assigned to it. Yet, Bardach thought the ICCs were better viewed as "virtual organizations," because "when it is functioning properly, an ICC also has intangible resources such as the cooperative dispositions and mutual understanding of the individuals who are trying to work together on a common task."[58] He also noted that ICCs typically had both objective and subjective components:

> The objective component includes formal agreements at the executive level, personnel, budgetary, equipment, and space resources assigned to collaborative tasks; delegation and accountability relationships that pertain to those tasks . . . . The subjective component is mainly the relevant individuals' expectations of others' availability for and competence at performing particular collaborative tasks. These expectations, in turn, are often built around beliefs in the legitimacy and desirability of collaborative action directed at certain goals, the readiness to act on this belief, and trust the other persons whose cooperation must be relied upon for success.[59]

The fact that such collaborations were much needed did not mean that they would inevitably arise. Indeed, significant obstacles to their development existed. Bardach observed:

> [One] major barrier to taking on the collaborative challenge is that resources [such as talented and purposive people and flexible funding] are always scarce . . . . Agencies do not want to give up control over these resources lest their own traditional missions be compromised. Moreover, if a manager wants to work on creating value, creating collaborative capacity may not appear as promising a way to invest time and energy as fixing agency capacity to do its own internal, self-contained tasks better.[60]

He also noted that once a manager or an organization made a commitment to collaborate there was no guarantee of success:

> Working cooperatively is often much more complicated than it sounds. It involves reconciling worldviews and professional ideolo-

gies that cluster within agency boundaries but differ across them. Moreover, it is often difficult to align agencies' work efforts in the face of governmental administrative systems that . . . favor specialization and separateness down to the smallest line item."[61]

A central problem in creating and managing effective interagency collaborations was overcoming the problem of distrust. In his view, distrust was a "corrosive presence in the creative process that ICC partners are necessarily engaged in." Further, distrust often "stood in the way of legitimating a leadership role and sometimes of legitimating the entry of particular persons into a leadership role."[62] In his view, one of the key ingredients necessary to establish an effective interagency collaboration was the emergence of leadership:

> Finding and motivating talented individuals to do the leadership job is a big and important challenge . . . . [Indeed] One might say that in many of the cases when ICCs do not arise, it is not just because agencies do not wish to give up resources and protect turf, but that leaders have not arisen to help organize the potential partners.[63]

Yet, it was by no means obvious where such leadership would come from. As he observed:

> Public management and public administration have no theory about what evokes purposiveness—a combination of public-spiritedness and creativity—in some situations but not in others, or what form it takes when it is invoked.[64]

Bardach's research indicated a significant gap between the number of interagency collaborations established and the number of those sustained within government, and it located the reasons. Bardach also concluded that the most effective single factor in ensuring that collaboration would develop was the emergence of a kind of collective leadership in which a group of individuals, for no particular reason other than that they shared a sense of urgency about dealing more effectively with a problem, took on the substantial risks and burdens of engaging in collaborative problem-solving efforts.

The Crime Prevention Literature: Interagency Collaboration

More recently, and closer to the subject at hand, experience with interagency efforts to prevent crime, including youth violence, has developed as

criminal justice agencies have looked for ways to prevent as well as respond
to crime. When they turned their attention to preventing crime, they
quickly found that they needed to reach beyond their individual boundaries if they hoped to succeed. In order to do so, they had to both reshape
their organizations and build their overall capacity to manage relationships
across organizational boundaries. It is worth exploring each of those steps:
the shift to crime prevention, the need to reshape criminal justice institutions, and the keys to success in managing interagency initiatives.

THE CHANGING PARADIGM OF CRIME CONTROL. Throughout much
of history, the social response to crime has been largely reactive: we have
waited for crimes to occur and then sought to find and punish the perpetrator.[65] That approach was consistent with the aim of doing justice: it
called offenders to account for their crime. It was also consistent with the
valued goal of minimizing state intrusiveness: the substantial power of the
state to interfere in private affairs—to stop citizens on the street, to investigate their activity, to bring charges against them, and so forth—would be
used only when an actual crime warranted its use. It may even have been
effective in preventing some crimes—by incapacitating offenders who
would otherwise continue to commit crimes, by deterring potential offenders with the prospect of punishment, or by rehabilitating offenders who
were caught.

To many, however, that response did not fully exploit the potential for
preventing crime. Initially, the drive to prevent as well as react to crime
focused on the importance of eliminating its "root causes," which were
thought to lie in the very structure of American society: in its economic
inequity, its racism, its cultural predilection for violence, and so on.[66]
Indeed, it was important to solve those problems for many reasons besides
the wish to reduce crime, but the root causes proved stubborn. Gradually,
then, different approaches to crime prevention emerged that lay somewhere between the reactive and the root causes approaches to crime control.[67] As the crime prevention movement developed, three different ideas
took hold.

The first was the idea that crime could be prevented by intervening in
the social processes that produced future offenders, which is closest to the
traditional idea that the root causes of crime should be eliminated.[68] Prevention would involve intervening in the lives of young people who were
growing up in adverse circumstances in order to make their lives better by
protecting them from domestic violence, providing them with more immediate access to a good education, giving them appropriate role models and
mentors, and so forth.

This approach differs from the root causes approach in that its focus— children at risk of becoming future dangerous offenders and their families—is narrower. What made this narrower approach possible were two factors. The first was the development of indicators to help identify children and families that are particularly at risk.[69] Some of those indicators focus on the background of the children, such as living in poverty, coming from a broken home, or having antisocial or abusive parents.[70] Others focus on the behavior of the children themselves at early stages, such as misconduct in school or substance abuse.[71] The second factor was the development of interventions that seem to reduce the probability that such children would become offenders in the future. Both prenatal care and early childhood education seem to be able to deter at-risk children from taking paths that lead to dangerous offending.[72] It may also be true that mentoring programs and certain kinds of juvenile justice programs can succeed in deflecting the trajectories of these children.

The second preventive idea focuses not on intervening in the social processes that produce offenders but in the social processes that produce occasions for offending.[73] In this conception, criminal offending (and perhaps even the development of criminal offenders) can be reduced by reducing opportunities for offending. This approach focuses on intervening in "hot spots" where crimes seem to occur—such as bars, drug markets, housing projects, or disputed gang turf[74]—and an intervention could be any action that seems to be plausibly effective in controlling crime at a particular place and time. It could be a "directed patrol" to ensure a police presence at places and times where and when crimes are likely to be committed. Or it could involve a deeper, more preventive effort, such as using the licensing power of the state to insist on safer, more orderly conditions in bars; demanding that abandoned buildings that serve as shelters for drug dealers be razed; or evicting tenants whose violence has turned a housing project into a threatening place.[75] Crime prevention also could involve efforts to mediate the festering disputes within families, between landlords and tenants, between warring gangs, or between racial groups. It could involve other kinds of creative problem-solving initiatives that make situations that were once criminogenic less so.[76]

The third crime prevention idea focuses not on the target of the intervention (future offenders or opportunities for offending) but on the character of the intervening agent. This idea suggests that crime prevention can best be accomplished not through the formal social control exercised by the agencies of the criminal justice system but through the informal social control exerted by community residents, groups, and associations.[77] In one limited manifestation of this idea, the community becomes the eyes and ears of the criminal justice system, broadening and reinforcing its response to crime. In the broader view, however, it is the power of the members of a community to establish norms and sanction misconduct when they see it that actually does the work of regulating most social behavior.[78] If that energy can be mobilized and channeled to meet crime prevention objectives, then there may be less need for formal social interventions, whether they come from criminal justice or social service agencies.

Taken together, these three approaches add up to a paradigm for crime prevention that differs markedly from both an attack on root causes and a criminal justice response restricted to catching offenders. We have, instead, the idea of using community groups, social service agencies, and criminal justice agencies to intervene early in the lives of at-risk children and to use their collective powers to resolve problems that seem to be occasioning crimes in the community.

Organizing to Act in Accord with the New Paradigm

Because these new crime prevention opportunities involve collaborations across government agencies and between government agencies and community groups, they require new organizational forms. At the outset, that is a serious problem, for, as a British Home Office report on crime prevention observed, "At present crime prevention is a peripheral concern for all the agencies involved and a truly core activity for none of them."[79] Efforts to develop crime prevention capabilities face a dual challenge. On one hand, they have to build an interest in and capacity for focusing on crime prevention within existing organizations; on the other, they have to build the structures that keep the partnerships going.

With respect to building the necessary structures to prevent crime through existing agencies, criminal justice organizations are probably the most advanced. Among criminal justice organizations, the police are probably more advanced than prosecutors, courts, or correctional agencies. Most social service and community-based organizations do not start with a well-developed focus on crime prevention because that is not their principal purpose. On the other hand, many criminal justice agencies have begun to take an interest in finding ways to prevent crime besides arresting offenders. The police, in particular, have taken up efforts to prevent as well as respond to crime. They have focused on serious juvenile offenders, hoping to interrupt their progress toward adult serious offending.[80] They have concentrated problem-solving efforts on hot spots that seem to generate criminal activity.[81] And they have reached out to form community partnerships under the banner of community policing.[82]

Recently prosecutors and the courts also have experimented with efforts to prevent future crime as well as process the cases that come to them. Prosecutors have developed special offices to deal with family violence, and they have begun to consult communities to discern the impact that particular kinds of crime have on the community in order to adjust their prosecutorial priorities.[83] Judicial authorities have turned to drug courts and community courts to supplement the standard case processing that goes on in adult felony courts in an attempt to be more effective in preventing crime and reducing fear than they would be by relying on traditional models.[84] Now, corrections and probation officials also are considering the potential of crime prevention—not through more effective rehabilitation of offenders but through partnerships with communities that can help them both monitor and support offenders following their conviction or release from prison.[85] As a result, criminal justice agencies now have the inclination and the capability to lead and join crime prevention enterprises. But what kind of enterprises are available for them to join? England's Home Office has spent the last decade studying crime prevention efforts initiated under the Safer Cities Program, established in 1991. Nick Tilley, who evaluated many of those programs, described their typical administrative and organizational structure:

> Each project (27 Safer Cities Programmes) has three members of staff including a co-ordinator, an assistant co-ordinator, and a personal assistant. All are temporary appointments of people with a good knowledge of the area. In addition, each project has a steering group, drawn from local authorities, the private sector, voluntary organizations, and government agencies active in the area, though there are quite wide variations in who is included within this general framework. Care was taken to ensure where possible that there was ethnic minority representation. The project staff service the steering group
> . . . . [The steering group's] terms of reference are: a) to act as a focus for the local multi-agency crime prevention partnership; b) set priorities for the project and oversee the implementation of community safety measures; c) to facilitate contact and co-operation between local agencies and interests.[86]

Those responsible for initiating and leading cross-agency partnerships found the same difficulties that many others before them had found:

[P]articipants in multi-agency work are usually quick to recognize [that] agencies having an interest in crime prevention seldom share the same priorities, working practices, definitions of the problem, power, or resource base. While interagency relations . . . can obviously be both positive and productive, our research . . . suggests that they are also highly complicated, seldom static, and influenced by a variety of institutional, individual, and local/historical factors.[87]

For purposes of analyzing how the interagency initiatives were structured and worked, the British researchers Liddle and Gelsthorpe relied on five models of a cooperative relationship, each one representing a higher level of integration:
—the communication model (parallel play)
—the cooperation model (parties agree to work on a problem together)
—the coordination model (parties combine their resources but retain individual control of them)
—federation model (services are integrated)
—merger model (collective resources are pooled and allocated according to the purposes of the integrated group).[88]
They also made the important observation that levels of cooperation could vary dramatically across and between hierarchical levels in the partnership as well as across the different agencies. They noted that

a spirit of cooperation among representatives on a strategic level . . . might coexist with acrimonious relations at the line worker level . . . . Research conducted at the Cambridge Institute of Criminology . . . suggests that productive cross-agency links are sometimes accompanied by lack of support at higher levels, while in some crime prevention schemes of a more 'top down' sort high-level resolutions concerning interagency cooperation in a few cases ran into major difficulties at implementation levels.[89]

On the basis of several years of experience with these various initiatives, Liddle and Gelsthorpe presented their conclusions regarding the kinds of structure that were consistent with successful interagency collaborations, the number and types of participants to be included in the initiatives, the forms of leadership that were necessary, and the stages of development that many of the initiatives went through.[90]
With respect to *structure*, the team reached four important conclusions:

—Effective multiagency crime prevention cannot be undertaken in the absence of some form of structure, although that structure can vary in its level of formality.

—Informal multiagency structures can have the advantage of allowing for quick response, but they also tend to be less durable and less well-adapted to policy coordination than formal structures.

—Crime prevention measures delivered throught informal multiagency networking tend to be difficult to monitor and evaluate. Informal networking can also give rise to questions concerning accountability and confidentiality.

—Top-tier multiagency groups having jurisdiction throughout a local authority can maximize the benefits of multiagency crime prevention initiatives.[91]

With respect to the *number and character of participants*:

—Membership should be just broad enough to facilitate the intended crime prevention effort.

—Questions about community and ethnic representation require careful consideration by participants; those questions affect both the identity of the group and subsequent ownership of group actions.

—Imbalance in the bureaucratic rank of members can lead to tensions in the group and to higher-level members dropping out.

—Front tier (high-level) representatives are preferable, since they have the authority to commit resources. Lower-level actors are valuable in action/implementation, but they need support from upper levels if their engagement is to remain solid.[92]

With respect to *authorized leadership* :

—Perceptions about which agency is in the lead often vary considerably among participants; leadership tends to change over time.

—The concept of lead agencies sits uneasily with the more recent notion of "partnerships" in multiagency work because it suggests the creation of a hierarchy instead of a partnership.

—Some current crime prevention work is best described in terms of a corporate model, in which coordination, decisionmaking, and implementation of work are regarded for the most part as being the responsibility of the multiagency group as a whole.

—The corporate approach seems to be becoming more popular in the field of crime prevention?[93]

Liddle and Gelsthorpe were particularly interested in how leadership was sustained over time and in the way that the leadership acquired full capability in coordinating (in the sense of directing and controlling) the operations of a group whose members remained accountable to their home organizations. They judged this kind of direction and control to be "essential for effective multiagency crime prevention work" and the lack of adequate coordination to be "one of the most common difficulties encountered." They also thought that while coordination is "ideally provided through a dedicated individual, it can also be taken on by members of a multiagency group on a rotating basis, or by the group as a whole."[94]

The problem of creating and sustaining leadership in the initiatives studied was particularly difficult since many of the programs did not emerge organically from the communities in which they were operating. They were established by the Home Office. A crime prevention coordinator was then appointed, who faced the difficult problem of establishing himself or finding someone else who could exercise effective leadership of the group. Nick Tilley reached back to sociologist George Simmel's notion of a "stranger," someone who would have special advantages and disadvantages in exercising leadership, to hold the crime prevention initiatives together:

> According to Simmel, a stranger is someone who is in but not of a particular social setting, close and far at the same time. The stranger can achieve, and be seen to achieve a kind of objectivity. The stranger enjoys the freedom which flows from independence from the restraints of membership in indigenous institutions. The stranger is often asked to arbitrate disputes. The stranger can act as a go-between. The stranger can enjoy trust, being detached from the interests at play inside a social setting. The stranger is not part of the hierarchies of those amongst whom he or she moves and can thus connect with them at various levels. What is not entailed by this, however, is any particular behavior on the part of the stranger; rather the position presents different opportunities and constraints from those which obtain for the insider . . . . Safer Cities Projects can be understood as stranger institutions, and their staff as embodiments of that stranger status.[95]

This model also influenced Tilley's understanding of how crime prevention initiatives might develop over time. He saw five distinct phases:
—1. The suspicious incomer: building trust
—2. The honest broker: building motivation/capacity

—3. The necessary catalyst: building structure

—4. The faithful servant: nurturing structure/strategy

—5. The guest who stayed too long: exiting.[96]

Finally, Tilley developed a "set of guidelines [drawn from the experience of sixteen Safer Cities sites] formulated for the sake of clarity and directness as 'rules'."[97] In publishing the guidelines as rules, he cautioned the reader to bear in mind three important limitations: "First, that to date progress everywhere is limited—no fully worked-out exemplars were found among the Safer City areas; second, that only Safer Cities were examined; third, this was a quick piece of work."[98] The guidelines for developing local crime prevention strategies are summarized and paraphrased below for an American audience:

—Do not expect immediate acceptance.

—Make and maintain contact with key policymakers.

—Foster network development among agencies.

—Take special care not to alienate local political authority or the police.

—Diagnose the local setting in terms of politics, personalities, structure, and finance.

—Expect and accept the commitment of agencies to their particular mission.

—Become substantively knowledgeable in crime prevention.

—Develop the credibility of the idea of crime prevention.

—Start with "low-hanging fruit."

—Keep in touch with operations at point of delivery; be aware of actions, not just agreements.

—Engage the public.

—Use a pincers approach: both bottom up and top down.

—Frame approaches to align with agencies' existing goals.

—Be alert to situations in which the potential for effective joint action is undermined by lack of confidence that a necessary partner will cooperate, and when such situations are found, move to ensure trust.

—Work with existing crime prevention partnerships.

—Develop competence and interest in partner agencies through discussion, shared work, and training.

—Get publicity and share credit.

—If the initiative gets stuck, either because partners cannot figure out what works or because they become locked in conflict, bring in new outsiders.

—Exploit opportunities at the national level.

—Align sources of data.

—Be patient in developing the strategy to be pursued by the partnership.[99]

Lessons for the Management of Strategies for Preventing and Responding to Youth Violence

What does all of this literature have to say about the managerial task of mounting an effective response to local outbreaks of youth violence in communities across the country? The general conclusion is that it is hard. It is hard not just because no institution by itself can solve the problem; it is hard primarily because it is difficult to mount and sustain an initiative that draws on assets and capabilities distributed across different institutions. The literature reviewed above provides many hints about how to maximize the chances of success, however. It might be helpful to organize those different ideas in a simple, overarching conception to guide those who manage such initiatives.

The Strategic Triangle

In other work on public sector management, a relatively simple concept has proven to be remarkably useful—the "strategic triangle," first developed at the Kennedy School of Government.[100] It was originally created as a guide on how to position an entire public organization in its particular environment. It turns out to be equally useful, however, when used to position a subordinate unit of an organization or, more relevant to our purposes here, to consider the feasibility of a particular policy initiative and the steps needed to ensure its effective implementation. The triangle, illustrated in figure 12-1, points to three calculations that leaders and managers must make as they commit themselves and their organizations to particular purposes. One point of the triangle focuses attention on the "public value" that they are seeking to produce. In the case of youth violence, it would be a reduction in the rate at which young people become victims or perpetrators of violence. It might also be a reduction in any events that contribute to violence, such as drive-by shootings (regardless of whether anyone is injured), or perhaps even in the existence of violent gangs. One could also think of the value of reducing the level of fear in both the youth and adult populations, including those close to the violence and those further removed. Those things might be valued as means to the end of reducing violence through prevention, or they might be valued as ends in themselves because they are intrinsically more pleasurable than their opposites.

Figure 12-1. *Strategy in the Public Sector*

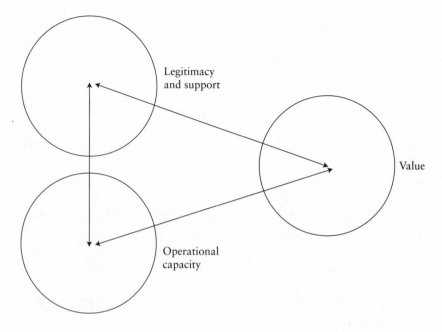

Legitimacy
and support

Value

Operational
capacity

The second point of the triangle focuses attention on the legitimacy of and support for a particular initiative. The diagnostic question is simply this: where will the resources—the money, the people, the energy, the continuing support—needed to achieve the goal come from? Often, money is the important issue. But in many initiatives to control youth violence, the important resources may be instead the willingness of partners to contribute resources that they already have to the goals of the initiative. Families have to refocus on supervising their children and preventing easy access to weapons. Church leaders have to use their considerable powers of moral suasion to help mobilize informal social controls designed to reduce violence. Schools have to stop denying the reality of violence in their classrooms and schoolyards and find effective ways of responding to it, with or without the help of police departments. And so on.

It is hard to legislate coalitions into existence. It is easier to put some money on the table to start a coalition or for someone in authority to authorize someone else to organize one. But those are hardly foolproof methods. Many antiviolence initiatives that begin with a grant or the appointment of a violence prevention czar will fail. Many others will succeed without that kind of support. It is by no means obvious what resources are required to sustain the commitment of a loose coalition. However, what seems to be crucial in sustaining an enterprise long enough to make a difference is the effective use of information about the scope and nature of the problem. That information is important first in dramatizing the significance of the problem and galvanizing people into action. It is important second in finding plausibly effective points of intervention. And it is important third in monitoring the coalition's efforts and accomplishments in dealing with the problem. In effect, it is the promise of the value to be realized through a sustained initiative that is crucial in mobilizing support, and a vivid display of that value, based on solid information, does the work of mobilizing the required material resources.

Public initiatives often need more than money and other kinds of material resources; those focused on responding to youth violence, in particular, often need the authority of the state to make arrests and prosecute those accused of civil and criminal violations. And if the formal authority of the state is complemented by the emergence of informal social controls whose aims are closely aligned with those of the state, the impact of an initiative often can be reinforced. It is one thing for an alien police force to sweep through a housing project arresting people whom the police judge to be threats to the community. It is quite another for the community itself, because it feels responsible for maintaining order within its own sphere, to ask the police for assistance in protecting it from an individual whose drug dealing and extortion have terrorized residents for months.

To magnify the effect of state action, whether that action provides services to or imposes obligations on citizens, it is necessary to earn the consent and support of the community as well as to have a continuing flow of money, material, and people. In effect, the enterprise needs legitimacy in the eyes of those affected, and it needs the capacity to exert formal and informal social control as well as to provide services of various kinds.

The third point of the triangle focuses attention on the operational capacity of an initiative to achieve the desired results. It is one thing to have an attractive purpose; it is another to have enthusiastic support and a supply of resources dedicated to achieving that purpose; and it is quite another to build the actual operational capacity needed to get the job done. This is partly a matter of knowing which interventions might have an effect; it is also a matter of using that knowledge to turn the flow of fungible resources into actual operations that produce results. Note that this point of the triangle is labeled "operational capacity" rather than "organizational capacity" because in the public sector, managers nearly always must try to supplement the capabilities of the organizations they lead with contributions from other agencies. For example, if one is trying to keep the streets clean, one can deploy a fleet of garbage trucks and street sweepers. But it is also valuable to persuade citizens to take their garbage to the curb in sealed containers, to refrain from littering, and to sweep their own sidewalks. Similarly, if one is trying to educate children, one can concentrate on classrooms, teachers, and curriculums. But those efforts are nearly always more effective if parents can be engaged to persuade children to do their homework faithfully. If it is important for a single organization to enlist outside agencies in the "coproduction" of its mission, it is particularly important to do so when one is trying to assemble a coalition to prevent and control youth violence. In this case, no single organization has the principal "operational capacity" needed. Instead, the required operational capacity is distributed across various organizations, and the managerial challenge is to consolidate and apply it to achieve the desired results.

The strategic triangle indicates that in initiating an antiviolence initiative, it is important to address the value to be produced (and how to measure it); the legitimacy and support needed to mount and sustain the enterprise; and the operational capability necessary to achieve the result. But *all* of those issues must be addressed in a consistent way or the enterprise as a whole will fail. There may be significant public value to be produced by mounting an antiviolence initiative, but that does little good if those with the resources needed for the effort do not agree. Similarly, the purpose may be attractive and the resources necessary to produce the result may be plentiful, but without an effective program, the enterprise will fail.

The Locus of Initiative and Leadership

In presenting the strategic triangle as a simple planning and management tool, I have implicitly assumed that someone or some group has taken or accepted the responsibility to do something to control youth violence—that leadership has emerged or managerial accountability for undertaking an initiative has been established. Yet, as noted above, one of the problems that must be overcome in creating such initiatives is to find someone, or some group, to take that kind of responsibility.

A leader, or a leadership group, could arise spontaneously among those concerned about the problem. That leadership could emerge among the people most affected by the violence—the families of the victims or the youths themselves—or it could emerge among those who feel close to them—for example, community or church leaders, schoolteachers, or coaches. It also could emerge among people who feel a professional responsibility for the problem, such as city council members, mayors, police officers, or prosecutors. Alternatively, the leadership role could be assigned to someone by a responsible government official. The attorney general of the United States, for example, could ask U.S. attorneys to take responsibility for mounting a youth violence program in their areas of responsibility, or a mayor could establish a youth violence task force. However the leadership emerges, one could say that leadership is a necessary, but not necessarily sufficient, component of an effective antiviolence initiative. We are accustomed to thinking that leadership is essential and that only an individual who has been formally and informally authorized to exercise leadership can do so. Yet it may be unreasonable to expect that form of leadership in producing youth violence initiatives, and it may not be particularly helpful.

It is important to consider how concentrated, stable, and formal the leadership must be for the enterprise to succeed. The evidence seems to suggest that successful initiatives are produced by groups whose leadership changes over time rather than those that have only one stable leader. There may be a need for a continuing presence and sufficient institutional memory to support the work of an interagency initiative, but that comes more often from someone in a staffing and enabling role than from someone who stands out front as the formal leader. One can hypothesize that the strongest form of leadership for an interagency initiative would be one in which

—the chairperson has significant formal and informal authority but not a particularly strong agenda of his or her own;

—enabling staff record the agreements reached by the group and check on the execution of the agreed-upon actions; and

—a group of people with purposes and resources of their own voluntarily commit themselves to a combined effort in the belief that it will be more effective than they would be on their own.

In effect, leadership takes the form of a forum in which value-creating deals can be struck among independent actors. The glue that holds the enterprise together, in the absence of formal authority, comes from

—some degree of shared commitment to dealing with the problem;

—some recognition of operational interdependence; and

—a whole lot of creative deal making, in which the deals are public and the parties' reliability in living up to the deals is made apparent.

Individual members' sense of accountability to the team for doing what they say they will do to deal with the problem takes the place of the formal authority of a "boss."

Creating the Governing and Operating Structures

Once a leader or leadership team takes or is given the responsibility for action, the leadership must figure out who else needs to be involved, either as authorizers or as doers. This is an important strategic calculation that focuses on
—the number of principals in the enterprise
—the hierarchical level of the principals
—the cultural divides that exist within the team.

Obviously, if one wants to mount a truly comprehensive attack on the problem of youth violence, one is tempted to reach for a large number of high-level people. One is also tempted to view cultural divides—such as those that might exist among community groups, business leaders, and government officials or between social service and criminal justice agencies—as problems to be solved rather than as fundamental differences that might actually threaten the effectiveness of the initiative. But, again, the evidence seems to indicate that there are real limits to the number of people that can be involved in a coherent partnership, especially when it is getting started. The basic operating principles seem to be the following:

—First, the partnership should include those people who can commit the kind and level of resources needed to make some significant dent in the problem. Otherwise, the partnership will find itself unable to act.

—Second, if one is tempted to create a large and diverse group of principals, one must recognize that the cost of staffing and sustaining the partnership will increase dramatically and the speed with which it can act will decrease. That is probably especially true if the partnership has its own resources to allocate, because conflicts over funding priorities may threaten the cohesiveness of the group.

—Third, it may be best to balance the interest in authorization with the desire for fast action and reliable execution by creating different partnerships at different levels. In the foreign policy world, for example, it is customary to pair a high-level group of principals who commit their collective authority to support an interagency initiative with a lower-level working group that actually implements the initiative.

Because potential participants might be committed to both a particular purpose and a particular way of achieving it, the desired overall strategy of the partnership guides the leadership group in deciding which principals to include. For example, if a youth violence task force is composed largely of police, prosecutors, and judges, in all likelihood the problem will be defined as one of dangerous offenders and youth gangs and the most appropriate intervention as the arrest and prosecution of those involved. If, on the other hand, a youth violence initiative is rooted in the school system or in community groups, the definition of the problem and the solution might be quite different. However, once the members of the group begin to work with one another to solve the problem, the overall strategy of the group might begin to change. As the strategy changes, the group may decide to include different people; it may even decide that some people who were originally included are no longer needed. So, while the initial set-up is important and probably exercises a profound effect on the path that a youth violence initiative takes, it is not set in stone. It adapts and changes over time.

Negotiating and Coordinating Interests and Actions

If a youth violence initiative is in fact a group of interdependent actors held together by a more or less shared commitment to the group's goal and some sense of operational interdependence in achieving that goal, then much of the effectiveness of the group will depend on the skill that each member has in negotiating agreements with his or her colleagues about what they will do to achieve it. Negotiating agreements with peers is different from both directing and controlling subordinates and being directed and controlled by a boss. Negotiating in front of an audience that expects a good-faith negotiating effort and reliable execution also is challenging. Creating favorable conditions for making deals and reliably executing them is probably the primary task of those who assume the responsibility for keeping the enterprise going.

While this sort of mutual contracting capability may be difficult to create in the beginning, it may very well get easier over time and as the partnership records some successes. At the outset, the parties to the negotiation may not know what they can count on from one another, in terms of either negotiating style or reliability in living up to agreements. Some may enter the negotiating process with a great deal of suspicion; that suspicion, in turn, may drag out the negotiations and prevent valuable deals from being struck. Once a few deals are done, however, the overall contracting capacity of the group might go up significantly. Members may become more adept at coordinating their negotiating styles and more confident that, once made, a deal will be honored. Indeed, over time, the group's approach might change from deal making to joint problem solving. At that stage, the overall performance of the group should dramatically improve and the rate at which it adapts, innovates, and shares resources should go up dramatically.

The Role of Information Systems

An information system that can monitor both the state of the problem and the efforts made to solve it is essential to the success of an interagency partnership. Accurate information about the state of the problem helps keep the problem in sharp focus, reminding the partners why they came together and what they are trying to accomplish. Partnerships also need some evidence of success to stay together. To the extent that the data describing the problem reveal some desired results, the feedback helps sustain and expand the capacity of the group to act. Information on actions taken by the partnership to deal with the problem also is important because each member needs to know what other members are doing in order to be confident that everyone is pulling his own weight and living up to the agreements made. Both kinds of information may have external importance as well. Public initiatives such as a youth violence partnership are always broadly accountable to the public, and their actions and accomplishments will be reported by the media. If the partnership has been funded by foundations, other donors, or higher levels of government, the funders may demand an accounting of the group's actions and accomplishments—or they may simply respond favorably if that information is provided. In addition, the partnership itself may value the public's favorable perception of its work and benefit from making itself publicly accountable. For all these reasons, the partnership must pay special attention to the development of its information processing capabilities.

Project Management Skills

The development of significant project management skills, like the development of negotiation skills and high-quality information systems, is important in an interagency partnership. Project management requires the ability to translate negotiated deals into a set of scheduled activities to be undertaken by members of the team. Ideally, these activities could be shown in some sort of chart. The chart would provide a handy way of indicating what key pieces of information would have to be collected to show whether members of the partnership had in fact taken the steps they promised to take to further the goals of the partnership. Such a chart would also provide a graphic illustration of the interdependence of the independent members of the group. A strong sense of interdependence, in turn, would help create the sense of mutual accountability that substitutes for formal authority in the group. It is hard work to create and keep a schedule of activities, with assigned responsibilities, up to date. But such a device is very effective in keeping an interagency team focused on the work that they need to do *together* instead of the work that their home agency plans for them to do in addition to their interagency work. Along with the creation of a first-rate information processing capacity, the development of a schedule might be the most important job for those who staff the interagency collaboration over time.

Conclusions

There are strong reasons for relying on collaborations that span the boundaries dividing levels of government from one another, agencies of government from one another, and private agencies from government agencies in efforts to deal with youth violence. Such collaborations are necessary to legitimize, fund, equip, and operate the complex strategies that are most likely to succeed in both controlling and preventing the problem. The difficulty, however, is that collaborative efforts are expensive, fragile, and unreliable. Moreover, their development and management requires not only a different outlook, but also different managerial skills from those needed in established, hierarchical organizations. They need people who take responsibility rather than wait to have it assigned to them; people who are good at finding and exploiting value-creating deals among peers rather than supervising subordinates; people who are committed to using information about efforts and results instead of complying with procedures; and people who are fanatic about operational details and living up to agreements rather than people who cover up conflicts and disagreements by being vague about their commitment. If such people can be recruited or developed, then the cost of interagency partnerships will go down and their robustness and effectiveness will be dramatically enhanced.

The United States has always been able to rely on its citizens and officials to respond to important public problems when they emerged. It has always been able to rely on a resourceful commitment to practical experimentation to find solutions to problems that initially seemed intractable. We have plenty of evidence that such an approach can work as we face the problem of dealing with youth violence. The challenge facing those of us who care about and act upon the problem is to accelerate the rate at which we are able to learn from our experience. We must document what we have done, share it with others, and reflect upon and talk about what we have learned—not only about which programs seem to work, but also about the leadership and management questions that face those who try to initiate and sustain complex, interagency problem-solving initiatives.

Notes

1. Philip J. Cook and John H. Laub, "The Unprecedented Epidemic in Youth Violence," in Michael Tonry and Mark H. Moore, eds., *Youth Violence* (University of Chicago Press, 1998), pp. 27–64.

2. Children's Defense Fund, *Wasting America's Future: The Children's Defense Fund Report on the Costs of Child Poverty* (Boston: Beacon Press, 1994).

3. Following a line of argument developed in Mark H. Moore and others, eds., *From Children to Citizens: The Mandate for Juvenile Justice*, vol. 1 (New York: Springer Verlag, 1987).

4. For a review, see Lisbeth B. Schorr, *Within Our Reach: Breaking the Cycle of Disadvantage* (Doubleday, 1988).

5. Martha Minow, ed., *Family Matters: Readings on Family Lives and the Law*, 1st ed. (New Press, 1993).

6. David T. Ellwood, *Poor Support: Poverty in the American Family* (Basic Books, 1988).

7. Schorr, *Within Our Reach*.

8. Jane Waldfogel, *The Future of Child Protection: How to Break the Cycle of Abuse and Neglect* (Harvard University Press, 1998).

9. Schorr, *Within Our Reach*, pp. 179–214.

10. Ibid., pp. 215–55.

11. Mark H. Moore and Stewart Wakeling, "Juvenile Justice: Shoring Up the Foundations," *Crime and Justice: A Review of Research*, vol. 22 (1997), pp. 253–55.

12. On tensions among professional communities, see Mark H. Moore and others, *Violence and Intentional Injuries: Criminal Justice and Public Health Perspectives on an Urgent National Problem*, pp. 167–216. Also, Mark H. Moore, Jeffrey A. Roth, and Patricia Kelly, "Responding to Violence in Cornet City: The Problem-Solving Enterprise" (National Institute of Justice, 1994).

13. See, for example, Shay Bilchik, "Delinquency Prevention Works: Program Summary," Office of Juvenile Justice and Delinquency Prevention (1995). Also, Kenneth E. Powell and Darnell Hawkins, eds., *Youth Violence Prevention: Descriptions and Baseline Data from 13 Evaluation Projects* (Oxford University Press, 1996).

14. Cabinet Council on Criminal and Juvenile Justice, "Maryland Crime Control and Prevention Strategy" (State of Maryland, 1998). City of Oakland, Calif., "Three Year Strategic Plan for Violence Prevention," 1996.

15. See, in general, Moore and others, "Responding to Violence in Cornet City."

16. Jeffrey A. Roth and Mark H. Moore, "Violence in Urban America: Mobilizing a Response" (National Research Council and Kennedy School of Government, Harvard University, 1994).

17. See, in general, Moore and others, *From Children to Citizens*.

18. Malcolm K. Sparrow, *Imposing Duties: Government's Changing Approach to Compliance* (Westport, Conn.: Praeger, 1994).

19. See, in general, Moore and others, *From Children to Citizens*.

20. Franklin E. Zimring and Gordon J. Hawkins, *Deterrence: The Legal Threat in Crime Control* (University of Chicago Press, 1973).

21. David M. Kennedy, "Pulling Levers: Chronic Offenders, High-Crime Settings, and a Theory of Prevention," *Valparaiso University Law Review*, vol. 31 (1997), pp. 449–84.

22. Steven C. Wheelwright and Kim B. Clark, *Revolutionizing Product Development: Quantum Leaps in Speed, Efficiency, and Quality* (Free Press, 1992), pp. 188–217.

23. Martin Linsky, *Impact: How the Press Affects Federal Policymaking* (W.W. Norton, 1986).

24. Hugh Heclo, *A Government of Strangers: Executive Politics in Washington* (Brookings, 1977).

25. Erwin C. Hargrove and John C. Glidewell, eds., *Impossible Jobs in Public Management* (University Press of Kansas, 1990). Also, James Q. Wilson, *Bureaucracy: What Government Agencies Do and Why They Do It* (Basic Books, 1989).

26. James Q. Wilson, "The Problem of Defining Agency Success," *Performance Measures for the Criminal Justice System* (U.S. Department of Justice, Bureau of Justice Statistics, 1993), pp. 157–67.

27. Paul R. Lawrence and Jay W. Lorsch, "New Management Job: The Integrator," *Harvard Business Review*, vol. 45, no. 6 (November–December 1967), pp. 142–51.

28. Lawrence and Lorsch, "New Management Job," pp. 142–43.

29. Ibid., p. 143.

30. John M. Stewart, "Making Project Management Work" (n.d., copy in author's possession), p. 7.

31. Ibid., pp. 8–14.

32. Lawrence and Lorsch, "New Management Job," pp. 145–46.

33. Ibid., p. 150.

34. Ibid., pp. 148–49.

35. Richard Hackman, "The Design of Work Teams," in J. Lorsch, ed., *Handbook of Organized Behavior* (Englewood Cliffs, N.J.: Prentice Hall, 1987), pp. 315–42.

36. Michael D. Watkins and Kim B. Clark, "Strategies for Managing a Project Portfolio" (Harvard Business School, Division of Research, 1992).

37. Eugene Bardach, *Getting Agencies to Work Together: the Practice and Theory of Managerial Craftsmanship* (Brookings, 1998).

38. Recently a literature has developed in private sector management about the management of partnerships and the management of firms that seem more like complex networks of partnerships than traditional firms consisting of employees directed by managers to fulfill a well-defined, common purpose. This literature undoubtedly has important insights for public managers who are trying to operate across organizational boundaries as well as functional or programmatic boundaries within organizations. Unfortunately, I have not been able to review this literature for the purposes of this chapter, which is already long

enough. I am indebted to my colleague David Brown for reminding me of the existence of this important literature.

39. Jeffrey L. Pressman and Aaron B. Wildavsky, *Implementation: How Great Expectations in Washington Are Dashed in Oakland; Or, Why It's Amazing That Federal Programs Work at All, This Being a Saga of the Economic Development Administration as Told by Two Sympathetic Observers Who Seek to Build Morals on a Foundation of Ruined Hopes*, Oakland Project Series (University of California Press, 1984).

40. Laurence J. O'Toole Jr., "Policy Recommendations for Multi-Actor Implementation: An Assessment of the Field," *Journal of Public Policy*, pp. 181–210; Daniel A. Mazmanian and Paul A. Sabatier, *Implementation Analysis* (Lexington, Mass.: Lexington Books); Pressman and Wildavsky, *Implementation*.

41. Eugene Bardach, "On Designing Implementable Programs," in Giandomenico Majone and E. S. Quade, eds., *Pitfalls of Analysis* (John Wiley, 1980), pp. 138–58.

42. Milbrey Wallin McLaughlin, "Implementation as Mutual Adaptation: Change in Classroom Organization," *Teachers College Record*, vol. 77 (1976), pp. 339–51.

43. Olivia Ann Golden, "Management without Control: Federal Managers and Local Service Delivery under the Comprehensive Employment and Training Act," Ph.D. dissertation, Harvard University, 1983.

44. Malcolm K. Sparrow, Mark H. Moore, and David M. Kennedy, *Beyond 911: A New Era for Policing* (Basic Books, 1990).

45. Sparrow, *Imposing Duties*.

46. Mark H. Moore, *Creating Public Value: Strategic Management in Government* (Harvard University Press, 1995).

47. Daniel P. Moynihan, *Maximum Feasible Misunderstanding: Community Action in the War on Poverty* (Free Press, 1970).

48. Frank Farrow, with the Executive Session on Child Protection, "Child Protection: Building Community Partnerships" (John F. Kennedy School of Government, Harvard University, 1997).

49. Steven Rathgeb Smith and Michael Lipsky, *Nonprofits for Hire: The Welfare State in the Age of Contracting* (Harvard University Press, 1993).

50. Alexander L. George, *Presidential Decisionmaking in Foreign Policy: The Effective Use of Information and Advice* (Boulder, Colo.: Westview, 1980).

51. United States, President's Special Review Board, "Report of the President's Special Review Board," 1987. Karl F. Inderfurth and Loch K. Johnson, eds., *Decisions of the Highest Order: Perspectives on the National Security Council* (Pacific Grove, Calif.: Brooks/Cole, 1988).

52. National Model Cities Directors Association, "Model Cities: The Lessons Learned" (1972).

53. W. Earl Sasser Jr. and David C. Rikert, "Burger King Corp." (Harvard Business School, 1998); W. Earl Sasser Jr. and David C. Rikert, "McDonald's Corp." (Harvard Business School, 1998).

54. Bardach, *Getting Agencies to Work Together*.

55. Ibid., p.17.

56. Ibid., p.11; Mary Jo Bane, *Management as Community Leadership: The Challenge of Welfare Reform*, lecture to the Academy of Management, August 11, 1997, Cambridge, Kennedy School of Government, 1997.

57. Bardach, *Getting Agencies to Work Together*, p. 20.

58. Ibid., p. 307.

59. Ibid., pp. 20–21.

60. Ibid., pp. 307–08.

61. Ibid., pp. 306–07.

62. Ibid., p. 309.

63. Ibid., pp. 308–09.

64. Ibid., p. 6.

65. Mark H. Moore, "Invisible Offenses: A Challenge to Minimally Intrusive Law Enforcement," in Gerald M. Caplan, ed., *ABSCAM Ethics: Moral Issues and Deception in Law Enforcement* (Police Foundation, 1983), pp. 17–42.

66. James Q. Wilson, "Criminologists," *Thinking About Crime* (Basic Books, 1975), pp. 43–63.

67. Lawrence W. Sherman and others, "Preventing Crime: What Works, What Doesn't, What's Promising" (U.S. Department of Justice, Office of Justice Programs, 1997).

68. J. David Hawkins and others, " A Review of the Predictors of Youth Violence," in Rolf Loeber and David P. Farrington eds., *Serious and Violent Juvenile Offenders: Risk Factors and Successful Interventions* (Thousand Oaks, Calif.: Sage Publications, 1998).

69. Hawkins and others, "A Review of the Predictors of Youth Violence."

70. Ibid., p. 94.

71. Ibid.

72. James Q. Wilson and Glenn C. Loury, eds., *From Children to Citizens: Families, Schools, and Delinquency Prevention*, vol. 3 (New York: Springer Verlag, 1987).

73. Ronald V. Clarke, *Situational Crime Prevention: Successful Case Studies* (Harrow & Heston, 1997).

74. Lawrence W. Sherman, *Cooling the Hot Spots of Homicide: A Plan for Action* (National Institute of Justice, Executive Office for Weed and Seed, January 1998), pp. 41–44.

75. Herman Goldstein, *Problem-Oriented Policing* (Police Executive Research Forum, 1990).

76. See discussion of COPE unit's handling of racial unrest among high school students in David M. Kennedy, "Fighting Fear in Baltimore County," Kennedy School of Government Case Program, 1990.

77. Laurie Robinson, "Linking Community-Based Initiatives and Community Justice: The Office of Justice Programs," *National Institute of Justice Journal*, no. 231 (August 1996), pp. 4–7.

78. Kennedy, "Pulling Levers."

79. Home Office, "Safer Communities: The Local Delivery of Crime Prevention through the Partnership Approach" (Home Office, 1991); Nick Tilley, "Safer Cities and Community Safety Strategies" (Home Office Crime Prevention Unit, 1992), p. 3.

80. T. S. Paine and D. M. Raymond, "Juvenile Serious Habitual Offenders/Drug Involved," Colorado Springs Police Department, 1985.

81. Sherman, *Cooling the Hot Spots*, pp. 41–44.

82. Wesley G. Skogan and Susan M. Hartnett, *Community Policing, Chicago Style* (Oxford University Press, 1997).

83. Catherine M. Coles and George L. Kelling, "Prosecution in the Community: A Study of Emergent Strategies," John F. Kennedy School of Government, Harvard University, 1998.

84. Jeff Tauber and C. West Huddleston, "Development and Implementation of Drug Court Systems," Monograph Series 2 (National Drug Court Institute, May 1999).

85. Michael Tonry, "The Fragmentation of Sentencing and Corrections in America," *Sentencing and Corrections: Issues for the 21st Century* (National Institute of Justice, 1999).

86. Tilley, "Safer Cities," p. 1.

87. Mark A. Liddle and Loraine R. Gelsthorpe, "Crime Prevention and Inter-Agency Cooperation" (London: Home Office, Crime Prevention Unit, 1994), p. 2.

88. Liddle and Gelsthorpe, "Crime Prevention," p. 2.

89. Ibid., p. 3.

90. Mark A. Liddle and Loraine R. Gelsthorpe, "Inter-Agency Crime Prevention: Organising Local Delivery" (London: Home Office, Crime Prevention Unit, 1994), pp. 29–31.

91. Liddle and Gelsthorpe, "Inter-Agency Crime Prevention," p. 29.

92. Liddle and Gelsthorpe, "Crime Prevention," p. 26.

93. Liddle and Gelsthorpe, "Inter-Agency Crime Prevention," p. 30.

94. Ibid.

95. Tilley, "Safer Cities," p. 5.

96. Ibid., pp. 6–10.

97. Ibid., pp. 30–34.

98. Ibid., p. 30.

99. Ibid., pp. 30–34.

100. Moore, *Creating Public Value.*

13

GARY S. KATZMANN

Conclusion: A New
Framework and Agenda

OLD WAYS OF THINKING about the problems of youth violence are giving
way to promising experimental approaches that focus on more than just
particular institutions or sets of institutions. As the next step, the research
and experience of the past decade must be synthesized and the lessons
learned applied within a framework for handling those problems. This
framework's components and proposals must be concrete and its essential
purposes practical—to rethink the roles of a variety of institutions and to
harness their collective energies in meeting the very considerable challenges
that youth violence presents. What follows is a description of such a framework and the presentation of an agenda for future action.

A New Framework

Central to meeting the challenges ahead is the ongoing redefinition of
institutional and professional roles, which entails new responsibilities for
the federal government and reshaped ones for the police, prosecutors, the
defense bar, the courts, probation and corrections departments, aftercare
programs, schools, nonprofit organizations, the private sector, and the
media. At the core of the emerging framework for addressing youth violence is the creation of cross-systemic and interagency initiatives:[1]

Federal-State Interface

Historically, juvenile justice and the problems of youth have been largely the domain of state and local entities. To the extent that there was federal intervention, it focused on providing program grants and some research capability.[2] Recent experience has demonstrated that an effective youth violence strategy requires a more dynamic and participatory federal role. Such a role does not signal greater federalization of crime prevention and control, which has posed concern to some analysts who fear that increased federal involvement would undermine traditional state and local authority and accountability.[3] Rather, the type of federal involvement contemplated involves enforcing statutes in ways that strengthen and provide important supplementary capabilities to state and local governments.[4] The federal government also can play an important part in forging partnerships with state and local entities and in stimulating involvement by the nonprofit and private sectors. Illustrating the new federal role is the deployment of federal prosecutorial and investigative resources to attack organized offenders and gangs in such cities as in Boston, Baltimore, Los Angeles, and Indianapolis,[5] as well as the active prosecution of gun law violators through federal partnerships with local law enforcement agencies, such as Project Safe Neighborhoods and Virginia's Project Exile.[6] The federal government would continue as before to support and stimulate state and local youth violence initiatives tested against effectiveness measures by providing research capacity and block grants and program funding.[7] At the same time, states and localities ought, for their part, to be creative in establishing integrated planning and management mechanisms that will operate synergistically when combined with federal funding and program assistance and minimize unnecessary duplication of programs and expenses.[8]

The Police

The traditional concept of the police as reactive agents who deal only with misbehaving youth—often by arresting them—has been supplanted by one in which they intervene in a proactive way to prevent the development of serious problems. A familiar reflection of the new organizational philosophy is community policing, which trains police officers to become more aware of the problems of individual youths as well as to develop the dynamic capacity to identify and map crime trends, such as those evidenced by "hot spots."[9] The new framework is marked by innovative collaborations, such as community-based justice programs in which police, prosecutors, and schools share information about at-risk children; partnerships with schools in which police serve as on-site resource officers at schools; and police-probation partnerships in which the police help to enforce probation conditions and provide protection to probation officers as they supervise their charges.[10] Moreover, under the new framework, the police recognize the importance of understanding the context in which youth violence occurs and of addressing the needs of at-risk youth.

Illustrating the innovative initiatives is a partnership between police officers and mental health professionals in New Haven, Connecticut, that sensitizes police to the need for clinical services for young people who are exposed to domestic violence and abuse and who themselves are therefore at heightened risk of developing criminal careers.[11] Another example of the new police role in providing alternative resources to troubled youth is Boston's Youth Services Providers Network, a collaboration of the police, youth service organizations such as the Boys and Girls Clubs, nonprofit social and human services providers, and city agencies. Through the network, an officer who comes in contact with a youth in need of services can refer the youth to a licensed clinical social worker based at the police station house, who can then evaluate and refer the youth to the appropriate network provider agency.[12]

Prosecutors

The formalization of legal process with respect to juveniles, legislation permitting or requiring prosecution of serious juvenile offenders as adults, and heightened concerns about violent trends among youth have come together to create a new leadership role for the prosecutor. Once confined to the largely gatekeeping role of court intake officer or processor of wayward youth, the prosecutor has been transformed into a problem solver.[13] Although the prosecutor remains a law enforcement official who pursues the traditional missions of enforcement, intervention, and prevention, he or she does so in a broader social and strategic context. The keystones of the new approach are identifying and pursuing lower-level misbehavior, which may be a precursor of more serious violent behavior if left unchecked, and working with investigators to monitor "hot spots," analyze trends, communicate successful enforcement results to the street level, and deploy aggressive enforcement in order to incapacitate serious offenders and bring down gangs and other dangerous groups of youth.[14] It also calls for reaching out and coordinating with community partners—from nonprofit groups to schools and government agencies—in developing intelligence, identifying at-risk youth, and implementing policies that include effective sanctions as well as responsive preventive programs.[15] The new prosecutorial role envisions not only organizational change within the prosecutor's office—for example, specialized units that focus on juvenile offenders—but also broader-based approaches to the problems of youth that relate to family issues such as domestic violence and child abuse and neglect.[16]

Defense Bar

The defender's role also has changed as a result of the expansion of criminal sanctions to young offenders and the formalization of legal process. Under the new framework the defender, like the prosecutor, must adopt broader approaches—apart from fulfilling the traditional role of advocate for his or her client, the defender must also present the defense's perspective in the public policy forum. This approach not only entails "holistic advocacy for the client," which involves presenting the court with appropriate psychological, clinical, and other support plans for the client, but also community outreach and education programs that broaden the avenues of communication between defender and community.[17] Moreover, it contemplates the development of partnerships between defenders and other criminal justice stakeholders so that defenders can better participate in the formation of social and political policies that bear on youth. The broader defense role, which is promoted and supported by innovative advocacy centers and law school clinical programs,[18] presents new challenges: in managing cases, the defender must combine elements of traditional litigation with new disciplines, and both the public defender and the private bar may have to reconsider their professional mission as they seek both to serve the best interests of their clients and to meet their community responsibilities.

Courts

Perhaps no institution of government has been subject to greater scrutiny and criticism in dealing with the problems of youth violence than the judiciary. The courts, particularly the juvenile courts, have been faulted for subscribing to the notion that youth are not simply "little adults" and that adult criminal justice is not appropriate for juveniles. It is interesting to note, however, that the juvenile courts were set up not only because, in part, youth were viewed as having lesser capacities than adults and so warranted a different legal system, but also because youth often escaped punishment in an adult system that was reluctant to mete out justice to the young.[19] The missions of protecting society and correcting the young are

not incompatible. The new framework recognizes that courts have an obligation to protect society from youthful offenders as well as to correct those
offenders through a continuum of sanctions extending to appropriate punishment. This paradigm holds that the young should be held accountable
for their actions and recognizes the importance of addressing not only violent offenses but also precursor offenses, such as status offenses, which often
presage more antisocial behavior. At the same time, in dealing with youth
violence on an individual basis, courts must address conditions that create
a context for future violent offending. In protecting children from abuse
and neglect and in punishing domestic violence, courts are mindful of the
reality that victims may themselves become perpetrators of violence if the
risk factors are not addressed promptly. By fulfilling their mission of protecting and preserving families, courts also respect the reality that a nurturing family can provide the kind of support that reduces those risks.[20]

The judiciary's interrelated missions inform the discussion of how the
courts should be organized to deal with youth violence and its precursors.
First, the juvenile court should include the functions of a family court,
encompassing delinquency, child abuse and neglect, domestic violence,
and dependency jurisdictions. This "one family/one judge concept," exemplified by the Bronx Integrated Domestic Violence Court, seeks to develop
a comprehensive approach to family problems while ending overlap among
courts.[21] Less ambitiously, a system that facilitates the coordination of the
jurisdiction of separate courts could be instituted.[22] Second, it is imperative
to implement management information systems that ensure that all relevant information regarding an offender is consolidated in a central database
to facilitate informed decisionmaking by the court, not scattered among
various jurisdictions. For example, when fashioning a disposition, the court
should be fully apprised if a delinquent offender has been subject to abuse
or neglect or has witnessed domestic violence; indeed, the court should be
involved in directing interventions to deal with those issues.[23] Management information systems should not only provide information about
offenders but also yield data that facilitate the establishment of objective
criteria for allocating resources in the court system and measuring workload and performance. As Chief Justice Margaret Marshall of the Supreme
Judicial Court of Massachusetts has stated regarding the management of
the judiciary generally, "No organization could survive without such basic
information."[24]

Third, it must be recognized that when courts address the youthful
offender in the larger context of family dysfunction, they increasingly

become immersed in social service delivery. Dispositional juvenile delinquency orders, for example, might require attendance in substance abuse programs; child abuse and neglect orders might require participation in therapy sessions subject to the supervision of the state's child welfare agency.[25] In their efforts to foster appropriate interventions by social service agencies for children and families, courts must employ skills and management capabilities that go well beyond the traditional scope of legal education and practice. Courts therefore must be provided adequate resources and the management training necessary to ensure effective social service delivery.[26] Fourth, legislatures need to affirm the vital role of juvenile and family courts and to provide them with appropriate funding. Fifth, the new framework recognizes the role of the judge as a leader in dealing with the problems of youth violence, supported by a comprehensive system that seeks to ensure that each youth who commits a delinquent act or status offense is held accountable and that there is appropriate intervention whenever a child is abused or neglected.[27] In this leadership capacity, a judge can bring together participants from relevant public, nonprofit, and private organizations to identify the services required for each type of case and to develop a plan for the delivery of those services.[28] Chief Judge Judith Kaye of the New York State Court of Appeals has called for "problem-solving courts" that "bring together prosecution and defense, criminal justice agencies, treatment providers and the like, all working with the judge toward a more effective outcome than the costly revolving door."[29] Promising returns from innovative domestic violence courts in Massachusetts, Wisconsin, and Michigan—which institutionalize the judge's community leadership role—are supportive of such a broader role for the judiciary.[30]

Probation

The new framework contemplates the return in a very real sense of probation officers to their traditional role of actively supervising probationers in the community with the goal of promoting public safety.[31] By actively supervising probationers in their neighborhoods, not passively meeting with them in the office, probation officers gain greater understanding of the challenges youthful offenders face and they come to know their probationers' family situation and associates. Under this model, the probation officer maintains a visible presence in the community, works nontraditional hours, including evenings, and makes clear to the youthful offender that all conditions of probation will be enforced and that all violations will be addressed swiftly. In the "place-based" model of supervision, cases are not assigned at random but according to geography, thereby promoting the development of strategic relationships and the accumulation of intelligence about criminal activity in a particular community. Partnerships between probation and police departments, such as Operation Night Light in Boston, as well as partnerships of schools and prosecutors in which information is shared regarding at-risk youth and probationers, are all part of the new role of the probation officer as community leader in addressing youth violence.

Corrections

The challenges for corrections in addressing youth violence are particularly formidable given the variety of correctional settings, including residential homes, training centers, group homes, detention facilities, jails, and prisons. The task is further compounded because many of these facilities are private. The new model, embraced by agencies such as the Texas Youth Commission,[32] contemplates use of sensitive classification instruments to determine the most appropriate type of confinement as well as ongoing programming and supervision designed to promote the maturation and personal development of the youthful offender. Programming and supervision would include educational and vocational programs, violent offender and sex offender programs, conflict management programs, and substance abuse programs. When youthful offenders are sentenced to adult prisons, corrections would assess various housing strategies, including separating youth from the adult population.[33] The new framework envisions ongoing monitoring and assessment of the histories of juveniles sentenced to adult prisons in order to aid public officials as they weigh the effectiveness of penal policies.

Aftercare

The new framework recognizes that juveniles released from confinement, like their adult counterparts, face serious difficulties in their efforts to become reintegrated into the community and to avoid returning to crime. Juvenile justice must therefore include a dynamic aftercare component, which ought to be viewed as part of the continuum of corrections. While confined and prior to release, juvenile offenders should participate in programs to help them become reintegrated in the community, followed by a structured transition to community living involving intensive day-release supervision during "step-down" confinement and culminating in active supervision and treatment services when they again become community residents.[34]

Schools

The new framework envisions schools that produce violence and crime prevention and intervention strategies by working with law enforcement agencies, for example, to identify mechanisms to ensure the safety of the school environment (such as use of metal detectors where appropriate) and surrounding neighborhoods and to create emergency response plans. In their new role, schools also develop curricula designed specifically to teach students how to manage their anger and resolve disputes peaceably and to recognize the inappropriateness of antisocial behavior such as bullying.[35] Teachers learn how to identify students who are at risk of violent behavior, and schools develop channels of communication with social service agencies, mental health agencies, and police and prosecutors in order to assist youths and prevent violent behavior.[36] Schools' participation in community-based justice programs as well as in initiatives that place probation officers and school resource or security officers in schools exemplify their new role in dealing with youth violence. Extending the hours of the school day to provide a haven for youth who do not have stable family relationships and collaborating with the nonprofit and private sector to fund programs for at-risk youth also are part of the broadened school role.[37]

Nonprofits, Faith-Based Organizations, and Private Sector

The new framework recognizes that the effort to fight youth violence is not government's alone; nonprofits, faith-based organizations, and the private sector also will figure prominently in the effort.

Nonprofits—ranging from service organizations to philanthropic foundations— play an important role in developing innovative approaches to dealing with youth violence.[38] For example, organizations such as the Boys and Girls Clubs or the Beacon Schools provide youth with multiservice havens and alternatives to violent environments;[39] "action tanks" such as City Year promote youth national service and leadership;[40] initiatives such as Common Sense About Kids and Guns disseminate information and provide resources to help reduce youth violence;[41] community coalitions bring together the nonprofit, public and private sectors to reduce violence;[42] and nonprofit corporations stimulate investment in at-risk neighborhoods.[43] Nonprofits such as the Project Exile Citizen Support

Foundation also make a significant contribution in promoting education, public outreach, and media initiatives to support law enforcement efforts.[44] In the future, the challenge for nonprofits will be not only to maximize the value of their contributions, but also to transform and adapt their organizational capacity to address new problems as initial program goals are met.[45]

As the Ten Point Coalition has demonstrated, faith-based organizations also have shown great promise in promoting the reduction of youth violence. Some commentators have suggested that the success of faith-based organizations in antiviolence strategies arises primarily from their grassroots knowledge of their community and their legitimacy within it, which permit them to build bridges between the legal system, youth, and the community to help those who are at risk; others have suggested that the transformational power of faith has been the motive force.[46] The efforts of faith-based organizations to build congregational capacity to implement programs and to engage non–faith-based organizations in partnerships are attracting much attention from both practitioners and scholars.[47] In the years ahead, the national Ten Point Coalition (which seeks to export the Boston success to other venues) and other faith-based endeavors such as Public/Private Ventures and the Jeremiah Project will no doubt be watched with great interest.[48]

The private sector also has played an important role in developing youth violence initiatives.[49] Its motives for involvement vary: they include civic conscience, the recognition that safe communities improve the economic environment, and the desire to foster a positive business image or brand name.[50] Perhaps the most highly visible examples of private sector involvement in youth issues have been in the schools, which businesses have provided with tutors, mentors, and equipment. The private sector also has partnered with law enforcement and government agencies, providing such resources as technical and management expertise. Initiatives in which business joins the community in violence prevention efforts, such as the National Campaign Against Youth Violence and America's Promise, exemplify this thrust.[51]

The new framework also recognizes the interrelationship of the components of the nongovernment sector. The economic strength of the nonprofit sector, for example, very much depends on funding from the private sector as well as government.[52] The challenge for nonprofits, faith-based institutions, and the private sector will be to maximize their contributions to youth violence initiatives by integrating their programmatic efforts, leveraging their resources, and avoiding duplication and counterproductive competition.

Media

In the new framework, the media will play a significant role, not only by restraining the dissemination of violent messages, but also through programming geared toward reducing youth violence. The disclosure that the perpetrators of the mass shootings at Columbine High School had been immersed in the world of violent video games, music, and movies has intensified Americans' concern about the impact on youth of violence in the media (defined as movies, television, music, and electronic games). The debate over the impact of the media has led to examination of the degree and extent to which media violence leads to violent behavior in young people. The Federal Trade Commission (FTC), in a study prompted by Columbine, observed that "[e]ven those who disagree that media violence causes violent behavior . . . concede that a child's exposure to violence in the media can be a concern."[53] In its study of the motion picture, music recording, and electronic game industries, the FTC noted that through their varying self-regulatory rating systems and labeling, all three industries recognized the public's concern about exposure of the young to violence. However, the commission noted that all three industries, in varying degrees, routinely marketed "to children the very products that have industries' self-imposed parental warning or ratings with age restrictions due to violent content." The FTC recommended that all three industries enhance their regulatory efforts—by improving the usefulness of ratings and labels, expanding codes that prohibit target marketing to children and impose meaningful sanctions for noncompliance, restricting children's access at the retail level to entertainment with violent content, and educating parents about ratings and labels so that they can better guide their children's choices.

Apart from these worthy measures, the media can further help to reduce youth violence by producing programs and public service announcements that teach children about the consequences of violence, transmit antiviolence messages, and address such issues as bullying.[54] Moreover, the media can be a powerful partner in spreading the word about law enforcement policy. In Project Exile, for example, not only the "free media" (such as news reports and public access cable) but also privately supported commercial media were used to communicate the message that "an illegal gun gets you five years in federal prison" and to seek anonymous tips about violations from citizens.[55] In sum, the new framework contemplates that the media and law enforcement and juvenile justice agencies will maintain active channels of communication and that they will discuss such issues as the impact of violence, both in news and entertainment programming; whether and to what extent violence generates "copycat" violence; and whether protocols addressing media coverage of juvenile crime ought to be established, particularly because intense coverage of juvenile crime may have distorted the extent of the problem and at times led to unrealistic public perceptions of its severity.[56]

Cross-Systemic and Interagency Initiatives

Recent efforts to address youth violence have been marked by a variety of collaborations among government bodies (including a full range of law enforcement, social service, and court agencies), nonprofit and private entities, and schools. This volume has described some of those initiatives, such as Operation Cease Fire in Boston.[57] The Office of Juvenile Justice and Delinquency Prevention (OJJDP) Comprehensive Strategy is another such initiative. The comprehensive strategy seeks to mobilize all segments of the community to develop and implement a research-based strategy to combat youth violence; its preventive component focuses on at risk-youth, seeking to identify the risk factors associated with youth violence and strengthen the factors that protect children from its effects.[58] Illustrating the new collaborations are the Safe Futures initiative, a community-wide program;[59] the Strategic Approaches to Community Safety Initiative (SACSI) supported by the United States Department of Justice;[60] and various corporate-community partnerships identified by the National Campaign Against Youth Violence.[61] San Diego, Forth Worth, Denver, and Hartford are among the cities whose partnerships have been cited for their efficacy.[62] To be sure, because community needs and capacities vary, efforts may differ; for example, they may focus on neighborhoods or on individual offenders.[63] All of the efforts, however, share several elements: creating a sense of urgency; forming a coalition or interagency working group that brings together all key stakeholders; identifying the problem to be addressed; gathering data and information about the youth violence problem; designing a strategic intervention or plan, including goals, timetable, and allocation of human, financial, and material resources; developing dynamic research capacity, with ongoing evaluation of the effectiveness of a strategy and responsive modification of the strategy as circumstances warrant; and celebrating the strategy's successes.[64]

In the years ahead, the various coordinated initiatives—differing in scope and form and operating in different environments and cultures—will surely be studied closely as we seek to learn from experience.

Agenda for the Future

As we apply the new framework in addressing youth violence, some areas of inquiry warrant particular focus. These include building bridges between the juvenile justice system and the child welfare and protection system; enhancing mental health outreach programs; developing a better understanding of collaboration and partnership in youth violence strategies; strengthening the research mission and the integration of research with action; and creating a presidential "State of the Young" address. We consider each in turn.

Bridging Systems

In addressing youth violence, the juvenile justice and criminal justice systems traditionally have been concerned only with the control of offenders whose conduct has brought them to the systems' attention. Unlike the classic public health disease prevention model, the law enforcement "control" model focuses on enforcement and deterrence through punishment, not on identifying and reducing risk factors and fostering protective factors.[65] A major theme of this volume has been the need to redefine institutional roles within the juvenile justice and criminal justice systems in order not only to enhance control and deterrence, but also to identify and reinforce risk reduction and protective factors. Apart from redefining roles and improving communication among the institutions within those systems, there needs to be enhanced communication and dialogue with other systems. In particular, greater attention must be given to the relationship between the child welfare and juvenile justice systems.

Studies on the "cycle of violence" have clearly established that childhood abuse and neglect increase the likelihood of future delinquency and adult criminality as well as the likelihood of violent criminal behavior.[66] The maltreated children who fall under the charge of the child welfare and protection agencies therefore are at greater risk of eventual delinquent or adult criminal behavior. (Indeed, nondelinquent children who may not be maltreated but are deemed "in need of supervision" because they are runaways, truants, school offenders, or disobedient may also be candidates for delinquency.) In a sense, the child welfare and protection system can be viewed as an early warning system;[67] greater resources therefore need to be devoted to improving and strengthening the mechanisms for dealing with maltreatment of children. Police officers, school staff, and mental health professionals need to be trained to identify children who are neglected or abused so that there can be appropriate early intervention.[68] Moreover, focused programs, such as specialized foster care, that are directed at children who have exhibited violent propensities ought to be developed within the child welfare and protection system.[69] At the same time, there should be communication and sharing of information with the child welfare and protection system about youths who already have moved into the juvenile or adult criminal justice systems to facilitate interventions in situations in which, for example, the offender has siblings who also may be at risk of maltreatment and criminality.[70] California, Rhode Island, and New York have initiated efforts to allow sharing of the databases of their dependency and delinquency systems and to promote interagency planning in particular cases.[71] In sum, structures that link the child welfare system with the juvenile justice and criminal justice systems are cornerstones of the new framework.[72]

Enhancing Mental Health Outreach

In recent years, the spate of spree killings by juveniles has brought new attention to the question of the mental health of the nation's young people.[73] Studies have indicated that mental health disorders are substantially more prevalent among youths in the juvenile justice system than among those in the general population. Yet, in some jurisdictions, when a youth is judged to be a delinquent or a criminal, he or she is barred from admission to the state's mental health system for abused children.[74] While there have been efforts to establish profiles of types of violent young offenders for predictive purposes,[75] there has been a dearth of research on mental health disorders among juveniles. Compounding the problem has been the inadequacy of the mental health services provided to juveniles. Much work needs to be done to develop a coordinated strategy for assessing and treating children in need of mental health services as well as those who have already entered the legal system.[76]

Partnerships and Collaboration

As policymakers contemplate the successes and failures of coalitions in dealing with youth violence, they would do well to note that the notions of "collaboration," "partnership," and "teamwork" have assumed a variety of meanings. Indeed, Paul Light has reminded us that "[c]ollaboration may be one of those rare and celebrated goals of organizational life, but it can mean everything from minimal information sharing to full-blown merger."[77] Thus, partnership may signify collaboration (collective problem solving that blurs the lines between agencies); cooperation (which involves a common goal but separate action); or coordination (which involves a limited sharing of resources and information).[78] Differences in definition have very real and obvious implications for implementation. Does collaboration signify collective on-site management, shared or blended roles regarding a client, or the contribution by each service provider of a separate but important component of the program?[79] Other important questions also arise. For example, to what extent do partners' different organizational cultures—whether government, nonprofit, or private sector—and their different measures of success impede the implementation and management of initiatives? Can the collaborative mechanisms and innovations for addressing youth violence that they generate be sustained? Can they be replicated? These questions will continue to loom large in the years ahead, as policymakers, practitioners, and researchers assess various collaborative efforts.

Research

As has been noted, research plays a crucial role in developing problem-solving approaches to youth violence. The independent researcher has been integral to both the ongoing evaluation of initiatives and ongoing discussions with practitioners to shape strategies that integrate both research and action.[80] Offices that collect, evaluate, and interpret data; identify trends; and monitor hot spots should be established and supported in each state. Organizations such as the National Institute of Justice, which promotes the integration of research and action, need to be supported.

The research agenda for the future is as diverse as it is challenging. Priorities include the continuing exploration of how best to measure "success" in evaluating programs and strategies[81] and ongoing analysis of "best practices," or blueprints for success in dealing with youth violence.[82] As suggested, further research also should examine the design and implementation of collaborative youth violence strategies, which are of recent vintage and often limited in scope and geographic domain. We also need to learn more about replication of programs and expanding small, pilot initiatives into full-scale programs —known in the parlance as "going to scale." Moreover, empirical inquiry could enlighten us about the challenges of management and leadership when an initiative involves a mix of public and private entities. Therefore the research agenda also should consider how the redefinition of traditional institutional roles affects the mission and integrity of institutions.

Apart from the organizational and institutional issues that have been the subject of this volume, research is needed on many other important issues that affect how resources ought to be deployed and allocated in addressing youth violence.[83] A successful gun violence reduction program, for example, requires not only law enforcement, interdiction, gun trafficking control, and prevention efforts, but also a greater understanding of the mix of factors—including fear, self-defense, poor academic performance, alcohol and drug use, and smoking—that may be linked to gun carrying by youth. [84] In addition, we need to learn more about how changing the environment of crime and modifying the dynamics of groups such as gangs can affect the "tipping point" that leads to crime "epidemics."[85] Other important research areas include the continuing examination of pathways to delinquency, which has bettered our understanding of which kinds of interventions may be most effective in dealing with youth violence.[86] Studies have suggested that early childhood interventions, defined as "formal attempts by agents outside the family to maintain or improve the quality of life of youngsters, starting with the prenatal period and continuing through entry into school," have long-term beneficial effects in reducing youth violence.[87] More research needs to be dedicated to the question of how to rebuild weak family structures.[88] As James Q. Wilson has observed, pointing to the works of pioneering criminologists Sheldon and Eleanor Glueck and contemporary scholars Richard Catalono and colleagues, crime prevention confronts the "central social question of our time" in its efforts to learn how to sustain a healthy family life in a culture that undermines family life.[89] Other important avenues for research include increasing our understanding of the relationship between biology and behavior, as suggested by the influence of prenatal care on the social behavior and well-being of children.[90] We also need to learn more about the increasing involvement of girls and young women in violence.[91] School shooting spree behavior presents another important research subject.[92] Furthermore, the disproportionate representation of minorities in the juvenile justice system must be the subject of renewed scrutiny and study.

The State of the Young Address

It is perhaps beyond dispute that no resource is as important to a country as its young people. In recognition of that reality, as well as of the symbolic significance of showing appreciation of the nation's youth and concern for their status, the U.S. president should consider delivering an annual report to Congress on the state of the country's youth.[93] An important component of this report would be a discussion of the state of the juvenile justice system, to which the various components of the expanded networks described in this volume would contribute their views regarding the system's problems, progress, and future direction. To highlight the importance of the effort and the Executive Office's concern, a prominent citizen would be appointed special assistant for youth to serve as a conduit between the White House and youth practitioners and policymakers. Similarly, such efforts could take place in each of the states, with the governor charged with the delivery of the "State of the Young" address and submission of the report. [94]

* * *

Today, initiatives to deal with youth violence take place in a world marked by contrasts and creative tensions. In a very fundamental sense, the sphere of the child and the family traditionally has been private domain; yet, the imperative of ensuring a child's safety and well-being is firmly established and widely accepted as justification for government intervention when the family fails. Collaboration and partnership efforts that bring together public and private organizations present new questions of institutional accountability. Redefinition of institutional roles has posed further questions regarding institutions' mission, integrity, and competence. As we consider new arrangements and missions, we must also be alert to unintended consequences, particularly mission creep, mission distortion, and the haphazard engrafting of organizational functions in the purported pursuit of partnership or collaboration.[95] The merging of law enforcement and public health efforts has changed the content and tone of the public policy debate, shifting the focus somewhat from the legitimacy of the purposes for which resources ought to be allocated to a discussion of priorities and of which entities ought to carry out those priorities, to what extent.[96] Yet, we should be mindful of Franklin Zimring's caution that youth development policy possesses its own vital, optimistic, and independent value and that it may be undermined if it is defined simply by its claimed benefit in crime control.[97]

Promising statistical indications of a decline in youth violence should not give rise to complacency; indeed, youth violence has shown signs of a new upswing.[98] Now, as much as ever, we require leaders who can define the direction of future youth policy and who can effectuate the management capabilities needed to organize and operate institutions and initiatives.[99] In dealing with youth violence, leadership requires vision for action, not only in particular institutions and organizations but also in forming partnerships and collaborations across institutions. In fostering innovation, leaders should promote, in Rosabeth Kanter's evocative image, "kaleidoscopic" thinking in their organizations; that is, organizations should "imagine possibilities outside of conventional categories, to envision actions that cross traditional boundaries, to anticipate repercussions and to take advantage of interdependencies, to make new connections or invent new combinations."[100] Leaders must also have the courage to undertake a continuing self-assessment, to act as reflective practitioners taking stock of experience while also fostering the momentum that builds on success instead of calcifying in the nostalgic celebration of old triumphs.[101] Such leaders recognize that the problems of youth violence are complex, that there is no magic bullet or organizational "fix," and, indeed, that there are limits to what institutions can achieve.

As leaders contemplate the most effective ways to address youth violence, they must realize that any strategy must be based not simply on promoting safety but also on recognizing each individual's worth and society's responsibility to advance and protect an individual's promise. President George W. Bush recounted the following haunting encounter when governor of Texas:

> A couple of years ago, I visited a juvenile jail in Marlin, Texas, and talked with a group of young inmates. They were angry, wary kids. All had committed grown-up crimes.
>
> Yet when I looked in their eyes, I realized some of them were still little boys.
>
> Toward the end of conversation, one young man, about 15, raised his hand and asked a haunting question . . . "What do you think of me?"
>
> He seemed to be asking, like many Americans who struggle . . . "Is there hope for me? Do I have a chance?" And, frankly . . . "Do you, a white man in a suit, really care what happens to me?"
>
> A small voice, but it speaks for so many. Single moms struggling to feed the kids and pay the rent. Immigrants starting a hard life in a new world. Children without fathers in neighborhoods where gangs seem like friendship, where drugs promise peace, and where sex, sadly, seems like the closest thing to belonging. We are their country, too.
>
> And each of us must share in its promise, or that promise is diminished for all.
>
> If that boy in Marlin believes he is trapped and worthless and hopeless—if he believes his life has no value—then other lives have no value to him and we are *all* diminished.[102]

In a time marked by solitary tendencies and lifestyles,[103] the movement to anticipate and prevent youth violence—before that boy in Marlin pursues a criminal path—depends on a vigorous sense of community, strengthened by the mediating institutions that make up civil society.[104] This notion of community is marked by the concept of nurturing, which encompasses not only supporting the young but also enforcing those norms of behavior upon which society relies for order—and from which the young are not exempt. We can do no less to secure our children's future—and, ultimately, the future of our society.

Notes

1. It is instructive to take note of a study from an earlier era, the 1967 report of the President's Commission on Law Enforcement and Administration of Justice, entitled *The Challenge of Crime in a Free Society* (Government Printing Office, 1967). In press just as *Gault* was issued, this important report could not foresee the significant changes in procedural process that would impact the juvenile justice system in the ensuing years, nor could it anticipate a central role for prosecution or law enforcement or problem-solving cross boundary partnerships in dealing with youth violence. See also President's Commission on Law Enforcement and Administration of Justice, *Task Force Report: Juvenile Delinquency and Youth Crime* (Government Printing Office, 1967).

2. For a statistical reference on the few juvenile delinquency cases in the federal court system, see chapter 1 in this volume.

3. American Bar Association, *Federalization of Criminal Law* (Washington: Task Force on Federalization of Criminal Law, 1998), pp. 49–50. On federal-state allocation of law enforcement responsibilities, generally, see Gary S. Katzmann, *Inside the Criminal Process* (W.W. Norton, 1991), pp. 157–58.

4. The issues of the appropriate federal role and comity are not new. For example, more than thirty years ago, Daniel Patrick Moynihan urged that a primary goal of federal urban policy should be to restore the vitality of urban government and to encourage the "indispensible role of state government in the management of urban affairs." Daniel P. Moynihan, "Toward a National Urban Policy," in *Violent Crime: Homicide, Assault, Rape, Robbery—The Report of the National Commission on the Causes and Prevention of Violence* (New York: George Braziller, 1969).

5. Veronica Coleman and others, "Using Knowledge and Teamwork to Reduce Crime," *National Institute of Justice Journal*, October 1999.

6. Remarks of Attorney General John Ashcroft at the unveiling of Project Safe Neighborhoods, May 14, 2001 (www.usdoj.gov/ag/speeches/2001/0514safe_neighborhoods.htm [April 19, 2002]); *Review of Department of Justice Firearms Prosecutions: Hearing before the Senate Subcommittee on Criminal Justice Oversight and Subcommittee on Youth Violence*, 106th Cong., 1st sess., March 22, 1999, testimony and prepared statement of Colonel Jerry A. Oliver, serial no. J-106-7, pp. 50–54.

7. American Bar Association, *Federalization of Criminal Law*, p. 54; Philip B. Heymann and Mark H. Moore, "The Federal Role in Dealing with Violent Street Crime:

Principles, Questions, and Cautions," *Annual of American Academy of Political & Social Sciences*, vol. 543, no. 103 (1996).

8. For example, the state of Maryland, under the direction of Lieutenant Governor Kathleen Kennedy Townsend, has established the Youth Strategies Initiative, which consolidates state and federal funding to implement a coordinated, research-based youth prevention strategy at the local level. This effort was aided by the State Advisory Group, established by the federal Juvenile Justice and Delinquency Prevention Act of 1974 and chaired by Martha Mazzone; the advisory group was charged with assisting in developing and implementing a three-year plan under the act.

9. John Eck and Edward Maguire, "Have Changes in Policing Reduced Violent Crime? An Assessment of the Evidence," in Alfred Blumstein and Joel Wallman, eds., *The Crime Drop in America* (Cambridge University Press, 2000), pp. 207–65.

10. Dennis J. Kenney and T. Steuart Watson, *Crime in the Schools* (Washington: Police Executive Research Forum, 1998).

11. Stephen Marans and Mark Schaefer, "Community Policing, Schools, and Mental Health: The Challenge of Collaboration," in Delbert S. Elliott, Beatrix A. Hamburg, and Kirk R. Williams, eds., *Violence in American Schools: A New Perspective* (Cambridge University Press, 1998), pp. 312–47.

12. Boston Strategy to Prevent Youth Violence, "The Youth Service Providers Network" (http://www.bostonstrategy.com/programs/15_YSProvidersNet.html [June 27, 2002]). Boston police commissioner Paul Evans has been a strong proponent of the Youth Service Providers Network.

13. Elizabeth Glazer, "How Prosecutors Can Reduce Crime," *Public Interest*, vol. 136 (Summer 1999), pp. 85–99.

14. In the Southern District of New York, for example, U.S. attorney Mary Jo White set up a crime control unit in order to implement a strategic coordinated approach to crime that uses advanced technologies such as computer mapping. Glazer, "How Prosecutors Can Reduce Crime," pp. 86, 94–95. In Boston, an example of the strategic targeted enforcement approach was the prosecution of Freddie Cardoza, considered to be one of the city's most dangerous gang members. Cardoza was arrested while in possession of a single round of handgun ammunition and was prosecuted successfully as a federal armed career criminal by assistant U.S. attorney Ralph Boyd Jr.

15. For example, Deborah Daniels (now assistant attorney general for the Department of Justice's Office of Justice Programs) developed Project Weed and Seed in Indianapolis when she was U.S. attorney from 1988–1993. That program sought to integrate law enforcement, violence prevention, community policing, and neighborhood restoration efforts. As noted in chapters 2 and 6 of this volume, former Middlesex County district attorney Tom Reilly, now Massachusetts attorney general, brought together community groups, schools, law enforcement, state social service agencies, and human health resources in developing innovative, proactive programmatic efforts through his Community Based Justice program. Middle Dakota County district attorney James Backstrom, of Hastings, Minnesota, has also long been active in building community partnerships for the prevention of youth violence and has recorded his experiences in a series of publications that make useful teaching guides. In other offices, such as the Windsor County, Vermont, state's attorney's office, prosecutors also are pursuing a balance prosecution and outreach agenda, placing a prosecuctor's office in the neighborhood as part of their community

prosecution program. (Author's conversation with Robert Sand, Windsor County state's attorney, October 2001.)

Boston also serves as a case study. In the early 1990s, then U.S. attorney Wayne Budd vigorously promoted such law enforcement efforts as Operation Triggerlock, a gun interdiction initiative, while also reaching out to community groups, local offices of district attorney and police, to establish channels of communication between law enforcement and the neighborhoods. His successor, Donald Stern, also pursued an aggressive law enforcement effort, strategically attacking gangs and serving as an active partner in Operation Ceasefire. At the same time, Stern's executive assistant, U.S. attorney Joy Fallon, was charged with responsibility for developing community outreach and youth violence initiatives. Stern's successor, Michael J. Sullivan, previously Plymouth County district attorney, see note 16, below, has formed the Community Prosecution and Crime Reduction Unit, which seeks to develop highly targeted gun violence reduction strategies consistent with the Project Safe Neighborhood's initiative and to work with local, state, and federal law enforcement officials in reducing community violence.

16. For example, from 1999 to 2001, former Plymouth County district attorney Michael J. Sullivan (now United States attorney) led an effort to reduce domestic violence, bringing together teams of law enforcement professionals, neighborhood groups, and social service agencies. The collection of research data enabled law enforcement officials to identify serious domestic offenders with the goal of holding repeat offenders accountable while providing victims with appropriate services. See Community Resources for Justice, "Brockton Safety First: Strategies to Reduce Domestic Violence," unpublished action document (Boston: December 1999).

17. Cait Clarke, "Problem-Solving Defenders in the Community: Expanding the Conceptual and Institutional Boundaries of Providing Counsel to the Poor," *Georgetown Journal of Legal Ethics*, vol. 14 (2001), pp. 401–58. See also Charles Ogletree Jr. (noting the juvenile defender's social worker and litigation roles), "Public Defender, Public Friend: Searching for the 'Best Interests' of Juvenile Offenders," in Gary Bellow and Martha Minow, eds., *Law Stories* (University of Michigan, 1996), pp. 131–58.

18. Suffolk University Law School's Juvenile Justice Center and Fordham University's Interdisciplinary Center for Family and Child Advocacy are examples of innovative, broad-based programs.

19. Jeffrey A. Butts and Adele V. Harrell, *Delinquents or Criminals: Policy Options for Young Offenders* (Washington: Urban Institute, 1998).

20. National Council of Juvenile and Family Court Judges, "The Janiculum Project: Recommendations" (www.ncjfcj.unr.edu/homepage/today/Janiculum.htm [April 19, 2002]).

21. "First Integrated Domestic Violence Court to Open in New York City," New York State Unified Court System, press release, November 26, 2001 (www.courts.state.ny.us/pr2001_20.html [April 19, 2002]).

22. Leonard P. Edwards, "The Juvenile Court and the Role of the Juvenile Court Judge," *Juvenile and Family Court Journal*, vol. 43, no. 2 (1992), pp. 38–39.

23. Jennifer Trone, Molly Armstrong, and Mercer Sullivan, *Beyond Blame and Panic: Institutional Strategies for Preventing and Controlling Adolescent Violence* (New York: Vera Institute of Justice, 1998), p. 14.

24. Address by Margaret H. Marshall, chief justice, Supreme Judicial Court of Massachusetts, Massachusetts Bar Association, January 26, 2002.

25. Trone, Armstrong, and Sullivan, *Beyond Blame and Panic*, p. 14.

26. United States District Court Judge Rya W. Zobel, former director of the Federal Judicial Center (the training and research arm of the federal courts), has been addressing in her teaching at Harvard's John F. Kennedy School of Government how the multiple roles of judges generally—including adjudicator and manager—affect the work of the judiciary.

27. The National Council on Juvenile and Family Court Judges, for example, has instituted a juvenile graduated sanctions program to promote "early responses to the first signs of delinquent behaviors in kids" (http://training.ncjfcj.unr.edu/juvenile_sanctions_center.htm [March 2002]).

28. Leonard P. Edwards, "The Future of the Juvenile Court: Promising New Directions," *Future of Children*, vol. 6, no. 3 (Winter 1996), pp. 131–37. Judge Edwards's dynamic efforts as the presiding judge of the Santa Clara County (California) Juvenile Court are detailed in John Hubner and Jill Wolfson, *Somebody Else's Children: The Courts, the Kids, and the Struggle to Save America's Troubled Families* (New York: Three Rivers Press, 1996). For an account of juvenile court in Los Angeles, see Edward Humes, *No Matter How Loud I Shout: A Year in the Life of Juvenile Court* (New York: Simon and Schuster, 1996).

29. Judith S. Kaye, *The State of the Judiciary: 2002* (New York State Unified Court System, 2002), p. 12.

30. Christine DeStefano and others, *Evaluation of the Judicial Oversight Demonstration Initiative: Baseline and Implementation Report* (Washington: Urban Institute, 2001). Dorchester District Court first justice Sydney Hanlon has noted that in the Massachusetts Domestic Violence Court, the court aggressively supervises batterers after conviction by enhancing the judiciary's management of offenders' conduct; using specialized probation officers to supervise offenders; enlarging the court's role in promoting victim safety; and helping victims by bringing together victim services, including those of government and nonprofit agencies. Meghan Laska, "The Domestic Violence Court," *Massachusetts Lawyer*, October 16, 2000, p.B1, B7–8; author's conversation with assistant U.S. attorney Marianne Hinkle, chief of Community Prosecution and Crime Reduction Unit, Boston, March 2002.

31. "'Broken Windows' Probation: The Next Step in Fighting Crime," Center for Civic Innovation, Manhattan Institute Civic Report 7 (August 1999) (www.manhattan-institute.org/html/cr_7.htm) [April 19, 2002]).

32. Texas Youth Commission, "Basic Correctional Treatment: Resocialization," (http://www.tyc.state.tx.us/programs/resocial.html [April 2000]).

33. Jane Austin, Kelly Johnson, and Marie Gregorious, *Juveniles in Adult Prisons and Jails: A National Assessment* (U.S. Department of Justice, Office of Juvenile Justice and Delinquency Prevention, 2000).

34. See David M. Altschuler, Troy L. Armstrong, and Doris Layton MacKenzie, "Reintegration, Supervised Release, and Intensive Aftercare," *Juvenile Justice Bulletin* (U.S. Department of Justice, Office of Juvenile Justice and Delinquency Prevention, July 1999). For a discussion of the Gulf Coast Trades Center, a Waverly, Texas, residential program for serious juvenile offenders that provides active aftercare support, see Richard A. Mendel, *Less Cost, More Safety: Guiding Lights for Reform in Juvenile Justice* (Washington: American Youth Policy Forum, 2001). On postrelease adult supervision, see Anne M. Piehl, *From Cell to Street: A Plan to Supervise Inmates After Release* (Boston: MassInc., 2002).

35. New York State Attorney General Eliot Spitzer has established the Students against Violence Initiative (SAVI), which partners the office of the attorney general with public

schools in order to develop and implement programs that give students a greater role in promoting nonviolent resolution of conflicts. Students, school staff, and staff of the office of the attorney general work together in discussing scenarios for nonviolent resolution of disputes and explore issues such as bullying, relationship violence, gangs, and weapons. SAVI is administered by four student leaders per grade level, a facilitator provided by the attorney general, and at least one faculty advisor.

36. The challenge of identifying the risk of violence posed by juveniles was considered by the Massachusetts Supreme Judicial Court in *Commonwealth* v. *Milo M.*, 433 Mass. 149 (2001). In that case, the court affirmed an adjudication of delinquency, ruling that "a drawing that depicts a student pointing a gun at his teacher constitutes a threat." Ibid. at 150. Writing for the court, Justice Roderick Ireland, the author of a leading treatise on juvenile justice law, observed: "[G]iven the recent highly publicized, school-related shootings by students, we take judicial notice of the actual and potential violence in public schools. Although we note that schools remain very safe places for children to be, such violent episodes are matters of common knowledge, particularly within the teaching community." Ibid. at 156.

37. Kenney and Watson, *Crime in the Schools*; Elliott, Hamburg, and Williams, *Violence in American Schools*, pp. 159–386; Ira Pollock and Carlos Sundermann, "Creating Safe Schools: A Comprehensive Approach," *Juvenile Justice Journal*, vol. 8, no. 1 (June 2001).

38. Writing generally about nonprofit organizations, Derek Bok has suggested that they are an "ingenious invention" that can provide valuable social programs that can be adapted to local conditions without the encumbrance of government bureaucracy. Derek Bok, *The Trouble with Government* (Harvard University Press, 2001), p. 219.

39. The Boys and Girls Clubs (BGC) provide program activities and support services to help the development of six- to eighteen-year-olds, generally from disadvantaged backgrounds. The Chelsea Clubhouse in Boston, for example, directed by Joshua Kraft, has spearheaded a teen leaders program in which teens are trained in such subjects as youth development, anger management, dating violence, teen pregnancy, and parenting. As noted above, the Youth Service Providers Network, a partnership between the BGC and the Boston Police Department, houses clinical social workers in police stations and in BCG clubhouses in an effort to connect at-risk youth with prevention and intervention services. (http://www.bgcb.org [May 2002]). The Beacon Schools, founded by Geoffrey Canada, president of the Rheedlen Centers for children and families, are open seven days a week from 9:00 a.m. to 11:00 p.m. or midnight. They integrate social services for high-risk families with educational and recreational activities. See, generally, Lisbeth B. Schorr, *Common Purpose: Strengthening Families and Neighborhoods to Rebuild America* (New York: Doubleday, 1997), pp. 47–55.

Another example of a nonprofit initiative that seeks to provide direction to at-risk youth is the Cambodian Mutual Assistance Association of Greater Lowell, Inc. (CMAA). CMAA sponsors a "Future Stars Sports Leadership" summer camp for Cambodian refugee students, many of whom are candidates for gang membership. This community-based effort has depended in part on aggressive solicitation of funds from foundations. John Tomase, "Helping Others Help Themselves: Weston Trio Volunteers in Lowell at Camp for Cambodian Youths," *Weston Town Crier and Tab* (July 30, 1998), p. 23, and author's conversation with Matthew Wolf, co–camp coordinator, February 2001.

40. City Year, co-founded by president Michael Brown and CEO Alan Khazei, operates

a national youth service corps and provides technical assistance to national and community initiatives. A member of the AmeriCorps network, its mission is to "put idealism to work by tapping the civic power of young people for an annual campaign of idealism that generates transformative community service, breaks down social barriers, inspires citizens to civic action, develops new leaders for the common good, and improves and promotes the concept of voluntary national service." City Year, *Annual Report 2000*, p. 9. While not established specifically to deal with youth violence, its activities encourage the development of leadership skills and grassroots community engagement, which can help reduce youth violence.

41. Common Sense about Kids and Guns, headed by Victoria Reggie Kennedy, is a nonprofit, nonpartisan organization that seeks to educate adults about safety steps they can take to protect children from gun violence. See http://www.kidsandguns.org [April 19, 2002]. Another nonprofit that addresses prevention issues is "I Am Your Child," a "national public awareness and engagement campaign to make early childhood development a top priority for our nation." See http://www.iamyourchild.com [April 19, 2002]. Actor and director Rob Reiner is one of the founders of that organization. An initiative that is not directed at youth violence but that may serve as a model for future philanthropic efforts in that area is Children for Children. Led by Silda Wall, this foundation seeks to encourage children to develop a sense of community responsibility and philanthropy by aiding selected New York City public or independent schools "struggling to provide quality education without adequate resources." Families donate a portion of their child's birthday party costs to the foundation. The families, including the children, select from a list provided by the foundation which New York City public or independent schools they want to receive their donation (http://www.childrenforchildren.org [May 2002]).

42. For example, the Boston Coalition against Drugs and Violence, chaired by John P. Driscoll Jr., has brought together community, philanthropic, government, corporate, religious, and education groups in the city to reduce violence, assist the criminal justice system, and fight substance abuse. The coalition founded the state's first drug court and has mentored other cities.

43. See, for example, the Local Initiatives Support Corporation (LISC), which serves as a conduit in providing funding to community development corporations. It has partnered with community development corporations and police departments in Seattle and Kansas City. The chairman of its board is Robert Rubin, former United States secretary of the treasury. See Christopher Swope, "Robert Rubin's Urban Crusade," *Governing* (August 2000), p. 24.

44. See Jim Comey and Stephen Miller, "Project Exile," *United States Attorneys' Bulletin*, vol. 50, no. 1 (January 2002), pp. 11, 14–15.

45. See Christine W. Letts, William P. Ryan, and Allen Grossman, *High-Performance Nonprofit Organizations: Managing Upstream for Greater Impact* (John Wiley & Sons, 1999).

46. These ideas are being examined by professor Tracey Meares of the University of Chicago Law School.

47. Harold Dean Trulear, "Faith-Based Institutions and High-Risk Youth," *Field Report Series* (Philadelphia: Public/Private Ventures, 2000), p. 6.

48. E. J. Dionne Jr. and John J. DiIulio Jr., eds., *What's God Got to Do with the American Experiment?* (Brookings, 2000); David B. Larson and Byron R. Johnson, "Religion: The Forgotten Factor in Cutting Youth Crime and Saving At-Risk Urban Youth," *The Jere-*

miah Project: Report 98-2, Manhattan Institute for Policy Research (www.manhattan-institute.org/html/jpr-98-2.htm). Former Indianapolis mayor Stephen Goldsmith, now chairman of the Corporation for National and Community Service, discusses his work with faith-based and neighborhood organizations in *Faith in Neighborhoods: Making Cities Work through Grassroots Empowerment* (Washington: Hudson Institute, 2002), with a case study by Ryan Streeter. See also Stephen Goldsmith, *The Twenty-First Century City: Resurrecting Urban America* (Washington: Regenery Publishing, 1997).

49. U.S. Department of Justice, *Corporate-Community Partnerships for Public Safety: The Role of Business in Building Safe and Sustainable Communities* (Washington: April 2000). The report cites corporations such as John Hancock Mutual Life Insurance Company, which sponsored "Freedom Summer" for at-risk youths, and Honeywell, General Mills, and Allina Health Care System, whose executives in Minneapolis met with the state governor, resulting in the partnership known as "Minnesota HEALS."

50. In his wide-ranging study of business leadership, Dean Garten, of the Yale School of Management, urges a more aggressive role for business, but not because he equates "the private interests of business with the public interest." Rather, he suggests "that the definition of the public interest has become too complex to draw bright lines between the public and private sectors as we have tended to do in recent years." Jeffrey E. Garten, *The Mind of the C.E.O.* (Basic Books, 2001), p. 17.

Ira Jackson, director of the Center for Business and Government at Harvard's John F. Kennedy School of Government, explores emerging trends in harnessing business to advance public values in his forthcoming book, *Capitalism with a Conscience*. The efforts of New York mayor Michael Bloomberg to apply a service-oriented business management strategy to the city will no doubt be watched with great interest. On his business philosophy, see Michael Bloomberg, *Bloomberg by Bloomberg* (John Wiley, 2001).

51. America's Promise—The Alliance for Youth, founded by General Colin Powell, seeks "to mobilize people from every sector of American life to build the character and competence of our nation's youth by fulfilling five promises: caring adults, safe places, healthy start, marketable skills, opportunities to serve" (http://www.americaspromise.org [April 2002]).

A model for private sector encouragement and support of service to the community is provided by the Timberland Company, the publicly traded shoe and apparel company. Under the leadership of president and CEO Jeffrey Swartz, Timberland has established the Path of Service program, which gives employees forty hours of paid time off to serve in their communities. Its strategic partners include City Year, Share Our Strength, and Harlem Children's Zone, and it has a variety of service partners, including America's Promise, AmeriCorps, and the Points of Light Foundation. See http://www.timberland.com [April 2002].

52. Peter B. Goldberg, "Nonprofits and the Public Sector: An Evolving Relationship," in Nonprofit Sector Research Fund, *Competing Visions: The Nonprofit Sector in the Twenty-First Century* (Aspen Institute, 1995), pp. 83–91.

53. *Marketing Violent Entertainment to Children: A Review of Self-Regulation and Industry Practices in the Motion Picture, Music Recording, and Electronic Game Industries: Report of the Federal Trade Commission* (Washington: September 2000), p. 2.

54. On media literacy initiatives and opportunities for action, see Sissela Bok, *Mayhem: Violence as Public Entertainment* (Reading, Mass.: Addison-Wesley, 1998), pp. 140–158.

55. Comey and Miller, "Project Exile," pp. 13–14.

56. In 1996, KVUE-TV, then the top-rated local news station in Austin, Texas, established criteria to determine whether to cover crime stories. The criteria included whether action needed to be taken, whether there was an immediate threat to safety or threat to children, whether the crime had a significant community impact, and whether the story would promote crime prevention. Robert E. Shepherd, Jr., "Film at Eleven: The News Media and Juvenile Crime," *Quinnipiac Law Review*, vol. 18 (1999), pp. 696–97. On the commercial pressures confronting the media to follow the adage "If it bleeds, it leads," see Leonard Downie Jr. and Robert G. Kaiser, *The News about the News: American Journalism in Peril* (Knopf, 2002), p. 178.

57. See also David M. Kennedy, Anthony A. Braga, and Anne M. Piehl, *Reducing Gun Violence: The Boston Gun Project's Operation Cease Fire* (National Institute of Justice, 2001).

58. Kathleen Coolbaugh and Cynthia J. Hansel, "The Comprehensive Strategy: Lessons Learned from the Pilot Sites," *OJJDP Juvenile Justice Bulletin* (U.S. Department of Justice, Office of Juvenile Justice and Delinquency Prevention, March 2000).

59. Elaine Morley and others, "Comprehensive Responses to Youth at Risk: Interim Findings from the SafeFutures Initiative," *OJJDP Summary* (U.S. Department of Justice, Office of Juvenile Justice and Delinquency Prevention, November 2000).

60. Coleman and others, "Using Knowledge and Teamwork to Reduce Crime."

61. National Campaign Against Youth Violence (www.noviolence.net [April 2002]).

62. National Crime Prevention Council, "Initiatives" (http://www.ncpc.org/comm.htm#success [May 2002]).

63. Anthony A. Braga, David M. Kennedy, and George E. Tita, "New Approaches to the Strategic Prevention of Gang and Group-Involved Violence," in C. Ronald Huff, ed., *Gangs in America* (Thousand Oaks, Calif.: Sage, 2002), pp. 271–85.

64. Interestingly, these elements are very similar to those identified by Harvard Business School professor John P. Kotter as necessary for creating major change in organizations. He identifies "the eight-stage process of creating major change" as follows: "establishing a sense of urgency; creating the guiding coalition; developing a vision and strategy; communicating the change vision; empowering broad-based action; generating short-term wins; consolidating gains and producing more change; anchoring new approaches in the culture." John P. Kotter, *Leading Change* (Harvard Business School Press, 1996), pp. 20-23.

65. Rolf Loeber and David P. Farrington, "Conclusions and the Way Forward," in Rolf Loeber and David P. Farrington, eds., *Serious and Violent Juvenile Offenders: Risk Factors and Successful Interventions* (Thousand Oaks, Calif.: Sage, 1998), pp. 405–27.

66. Cathy S. Widom and Michael G. Maxfield, "An Update on the 'Cycle of Violence,'" *National Institute of Justice Research in Brief*, no. 184894 (National Institute of Justice, February 2001), p. 1.

67. Richard Wiebush, Raelene Freitag, and Christopher Baird, "Preventing Delinquency through Improved Child Protection Services," *Juvenile Justice Bulletin*, NCJ 187759 (U.S. Department of Justice, Office of Juvenile Justice and Delinquency Prevention, July 2001).

68. Widom and Maxfield, "An Update on the 'Cycle of Violence,'" p. 7.

69. Jennifer Toth, *What Happened to Johnnie Jordan? The Story of a Child Turning Violent* (New York: Free Press, 2002), p. 268. Toth notes recommendations that a specialized foster care service be staffed by professionals and that anger management and empathy training as well as individual and group therapy be standard.

70. For a discussion by an associate justice of the Massachusetts District Court calling for modification of confidentiality rules in order to promote interagency collaboration, see Gordon A. Martin Jr., "Open the Doors: A Judicial Call to End Confidentiality in Delinquency Proceedings," *Criminal and Civil Confinement*, vol. 21, no. 2 (1995), pp. 406–10. Justice Martin has also served since 1994 as a member of the Federal Coordinating Council on Juvenile Justice and Delinquency Prevention.

71. Trone, Armstrong, and Sullivan, *Beyond Blame and Panic*. See also M. L. Armstrong, *Adolescent Pathways: Exploring the Intersections between Child Welfare and Juvenile Justice, PINS, and Mental Health* (New York: Vera Institute of Justice, May 1998).

72. Under the leadership of president and CEO Shay Bilchik, the Child Welfare League of America, the nation's largest and oldest membership-based child welfare organization, is expanding partnerships with law enforcement, juvenile justice, and the mental health system.

73. Joseph J. Cocozza and Kathleen R. Skowyra, "Youth with Mental Health Disorders: Issues and Emerging Responses," *Juvenile Justice*, vol. 7, no. 1 (April, 2000), pp. 3–11 (U.S. Department of Justice, Office of Juvenile Justice and Delinquency Prevention).

74. Toth, *What Happened to Johnnie Jordan?*, p. 265.

75. See, for example, Federal Bureau of Investigation, *The School Shooter: A Threat Assessment Perspective: 2000*, a report sponsored by the Critical Incident Response Group and the National Center for the Analysis of Violent Crime.

76. For a survey of mental health issues in juvenile court compiled by an associate justice of the Massachusetts Juvenile Court and founding attorney of the Youth Advocacy Project, see Jay Blitzman, "Mental Health and Forensic Issues in Juvenile Court," in Suffolk University Law School, *Children on Trial: Understanding the Juvenile Justice System* (Boston: 1999), pp. 305–25. See also Coalition for Juvenile Justice, *Handle with Care: Serving the Mental Health Needs of Young Offenders—2000 Annual Report* (Washington: 2000).

77. Paul C. Light, *Making Nonprofits Work: A Report on the Tides of Nonprofit Management Reform* (Brookings, 2000), p. 60.

78. Ibid.

79. Jodi Lane and Susan Turner, "Interagency Collaboration in Juvenile Justice: Learning from Experience," *Federal Probation*, vol. 63, no. 2 (December 1999), pp. 33, 36–38.

80. David Kennedy, "Research for Problem Solving and the New Collaborations," pp. 1–8, and J. Phillip Thompson, "The Changing Role of the Researcher in Working with Communities," pp. 9–16, in *Viewing Crime and Justice from a Collaborative Perspective: Plenary Papers of the 1998 Conference on Criminal Justice Research and Evaluation*, NCJ publication 176979 (National Institute of Justice, July 1999); Coleman and others, "Using Knowledge and Teamwork to Reduce Crime."

81. Lawrence W. Sherman and others, *Preventing Crime: What Works, What Doesn't, What's Promising*, Office of Justice Programs research report NCJ 165366 (U.S. Department of Justice, Office of Justice Programs, February 1997).

82. Sharon Mihalic and others, "Blueprints for Violence Prevention," *OJJDP Juvenile Justice Bulletin*, NCJ 187079 (U.S. Department of Justice, Office of Juvenile Justice and Delinquency Prevention, July 2001). See also National Campaign Against Youth Violence, Academic Advisory Council Report of Initial Meeting (December 2000, unpublished report on file with author).

83. Loeber and Farrington, "Conclusions and the Way Forward," pp. 405–27.

84. Jeffrey Butts and others, *Youth, Guns, and the Juvenile Justice System* (Washington: Urban Institute, 2002), pp. 18–20.

85. Malcolm Gladwell, *The Tipping Point: How Little Things Can Make A Big Difference* (Little, Brown, 2000), pp. 140–151.

86. Mark W. Lipsey, David B. Wilson, and Lynn Cothern, "Effective Intervention for Serious Juvenile Offenders," *OJJDP Bulletin*, NCJ 181201 (U.S. Department of Justice, Office of Juvenile Justice and Delinquency Prevention, April 2000); Peter W. Greenwood and others, *Diverting Children from a Life of Crime: Measuring Costs and Benefits* (Santa Monica, Calif.: Rand, 1996); J. David Hawkins, ed., *Delinquency and Crime: Current Theories* (Cambridge University Press, 1996).

87. Lynn A. Karoly and others, *Investing in Our Children: What We Know and Don't Know about the Cost and Benefits of Early Childhood Interventions* (Rand, 1998), pp. 4, 11–71.

88. Amplifying her work with William Galson on the disintegration of family structure, Elaine Kamarck has observed that "[t]he relationship between crime and one-parent families, in fact, is so strong that controlling for family configuration erases the relationship between race and crime and between low income and crime." Elaine Kamarck, "Family Policy," in *The Citizen Transition Project: Changing America: Blueprints for the New Administration* (New York: Newmarket Press, 1992), p. 445.

89. James Q. Wilson, "Foreword: Never Too Early," in Loeber and Farrington, *Serious and Violent Juvenile Offenders*, p. xi.

90. Patricia A. Brennan, "Biosocial Risk Factors and Juvenile Violence," *Federal Probation*, vol. 63, no. 2 (December 1999).

91. See, generally, "Investing in Girls: A 21st Century Strategy," *Juvenile Justice Journal*, vol. 6, no. 1 (October 1999); Joyce London Alexander, "Aligning the Goals of Juvenile Justice with the Needs of Young Women Offenders: A Proposed Praxis for Transformational Justice," *Suffolk University Law Review*, vol. 32 (1999), pp. 557–611; American Bar Association and National Bar Association, *Justice by Gender: The Lack of Appropriate Prevention, Diversion, and Treatment Alternatives for Girls in the Justice System* (Washington: 2001). The dearth of knowledge about young female offenders is to be contrasted with the substantial literature that has developed regarding young boys and violence. See, for example, William Pollack, *Real Boys: Rescuing Our Sons from the Myths of Boyhood* (New York: Henry Holt, 1998); James Garbarino, *Lost Boys: Why Our Sons Turn Violent and How We Can Save Them* (Anchor, 1999); Richard Rhodes, *Why They Kill* (Random House, 1999).

92. See, for example, James Alan Fox and Jack Levin, "Helping Set the Stage for Copycat School Shootings," *Boston Globe*, March 11, 2001, p. E1.

93. One accounting has identified eight White House conferences concerning children over the last 100 years. See American Bar Association Steering Committee on the Unmet Legal Needs of Children, *America's Children Still at Risk* (Chicago: ABA, 2001), p. 467.

94. Some states, of course, have been quite active in generating reports regarding youth violence. See, for example, North Carolina Governor's Task Force on Youth Violence and School Safety Report, August 11, 1999 (http://www.nccrimecontrol.org/taskforce/finalreport.html [April 19, 2002]); Scott Harshbarger and Jay Winsten, *No Time to Lose: A Comprehensive Action Plan to Prevent Youth Violence* (Boston: Commonwealth of Massachusetts, 1997), a report by the attorney general and the associate dean of Harvard School of Public Health; Governor's Advisory Council on Youth Violence, *Analysis and Recommendations Regarding Violence in Massachusetts Schools* (Boston, 1999).

95. See Ronald Corbett Jr., chapter 6 in this volume.

96. The commonality of the language of the discussion concerning youth violence can be seen in the views expressed about the Violent and Repeat Juvenile Offender Act of 1997, S. 10, which was not enacted. The committee report submitted by Senator Orrin Hatch for what was then the majority stated the following:

> There has been considerable debate within the criminal justice system and among members of the public over the appropriate emphasis to be placed on the importance of punishment and prevention. Some believe that increasing punishments cannot solve the juvenile crime problem . . . . By contrast, others maintain that the focus should be on punishment rather than on prevention, because punishment itself prevents crime, through its incapacitative and deterrent effects . . . . The Committee believes that both theories have their place in the juvenile justice system, but that the time has come to reassess the theoretical underpinnings of that system. The theory that "there is no such thing as a bad kid" no longer has merit in a day when juveniles commit the type of horrific crimes that are seen daily. At the same time, the Committee does not believe that all efforts at prevention should be abandoned. The bill that the Committee recommends therefore does nothing of the kind. On the contrary, the bill reported by the Committee is quite generous regarding the amount of money that may be spent on juvenile crime prevention programs.

Violent and Repeat Juvenile Offender Act of 1997: Report of the Committee on the Judiciary together with Additional, Minority, and Supplemental Views to Accompany S. 10, S. Rept. 105-108, 105th Cong., 1st. sess. (GPO, 1997), pp. 68–69.

Senator Charles Grassley, then in the majority, added: "I support smart crime prevention programs and I am pleased that the Violent and Repeat Juvenile Offender Act of 1997 includes significant resources for prevention programs. However, it seems to me that many who blindly advocate prevention programs fail to understand that incarceration is the best form of crime prevention." Ibid. at p. 191.

The views of the then minority (Senators Leahy, Kennedy, Biden, Kohl, Feingold, and Durbin), followed:

> [T]here is no need to reinvent the wheel on juvenile crime control. In response to the explosion of juvenile crime that began in 1985, states and localities across the country have been crafting comprehensive approaches to this problem. These efforts are now beginning to bear fruit . . . . Boston has achieved these results without adopting any of the strategies S. 10 seeks to impose on the entire country—such as prosecuting more juveniles as adults, housing nonviolent juvenile offenders in adult facilities, and spending huge sums of money on new facilities and juvenile recordkeeping. Rather, the key to success in Boston is a comprehensive strategy—neither a "liberal" nor "conservative" approach—that involves the entire community, police and probation officers, clergy and community leaders, even the gang members themselves. The strategy is based on three parallel strong commitments—tough, targeted enforcement; heavy emphasis on afterschool prevention programs that provide alternatives to criminal gang membership for at-risk youth; and aggressive steps to take guns out of the hands of criminal gang members and other violent juvenile offenders. Neglecting any of these commitments unravels the whole strategy . . . . [I]f we focus exclusively on our most

violent youth and neglect those we can still influence positively, we will inevitably return to this subject a decade from now, and face increasing youth crime rates. Similarly, if we indiscriminately tear down principles and institutions that have worked well to divert young people from crime and delinquency, we will be making things worse for future generations, not better.

Ibid. at pp. 144–45. Senator Joseph Biden added: "When addressing the problem of juvenile crime and violence, national policymakers should be taking aim at three different groups of youth: the relatively small numbers of juveniles who have committed serious violent crimes, minor offenders who are still capable of being turned around, and the burgeoning population of at-risk youth who will soon be entering their most crime prone years . . . . [S. 10] falls far short of delivering what is needed for each of the three populations." Ibid. at p. 196.

97. Franklin E. Zimring, *American Youth Violence* (Oxford University Press, 1998), pp. 177–95.

98. See, for example, Francis Latour, "Crackdown on Crime in Dorchester Set to Start," *Boston Globe* (October 30, 2001), p. B1. See also Dan Eggen, "Major Crimes in U.S. Increase," *Washington Post*, June 23, 2002, p. A1 (quoting professor James Alan Fox as stating that "[t]he great 1990s crime drop ended with the 1990s; the new millenium brings a different picture"); Federal Bureau of Investigation, *Crime Trends: 2001 Preliminary Figures* (Washington, 2002) (the volume of violent crime generally, not broken down by age, increased 0.6 percent in 2001 from the 2000 figure; murder volume increased 26.4 percent).

99. It has become increasingly common to distinguish the leadership and management functions. See Ronald A. Heifetz, *Leadership without Easy Answers* (Harvard University Press, 1994), p. 15. Thus, management has been defined as a "set of processes that can keep a complicated system of people and technology running" through such functions as "planning, budgeting, organizing, staffing, controlling, and problem solving." Kotter, *Leading Change*, p. 25. By contrast, "[l]eadership is a set of processes that creates organizations in the first place or adapts them to significantly changing circumstances." Ibid. For a discussion of various concepts of leadership, including transformational and adaptive notions, see Heifetz, *Leadership without Easy Answers*, pp. 13–27. See also David Gergen, *Eyewitness to Power: The Essence of Leadership, Nixon to Clinton* (Simon and Schuster, 2000).

100. Rosabeth Moss Kanter, "Creating the Culture for Innovation," in Frances Hesselbein, Marshall Goldsmith, and Iain Somerville, eds., *Leading for Innovation and Organizing for Results* (San Francisco: Jossey-Bass, 2002), p. 74. Peter Drucker has defined innovation as "change that creates a new dimension of performance." Ibid. at xi. See also Alan A. Altschuler and Robert D. Behn, eds., *Innovation in American Government: Challenges, Opportunities, and Dilemmas* (Brookings, 1997).

101. See Ellen Schall, "Notes from a Reflective Practitioner of Innovation," in Altschuler and Behn, eds., *Innovation in American Government*, pp. 360–77, where the author discusses her tenure as commissioner of the New York City Department of Juvenile Justice.

102. Presidential Nomination Address, *New York Times*, August 04, 2000, p. A24.

103. See Robert D. Putnam, *Bowling Alone* (Simon and Schuster, 2000).

104. E. J. Dionne Jr., ed., *Community Works: The Revival of Civil Society in America* (Brookings, 1998), pp. 1–14.

Contributors

Jenny Berrien is an analyst at Abt Associates in the area of housing and community revitalization. Before joining Abt she was a program and policy analyst at Public/Private Ventures, working on P/PV's faith-based initiative. She received a bachelor of arts degree from Harvard University and is now enrolled in the joint MPP/MBA degree program of Harvard's John F. Kennedy School of Government and the Harvard Business School.

Amalia V. Betanzos is president of Wildcat Service Corporation, a non-profit, multimillion-dollar employment program, and the founder of the Wildcat Academy, an alternative high school program. She has served as commissioner of the New York City Youth Services Agency, chairperson of the National Puerto Rican Coalition, chairperson of the NYC Commission on the Status of Women, chairperson of the Rent Guidelines Board, and vice president of the United Parents Association. She has been a member of former Mayor Rudolph Giuliani's Commission on School Safety, the NYC Board of Education, the NYC Private Industry Council, the NYC Housing Authority, the Mayor's Advisory Committee on Police Management and Personnel Safety, and the NYC Charter Revision Commission and a trustee of Catholic Charities.

Catherine M. Coles is a fellow in criminal justice at the Kennedy School of Government, Harvard University, and has taught local governmental studies at Ahmadu Bellow University, Nigeria, and anthropology and African studies at Dartmouth College. She has studied community policing and the changing roles of American prosecutors, and she also is interested in courts, constitutional and criminal law, community justice, and order maintenance and public policy in these areas. Coles has published widely on these subjects and is co-author with George Kelling of *Fixing Broken Windows: Restoring Order and Reducing Crime in Our Communities.*

Ronald Corbett is executive director of the Supreme Judicial Court of Massachusetts. He previously worked in corrections for twenty-five years, including service as second deputy commissioner of the Massachusetts Probation Department, and he is a past president of the National Association of Probation Executives. He has taught and published widely. He is editor of *Perspectives*, the journal of the American Probation and Parole Association, and co-editor of the "Up to Speed" column in *Federal Probation*. He has been the recipient of the American Probation and Parole Association's Sam Houston State University Award (1990), the Manson-Robinson Award (1994) of the New England Council on Crime and Delinquency, and the Probation Executive of the Year Award (1997) from the National Association of Probation Executives (NAPE).

Barbara Fedders is currently a staff attorney for the Roxbury Defenders Office of the Massachusetts Committee for Public Counsel Services. She worked previously as a clinical staff attorney for the Boston College Law School Juvenile Rights Advocacy Project, as a Soros Justice Fellow, and as a staff attorney at the Youth Advocacy Project, which provides direct representation to low-income young people in the Massachusetts juvenile courts. She is a graduate of New York University School of Law.

Gerald G. Gaes is a principal research associate at the Urban Institute. He was director of the Office of Research, Federal Bureau of Prisons, from 1988 until July 2002. His most recent publications include "Adult Correctional Treatment," a co-authored chapter in *Prisons, Crime, and Justice: A Review of Research*; "Correctional Treatment," in *The Handbook of Crime and Punishment*; and "Private Adult Prisons: What Do We Really Know and Why Don't We Know More?" a co-authored chapter in *Privatization in Criminal Justice*. His current research interests include

prison privatization, evaluation methodology, inmate gangs, inmate classification, simulating criminal justice processes, prison crowding, prison violence, and the effectiveness of prison program interventions on post-release
outcomes.

Francis X. Hartmann is executive director and senior research fellow of the
Program in Criminal Justice Policy and Management, Kennedy School of
Government, Harvard University; executive director of the Malcolm
Wiener Center for Social Policy; and adjunct lecturer in public policy at
the Kennedy School of Government. His current research explores com-
munity policing and how communities work to promote and ensure safety.
Formerly he was director of the Hartford Institute of Criminal and Social
Justice, director of research and evaluation for New York City's Addiction
Services Agency, and program officer at the Ford Foundation.

Randy Hertz is a professor at New York University Law School, where he
is a supervising attorney of both the law school's Capital Defender Clinic
and Juvenile Rights Clinic. A former staff attorney of the Public Defender
Service for the District of Columbia, he is a co-author of *Federal Habeas
Corpus Law and Practice*, a two-volume treatise on habeas corpus for
lawyers in capital cases; co-author of *Trial Manual for Defense Attorneys in
Juvenile Court*, a two-volume trial manual on juvenile court practice for
defense attorneys; and author of articles on various aspects of criminal and
juvenile law and practice. He regularly provides training lectures on crim-
inal and juvenile delinquency procedure to judges, appellate defenders, and
trial-level defenders. He is a recipient of the American Bar Association's
Livingston Hall Award for Juvenile Justice Advocacy and the New York
City Bar Association's Thurgood Marshall Award for Capital Punishment
Representation.

Gary S. Katzmann is director of the Governance Institute project on juvenile justice and youth violence. He is a research fellow at the John F.
Kennedy School of Government at Harvard University and a fellow of the
Governance Institute. He has been an assistant U.S. attorney in the district
of Massachusetts, where he has been chief appellate attorney, deputy chief
of the criminal division, and chief legal counsel, and he has engaged in
criminal and civil litigation in the trial and appellate courts. He has served
on detail in Washington, D.C., as an associate deputy attorney general
focusing on criminal justice (including service as the Justice Department's

representative to the Sentencing Commission) and also on detail to the FBI, where he drafted major health care fraud legislation. He is a recipient of the Department of Justice's Director's Award. Among his publications is *Inside the Criminal Process*, a book that, translated into Russian, was used to teach Russian law enforcement and judicial officers. He has been a lecturer on law at Harvard University, and he also taught at Yale and at the Russian Procuracy Institute program. Katzmann received an A.B. from Columbia College, an M.Litt. from Oxford University, an M.P.P.M. from Yale University, and a J.D. from Yale Law School, where he was an editor of the *Yale Law Journal*. He served as a law clerk to then U.S. Circuit Court Judge Stephen G. Breyer and to U.S. District Court Judge Leonard B. Sand.

George L. Kelling is a professor in the School of Criminal Justice at Rutgers University; a research fellow in the Program in Criminal Justice Policy and Management, Kennedy School of Government, Harvard University; a senior fellow at the Manhattan Institute; and professor emeritus, College of Criminal Justice, Northeastern University. He has been a child care social worker and a probation officer, and he has administered residential care programs for aggressive and disturbed youths, conducted large-scale experiments in policing, and developed the order maintenance policies adopted by New York City's subway system and police department. His publications include the *Kansas City Preventive Patrol Experiment*; "Broken Windows," with James Q. Wilson; and *Fixing Broken Windows: Restoring Order and Reducing Crime in Our Communities*, with Catherine M. Coles. He currently is studying organizational change in policing and the development of comprehensive community crime prevention programs.

David M. Kennedy is a senior researcher at the Program in Criminal Justice Policy and Management, Kennedy School of Government, Harvard University. He has written and consulted extensively in the areas of community and problem-solving policing, police corruption, and neighborhood revitalization, and he is the founder and director of the Boston Gun Project. He is the co-author of *Beyond 911: A New Era for Policing* and of numerous articles on police management, illicit drug markets, and gun control. He currently is focusing on the problem of violence and strategies for preventing violence, with a special emphasis on the role of fear in driving cycles of urban violence; the nature of the illicit markets supplying guns to criminals; and the possibilities for city-specific strategies to disrupt gun markets and reduce fear.

Sara Kropf is an attorney in private practice in Washington, D.C. She holds graduate and professional degrees from Georgetown University and wrote her doctoral dissertation on the subject of juvenile justice and race. She also has served as a law clerk on the U.S. Court of Appeals for the Fourth Circuit.

David B. Mitchell is the executive director of the National Council of Juvenile and Family Court Judges. From 1984 to November 2001, he served as an associate judge on the circuit court for Baltimore City. As the administrative judge of the juvenile court for eleven years, he enlisted volunteer advocates for children in the system, computerized court records, and worked for a new Juvenile Justice Center. He also was in charge of the criminal docket of the court and was instrumental in reviving the Criminal Justice Coordinating Council to address the many issues facing the courts today. He serves on many boards and associations dealing with juvenile issues as well as judicial reform.

Mark H. Moore is the director of the Hauser Center for Nonprofit Organizations; the faculty chairman of the Kennedy School of Government's Program in Criminal Justice Policy and Management at Harvard University; and the Guggenheim Professor of Criminal Justice Policy and Management at the Kennedy School. He was the founding chair of the school's Committee on Executive Programs, serving in that role for more than a decade. His research interests are in public management and leadership; civil society and community mobilization; criminal justice policy and management; nonprofit enterprises; and the intersection of those domains. His publications include *Creating Public Value: Strategic Management in Government*; *Buy and Bust: The Effective Regulation of an Illicit Market in Heroin*; *Dangerous Offenders: The Elusive Targets of Justice*; and (with others) *Public Duties: The Moral Obligations of Public Officials*; *Ethics in Government: The Moral Challenges of Public Leadership*; *Inspectors General: Junkyard Dogs or Man's Best Friend*; *From Children to Citizens: The Mandate for Juvenile Justice*; and *Beyond 911: A New Era for Policing*.

Ronald G. Slaby is a senior scientist at the Education Development Center and a lecturer on education and pediatrics at Harvard University, where he teaches the courses "Television and the Developing Child" and "Preventing Violence in America." A developmental psychologist, he brings more than thirty years of experience to the investigation of parent, peer, and media influences on the cognitive and social development of children. He is a fellow of the American Psychological Association. His books include *Early Violence Prevention: Tools for Teachers of Young Children*; *Aggressors, Victims, and Bystanders: Thinking and Acting to Prevent Violence*; *Viewpoints: A Guide to Conflict Resolution and Decision Making in Adolescence*; and *Social Development in Young Children*. He has served on children's media panels for the National Endowment for the Humanities, the National Endowment for the Arts, the National Campaign to Reduce Youth Violence, the Corporation for Public Broadcasting, and the American Children's Television Council, and he has co-authored a national plan for the prevention of violence for the Centers for Disease Control.

Stephen J. Weymouth, currently in private practice, was director of the Youth Advocacy Project in Boston. He joined YAP in 1996 with seventeen years of experience in all aspects of criminal and civil practice, including the representation of juveniles charged with serious offenses. Weymouth has been active in the Boston Bar Association, the Massachusetts Bar Association, the Massachusetts Association of Criminal Defense Attorneys, and a variety of community organizations.

Christopher Winship has been a professor of sociology at Harvard University since 1992 and also has been chair of the department. Previously he was a professor and chair of the sociology department at Northwestern University, a founding member of Northwestern's department of statistics, and director of the Economics Research Center at the National Opinion Research Center at the University of Chicago. He currently is doing research on several topics: the Ten Point Coalition; statistical models for causal analysis; the effects of education on mental ability; causes of the racial difference in performance in elite colleges and universities; and changes in the racial differential in imprisonment rates over the past sixty years.

Index